MW01687649

Kabbala Denudata, the Kabbalah Unveiled, Containing the Following Books of the Zohar. 1. the Book of Concealed Mystery. 2. the Greater Holy Assembly. 3. the Lesser Holy Assembly. Translated Into English from the Latin Version of Knorr Von Rosenroth and Co

Samuel Liddell MacGregor Mathers

Zohar

KABBALA DENUDATA

THE

KABBALAH UNVEILED

CONTAINING THE FOLLOWING BOOKS OF THE ZOHAR

1. THE BOOK OF CONCEALED MYSTERY.
2. THE GREATER HOLY ASSEMBLY.
3. THE LESSER HOLY ASSEMBLY.

TRANSLATED INTO ENGLISH FROM THE LATIN VERSION OF KNORR VON ROSENROTH, AND COLLATED WITH THE ORIGINAL CHALDEE AND HEBREW TEXT

BY

S. L. MAC GREGOR MATHERS

THIRD IMPRESSION

THE THEOSOPHICAL PUBLISHING COMPANY
OF NEW YORK
253, WEST 72ND STREET
1912

Tlo

KABBALAH.

INTRODUCTION.

1. THE first questions which the non-qabalistical reader will probably ask are: What is the Qabalah? Who was its author? What are its sub-divisions? What are its general teachings? And why is a translation of it required at the present time?

2. I will answer the last question first. At the present time a powerful wave of occult thought is spreading through society; thinking men are beginning to awake to the fact that "there are more things in heaven and earth than are dreamed of in their philosophy;" and, last but not least, it is now felt that the Bible, which has been probably more misconstrued than any other book ever written, contains numberless obscure and mysterious passages which are utterly unintelligible without some key wherewith to unlock their meaning. THAT KEY IS GIVEN IN THE QABALAH. Therefore this work should be of interest to every biblical and theological student. Let every Christian ask himself this question: "How can I think to understand the Old Testament if I be ignorant of the construction put upon it by that nation whose sacred book it formed; and if I know not the meaning of the Old Testament, how can I expect to understand the New?" Were the real and sublime philosophy of the Bible better known, there would be

fewer fanatics and sectarians. And who can calculate the vastness of the harm done to impressionable and excitable persons by the bigoted enthusiasts who ever and anon come forward as teachers of the people? How many suicides are the result of religious mania and depression! What farragos of sacrilegious nonsense have not been promulgated as the true meanings of the books of the Prophets and the Apocalypse! Given a translation of the sacred Hebrew Book, in many instances incorrect, as the foundation, an inflamed and an ill-balanced mind as the worker thereon, what sort of edifice can be expected as the result? I say fearlessly to the fanatics and bigots of the present day: You have cast down the Sublime and Infinite One from His throne, and in His stead have placed the demon of unbalanced force; you have substituted a deity of disorder and of jealousy for a God of order and of love; you have perverted the teachings of the crucified One. Therefore at this present time an English translation of the Qabalah is almost a necessity, for the Zohar has never before been translated into the language of this country, nor, as far as I am aware, into any modern European vernacular.

3. The Qabalah may be defined as being the esoteric Jewish doctrine. It is called in Hebrew QBLH, *Qabalah*, which is derived from the root QBL, *Qibel*, meaning "to receive." This appellation refers to the custom of handing down the esoteric knowledge by oral transmission, and is nearly allied to "tradition."

4. As in the present work a great number of Hebrew or Chaldee words have to be used in the text, and the number of scholars in the Shemitic languages is limited, I have thought it more advisable to print such words in ordinary Roman characters, carefully retaining the exact orthography. I therefore append a table showing at a glance the ordinary Hebrew and Chaldee alphabet (which is common to both languages), the Roman characters by

PLATE I.—TABLE OF HEBREW AND CHALDEE LETTERS.

Number	Sound or Power.	Hebrew and Chaldee Letters.	Numerical Value.	Roman character by which expressed in this work.	Name.	Signification of Name.
1.	*a* (soft breathing).	א	**1.** (Thousands are	**A.**	Aleph.	Ox.
2.	*b, bh* (*v*).	ב	**2.** denoted by a	**B.**	Beth.	House.
3.	*g* (hard), *gh.*	ג	**3.** larger letter ;	**G.**	Gimel.	Camel.
4.	*d, dh* (flat *th*).	ד	**4.** thus an Aleph	**D.**	Daleth.	Door.
5.	*h* (rough breathing).	ה	**5.** larger than the	**H.**	He.	Window.
6.	*v, u, o.*	ו	**6.** rest of the let-	**V.**	Vau.	Peg, nail.
7.	*z, dz.*	ז	**7.** ters among	**Z.**	Zayin.	Weapon, sword.
8.	*ch* (guttural).	ח	**8.** which it is,	**Ch.**	Cheth.	Enclosure, fence.
9.	*t* (strong).	ט	**9.** signifies not 1,	**T.**	Teth.	Serpent.
10.	*i, y* (as in *yes*).	י	**10.** but 1000.)	**I.**	Yod.	Hand.
11.	*k, kh.*	כ Final = ך	**20.** Final = **500**	**K.**	Caph.	Palm of the hand.
12.	*l.*	ל	**30.**	**L.**	Lamed.	Ox-goad.
13.	*m.*	מ Final = ם	**40.** Final = **600**	**M.**	Mem.	Water.
14.	*n.*	נ Final = ן	**50.** Final = **700**	**N.**	Nun.	Fish.
15.	*s.*	ס	**60.**	**S.**	Samekh.	Prop, support.
16.	*O, aa, ng* (gutt.).	ע	**70.**	**O.**	Ayin.	Eye.
17.	*p, ph.*	פ Final = ף	**80.** Final = **800**	**P.**	Pe.	Mouth.
18.	*ts, tz, j.*	צ Final = ץ	**90.** Final = **900**	**Tz.**	Tzaddi.	Fishing-hook.
19.	*q, qh* (guttur.).	ק	**100.** (The finals are not	**Q.**	Qoph.	Back of the head.
20.	*r.*	ר	**200.** always considered	**R.**	Resh.	Head.
21.	*sh, s.*	ש	**300.** as bearing an in-creased numeri-	**Sh.**	Shin.	Tooth.
22.	*th, t.*	ת	**400.** cal value.)	**Th.**	Tau.	Sign of the cross.

which I have expressed its letters in this work; also their names, powers, and numerical values. There are no separate numeral characters in Hebrew and Chaldee; therefore, as is also the case in Greek, each letter has its own peculiar numerical value, and from this circumstance results the important fact that *every word is a number, and every number is a word.* This is alluded to in Revelations, where "the number of the beast" is mentioned, and on this correspondence between words and numbers the science of Gematria (the first division of the so-called literal Qabalah) is based. I shall refer to this subject again. I have selected the Roman letter Q to represent the Hebrew *Qoph* or *Koph*, a precedent for the use of which without a following *u* may be found in Max Müller's "Sacred Books of the East." The reader must remember that the Hebrew is almost entirely a consonantal alphabet, the vowels being for the most part supplied by small points and marks usually placed below the letters. Another difficulty of the Hebrew alphabet consists in the great similarity between the forms of certain letters—*e.g.*, V, Z, and final N.

5. With regard to the author and origin of the Qabalah, I cannot do better than give the following extract from Dr. Ginsburg's "Essay on the Kabbalah," first premising that this word has been spelt in a great variety of ways—Cabala, Kabalah, Kabbala, &c. I have adopted the form Qabalah, as being more consonant with the Hebrew writing of the word.

6. "A system of religious philosophy, or, more properly, of theosophy, which has not only exercised for hundreds of years an extraordinary influence on the mental development of so shrewd a people as the Jews, but has captivated the minds of some of the greatest thinkers of Christendom in the sixteenth and seventeenth centuries, claims the greatest attention of both the philosopher and the theologian. When it is added that among its

captives were Raymond Lully, the celebrated scholastic metaphysician and chemist (died 1315); John Reuchlin, the renowned scholar and reviver of Oriental literature in Europe (born 1455, died 1522); John Picus de Mirandola, the famous philosopher and classical scholar (1463-1494); Cornelius Henry Agrippa, the distinguished philosopher, divine, and physician (1486-1535); John Baptist Von Helmont, a remarkable chemist and physician (1577-1644); as well as our own countrymen, Robert Fludd, the famous physician and philosopher (1574-1637); and Dr. Henry More (1614-1687); and that these men, after restlessly searching for a scientific system which should disclose to them 'the deepest depths' of the divine nature, and show them the real tie which binds all things together, found the cravings of their minds satisfied by this theosophy, the claims of the Kabbalah on the attention of students in literature and philosophy will readily be admitted. The claims of the Kabbalah, however, are not restricted to the literary man and the philosopher; the poet too will find in it ample materials for the exercise of his lofty genius. How can it be otherwise with a theosophy which, we are assured, was born of God in Paradise, was nursed and reared by the choicest of the angelic hosts in heaven, and only held converse with the holiest of man's children upon earth. Listen to the story of its birth, growth, and maturity, as told by its followers.

7. "The Kabbalah was first taught by God himself to a select company of angels, who formed a theosophic school in Paradise. After the Fall the angels most graciously communicated this heavenly doctrine to the disobedient child of earth, to furnish the protoplasts with the means of returning to their pristine nobility and felicity. From Adam it passed over to Noah, and then to Abraham, the friend of God, who emigrated with it to Egypt, where the patriarch allowed a portion of this mysterious doctrine to ooze out. It was in this way

that the Egyptians obtained some knowledge of it, and the other Eastern nations could introduce it into their philosophical systems. Moses, who was learned in all the wisdom of Egypt, was first initiated into the Qabalah in the land of his birth, but became most proficient in it during his wanderings in the wilderness, when he not only devoted to it the leisure hours of the whole forty years, but received lessons in it from one of the angels. By the aid of this mysterious science the law-giver was enabled to solve the difficulties which arose during his management of the Israelites, in spite of the pilgrimages, wars, and frequent miseries of the nation. He covertly laid down the principles of this secret doctrine in the first four books of the Pentateuch, but withheld them from Deuteronomy. Moses also initiated the seventy elders into the secrets of this doctrine, and they again transmitted them from hand to hand. Of all who formed the unbroken line of tradition, David and Solomon were the most deeply initiated into the Kabbalah. No one, however, dared to write it down, till Schimeon Ben Jochai, who lived at the time of the destruction of the second temple. . . . . After his death, his son, Rabbi Eleazar, and his secretary, Rabbi Abba, as well as his disciples, collated Rabbi Simon Ben Jochai's treatises, and out of these composed the celebrated work called ZHR, *Zohar*, splendour, which is the grand storehouse of Kabbalism."

8. The Qabalah is usually classed under four heads:

(α) The practical Qabalah.
(β) The literal Qabalah.
(γ) The unwritten Qabalah.
(δ) The dogmatic Qabalah.

9. The practical Qabalah deals with talismanic and ceremonial magic, and does not come within the scope of this work.

10. The literal Qabalah is referred to in several places,

and therefore a knowledge of its leading principles is necessary. It is divided into three parts: GMTRIA, *Gematria*; NVTRIQVN, *Notariqon*; and ThMVRH, *Temura*.

11. Gematria is a metathesis of the Greek word *γραμματεια*. It is based on the relative numerical values of words, as I have before remarked. Words of similar numerical values are considered to be explanatory of each other, and this theory is also extended to phrases. Thus the letter *Shin*, Sh, is 300, and is equivalent to the number obtained by adding up the numerical values of the letters of the words RVCh ALHIM, *Ruach Elohim*, the spirit of the Elohim; and it is therefore a symbol of the spirit of the Elohim. For R=200, V=6, Ch=8, A=1, L=30, H=5, I=10, M=40; total=300. Similarly, the words AChD, *Achad*. Unity, One, and AHBH, *Ahebah*, love, each=13; for A=1, Ch=8, D=4, total=13; and A=1, H=5, B=2, H=5, total=13. Again, the name of the angel MTTRVN, *Metatron* or *Methraton*, and the name of the Deity, ShDI, *Shaddaï*, each make 314; so the one is taken as symbolical of the other. The angel Metraton is said to have been the conductor of the children of Israel through the wilderness, of whom God says, "My Name is in him." With regard to Gematria of phrases (Gen. xlix. 10), IBA ShILH, *Yeba Shiloh*, "Shiloh shall come"= 358, which is the numeration of the word MShICh, *Messiah*. Thus also the passage, Gen. xviii. 2 VHNH ShLShH, *Vehenna Shalisha*, "And lo, three men," equals in numerical value ALV MIKAL GBRIAL VRPAL, *Elo Mikhael Gabriel Ve-Raphael*, "These are Mikhael, Gabriel and Raphael;" for each phrase=701. I think these instances will suffice to make clear the nature of Gematria, especially as many others will be found in the course of the ensuing work.

12. Notariqon is derived from the Latin word *notarius*, a shorthand writer. Of Notariqon there are two forms

In the first every letter of a word is taken for the initial or abbreviation of another word, so that from the letters of a word a sentence may be formed. Thus every letter of the word BRAShITh, *Berashith*, the first word in Genesis, is made the initial of a word, and we obtain BRAShITh RAH ALHIM ShIQBLV IShRAL ThVRH, *Besrashith Rahi Elohim Sheyequebelo Israel Torah:* "In the beginning the Elohim saw that Israel would accept the law." In this connection I may give six very interesting specimens of Notariqon formed from this same word BRAShITh by Solomon Meir Ben Moses, a Jewish Qabalist, who embraced the Christian faith in 1665, and took the name of Prosper Rugers. These have all a Christian tendency, and by their means Prosper converted another Jew, who had previously been bitterly opposed to Christianity. The first is BN RVCh AB ShLVShThM IChD ThMIM, *Ben, Ruach, Ab, Shaloshethem Yechad Themim:* "The Son, the Spirit, the Father, Their Trinity, Perfect Unity." The second is, BN RVCh AB ShLVShThM IChD ThOBVDV, *Ben, Ruach, Ab, Shaloshethem Yechad Thaubodo*: "The Son, the Spirit, the Father, ye shall equally worship Their Trinity." The third is, BKVRI RAShVNI AShR ShMV IShVO ThOBVDV, *Bekori Rashuni Asher Shamo Yeshuah Thaubodo*: "Ye shall worship My first-born, My first, Whose Name is Jesus." The fourth is, BBVA RBN AShR ShMV IShVO ThOBVDV, *Beboa Rabban Asher Shamo Yesuah Thaubado*: "When the Master shall come Whose Name is Jesus ye shall worship." The fifth is, BThVLH RAVIH ABChRShThLDIShVOThAShRVH, *Bethulah Raviah Abachar Shethaled Yeshuah Thrashroah*: "I will choose a virgin worthy to bring forth Jesus, and ye shall call her blessed." The sixth is, BOVGTh RTzPIM ASThThR ShGVPI IShVO ThAKLV, *Beaugoth Ratzephim Assattar Shegopi Yeshuah Thakelo*: "I will hide myself in cake (baked with) coals, for ye shall eat Jesus, My Body." The Qabalistical importance of these sentences as bearing upon the doctrines of Christianity can hardly be overrated.

13. The second form of Notariqon is the exact reverse of the first. By this the initials or finals, or both, or the medials, of a sentence, are taken to form a word or words. Thus the Qabalah is called CHKMH NSTHRH, *Chokhmah Nesethrah*, "the secret wisdom;" and if we take the initials of these two words CH and N, we form by the second kind of Notariqon the word CHN, *Chen*, "grace." Similarly, from the initials and finals of the words MI IOLH LNV HSHMIMH, *Mi Iaulah Leno Ha-Shamayimah*, "Who shall go up for us to heaven?" (Deut. xxx. 12), are formed MILH, *Milah*, "circumcision," and IHVH, the Tetragrammaton, implying that God hath ordained circumcision as the way to heaven.

14. Temura is permutation. According to certain rules, one letter is substituted for another letter preceding or following it in the alphabet, and thus from one word another word of totally different orthography may be formed. Thus the alphabet is bent exactly in half, in the middle, and one half is put over the other; and then by changing alternately the first letter or the first two letters at the beginning of the second line, twenty-two commutations are produced. These are called the "Table of the Combinations of TzIRVP," *Tziruph*. For example's sake, I will give the method called ALBTH, *Albath*, thus:

11	10	9	8	7	6	5	4	3	2	1
K	I	T	CH	Z	V	H	D	G	B	A
M	N	S	O	P	Tz	Q	R	SH	TH	L

Each method takes its name from the first two pairs composing it, the system of pairs of letters being the groundwork of the whole, as either letter in a pair is substituted for the other letter. Thus, by Albath, from RVCH, *Ruach*, is formed DTzO, *Detzau*. The names of the other twenty-one methods are: ABGTH, AGDTH

ADBG, AHBD, AVBH, AZBV, AChBZ, ATBCh, AIBT, AKBI, ALBK, AMBL, ANBM, ASBN, AOBS, APBO, ATzBP, AQBTz, ARBQ, AShBR, and AThBSh. To these must be added the modes ABGD and ALBM. Then comes the "Rational Table of Tziruph," another set of twenty-two combinations. There are also three "Tables of the Commutations," known respectively as the Right, the Averse, and the Irregular. To make any of these, a square, containing 484 squares, should be made, and the letters written in. For the "Right Table" write the alphabet across from right to left; in the second row of squares do the same, but begin with B and end with A; in the third begin with G and end with B; and so on. For the "Averse Table" write the alphabet from right to left backwards, beginning with Th and ending with A; in the second row begin with Sh and end with Th, &c. The "Irregular Table" would take too long to describe. Besides all these, there is the method called ThShRQ, *Thashraq*, which is simply writing a word backwards. There is one more very important form, called the "Qabalah of the Nine Chambers," or AIQ BKR, *Aiq Bekar*. It is thus formed :

300	30	3	200	20	2	100	10	1
ooo	oo	o	ooo	oo	o	ooo	oo	o
Sh	L	G	R	K	B	Q	I	A
600	60	6	500	50	5	400	40	4
ooo	oo	o	ooo	oo	o	ooo	oo	o
M final	S	V	K final	N	H	Th	M	D
900	90	9	800	80	8	700	70	7
ooo	oo	o	ooo	oo	o	ooo	oo	o
Tz final	Tz	T	P final	P	Ch	N final	O	Z

I have put the numeration of each letter above to show the affinity between the letters in each chamber. Sometimes this is used as a cipher, by taking the portions of the figure to show the letters they contain, putting one point for the first letter, two for the second,

&c. Thus the right angle, containing AIQ, will answer for the letter Q if it have three dots or points within it. Again, a square will answer for H, N, or K final, according to whether it has one, two, or three points respectively placed within it. So also with regard to the other letters. But there are many other ways of employing the Qabalah of the Nine Chambers, which I have not space to describe. I will merely mention, as an example, that by the mode of Temura called ATHBSH, *Athbash*, it is found that in Jeremiah xxv. 26, the word SHSHK, *Sheshakh*, symbolizes BBL, *Babel.*

15. Besides all these rules, there are certain meanings hidden in the *shape* of the letters of the Hebrew alphabet; in the form of a particular letter at the end of a word being different from that which it generally bears when it is a final letter, or in a letter being written in the middle of a word in a character generally used only at the end; in any letter or letters being written in a size smaller or larger than the rest of the manuscript, or in a letter being written upside down; in the variations found in the spelling of certain words, which have a letter more in some places than they have in others; in peculiarities observed in the position of any of the points or accents, and in certain expressions supposed to be elliptic or redundant.

16. For example the shape of the Hebrew letter *Aleph*, A (see Plate I.), is said to symbolize a *Vau*, V, between a *Yod*, I, and a *Daleth*, D; and thus the letter itself represents the word IVD, *Yod.* Similarly the shape of the letter *He*, H, represents a *Daleth*, D, with a *Yod*, I, written at the lower left-hand corner, &c.

17. In Isaiah ix. 6, 7, the word LMRBH, *Lemarbah*, for multiplying, is written with the character for M final in the middle of the word, instead of with the ordinary initial and Medial M. The consequence of this is that the total numerical value of the word, instead of being $30 + 40 + 200 + 2 + 5 = 277$, is $30 + 600 + 200$

+2+5=837=by Gematria ThTh ZL, *Tat Zal*, the profuse Giver. Thus, by writing the M final instead of the ordinary character, the word is made to bear a different qabalistical meaning.

18. In Deuteronomy vi. 4, &c., is the prayer known as the "Shema Yisrael." It begins, "ShMO IShRAL IHVH ALHINV IHVH AChD, *Shemaa Yisrael, Tetragrammaton Elohino Tetragrammaton Achad:* "Hear, O Israel, Tetragrammaton your God is Tetragrammaton Unity." In this verse the terminal letter O in ShMO, and the D in AChD are written much larger than the other letters of the text. The qabalistical symbology contained in this circumstance is thus explained: The letter O, being of the value of 70, shows that the law may be explained in seventy different ways, and the D=4= the four cardinal points and the letters of the Holy Name. The first word, ShMO, has the numerical value of 410, the number of years of the duration of the first temple, &c. &c. There are many other points worthy of consideration in this prayer, but time will not permit me to dwell on them.

19. Other examples of deficient and redundant spelling, peculiarities of accent and pointing, &c., will be found in various places in the ensuing work.

20. It is to be further noted with regard to the first word in the Bible, BRAShITh, *Berashith*, that the first three letters, BRA, are the initial letters of the names of the three persons of the Trinity: BN, *Ben*, the Son; RVCH, *Ruach*, the Spirit; and AB, *Ab*, the Father. Furthermore, the first letter of the Bible is B, which is the initial letter of BRKH, *Berakhah*, blessing; and not A, which is that of ARR, *Arar*, cursing. Again, the letters of *Berashith*, taking their numerical powers, express the number of years between the Creation and the birth of Christ, thus: *B=2,000, R=200, *A=

* See note to the numerical values in the Table of the Hebrew Alphabet, &c., Plate I.

1000, SH = 300, I = 10, and TH = 400; total = 3910 years, being the time in round numbers. Picus de Mirandola gives the following working out of BRASHITH, *Berashith*:—By joining the third letter, A, to the first, B, AB, *Ab*=Father, is obtained. If to the first letter B, doubled, the second letter, R, be added, it makes BBR, *Bebar*=in or through the Son. If all the letters be read except the first, it makes RASHITH, *Rashith*=the beginning. If with the fourth letter, SH, the first B and the last TH be connected, it makes SHBTH, *Shebeth*=the end or rest. If the first three letters be taken, they make BRA, *Bera*=created. If, omitting the first, the three following be taken, they make RASH, *Rash*=head. If, omitting the two first, the next two be taken, they give ASH, *Ash*=fire. If the fourth and last be joined, they give SHTH, *Sheth*=foundation. Again, if the second letter be put before the first, it makes RB, *Rab*=great. If after the third be placed the fifth and fourth, it gives AISH, *Aish*=man. If to the two first be joined the two last, they give BRITH, *Berith*=covenant. And if the first be added to the last, it gives THB, *Theb*, which is sometimes used for TVB, *Thob*=good.

21. Taking the whole of these mystical anagrams in proper order, Picus makes the following sentence out of this one word BRASHITH:—*Pater in filio* (*aut per filium*) *principium et finem* (*sive quietum*) *creavit caput, ignem, et fundamentum magni hominis fœdere bono:* "Through the Son hath the Father created that Head which is the beginning and the end, the fire-life and the foundation of the supernal man (the Adam Qadmon) by His righteous covenant." Which is a short epitome of the teachings of the "Book of Concealed Mystery." This notice of the literal Qabalah has already extended beyond its proper limits. It was, however, necessary to be thus explicit, as much of the metaphysical reasoning of the ensuing work turns on its application.

22. The term "Unwritten Qabalah" is applied to certain

knowledge which is never entrusted to writing, but communicated orally. I may say no more on this point, not even whether I myself have or have not received it. Of course, till the time of Rabbi Schimeon Ben Jochai none of the Qabalah was ever written.

23. The Dogmatic Qabalah contains the doctrinal portion. There are a large number of treatises of various dates and merits which go to make up the written Qabalah, but they may be reduced to four heads:

(α) The Sepher Yetzirah and its dependencies.

(β) The Zohar with its developments and commentaries.

(γ) The Sepher Sephiroth and its expansions.

(δ) The Asch Metzareph and its symbolism.

24. The SPR ITZIRH, *Sepher Yetzirah*, or "Book of Formation," is ascribed to the patriarch Abraham. It treats of the cosmogony as symbolized by the ten numbers and the twenty-two letters of the alphabet, which it calls the "thirty-two paths." On these latter Rabbi Abraham Ben Dior has written a mystical commentary. The term "path" is used throughout the Qabalah to signify a hieroglyphical idea, or rather the sphere of ideas, which may be attached to any glyph or symbol.

25. The ZHR, *Zohar*, or "Splendour," besides many other treatises of less note, contains the following most important books, of which the three first are translated in this volume:

(α) The SPRA DTZNIOVTHA, *Siphra Dtzenioutha*, or "Book of Concealed Mystery," which is the root and foundation of the Zohar.

(β) The ADRA RBA QDISHA, *Idra Rabba Qadisha* or "Greater Holy Assembly:" this is a development of the "Book of Concealed Mystery."

(γ) The ADRA ZVTA QDISHA, *Idra Zuta Qadisha*, or "Lesser Holy Assembly;" which is in the nature of a supplement to the "Idra Rabba." These three books treat of the gradual development of the creative Deity, and with Him the

Creation. The text of these works has been annotated by Knorr von Rosenroth (the author of the "Qabalah Denudata,") from the Mantuan, Cremonensian, and Lublinensian Codices, which are corrected printed copies; of these the Mantuan and Cremonensian are the oldest. A species of commentary is also given, which is distinguished from the actual text by being written within parentheses.

(δ) The pneumatical treatise called BITH ALHIM, *Beth Elohim*, or the "House of the Elohim," edited by Rabbi Abraham Cohen Irira, from the doctrines of Rabbi Yitzchaq Loria. It treats of angels, demons, elemental spirits, and souls.

(ε) The "Book of the Revolutions of Souls" is a peculiar and discursive treatise, and is an expansion of Rabbi Loria's ideas.

26. The SPR SPIRVTH, *Sepher Sephiroth*, or "Book of the Emanations," describes, so to speak, the gradual evolution of the Deity from negative into positive existence.

27. The ASH MTzRP, *Asch Metzareph*, or "Purifying Fire," is hermatic and alchemical, and is known to few, and when known is understood by still fewer.

28. The principal doctrines of the Qabalah are designed to solve the following problems:—

(α) The Supreme Being, His nature and attributes.
(β) The Cosmogony.
(γ) The creation of angels and man.
(δ) The destiny of man and angels.
(ε) The nature of the soul.
(ζ) The nature of angels, demons, and elementals.
(η) The import of the revealed law.
(θ) The transcendental symbolism of numerals.
(ι) The peculiar mysteries contained in the Hebrew letters.
(κ) The equilibrium of contraries.

29. The "Book of Concealed Mystery" opens with these

words: "The Book of Concealed Mystery is the book of the equilibrium of balance." What is here meant by the terms "equilibrium of balance"? Equilibrium is that harmony which results from the analogy of contraries, it is the dead centre where, the opposition of opposing forces being equal in strength, rest succeeds motion. It is the central point. It is the "point within the circle" of ancient symbolism. It is the living synthesis of counterbalanced power. Thus form may be described as the equilibrium of light and shade; take away either factor, and form is viewless. The term balance is applied to the two opposite natures in each triad of the Sephiroth, their equilibrium forming the third Sephira in each ternary. I shall recur again to this subject in explaining the Sephiroth. This doctrine of equilibrium and balance is a fundamental qabalistical idea.

30. The "Book of Concealed Mystery" goes on to state that this "Equilibrium hangeth in that region which is negatively existent." What is negative existence? What is positive existence? The distinction between these two is another fundamental idea. To define negative existence clearly is impossible, *for when it is distinctly defined it ceases to be negative existence*; it is then negative existence passing into static condition. Therefore wisely have the Qabalists shut out from mortal comprehension the primal AIN, *Ain*, the negatively existent One, and the AIN SVP, *Ain Soph*, the limitless Expansion; while of even the AIN SVP AVR, *Ain Soph Aur*, the illimitable Light, only a dim conception can be formed. Yet, if we think deeply, we shall see that such must be the primal forms of the unknowable and nameless One, whom we, in the more manifest form speak of as God. He is the Absolute. But how define the Absolute? Even as we define it, it slips from our grasp, for it ceases when defined to be the Absolute. Shall we then say that the Negative, the Limitless, the Absolute are, logically speaking, absurd, since they are ideas which our reason

cannot define? No; for could we define them, we should make them, so to speak, contained by our reason, and therefore not superior to it; for a subject to be capable of definition it is requisite that certain limits should be assignable to it. How then can we limit the Illimitable?

31. The first principle and axiom of the Qabalah is the name of the Deity, translated in our version of the Bible, "I am that I am," AHIH AShR AHIH, *Eheieh Asher Eheieh*. A better translation is, "Existence is existence," or "I am He who is."

32. Eliphaz Levi Zahed, that great philosopher and Qabalist of the present century, says in his "Histoire de la Magie" (bk. i. ch. 7): "The Qabalists have a horror of everything that resembles idolatry; they, however, ascribe the human form to God, but it is a purely hieroglyphical figure. They consider God as the intelligent, living, and loving Infinite One. He is for them neither the collection of other beings, nor the abstraction of existence, nor a philosophically definable being. He is in all, distinct from all, and greater than all. His very name is ineffable; and yet this name only expresses the human ideal of His Divinity. What God is in Himself it is not given to man to know. God is the absolute of faith; existence is the absolute of reason, existence exists by itself, and because it exists. The reason of the existence of existence is existence itself. We may ask, 'Why does any particular thing exist?' that is, 'Why does such or such a thing exist?' But we cannot ask, without its being absurd to do so, 'Why does existence exist?' For this would be to suppose existence prior to existence." Again, the same author says (*ibid.* bk. iii. ch. 2): "To say, 'I will believe when the truth of the dogma shall be scientifically proved to me,' is the same as to say, 'I will believe when I have nothing more to believe, and when the dogma shall be destroyed as dogma by becoming a scientific theorem.'

That is to say, in other words: 'I will only admit the Infinite when it shall have been explained, determined, circumscribed, and defined for my benefit; in one word, when it has become finite. I will then believe in the Infinite when I am sure that the Infinite does not exist. I will believe in the vastness of the ocean when I shall have seen it put into bottles.' But when a thing has been clearly proved and made comprehensible to you, you will no longer *believe* it—you will *know* it."

33. In the "Bhagavadgîtâ," ch. ix., it is said: "I am Immortality and also death; and I, O Arguna! am that which is and that which is not." * And again (ch. ix.): "And, O descendant of Bharata! see wonders in numbers, unseen before. Within my body, O Gudâkesa! see to-day the whole universe, including everything movable and immovable, all in one." And again (*ibid.*) Arguna said: "O Infinite Lord of the Gods! O Thou who pervadest the universe! Thou art the Indestructible, that which is, that which is not, and what is beyond them. Thou art the Primal God, the Ancient One; Thou are the highest support of this universe. By Thee is this universe pervaded, O Thou of the infinite forms . . . . Thou art of infinite power, of unmeasured glory; Thou pervadest all, and therefore Thou art all!"

34. The idea of negative existence can then exist *as an idea*, but it will not bear definition, since the idea of definition is utterly incompatible with its nature. "But," some of my readers will perhaps say, "your term negative existence is surely a misnomer; the state you describe would be better expressed by the title of negative subsistence." Not so, I answer; for negative subsistence can never be anything but negative subsistence; it cannot vary, it cannot develop; for negative subsistence is literally and truly *no thing*. Therefore, negative subsistence cannot *be* at all; it never has existed, it never does exist, it never will exist. But negative existence bears hidden in

* Or, "which exists negatively."

itself, positive life; for in the limitless depths of the abyss of its negativity lies hidden the power of standing forth from itself, the power of projecting the scintilla of the thought unto the utter, the power of re-involving the syntagma into the inner. Thus shrouded and veiled is the absorbed intensity in the centreless whirl of the vastness of expansion. Therefore have I employed the term "Ex-sto," rather than "Sub-sto."

35. But between two ideas so different as those of negative and positive existence a certain nexus, or connecting-link, is required, and hence we arrive at the form which is called potential existence, which while more nearly approaching positive existence, will still scarcely admit of clear definition. It is existence in its possible form. For example, in a seed, the tree which may spring from it is hidden; it is in a condition of potential existence; is there; but it will not admit of definition. How much less, then, will those seeds which that tree in its turn may yield. But these latter are in a condition which, while it is somewhat analogous to potential existence, is in hardly so advanced a stage; that is, they are negatively existent.

36. But, on the other hand, positive existence is always capable of definition; it is dynamic; it has certain evident powers, and it is therefore the antithesis of negative existence, and still more so of negative subsistence. It is the tree, no longer hidden in the seed, but developed into the outer. But positive existence has a beginning and an end, and it therefore requires another form from which to depend, for without this other concealed negative ideal behind it, it is unstable and unsatisfactory.

37. Thus, then, have I faintly and with all reverence endeavoured to shadow forth to the minds of my readers the idea of the Illimitable One. And before that idea, and of that idea, I can only say, in the words of an ancient oracle: "In Him is an illimitable abyss of glory, and from it there goeth forth one little spark

which maketh all the glory of the sun, and of the moon, and of the stars. Mortal! behold how little I know of God; seek not to know more of Him, for this is far beyond thy comprehension, however wise thou art; as for us, who are His ministers, how small a part are we of Him!"

38. There are three qabalistical veils of the negative existence, and in themselves they formulate the *hidden ideas* of the Sephiroth not yet called into being, and they are concentrated in Kether, which in this sense is the Malkuth of the hidden ideas of the Sephiroth. I will explain this. The first veil of the negative existence is the AIN, *Ain*=Negativity. This word consists of three letters, which thus shadow forth the first three Sephiroth or numbers. The second veil is the AIN SVP, *Ain Soph* = the Limitless. This title consists of six letters, and shadows forth the idea of the first six Sephiroth or numbers. The third veil is the AIN SVP AVR, *Ain Soph Aur*=the Limitless Light. This again consists of nine letters, and symbolizes the first nine Sephiroth, but of course in their hidden idea only. But when we reach the number nine we cannot progress farther without returning to the unity, or the number one, for the number ten is but a repetition of unity freshly derived from the negative, as is evident from a glance at its ordinary representation in Arabic numerals, where the circle 0 represents the Negative, and the 1 the Unity. Thus, then, the limitless ocean of negative light *does not proceed from a centre, for it is centreless, but it concentrates a centre,* which is the number one of the manifested Sephiroth, Kether, the Crown, the First Sephira; which therefore may be said to be the Malkuth or number ten of the hidden Sephiroth. (See Plate II.). Thus, "Kether is in Malkuth, and Malkuth is in Kether." Or, as an alchemical author of great repute (Thomas Vaughan, better known as Eugenius Philalethes) says,*

* "Euphrates; or, The Waters of the East."

CLOUD VEILS OF THE AIN FORMULATING THE HIDDEN SEPHIROTH
AND CONCENTRATING IN KETHER, THE FIRST SEPHIRA

Plate II.

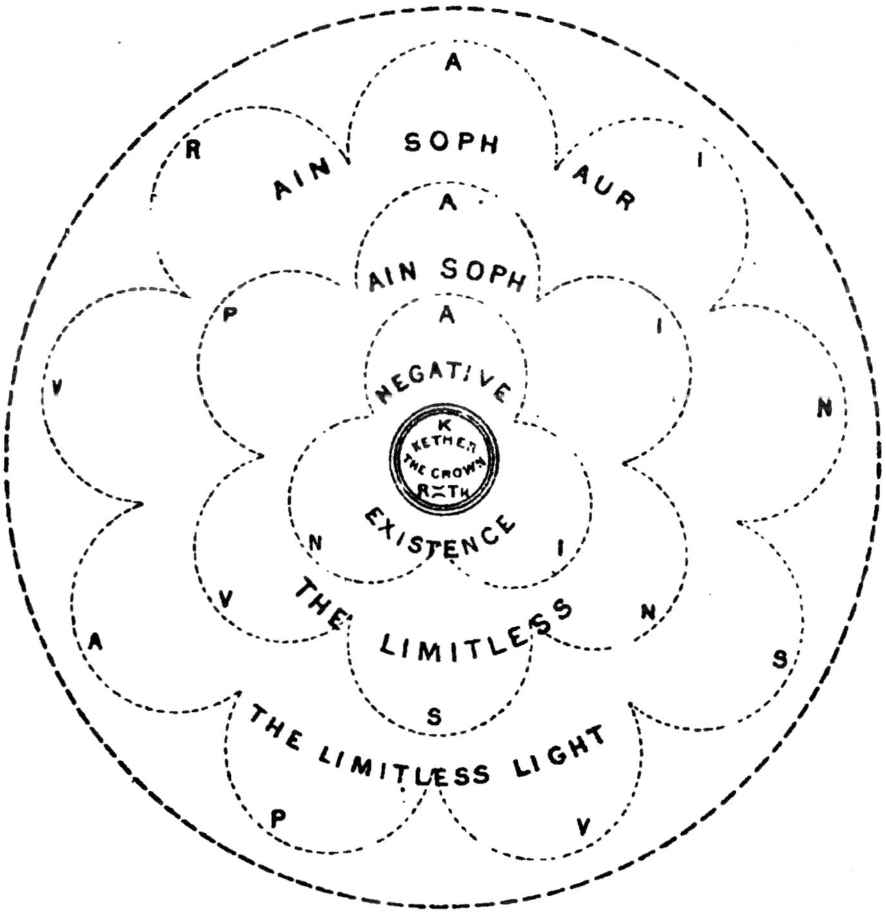

(To face page 20.)

apparently quoting from Proclus: "That the heaven is in the earth, but after an earthly manner; and that the earth is in the heaven, but after a heavenly manner." But inasmuch as negative existence is a subject incapable of definition, as I have before shown, it is rather considered by the Qabalists as depending back from the number of unity than as a separate consideration therefrom; wherefore they frequently apply the same terms and epithets indiscriminately to either. Such epithets are "The Concealed of the Concealed," "The Ancient of the Ancient Ones," the "Most Holy Ancient One," &c.

39. I must now explain the real meaning of the terms Sephira and Sephiroth. The first is singular, the second is plural. The best rendering of the word is "numerical emanation." There are ten Sephiroth, which are the most abstract forms of the ten numbers of the decimal scale—*i.e.*, the numbers 1, 2, 3, 4, 5, 6, 7, 8, 9, 10. Therefore, as in the higher mathematics we reason of numbers in their abstract sense, so in the Qabalah we reason of the Deity by the abstract forms of the numbers; in other words, by the SPIRVTH, *Sephiroth*. It was from this ancient Oriental theory that Pythagoras derived his numerical symbolic ideas.

40. Among these Sephiroth, jointly and severally, we find the development of the persons and attributes of God. Of these *some are male and some female.* Now, for some reason or other best known to themselves, the translators of the Bible have carefully crowded out of existence and smothered up every reference to the fact that the Deity is both masculine and feminine. They have translated *a feminine plural* by a *masculine singular* in the case of the word Elohim. They have, however, left an inadvertent admission of their knowledge that it was plural in Gen. iv. 26; "And Elohim said: Let Us make man." Again (v. 27), how could Adam be made in the image of the Elohim, male and female, unless the Elohim were male and female also? The word Elohim

is a plural formed from the feminine singular ALH, *Eloh*, by adding IM to the word. But inasmuch as IM is usually the termination of the masculine plural, and is here added to a feminine noun, it gives to the word Elohim the sense of a female potency united to a masculine idea, and thereby capable of producing an offspring. Now, we hear much of the Father and the Son, but we hear nothing of the Mother in the ordinary religions of the day. But in the Qabalah we find that the Ancient of Days conforms Himself simultaneously into the Father and the Mother, and thus begets the Son. Now, this Mother is Elohim. Again, we are usually told that the Holy Spirit is masculine. But the word RVCH, *Ruach*, Spirit, is feminine, as appears from the following passage of the Sepher Yetzirah: "ACHTH RVCH ALHIM CHIIM, *Achath* (*feminine, not Achad, masculine*) *Ruach Elohim Chiim*: One is *She* the Spirit of the Elohim of Life."

41. Now, we find that before the Deity conformed Himself thus—*i.e.*, as male and female—that the worlds of the universe could not subsist, or, in the words of Genesis, "The earth was formless and void." These prior worlds are considered to be symbolized by the "kings who reigned in Edom before there reigned a king in Israel," and they are therefore spoken of in the Qabalah as the "Edomite kings." This will be found fully explained in various parts of this work.

42. We now come to the consideration of the first Sephira, or the Number One, the Monad of Pythagoras. In this number are the other nine hidden. It is indivisible, it is also incapable of multiplication; divide 1 by itself and it still remains 1, multiply 1 by itself and it is still 1 and unchanged. Thus it is a fitting representative of the great unchangeable Father of all. Now this number of unity has a twofold nature, and thus forms, as it were, the link between the negative and the positive. In its unchangeable one-ness it is scarcely a number; but in its property of capability of addition

it may be called the first number of a numerical series. Now, the zero, 0, is incapable even of addition, just as also is negative existence. How, then, if 1 can neither be multiplied nor divided, is another 1 to be obtained to add to it; in other words, how is the number 2 to be found? *By reflection of itself.* For though 0 be incapable of definition, 1 is definable. And the effect of a definition is to form an Eidolon, duplicate, or image, of the thing defined. Thus, then, we obtain a duad composed of 1 and its reflection. Now also we have *the commencement of a vibration* established, for the number 1 vibrates alternately from changelessness to definition, and back to changelessness again. Thus, then, is it the father of all numbers, and a fitting type of the Father of all things.

The name of the first Sephira is KTHR, *Kether*, the Crown.

The Divine Name attributed to it is the Name of the Father given in Exod. iii. 4: AHIH, *Eheieh*, I am. It signifies Existence.

Among the Epithets applied to it, as containing in itself the idea of negative existence depending back from it, are:

TMIRA DTMIRIN, *Temira De-Temirin*, the Concealed of the Concealed.

OTHIQA DOTHIQIN, *Authiqa De-Authiqin*, the Ancient of the Ancient Ones.

OTHIQA QDISHA, *Authiqa Qadisha*, the Most Holy Ancient One.

OTHIQA, *Authiqa*, the Ancient One.

OTHIQ IVMIN, *Authiq Iomin*, the Ancient of Days.

It is also called:

NQDH RASHVNH, *Nequdah Rashunah*, the Primordial Point.

NQDH PSHVTH, *Nequdah Peshutah*, the Smooth Point.

RISHA HVVRH, *Risha Havurah*, the White Head.

RVM MOLH, *Rom Meolah*, the Inscrutable Height.

Besides all these there is another very important name applied to this Sephira as representing the great Father of all things. It is ARIK ANPIN, *Arikh Anpin*, the Vast Countenance, or Macroprosopus. Of Him it is said that He is partly concealed (in the sense of His connection with the negative existence) and partly manifest (as a positive Sephira). Hence the symbolism of the Vast Countenance is that of a profile wherein one side only of the countenance is seen; or, as it is said in the Qabalah, "in Him all is right side." I shall refer to this title again.

The whole ten Sephiroth represent the Heavenly Man, or Primordial Being, ADM OILAH, *Adam Auilah.*

Under this Sephira are classed the angelic order of CHIVTH HQDSH, *Chioth Ha-Qadesh*, holy living-creatures, the kerubim or sphinxes of Ezekiel's vision and of the Apocalypse of John. These are represented in the Zodiac by the four signs, Taurus, Leo, Scorpio, and Aquarius—the Bull, Lion, Eagle, and Man: Scorpio, as a good emblem, being symbolized by the eagle, as an evil emblem by the scorpion, and as of a mixed nature by the snake.

This first Sephira contained the other nine, and produced them in succession, thus:—

43. The number 2, or the Duad. The name of the second Sephira is CHKMH, *Chokmah*, Wisdom, a masculine active potency reflected from Kether, as I have before explained. This Sephira is the active and evident Father, to whom the Mother is united, who is the number 3. This second Sephira is represented by the Divine Names, IH, *Yah*, and IHVH; and among the angelic hosts by AVPNIM, *Auphanim*, the Wheels (Ezek. i.). It is also called AB, *Ab*, the Father.

44. The third Sephira, or Triad, is a feminine passive potency, called BINH, *Binah*, the Understanding, who is co-equal with Chokmah. For Chokmah, the number 2, is like two straight lines which can never enclose a space,

and therefore it is powerless till the number 3 forms the triangle. Thus this Sephira completes and makes evident the supernal Trinity. It is also called AMA, *Ama*, Mother, and AIMA, *Aima*, the great productive Mother, who is eternally conjoined with AB, the Father, for the maintenance of the universe in order. Therefore is she the most evident form in whom we can know the Father, and therefore is she worthy of all honour. She is the supernal Mother, co-equal with Chokmah, and the great feminine form of God, the Elohim, in whose image man and woman are created, according to the teaching of the Qabalah, *equal before God. Woman is equal with man, and certainly not inferior to him*, as it has been the persistent endeavour of so-called Christians to make her. Aima is the woman described in the Apocalypse (ch. xii.). This third Sephira is also sometimes called the great sea. To her are attributed the Divine names, ALHIM, *Elohim*, and IHVH ALHIM; and the angelic order, ARALIM, *Aralim*, the Thrones. She is the supernal Mother, as distinguished from Malkuth, the inferior Mother, Bride, and Queen.

45. The number 4. This union of the second and third Sephiroth produced CHSD, *Chesed*, Mercy or Love also called GDVLH, *Gedulah*, Greatness or Magnificence; a masculine potency represented by the Divine Name AL, *El*, the Mighty One, and the angelic name, CHSHMLIM, *Chashmalim*, Scintillating Flames (Ezek. iv. 4).

46. The number 5. From this emanated the feminine passive potency GBVRH, *Geburah*, strength or fortitude; or DIN, *Deen*, Justice; represented by the Divine Names, ALHIM GBVR, and ALH, *Eloh*, and the angelic name SHRPIM, *Seraphim* (Isa. vi. 6). This Sephira is also called PCHD, *Pachad*, Fear.

47. The number 6. And from these two issued the uniting Sephira, THPARTH, *Tiphereth*, Beauty or Mildness, represented by the Divine Name ALVH VDOTH, *Eloah*

Va-Daath, and the angelic names, *Shinanim*, SHNANIM (Ps. lxviii. 18), or MLKIM, *Melakim*, kings. Thus by the union of justice and mercy we obtain beauty or clemency, and the second trinity of the Sephiroth is complete. This Sephira, or "Path," or "Numeration"—for by these latter appellations the emanations are sometimes called—together with the fourth, fifth, seventh, eighth, and ninth Sephiroth, is spoken of as ZOIR ANPIN, *Zauir Anpin*, the Lesser Countenance, or Microprosopus, by way of antithesis to Macroprosopus, or the Vast Countenance, which is one of the names of Kether, the first Sephira. The sixth Sephiroth of which *Zauir Anpin* is composed, are then called His six members. He is also called MLK, *Melekh*, the King.

48. The number 7. The seventh Sephira is NTzCH, *Netzach*, or Firmness and Victory, corresponding to the Divine Name *Jehovah Tzabaoth*, IHVH TzBAVTH, the Lord of Armies, and the angelic names ALHIM, *Elohim*, gods, and THRSHISHIM, *Tharshisim*, the brilliant ones (Dan. x. 6).

49. The number 8. Thence proceeded the feminine passive potency HVD, *Hod*, Splendour, answering to the Divine Name ALHIM TzBAVTH, *Elohim Tzabaoth*, the Gods of Armies, and among the angels to BNI ALHIM, *Beni Elohim*, the sons of the Gods (Gen. vi. 4).

50. The number 9. These two produced ISVD, *Yesod*, the Foundation or Basis, represented by AL CHI, *El Chai*, the Mighty Living One, and SHDI, *Shaddaï*; and among the angels by ASHIM, *Aishim*, the Flames (Ps. civ. 4), yielding the third Trinity of the Sephiroth.

51. The number 10. From this ninth Sephira came the tenth and last, thus completing the decad of the numbers. It is called MLKVTH, *Malkuth*, the Kingdom, and also the Queen, Matrona, the inferior Mother, the Bride of Microprosopus; and SHKINH, *Shekinah*, represented by the Divine Name *Adonai*, ADNI, and among the angelic hosts by the kerubim, KRVBIM. Now, each of these Sephiroth will be in a certain degree androgynous, for

it will be feminine or receptive with regard to the Sephira which immediately precedes it in the sephirotic scale, and masculine or transmissive with regard to the Sephira which immediately follows it. But there is no *Sephira* anterior to Kether, nor is there a Sephira which succeeds Malkuth. By these remarks it will be understood how Chokmah is a feminine noun, though marking a masculine Sephira. The connecting-link of the Sephiroth is the Ruach, spirit, from Mezla, the hidden influence.

52. I will now add a few more remarks on the qabalistical meaning of the term MThQLA, *Metheqela*, balance. In each of the three trinities or triads of the Sephiroth is a duad of opposite sexes, and a uniting intelligence which is the result. In this, the masculine and feminine potencies are regarded as the two scales of the balance, and the uniting Sephira as the beam which joins them. Thus, then, the term balance may be said to symbolize the Triune, Trinity in Unity, and the Unity represented by the central point of the beam. But, again, in the Sephiroth there is a triple Trinity, the upper, lower, and middle. Now, these three are represented thus: the supernal, or highest, by the Crown, Kether; the middle by the King, and the inferior by the Queen; which will be the greatest trinity. And the earthly correlatives of these will be the *primum mobile*, the sun and the moon. Here we at once find alchemical symbolism.

53. Now in the world the Sephiroth are represented by:

(1) RAShITh HGLGLIM, *Rashith Ha-Galgalim*, the commencement of whirling motions, the *primum mobile*

(2) MSLVTh, *Masloth*, the sphere of the Zodiac.

(3) ShBThAI, *Shabbathai*, rest, Saturn.

(4) TzDQ, *Tzedeq*, righteousness, Jupiter.

(5) MADIM, *Madim*, vehement strength, Mars.

(6) ShMSh, *Shemesh*, the solar light, the Sun.

(7) NVGH, *Nogah*, glittering splendour, Venus.

(8) KVKB, *Kokab*, the stellar light, Mercury.

(9) LBNH, *Levanah*, the lunar flame, the Moon.

(10) CHLM ISVDVTH, *Cholom Yesodoth*, the breaker of the foundations, the elements.

54. The Sephiroth are further divided into three pillars—the right-hand Pillar of Mercy, consisting of the second, fourth, and seventh emanations; the left-hand Pillar of Judgment, consisting of the third, fifth, and eighth; and the middle Pillar of Mildness, consisting of the first, sixth, ninth, and tenth emanations.

55. In their totality and unity the ten Sephiroth represent the archetypal man, ADM QDMVN, *Adam Qadmon*, the Protogonos. In looking at the Sephiroth constituting the first triad, it is evident that they represent the intellect; and hence this triad is called the intellectual world, OVLM MVSHKL, *Olahm Mevshekal*. The second triad corresponds to the moral world, OVLM MVRGSH, *Olahm Morgash*. The third represents power and stability, and is therefore called the material world, OVLM HMVTBO, *Olahm Ha-Mevetbau*. These three aspects are called the faces, ANPIN, *Anpin*. Thus is the tree of life, OTz CHIIM, *Otz Chaiim*, formed; the first triad being placed above, the second and third below, in such a manner that the three masculine Sephiroth are on the right, three feminine on the left, whilst the four uniting Sephiroth occupy the centre. This is the qabalistical "tree of life," on which all things depend. There is considerable analogy between this and the tree Yggdrasil of the Scandinavians.

56. I have already remarked that there is one trinity which comprises all the Sephiroth, and that it consists of the crown, the king, and the queen. (In some senses this is the Christian Trinity of Father, Son, and Holy Spirit, which in their highest divine nature are symbolized by the first three Sephiroth, Kether, Chokmah, and Binah.) It is the Trinity which created the world, or, in qabalistic language, the universe was born from the

Plate III.

THE SEPHIROTH.

AIN SOPH THE LIMITLESS ONE

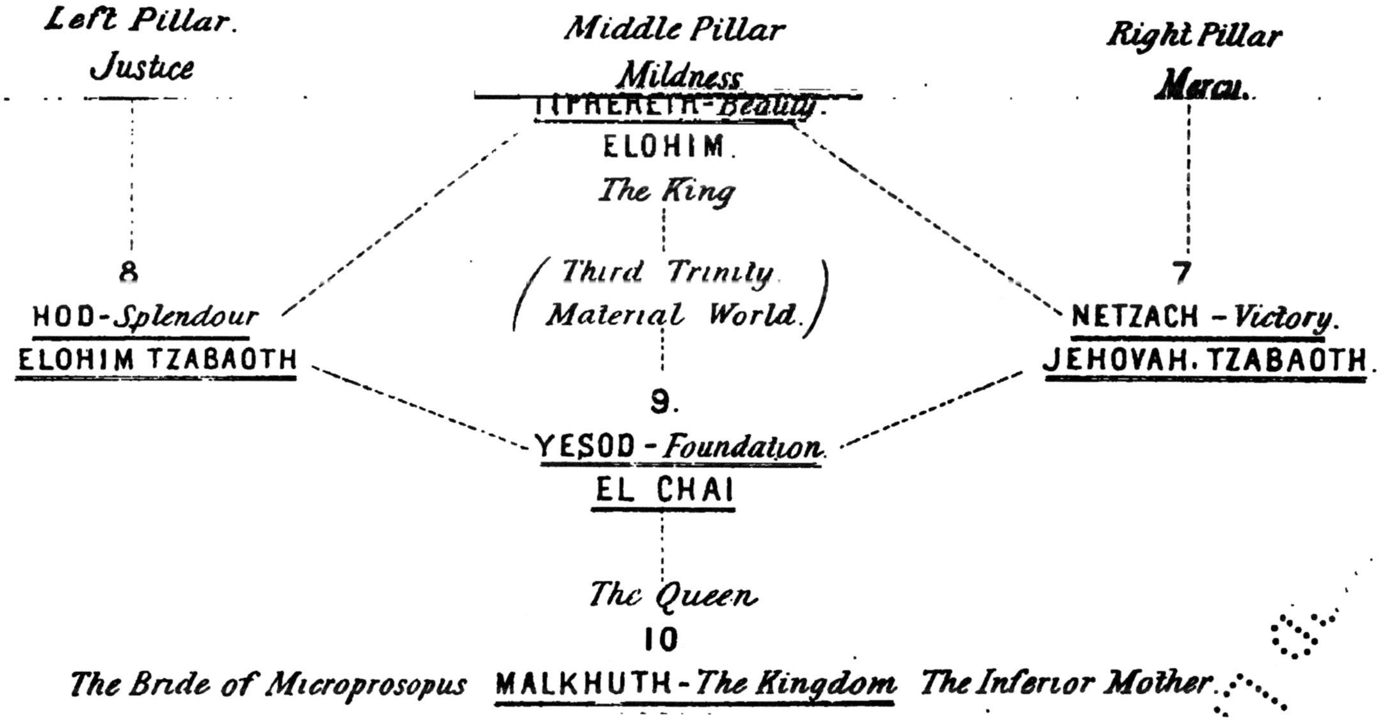

[redacted]

union of the crowned king and queen. But according to the Qabalah, before the complete form of the heavenly man (the ten Sephiroth) was produced, there were certain primordial worlds created, but these could not subsist, as the equilibrium of balance was not yet perfect, and they were convulsed by the unbalanced force and destroyed. These primordial worlds are called the "kings of ancient time," and the "kings of Edom who reigned before the monarchs of Israel." In this sense, Edom is the world of unbalanced force, and Israel is the balanced Sephiroth (Gen. xxxvi. 31). This important fact, that worlds were created and destroyed prior to the present creation, is again and again reiterated in the Zohar.

57. Now the Sephiroth are also called the World of Emanations, or the Atziluthic World, or archetypal world, OVLM ATzILVTh, *Olahm Atziloth;* and this world gave birth to three other worlds, each containing a repetition of the Sephiroth, but in a descending scale of brightness.

58. The second world is the Briatic world, OVLM HBRIAH, *Olahm Ha-Briah,* the world of creation, also called KVRSIA, *Khorsia,* the throne. It is an immediate emanation from the world of Atziloth, whose ten Sephiroth are reflected herein, and are consequently more limited, though they are still of the purest nature, and without any admixture of matter.

59. The third is the Jetziratic world, OVLM HITzIRH, *Olahm Ha-Yetzirah,* or world of formation and of angels, which proceeds from Briah, and though less refined in substance, is still without matter. It is in this angelic world where those intelligent and incorporeal beings reside who are wrapped in a luminous garment, and who assume a form when they appear unto man.

60. The fourth is the Asiatic world, OVLM HOShIH, *Olahm Ha-Asia,* the world of action, called

also the world of shells, OVLM HQLIPVTH, *Olahm Ha-Qliphoth*, which is this world of matter, made up of the grosser elements of the other three. In it is also the abode of the evil spirits which are called "the shells" by the Qabalah, QLIPVTH, *Qliphoth*, material shells. The devils are also divided into ten classes, and have suitable habitations. (See Table.)

61. The Demons are the grossest and most deficient of all forms. Their ten degrees answer to the decad of the Sephiroth, but in inverse ratio, as darkness and impurity increase with the descent of each degree. The two first are nothing but absence of visible form and organization. The third is the abode of darkness. Next follow seven Hells occupied by those demons which represent incarnate human vices, and torture those who have given themselves up to such vices in earth-life. Their prince is *Samael*, SMAL, the angel of poison and of death. His wife is the harlot, or woman of whoredom, ASHTH ZNVNIM, *Isheth Zenunim*; and united they are called the beast, CHIVA, *Chioa*. Thus the infernal trinity is completed, which is, so to speak, the averse and caricature of the supernal Creative One. Samael is considered to be identical with Satan.

62. The name of the Deity, which we call Jehovah, is in Hebrew a name of four letters, IHVH; and the true pronunciation of it is known to very few. I myself know some score of different mystical pronunciations of it. The true pronunciation is a most secret arcanum, and is a secret of secrets. "He who can rightly pronounce it, causeth heaven and earth to tremble, for it is the name which rusheth through the universe." Therefore when a devout Jew comes upon it in reading the Scripture, he either does not attempt to pronounce it, but instead makes a short pause, or else he substitutes for it the name *Adonai*, ADNI, Lord. The radical meaning of the word is "to be," and it is thus, like AHIH, *Eheieh*, a glyph of existence. It is capable of twelve transposi-

Plate IX

TABLE
SHOWING THE RECEPTION AND TRANSMISSION OF THE SEPHIROTH IN THE FOUR WORLDS.

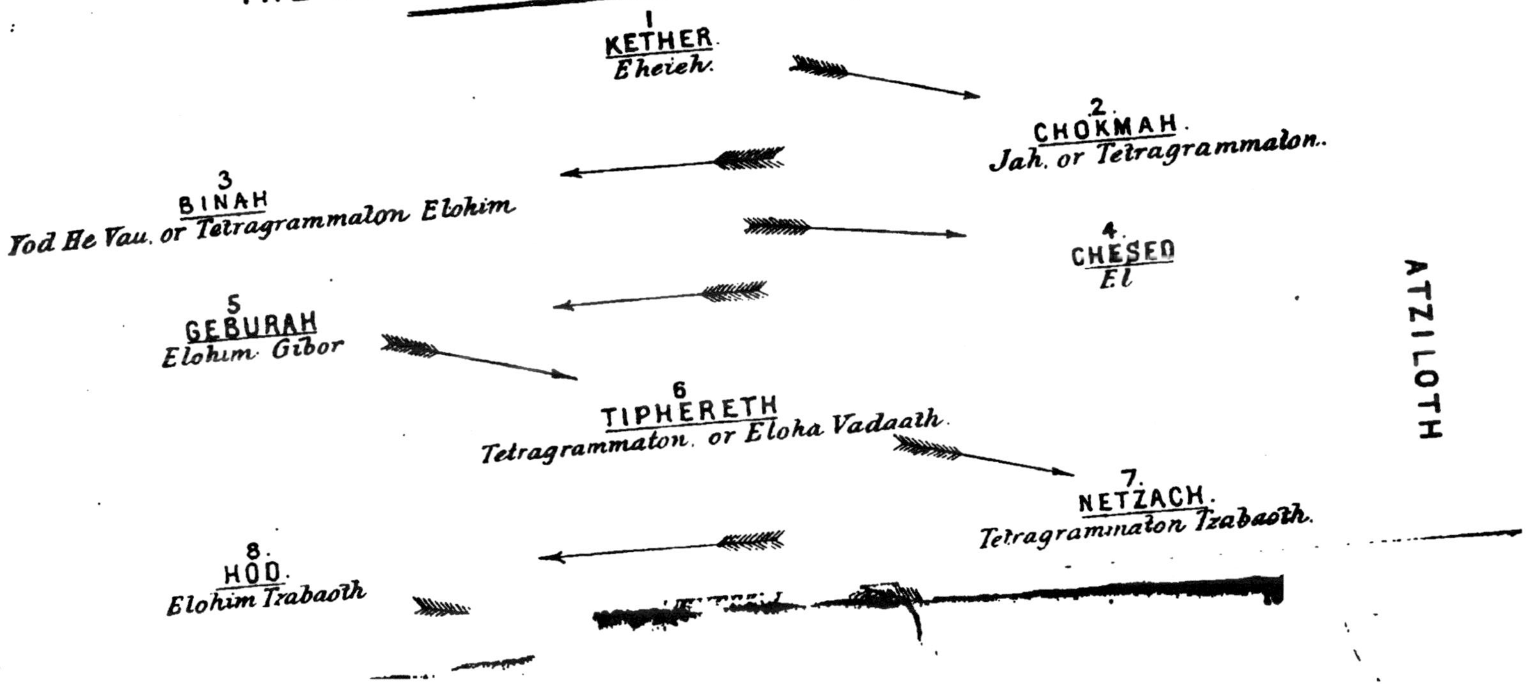

(In Ezekiel's Vision, the "Appearanc

also the world of shells, OVLM HQLIPVTH, *Olahm Ha-Qliphoth*, which is this world of matter, made up of the grosser elements of the other three. In it is also the abode of the evil spirits which are called "the shells" by the Qabalah, QLIPVTH, *Qliphoth*, material shells. The devils are also divided into ten classes, and have suitable habitations. (See Table.)

61. The Demons are the grossest and most deficient of all forms. Their ten degrees answer to the decad of the Sephiroth, but in inverse ratio, as darkness and impurity increase with the descent of each degree. The two first are nothing but absence of visible form and organization. The third is the abode of darkness. Next follow seven Hells occupied by those demons which represent incarnate human vices, and torture those who have given themselves up to such vices in earth-life. Their prince is *Samael*, SMAL, the angel of poison and of death. His wife is the harlot, or woman of whoredom, ASHTH ZNVNIM, *Isheth Zenunim;* and united they are called the beast, CHIVA, *Chioa*. Thus the infernal trinity is completed, which is, so to speak, the averse and caricature of the supernal Creative One. Samael is considered to be identical with Satan.

62. The name of the Deity, which we call Jehovah, is in Hebrew a name of four letters, IHVH; and the true pronunciation of it is known to very few. I myself know some score of different mystical pronunciations of it. The true pronunciation is a most secret arcanum, and is a secret of secrets. "He who can rightly pronounce it, causeth heaven and earth to tremble, for it is the name which rusheth through the universe." Therefore when a devout Jew comes upon it in reading the Scripture, he either does not attempt to pronounce it, but instead makes a short pause, or else he substitutes for it the name *Adonai*, ADNI, Lord. The radical meaning of the word is "to be," and it is thus, like A[illegible] a glyph of existence. It is capable of tw

TABLE
SHOWING THE RECEPTION AND TRANSMISSION OF THE SEPHIROTH IN THE FOUR WORLDS

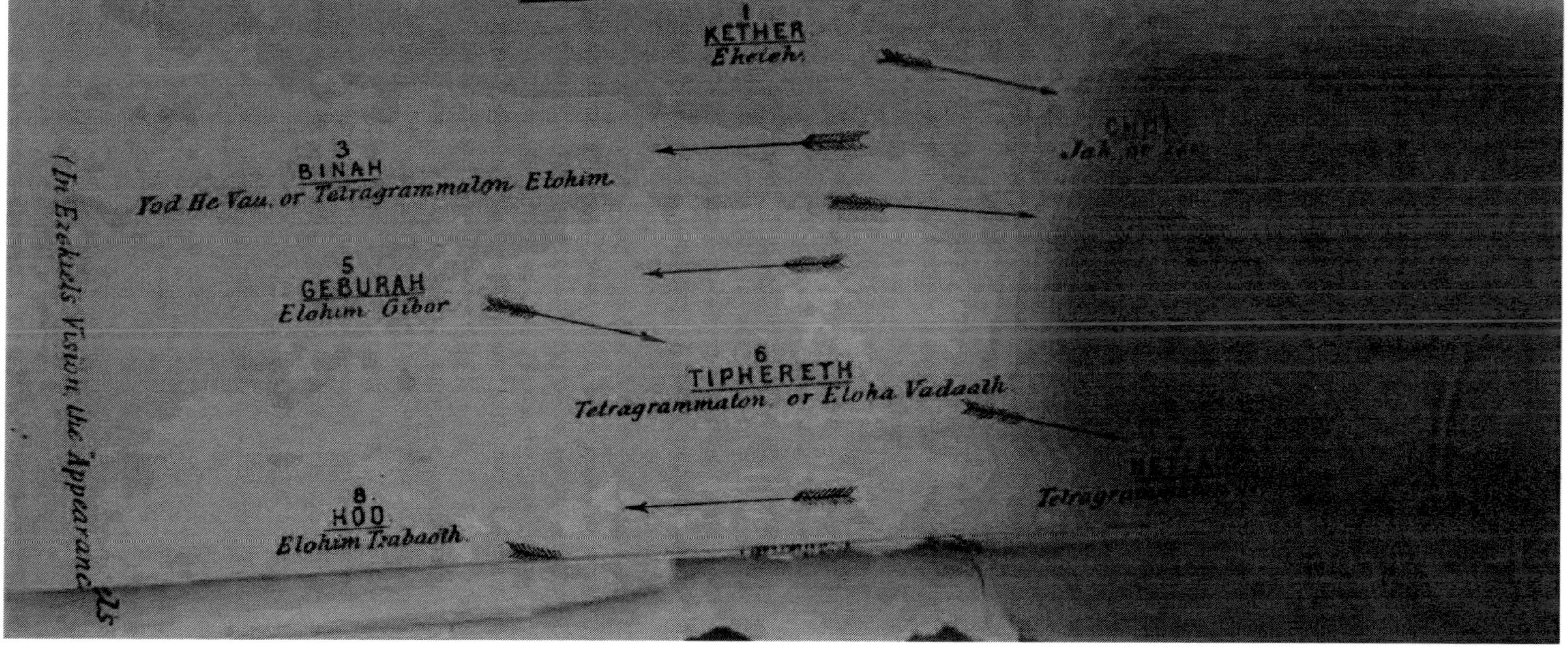

also the world of shells, OVLM HQLIPVTH, *Olahm Ha-Qliphoth,* which is this world of matter, made up of the grosser elements of the other three. In it is also the abode of the evil spirits which are called "the shells" by the Qabalah, QLIPVTH, *Qliphoth,* material shells. The devils are also divided into ten classes, and have suitable habitations. (See Table.)

61. The Demons are the grossest and most deficient of all forms. Their ten degrees answer to the decad of the Sephiroth, but in inverse ratio, as darkness and impurity increase with the descent of each degree. The two first are nothing but absence of visible form and organization. The third is the abode of darkness. Next follow seven Hells occupied by those demons which represent incarnate human vices, and torture those who have given themselves up to such vices in earth-life. Their prince is *Samael,* SMAL, the angel of poison and of death. His wife is the harlot, or woman of whoredom, ASHTH ZNVNIM, *Isheth Zenunim;* and united they are called the beast, CHIVA, *Chioa.* Thus the infernal trinity is completed, which is, so to speak, the averse and caricature of the supernal Creative One. Samael is considered to be identical with Satan.

62. The name of the Deity, which we call Jehovah, is in Hebrew a name of four letters, IHVH; and the true pronunciation of it is known to very few. I myself know some score of different mystical pronunciations of it. The true pronunciation is a most secret arcanum, and is a secret of secrets. "He who can rightly pronounce it, causeth heaven and earth to tremble, for it is the name which rusheth through the universe." Therefore when a devout Jew comes upon it in readi-
Scripture, he either does not attempt to pronou
instead makes a short pause, or else he subst
the name *Adonai,* ADNI, Lord. The radical
the word is "to be," and it is thus, li
a glyph of existence. It is capable o

Plate IX

TABLE
SHOWING THE RECEPTION AND TRANSMISSION OF THE SEPHIROTH IN THE FOUR WORLDS.

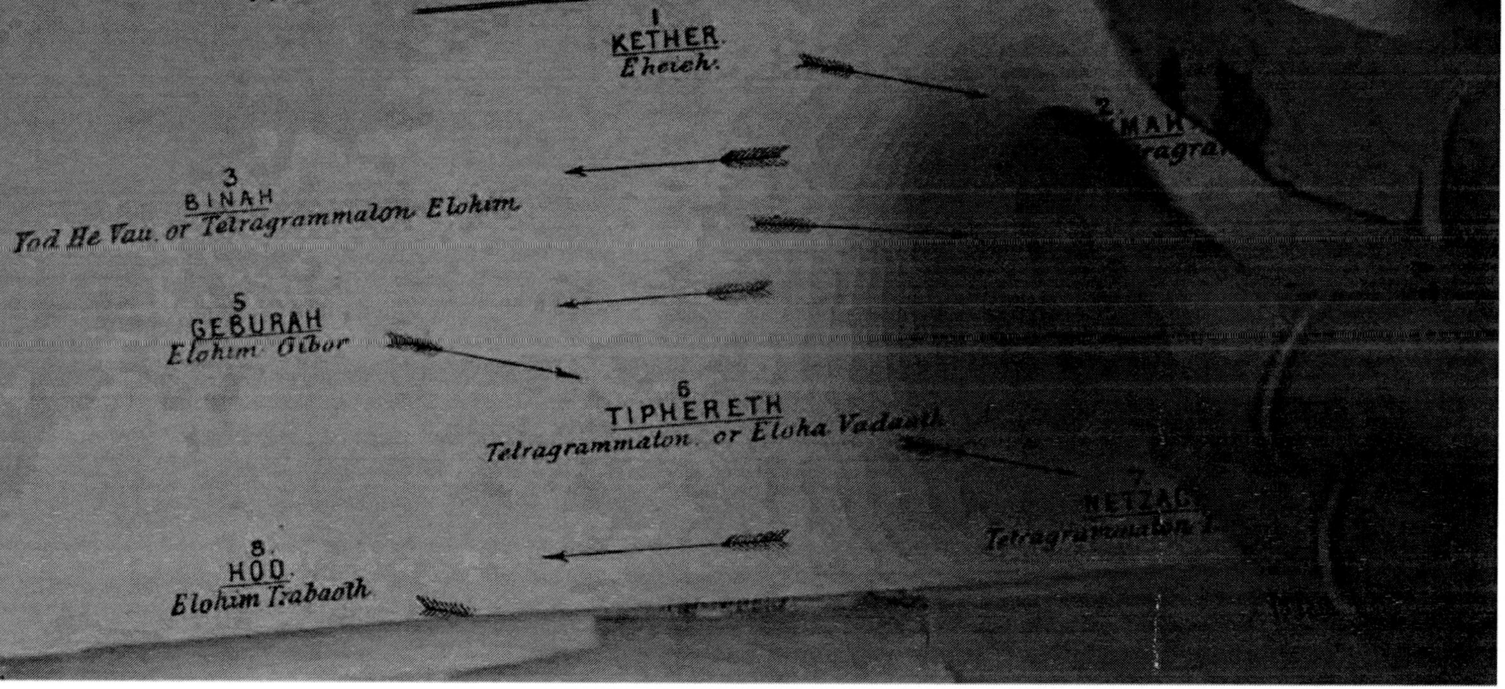

(In Ezekiel's Vision the Appearanc

ith the Fou

The

och.

I, Yod.

H, The

V, Vau

H, The

Plate VI

PLATE ILLUSTRATING THE ANALOGY BETWEEN THE SOUL, THE LETTERS OF TETRAGRAMMATON, & THE FOUR WORLDS

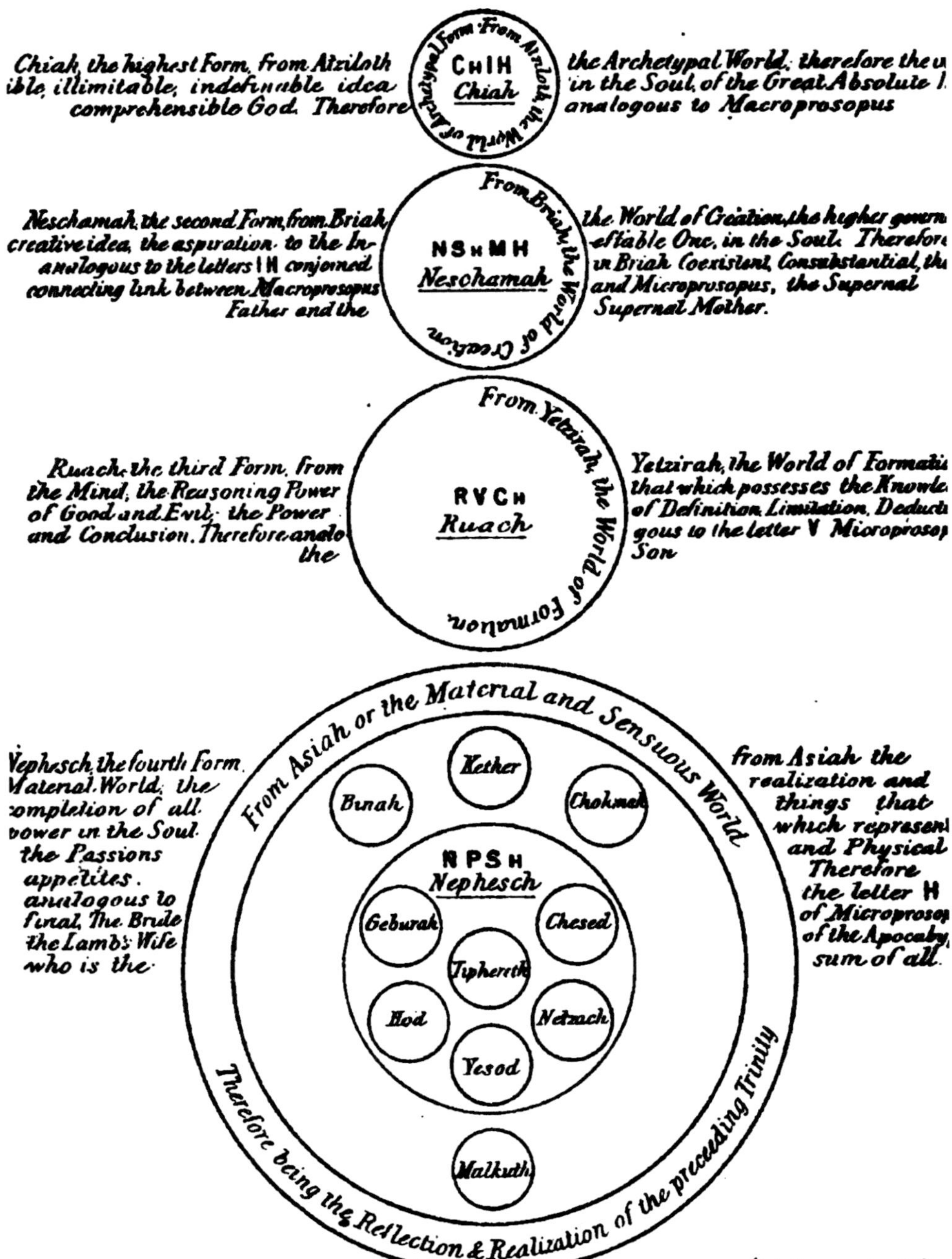

(To face page 35)

different bodies; if therefore in this mortal life the male half encounters the female half, a strong attachment springs up between them, and hence it is said that in marriage the separated halves are again conjoined; and the hidden forms of the soul are akin to the kerubim.

72. But this foregoing triple division of the soul is only applicable to the triple form of the intellectual, moral, and material. Let us not lose sight of the great qabalistical idea, *that the trinity is always completed by and finds its realization in the quaternary*; that is, IHV completed and realized in IHVH—the trinity of

Crown;	King;	Queen;
Father;	Son;	Spirit;
Absolute;	Formation;	Realization:

completed by the quaternary of—

Absolute One	Father and Mother	Son	Bride.—
Macroprosopus, the Vast Countenance	Father and Mother	Microprosopus, the Lesser Countenance	Malkuth, the Queen and Bride.
Atziloth Archetypal	Briah Creative	Yetzirah Formative	Asiah. Material.

And to these four the soul answers in the following four forms:—Chiah to Atziloth; Neschamah to Briah; Ruach to Yetzirah; and Nephesch to Asiah. See subjoined plate illustrating the analogy between the soul, the letters of the Tetragrammaton, and the four worlds.

73. But Chiah is in the soul the archetypal form analogous to Macroprosopus. Wherefore Neschamah, Ruach, and Nephesch represent as it were by themselves the Tetragrammaton, without Chiah, which is nevertheless symbolized "in the uppermost point of the I, *yod*," of the soul; as Macroprosopus is said to be symbolized by the uppermost point of the I, *yod*, of IHVH. For "*yod* of the Ancient One is hidden and concealed."

74. I select the following *résumé* of the qabalistical teachings regarding the nature of the soul from Eliphaz

Levi's "Clef des Mystères," as also the accompanying plate. This gives the chief heads of the ideas of Rabbi Moses Korduero and of Rabbi Yitzchaq Loria.

"The soul is a veiled light. This light is triple:

"Neschamah = the pure spirit;

"Ruach = the soul or spirit;

"Nephesch = the plastic mediator.

"The veil of the soul is the shell of the image.

"The image is double because it reflects alike the good and the evil angel of the soul.

"Nephesch is immortal by renewal of itself through the destruction of forms;

"Ruach is progressive through the evolution of ideas;

"Neschamah is progressive without forgetfulness and without destruction.

"There are three habitations of souls:—

"The Abyss of Life;

"The superior Eden;

"The inferior Eden."

"The image Tzelem is a sphinx which propounds the enigma of life.

"The fatal image (*i.e., that which succumbs to the outer*) endows Nephesch with his attributes, but Ruach can substitute the image conquered by the inspirations of Neschamah.

"The body is the veil of Nephesch, Nephesch is the veil of Ruach, Ruach is the veil of the shroud of Neschamah.

"Light personifies itself by veiling itself, and the personification is only stable when the veil is perfect.

"This perfection upon earth is relative to the universal soul of the earth (*i.e., as the macrocosm or greater world, so the microcosm or lesser world, which is man*).

"There are three atmospheres for the souls.

"The third atmosphere finishes where the planetary attraction of the other worlds commences.

Plate V

PLATE SHOWING THE FORMATION OF THE SOUL, &c.

(From "Clef des Mystères" by Eliphaz Lévi Zahed.)

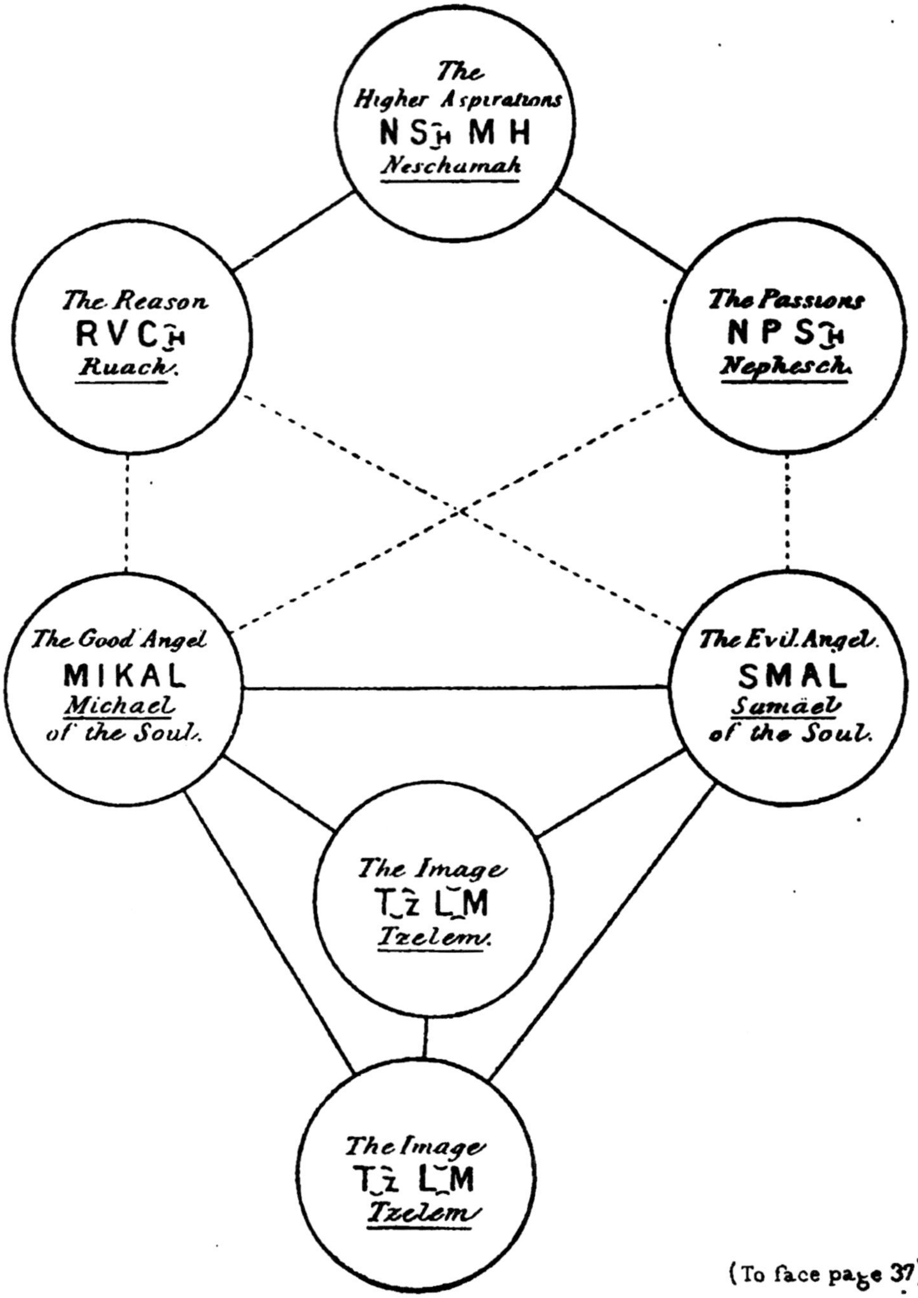

(To face page 37)

"Souls perfected on this earth pass on to another station.

"After traversing the planets they come to the sun; then they ascend into another universe and recommence their planetary evolution from world to world and from sun to sun.

"In the suns they remember, and in the planets they forget.

"The solar lives are the days of eternal life, and the planetary lives are the nights with their dreams.

"Angels are luminous emanations personified, not by trial and veil, but by divine influence and reflex.

"The angels aspire to become men, for the perfect man, the man-God,* is above every angel.

"The planetary lives are composed of ten dreams of a hundred years each, and each solar life is a thousand years; therefore is it said that a thousand years are in the sight of God as one day.

"Every week—that is, every fourteen thousand years—the soul bathes itself and reposes in the jubilee dream of forgetfulness.

"On waking therefrom it has forgotten the evil and only remembers the good."

75. In the accompanying plate of the formation of the soul there will be seen in the upper part three circles, representing the three parts known as Neschamah, Ruach, and Nephesch. From Ruach and Nephesch, influenced by the good aspirations of Neschamah, proceeds Michael, the good angel of the soul; that is to say, the synthetical hieroglyph of the good ideas, or, in the esoteric Buddhist phraseology, the "Good Karma" of a man. From Nephesch dominating Ruach, and uninfluenced by the good aspirations of Neschamah, proceeds Samäel, the evil angel of the soul; that is to say, the synthetical hieroglyph of the evil ideas, the "evil

* As distinguished from the God-man.

Karma" of a man. And the Tzelem, or image, is double, for it reflects alike Michael and Samäel.

76. The following is Dr. Jellinek's* analysis of the sephirotic ideas, according to the ethics of Spinoza:—

1. Definition.—By the Being who is the cause and governor of all things I understand the *Ain Soph* —*i.e.*, a Being infinite, boundless, absolutely identical with itself, united in itself, without attributes, will, intention, desire, thought, word, or deed.

2. Definition. — By *Sephiroth* I understand the potencies which emanated from the Absolute, *Ain Soph*, all entities limited by quantity, which, like the will, without changing its nature, wills diverse objects that are the possibilities of multifarious things.

I. Proposition.—The primary cause and governor of the world is the *Ain Soph*, who is both immanent and transcendent.

(*a*) Proof.—Each effect has a cause, and everything which has order and design has a governor.

(*b*) Proof.—Everything visible has a limit, what is limited is finite, what is finite is not absolutely identical; the primary cause of the world is invisible, therefore unlimited, infinite, absolutely identical—*i.e.*, he is the *Ain Soph.*

(*c*) Proof.—As the primary cause of the world is infinite, nothing can exist *without* (extra) him; hence he is immanent.

Scholion.—As the *Ain Soph* is invisible and exalted, it is the root of both faith and unbelief.

II. Proposition.—The *Sephiroth* are the medium between the absolute *Ain Soph* and the real world.

Proof.—As the real world is limited and not perfect, it cannot directly proceed from the *Ain Soph*; still the *Ain Soph* must exercise his influence over it, or his perfection would cease. Hence the *Sephiroth*, which, in their intimate connection with

* "Beiträge zur Geschichte der Kabbalah, Erstes Heft." Leipzig. 1852.

the *Ain Soph*, are perfect, and in their severance are imperfect, must be the medium.

Scholion.—Since all existing things originated by means of the *Sephiroth*, there are a higher, a middle, and a lower degree of the real world. (*Vide infra*, Proposition VI.)

III.—Proposition.—There are ten intermediate *Sephiroth*.

Proof.—All bodies have three dimensions, each of which repeats the other (3 × 3); and by adding thereto space generally, we obtain the *number ten*. As the *Sephiroth* are the potencies of all that is limited they must be *ten*.

(*a*) *Scholion.*—The number ten does not contradict the absolute unity of the *Ain Soph*; as *one* is the basis of all numbers, plurality proceeds from unity, the germs contain the development, just as fire, flame, sparks, and colour have *one* basis, though they differ from one another.

(*b*) *Scholion.*—Just as cogitation or thought, and even the mind as a cogitated object, is limited, becomes concrete, and has a measure, although *pure thought* proceeds from the *Ain Soph*; so limit, measure, and concretion are the attributes of the *Sephiroth*.

IV. Proposition.—The *Sephiroth* are emanations, and not creations.

1. Proof.—As the absolute *Ain Soph* is perfect, the *Sephiroth* proceeding therefrom must also be perfect; hence they are not created.

2. Proof.—All created objects diminish by abstraction; the *Sephiroth* do not lessen, as their activity never ceases; hence they cannot be created.

Scholion.—The first *Sephira* was in the *Ain Soph* as a power before it became a reality; then the second *Sephira* emanated as a potency for the intellectual world; and afterwards the other *Sephiroth* emanated for the moral and material worlds. This, however, does not imply a *prius* and *posterius*, or a gradation in the *Ain Soph*, but just as a light whose kindled lights, which shine sooner and later, and variously, so it embraces all in a unity.

V. Proposition.—The Sephiroth are both active and passive (MQBIL VMThQBL, *Meqabil Va-Metheqabel*).

Proof.—As the *Sephiroth* do not set aside the unity of the *Ain Soph*, each one of them must receive from its predecessor and impart to its successor—*i.e.*, be receptive and imparting.

VI. Proposition.—The first *Sephira* is called *Inscrutable Height*, RVM MOLH, *Rom Maaulah;* the second, *Wisdom*, ChKMH, *Chokmah;* the third, *Intelligence*, BINH, *Binah;* the fourth, *Love*, ChSD, *Chesed;* the fifth, *Justice*, PcHD, *Pachad;* the sixth, *Beauty*, ThPARTh, *Tiphereth;* the seventh, *Firmness*, NTzCh, *Netzach;* the eighth, *Splendour*, HVD, *Hod;* the ninth, *the Righteous is the Foundation of the World*, TzDIQ ISVD OVLM, *Tzediq Yesod Olahm;* and the tenth, *Righteousness*, TzDQ, *Tzedeq*.

(*a*) *Scholion*.—The first three *Sephiroth* form the world of thought; the second three the world of soul; and the four last the world of body; thus corresponding to the intellectual, moral, and material worlds.

(*b*) *Scholion*.—The first *Sephira* stands in relation to the soul, inasmuch as it is called a *unity*, IChIDH, *Yechidah;* the second, inasmuch as it is denominated *living*, ChIH, *Chiah;* the third, inasmuch as it is termed *Spirit*, RVCh, *Ruach;* the fourth, inasmuch as it is called *vital principle*, NPSh, *Nephesch;* the fifth, inasmuch as it is denominated *soul*, NShMH, *Neschamah;* the sixth operates on the blood, the seventh on the bones, the eighth on the veins, the ninth on the flesh, and the tenth on the skin.

(*c*) *Scholion*.—The first *Sephira* is like the concealed light, the second like sky-blue, the third like yellow, the fourth like white, the fifth like red,* the sixth like white-

* This mixture of white and red refers to Microprosopus, as will be seen in the greater and lesser Holy Assembly.

red, the seventh like whitish-red, the eighth like reddish-white, the ninth like white-red whitish-red reddish-white, and the tenth is like the light reflecting all colours.

77. I will now revert to the subject of Arikh Anpin and Zauir Anpin, the Macroprosopus and the Microprosopus, or the Vast and the Lesser Countenances. Macroprosopus is, it will be remembered, the first Sephira, or Crown Kether; Microprosopus is composed of six of the Sephiroth. (See subjoined plate.) In Macroprosopus all is light and brilliancy; but Microprosopus only shineth by the reflected splendour of Macroprosopus. The six days of creation correspond to the six forms of Microprosopus. Therefore the symbol of the interlaced triangles, forming the six-pointed star, is called the Sign of the Macrocosm, or of the creation of the greater world, and is consequently analogous to the two countenances of the Zohar. This, however, is not the only occult reason that I have placed this symbol in the plate, for it typifies other ideas upon which I shall not here enter. The "Book of Concealed Mystery" fully discusses the symbolism of Macroprosopus and Microprosopus; therefore it is well, before reading it, to be cognizant of their similarities and differences. The one is AHIH, *Eheieh;* the other is the V, *Vau,* of the Tetragrammaton. The first two letters, I and H, *Yod* and *He,* are the father and mother of Microprosopus, and the H final is his bride. But in these forms is expressed the equilibrium of severity and mercy;* severity being symbolized by the two Hs, *Hes,* the mother and the bride, but especially by the latter. But while the excess of Mercy is not an evil tendency, but rather conveys a certain idea of weakness and want of force, too great an excess of severity calls forth the executioner of judgment, the evil and oppressive force,

* Regarding the equilibrium of severity and mercy of which the universe is the result. See especially "Greater Holy Assembly," §838 *et seq.*

which is symbolized by Leviathan. Wherefore it is said, "Behind the shoulders of the bride the serpent rears his head:" of the bride, but not of the mother, for she is the supernal H, and bruises his head. "But his head is broken by the waters of the great sea." The sea is Binah, the supernal H, the mother. The serpent is the centripetal force, ever seeking to penetrate into Paradise (the Sephiroth), and to tempt the supernal Eve (the bride), so that in her turn she may tempt the supernal Adam (Microprosopus).

It is utterly beyond the scope of this Introduction to examine this symbolism thoroughly, especially as it forms the subject of this work; so I will simply refer my reader to the actual text for further elucidation, hoping that by the perusal of this introductory notice he will be better fitted to understand and follow the course of qabalistic teaching there given.

SPRA DTzNIOVThA

(SIPHRA DTZENIOUTHA);

OR,

THE BOOK OF CONCEALED MYSTERY.

CHAPTER I.

1. *Tradition.*—"The Book of Concealed Mystery" is the book of the equilibrium of balance.

[The word "Dtzenioutha" is difficult to translate, but I think its meaning is best expressed by the words "Concealed Mystery." I have explained in the Introduction the qabalistical meaning of the words "equilibrium" and "balance," § 29.]

2. *Tradition.*—For before there was equilibrium, countenance beheld not countenance.

[By the two countenances are meant Macroprosopus and Microprosopus. See Introduction, §§ 42, 47, 64, 65, 67, 73, and 77.]

3. And the kings of ancient time were dead, and their crowns were found no more; and the earth was desolate.

[The "kings of ancient time" mean the same thing as the "Edomite Kings;" that is, they symbolize worlds of "unbalanced force," which, according to the Zohar, preceded the formation of this universe. I have explained this also in the Introduction, §§ 41 and 56. This and the immediately following sections are supposed to trace the gradual development of the Deity from negative into positive existence; the text is here describing the time when the Deity was just commencing His manifestation from His primal negative form. Therefore, according to the qabalistical ideas, the universe is the garment as it were of the Deity; He not only contains all, but is Himself all, and exists in all.]

4. Until that head (which is incomprehensible) desired by all desires (proceeding from AIN SVP, *Ain Soph*, the infinite and limitless one), appeared and communicated the vestments of honour.

[This Head, which is here described as proceeding from the infinite and limitless One, the *Ain Soph*, is the first Sephira, the Crown *Kether*, otherwise called *Arikh Anpin*, or Macroprosopus, the Vast Countenance. From this first Sephira the other nine emanations are produced. I have explained all this in the Introduction, §§ 38-57, in treating of the Sephiroth.]

5. This equilibrium hangeth in that region which is negatively existent in the Ancient One.

[By the expression "This equilibrium hangeth in that region which is negatively existent in the Ancient One," is meant that the other nine Sephiroth (which are equilibrated by their formation in trinities) are as yet not developed in the first Sephira, but exist within it as the tree exists in the seed from which it springs. By "the Ancient One" is intended the first Sephira, the Crown Kether, one of whose appellations is *Autheqa*, the Ancient One. From this Sephira, as I have before remarked, the idea of negative existence depends back towards the AIN.]

6. Thus were those powers equiponderated which were not yet in perceptible existence.

[These powers are the other nine Sephiroth, which are, as it were, powers of the first Sephira; as soon as they are equated they become positively existent through correlation of force. The next two sections explain the manner of their equilibration while yet negative entities, or rather ideas.]

7. In His form (in the form of the Ancient One) existeth the equilibrium: it is incomprehensible, it is unseen.

[But the first idea of equilibrium is the Ancient One (the first Sephira, or Crown Kether), because it is the first potential limitation of the boundless light which proceeds from the Limitless One. That is, the central point of Kether is the equilibrium, because the balance does not yet exist, the two opposite poles which form the balance not being yet developed. We must not confuse these two terms, equilibrium and balance. The balance consists of two scales (opposing forces), the equilibrium is the central point of the beam.]

8. Therein have they ascended, and therein do they ascend—they who are not, who are, and who shall be.

[Therein (in the equilibrium of Kether) have they ascended (developed when they became positively existent), and therein (in the equilibrium) do they ascend (have their first existence), they (the Sephiroth) who are not (exist negatively), who are (then become positive), and who shall be (exist permanently, because they are counterbalanced powers). This triple expression "are not, are, and shall be," also refers to the triple trinity of the Sephiroth.] (See Introduction, §§ 52, 64, 65 and 66.)

9. The head which is incomprehensible is secret in secret.

[This head is Macroprosopus, the Vast Countenance, and is the same as the Ancient One, or Crown Kether. It is secret, for therein are hidden the other potentialities.]

10. But it hath been formed and prepared in the likeness of a cranium, and is filled with the crystalline dew.

[The crystalline dew is the creative lux or *Aur*, AVR, proceeding from the Limitless One. The Mantuan Codex calls the skull or cranium the first, and the crystalline dew the second conformation of Macroprosopus.]

11. His skin is of ether, clear and congealed.

12. (His hair is as) most fine wool, floating through the balanced equilibrium.

[The ether is the clear and insupportable brilliance of his glory. The hair is white—*i.e.*, spotless as wool—to denote the utter absence of matter and of shell. The Mantuan Codex calls the ether the third conformation, and the hair the fourth, which latter it refers to the Sephira Netzach, victory.]

13. (His forehead is) the benevolence of those benevolences which are manifested through the prayers of the inferior powers.

[The supernal benignity which transmits their qualities, powers and offices, to the lower Sephiroth (the inferior powers). It must be remembered that each Sephira *receives from* that which immediately precedes it, and *transmits to* that which next follows it. Thus, each Sephira is said to be feminine or passive as regards its predecessor, and masculine or active in respect to its successor. (See Introduction, §§ 43 and 51.) The Mantuan Codex calls this the fifth conformation, and refers it to the idea of the ninth Sephira, Yesod, foundation.]

14. His eye is ever open and sleepeth not, for it continually keepeth watch. And the appearance of the lower is according to the aspect of the higher light.

[Were the eye to close (the directing thought Divine to be abstracted from the Sephiroth), the whole universe would give way, for its mainspring would be withdrawn. Because the appearance (development) of the lower (nine Sephiroth) is according to (dependent on) the aspect (ruling thought) of the higher light (Kether, the first Sephira). The Mantuan Codex terms this the sixth conformation of Macroprosopus, and refers it, as in the case of the fourth conformation, to the primal idea of the Sephira Netzach, victory.]

15. Therein are His two nostrils like mighty galleries, whence His spirit rushes forth over all. (The Mantuan Codex adds that this is the seventh conformation, which refers to MLKVTH, *Malkuth*, or "the kingdom," the tenth emanation or Sephira of the Deity.)

[The creative spirit, or the "breath of life."]

16. (When, therefore, the Divine law beginneth) BRASHITH BRA ALHIM ATH HSHMIM VATH HARTZ, *Berashith Bera Elohim Ath Hashamaim Vaath Haaretz:* "In the beginning the Elohim created the substance of the heavens and the substance of the earth." (The sense is: Six members were created, which are the six numerations of Microprosopus—viz., benignity as His right arm; severity as His left arm; beauty as His body; victory as His right leg; glory as His left leg; and the foundation as reproductive.) For instead of BRASHITH, *Berashith*, "in the beginning," it may be read, BRA SHITH, *Bera*

Shith, "He created the six." Upon these depend all things which are below (principally the Queen, who is the lowest path, or the bride of Microprosopus, and all the three inferior worlds.)

[The view which the Siphra Dtzenioutha here follows out is that the beginning of Genesis describes *not only the creation of the world, but the development of God*, for it considers the universe as the outward and material expression of the power of the thought Divine. Microprosopus is as it were the reflection of Macroprosopus, for as Macroprosopus has six principal titles, so is Microprosopus composed of six of the Sephiroth. (See Introduction, §§ 42, 47 and 77.) SHITH, *Shith*, is the Chaldee form of the Hebrew SHSH, *Shash*, six. The queen is Malkuth, the tenth Sephira. The three inferior worlds are Briah, Yetzirah, and Asiah. See Introduction, §§ 57-60.]

17. And the dignity of dignity hangeth from the seven conformations of the cranium. (This is the beard of the venerable and Ancient One, which is divided into thirteen portions).

[The Ancient One is the first Sephira, Macroprosopus, as I have before remarked. The beard, in continuation of the symbolic representation of the head, is divided into thirteen portions, which answer by Gematria (see Introduction, § 11) to the idea of unity. For ACHD, *Achad*, unity, yields the number 13 by numerical value.]

18. And the second earth came not into the computation. (That is, the kingdom of the restored world, which elsewhere is called the Bride of Microprosopus, came not into the computation when the six members were said to be created. Or otherwise, when in Genesis iv. 2 it is said in another way, "And the earth," that earth is not to be understood of which mention hath been first made; since by the first is to be understood the kingdom of the restored world, and by the second the kingdom of the destroyed world), and this is elsewhere said.

[The kingdom of the destroyed world is that of unbalanced force. (See Introduction, §§ 41 and 56, and also note Section 3, foregoing.) This refers to a period prior to the development of the Sephiroth, and must therefore be referable to the Edomite kings.]

19. And it hath proceeded out of that which hath undergone the curse, as it is written in Genesis v. 29, "From the earth which the Lord hath cursed." (The meaning is: That the kingdom of the restored world was formed from the kingdom of the destroyed world, wherein seven kings had died and their possessions had been broken up. Or, the explanation of the world, of which mention is made elsewhere, proceedeth from the kingdom of the destroyed world.)

[These seven kings are the Edomite kings before mentioned in Section 3.]

20. It was formless and void, and darkness upon the face of the deep, and the Spirit of the Elohim vibrating upon the face of the waters. Thirteen (these words, from "it was formless" down to "of the waters," are thirteen in the Hebrew text of Genesis) depend from the thirteen (forms) of the dignity of dignity (that is, the beard of the Macroprosopus, or first formed head).

[I have before remarked that the number thirteen expresses unity. The author of "The Book of Concealed Mystery" here argues that the very number and order of the words in the Hebrew text refer to certain forms of the Deity. The terms "face of the deep" and "face of the waters" bear a striking analogy to Macroprosopus and Microprosopus, the Vast and the Lesser Countenances. In this sense the "face of (from) the deep (abyss)" is the countenance formed from Ain Soph, the Limitless One; namely, the first Sephira, the Crown Kether.]

21. Six thousand years depend from the six first. This is what the wise have said, that the world shall last six thousand years, and it is understood from the six numbers of Microprosopus. But also the six following words give occasion to this idea: VIAMR ALHIM IHI AVR VIHI AVR, *Veyomar Elohim Yehi Aur Vayehi Aur*: "And the Elohim said, Let there be light, and there was light."

[By an exegetical rule of numbers, not so often employed as the others, simple numbers or units signify divine things; numbers of ten, celestial things; numbers of a hundred, terrestrial things; and thousands signify the future, what shall be in an after-age. Hence are the "six thousand years" deduced from the six first words, which also are said to refer to the six Sephiroth of whom Microprosopus is formed; the idea of six being extended into as many thousands, to symbolise that number on the plane of a future age.]

22. The seventh (the millennium, and the seventh space, namely, the Kingdom), above that One which alone is powerful—(*i.e.*, when the six degrees of the members denote mercies and judgments, the seventh degree tendeth alone to judgment and rigour). And the whole is desolate (that is, the Kingdom, MLKVTH, *Malkuth*, in the higher powers, is the antitype of the sanctuary, and like as this is destroyed, so also the Schechinah, or Kingdom, is itself exiled) for twelve hours (for the Hebrews include all this time of their exile in the space of one day). Like as it is written: "It was formless and void, &c." (for from the word "it was formless," down to "upon the faces of," are twelve words in the Hebrew text of Genesis.)

[By the same rule, the millennium is deduced from the seventh word. The seventh space here means Malkuth, the kingdom, or the queen, which together with the six of Microprosopus, makes up the seven lower Sephiroth. (See Introduction, § 77, further, for the idea of the balance of mercy and judgment.)]

23. The thirteenth (that is, "of the waters," HMIM, *Hamim*, which is the thirteenth word) raiseth up these (that is, as well the sanctuary which is above as that which is below) through mercy (since the water symbolizeth that measure of mercy through which judgment and punishments are mitigated), and they are renewed as before (for the six words follow afresh, as in the beginning the six members are enumerated). For all those six continue and stand fast (they are the members of the Microprosopus, and are not as his bride, and from them is the restitution), since it is written BRA, *Bera*, "created" (which hath a sense of permanence), and then it is written HITʜH, *Hayitha*, "it was" (which also is a

phrase of permanence and not of interpolation), for it is very truth (plainly, therefore, the kingdom perished not, although it might be formless and void, but it retaineth hitherto the essence).

[Mercy and judgment are opposites, and from the side of judgment comes the execution of judgment, which is destruction.]

24. And at the end of the Formless and the Void and the Darkness (that is, at the end of the exile this saying shall have place: Isa. ii. 11). And the Tetragrammaton alone shall be exalted in that day (that is, in the time of Messiah).

[The Tetragrammaton (see Introduction, § 67) comprehends the whole ten Sephiroth, and consequently expresses their three trinities of balanced force also; consequently, when the Tetragrammaton appears, the formless and the void and the darkness disappear, and form, fulness, and light replace them.]

25. But there are excavations of excavations. (The excavation is the receptacle, like that which is hollowed out, or carved out, like a cave, or any other receptacle. Therefore all receptacles are inferior with respect to the superiors, among which the "shells" hold the last place, which here are described, which are) under the form of a vast serpent extending this way and that. (Concerning this serpent the author of the "Royal Valley" speaks thus in his "Treatise of the Shells." The fragments of the receptacles, which have fallen into the world of Creation, of Formation, and of Action, therein exist from the Outer; and judgments are more consonant to these, which are called profane, and have their habitation in the middle space between the Holy and the Unclean. And from the head is formed that great dragon which is in the sea, and is the sea-serpent, which is, however, not so harmful as the earthly one. And this dragon hath been castrated since his crest (or *membrum genitale*), together with his mate, have been repressed, and thence have been formed four hundred desirable worlds. And this dragon hath in his head a

nostril (after the manner of whales) in order that he may receive influence, and in himself he containeth all other dragons, concerning which it is said: "Thou hast broken the heads of the dragons upon the waters" (Ps. lxxiv. 13). And here the idea or universal form of all the shells is understood, which encompasseth the seven inferior emanations of the queen after the manner of a serpent, as well from the right as from the left and from every side.)

[The excavation or receptacle of a Sephira is that quality whereby it receives the supernal influence from that which immediately precedes it; hence each Sephira has a double quality of receiving and of transmitting, which passes through the four worlds, in each of which the Sephiroth exist, though in gradually decreasing light. (See Table subjoined.) The "shells," *Qlipoth*, are the demons, in whom again is a form of the Sephiroth, distorted and averse. This great dragon which is here described is evidently identical with the leviathan of Job. He is the executor of judgment, the centripetal force, the old serpent ever seeking to penetrate into Paradise; finally, in a more *exoteric* sense he is Satan and the devil, the accusing one. In the Sepher Yetzirah, a most important qabalistical book, he is called *Theli*, THLI, the dragon. Now, by Gematria, THLI = 400 + 30 + 10 = 440; and if we "repress his crest"—*i.e.*, take away the first letter, which is TH, *Tau*,—400, there will remain LI = 40 = M, *Mem*, the water. The "400 desirable worlds" are the numerical value of TH, and signify the power of the Tetragrammaton on the material plane (See note to section 21, foregoing). There is much alchemical symbolism contained in the "Siphra Dtzenioutha." The "Seven Inferior Emanations" of the queen, are the seven lower Sephiroth —viz., Chesed, Geburah, Tiphereth, Netzach, Hod, Yesod, and Malkuth; or Microprosopus and his bride, the king and queen. "Shells," *Qliphoth*, are the evil spirits.]

26. His tail is in his head (that is, he holdeth his tail in his mouth, in order that he may form a circle, since he is said to encompass holiness). He transferreth his head to behind the shoulders (that is, he raiseth his head at the back of the bride of Microprosopus, where is the place of most severe judgments), and he is despised (since in him is the extremity of judgments and severities, whence wrath is the attribute of his forms). He watcheth (that

is, he accurately searcheth out and seeketh in what place he may gain an entry into holiness. And he is concealed (as if laying traps; since he insinuateth himself into the inferiors, by whose sins he hath access to the holy grades, where the carrying out of judgments is committed to him.) He is manifested in one of the thousand shorter days. (Numbers are called days, and numbers of the inferior world short days; among which tens are attributed to the factive, on account of their decimal numeration; hundreds to the formative, since they are numbers of the light of their author, and draw their existence from the tens; but thousands to the creative, for the same reason. But that dragon hath about this his most powerful location, whence, if a defect occurreth only in one numeration of that system through the fault of the inferiors, he is immediately manifest, and thus commenceth his accusations before the throne of glory.)

[Here is the origin of the well-known symbol of a serpent holding his tail in his mouth, like a circle—the serpent of Saturn. The reason that he raiseth his head behind the shoulders of the bride (Malkuth) is because he is, so to speak, not only the executor of judgment, but also the destroyer; destruction as opposed to creation, death as opposed to life. For the whole Sephiroth are represented as being the balance of mercy and justice, and the tenth Sephira is especially of the nature of justice, as also is Geburah, the fifth. He is concealed, because he is not called into action till justice requires him. The term "decimal numeration" of course refers to the ten Sephiroth. The presence of the serpent when revealed, is an accusation, because it shows that the balance is destroyed; just as in a watch, if one of the wheels be injured, irregularity is at once manifested. Now, life, when it consists of birth into another form, necessarily implies death in the previous form. The throne of glory is the Briatic world.]

27. There are swellings in his scales (that is, like as in a crocodile; because great in him is the heaping together of judgments). His crest keepeth its own place (that is, there is in him no further power of hastening to things beyond in the Outer).

[There is in the destroyer no "hastening to the outer," because he is *centripetal* and not *centrifugal.*]

28. But his head is broken by the waters of the great sea. (The great sea is wisdom, the fountain of mercy and loving-kindness; which, if it sendeth down its influence, judgments are pacified, and the hurtful power of the shells is restricted); like as it is written, Ps. lxxiv. 13: "Thou hast broken the heads of the dragons by the waters."

["The waters of the great sea," are the influence of the supernal mother, Binah, of whom Malkuth is the reflection. But Binah receives the influence of Chokmah. See Introduction.]

29. They were two (male and female, whence the text of the Psalm speaketh of the dragons in the plural number; but when the plural number is given in its least form, two only are understood). They are reduced into one (for the female leviathan hath been slain, lest they should seek to multiply judgments). Whence the word THNINM, *Thenanim* (in the before-mentioned passage of the Psalm), is written in a defective form (purposely to denote that restriction).

[I may refer the reader to the Talmud for further information regarding Jewish ideas of the Leviathan. *Thenanim* is written in a defective form, because the letter I of the plural is omitted. Written fully, it should be THNINIM, instead of THNINM.]

30. (But it is said) heads (in the plural number, for the purpose of denoting a vast multitude, as well of species as of individuals in that genus); like as it is written, Ezek. i. 22: "And a likeness as a firmament above the heads of the living creature." (Where also the word living creature, CHIH, *Chiah*, is put in the singular as a genus of angels; and heads in the plural for the purpose of denoting species and innumerable individuals.)

["Thou hast broken the heads of the dragons (*Thenanim*) by the waters." It must be remembered that this dragon is said by the author of the "Royal Valley" to be the king of all the "shells" or demons. Now, the demons are divided into ten classes, corresponding to the ten Sephiroth, but in an averse form, and are called in the book, "Beth Elohim," the "impure Sephiroth." The heads of the leviathan (cf. the Lernaean Hydra which Hercules slew) are probably these. Compare the description of the beast in Revelation.]

31. "And the Elohim said, let there be light, and there was light." (The sense may be sought from that Psalm xxxiii. 9) where it is written, "Since He Himself spake, and it was done." (First, therefore, is commemorated) the Path HVA, *Hoa*, (that is, the mother of understanding, who is called ALHIM, *Elohim*, near the beginning of the verse. "And the Elohim said." She also is called HVA, *Hoa*, in the words of Psalm xxxiii. 9, on account of her truly secret nature) is alone (as well with Moses as with David). The word VIHI, *Vayehi*, "and it was done," is also alone. (As if the six members were considered separately, seeing that V, *Vau*, occupieth the first place in the word VIHI, *Vayehi*.

[This statement, that the supernal mother symbolized by the word Hoa, He, seems at first sight at variance with the statement in another place, that Hoa represents Macroprosopus. But the letter H in the Tetragrammaton symbolizes the supernal mother, and this is also the initial letter of Hoa. And again by Gematria (see Introduction) Hoa, $HVA=5+6+1=12$, and the digits of 12 $1+2=3$. And 3 symbolizes Binah because she is the third Sephira. "Seeing that V, *Vau*, occupies the first place in the word VIHI," because V stands for the number 6. See Table of the Alphabet, &c., in Introduction.]

32. Then are the letters inverted, and become one. (If, namely, in the word VIHI, *Vayehi*, the letters I, *Yod*, and H, *He*, be placed in front so that it may read IHVI, *Yahevi*, it maketh one Tetragrammaton, which exhausteth the whole Divinity. But since these belong to the mother, from whom arise the judgments, hence this tetragrammaton is here written in retrograde order, which mode of writing is referred by qabalists to the judgments, on account of the nature of averse things; whence this

ought to be written in this way: IHVI, *Yahevi*, IHV, *Yeho*, IH, *Yah*, I, *Yod*. But since in the path of understanding those judgments themselves do not exist, but only their roots, while in itself this path is only pure mercy; hence the retrograde order is inverted, in order that it may be posited entire in this manner as at first): I, *Yod*, IH, *Yah*, IHV, *Yeho*, IHVI, *Yahevi*. (But it is not written in the usual manner, IHVH, *Yod*, *He*, *Vau*, *He*; because the word is derived from VIHI, *Vayehi*, whose metathesis is here discussed. And nevertheless the letter) which is last (namely, I, *Yod*, which is put in the place of the last H, *He*, in the ordinary form of the Tetragrammaton, denoteth), the Schechinah (or the queenly presence) which is below (that is, a path of the kingdom, namely, MLKVTH, *Malkuth*, the tenth and last Sephira); like as (in the other instance) the letter H, *He*, is found to be the Schechinah.

[The reader will be utterly unable to follow the reasoning in this section, unless he reads carefully what I have said in the Introduction concerning the Literal Qabalah under the heads of Notariqon and Temurah, to which therefore I refer him. Any four-lettered name is of course a tetragrammaton, but this term is especially applied to the word of four letters called by biblical translators Jehovah. It must be remembered that the natural course of writing Hebrew and Chaldee is from *right to left*, and that when it is written from *left to right*, it is said to be written "backwards," "in retrograde order," or "averse." By the "path of understanding" is meant Binah, the third Sephira. Schechinah is of course the Divine Presence manifested in the path of Malkuth. I have explained in the Introduction the meaning of the term "path" as employed in the Zohar.]

33. But in one balance are they equiponderated. (The balance denoteth the male and the female; and the meaning is, that the letters I, *Yod*, and H, *He*—of which the former is masculine and referreth to the path of the foundation; and the latter is feminine, pertaining to the queen—are interchangeable; since whilst the equilibrium existeth there is an intercommunication between them,

and they are joined together as one. Add to this that the queen is also called ADNI, *Adonaï*, wherein the letter I, *Yod*, bringeth up the rearguard of the army, as it were; because also it is accustomed to be called the Lesser Wisdom.) And the living creatures rush forth and return. (This is what is said in Ezek. i. 14 concerning the living creatures, which it is accustomed to be said concerning those letters of the Tetragrammaton, which sometimes hold the last place and sometimes the first; as when I, *Yod*, rusheth forth unto the last place, and when it returneth unto the beginning again; and so also the letter H, *He*. Likewise, then, also the living creatures are said to rush forth, when the Tetragrammaton is written with the final H, *He*, because then the whole system of emanatives is exhausted. But they are said to return when the Tetragrammaton is written with the final I, *Yod*, so that the sense may be collected in such a manner as to return from the last path of the queen into the penultimate of the foundation, which is designated by this letter I, *Yod*.

[I have defined "balance" in the Introduction, § 29, which see. The "path of the foundation" is of course Yesod, the ninth Sephira, while the queen is Malkuth, the tenth. Yesod is therefore the connecting link between the Microprosopus and the bride. The letter I "bringeth up the rearguard as it were" in the name ADNI, *Adonai*, because it is the last letter. Ezek. i. 14: the Qabalists by the term CHIVTH HQDSH, *Chaioth Ha-Qadesch*, the Holy Living-Creatures, understand the letters of the Tetragrammaton. With regard to the "letters of the Tetragrammaton, which sometimes hold the last place and sometimes the first," the following are two examples—namely, as in the form IHVI, *Yod, He, Vau, Yod*, the letter I, *Yod*, is both at the beginning and end of the word; and in the form which is more usual IHVH, *Yod, He, Vau, He*, the letter H, *He*, is in the second and last place.]

34. Like as it is written: "And the Elohim saw the substance of the light, that it was good. (Here a reason is adduced from the proposed text itself, showing how the last letter of this form of the Tetragrammaton, namely, I, *Yod*, may be said to symbolize the bride, since

God himself might behold in that light the path of conjunctive foundation, which the word "goodness" pointeth out; but when the foundation is in the act of conjunction—that is, under the idea of communicating goodness—there then is the bride. But also that the word "goodness" denoteth the foundation is proved from Isa. iii. 10, where it is said, "Say ye unto the righteous man" (that is, to the path of foundation, because the first man is said to be the foundation of the world, Prov. x. 25), "that it shall be well with him." Therefore, then do they ascend within the equilibrium. (That is, these two letters, I, *Yod*, and H, *He*, mean one and the same thing. Or, again: But behold, how in balanced power ascend the letters of Tetragrammaton. That is, how those letters agree when in conjunction, which before were standing separated in the word VIHI, *Vayehi*.)

[The "path of foundation" is of course the ninth Sephira, Yesod, which is the sixth member of Microprosopus (see section 16, foregoing), and typifies reproductive power. Malkuth is the queen. We must remember that in the Tetragrammaton, IHVH, I, *Yod*, is the father (who is *not* Macroprosopus, though he is implied therein, as the top point of the Hebrew letter Yod is said to symbolize him); H, *He*, the supernal mother; V, *Vau*, the son (Microprosopus); and H, *He*, final, the bride (the queen). And this is their proper order. Other variations of the Tetragrammaton, therefore, alter the position of the letters with regard to each other; their normal and correct position being IHVH.]

35 (Whilst the spouse, Microprosopus) was at first alone (he was standing by, whilst the letter V, *Vau*, occupied the first place, then was he separated from his bride). But all things returned into the unity. (That is, not only were father and mother conjoined into one, because the two letters, I, *Yod*, and H, *He*, were combined; but also the Microprosopus returned to his bride, whilst V, *Vau*, was placed next to I, *Yod*, in the Tetragrammaton, IHVI, *Yahevi*. For) V, *Vau*, descendeth (when in the word VIHI, *Vayehi*, "and it was done," it occupieth the first

place; but in the proposed metathesis, it descended into the third place, in order that it might be IHVI, *Yahevi*). And they are bound together the one to the other (male and female, V, *Vau*, and I, *Yod*, the path of beauty and the queen), namely, I, *Yod*, and H, *He* (by which are shown wisdom and knowledge, father and mother), like unto two lovers who embrace each other. (By two lovers are understood either V, *Vau*, and I, *Yod*, only—that is, at the end; or I, *Yod*, and H, *He*, together—that is, at the beginning).

[The "path of beauty," or Tiphereth, the sixth Sephira, is sometimes represented by V, *Vau*, and therefore sometimes stands for Microprosopus by itself; it is really the *central* Sephira of the group of six Sephiroth which compose him. The numerical value of Vau is 6.]

36. (Now the author of the "Siphra Dtzenioutha" hasteneth to the latter explanation of these letters, I, *Yod*, and V, *Vau;* and concerning V, *Vau*, he saith): Six members are produced from the branch of the root of his body. (The body is Microprosopus; the root of the body is the mother, who is symbolized by the letter H, *He;* the branch of the root is the letter V, *Vau*, enclosed and hidden within the letter H, *He;* and from that very branch were produced the six members—that is, the entire letter V, *Vau*, now having obtained the head.)

[The mother here mentioned is of course the third Sephira, Binah. The six members of Microprosopus forming the entire letter Vau is an allusion to the numerical value of that letter being 6.]

37. "The tongue speaketh great things" (see Dan. vii, 8. And by the tongue is understood the foundation—namely, the letter I, *Yod*, joined with his bride; the speech is the marital influx flowing forth from the bride; for the queen is called the word; but the great things are the inferiors of all grades produced.)

[The inferiors of all "grades" or "paths" are the Sephiroth in the inferior worlds.]

38. This tongue is hidden between I, *Yod*, and H, *He*. (For father and mother are perpetually conjoined in ISVD, *Yesod*, the foundation, but concealed under the mystery of Daath or of knowledge.)

[The conjunction of the letters V and H at the end of the Tetragrammaton IHVH is similar to that of I and H at the beginning.]

39. Because it is written (Isa. xliv. 5): "That man shall say, I am of the Tetragrammaton." (The word ANI, *Ani*, I, when the discourse is concerning judgments, pertaineth to the queen. But whensoever mercy is introduced it referreth to the understanding, like as in this place. In order that the sense may be: The supernal path, which is called I, or the understanding in act of conjunction with the father, is for the purpose of the formation of the Tetragrammaton, and this is one conjunction between the father and the mother for the constitution of the six members.) And that shall be called by the name Jacob, IOQB, *Yaqob*. (To call by name is to preserve; and another conjunction of father and mother is introduced for the purpose of preserving the Microprosopus, which is called Jacob.) And that man shall write with his hand, "I am the Lord's." (To write belongeth to the written law, or the beautiful path, and the same also signifieth to flow in. "With his hand," BIDV, *Byodo*, is by metathesis BIVD, *Byod*, by I, *Yod*—that is, through the foundation; in order that the sense may be, it may be formed from his influx, so that the Tetragrammaton may be written with I, *Yod*, as we have above said.) And by the name of Israel shall he call himself. He shall call himself thus in truth. (For the conception of the Microprosopus is more properly under the name of Jacob, whose wife is Rachel; and his cognomen, as it were, is Israel, whose wife is Leah.)

[The understanding is Binan, the third Sephira, which is referred to the supernal H, *He*, The "beautiful path" is Tiphereth, the sixth. The foundation is Yesod, the ninth. It is the *final* Yod, I, of the form of the Tetragrammaton IHVI, which is referred to Yesod, and not the initial, which belongs to Chokmah, the second Sephira, the Father.]

40. That man shall say, I am the Lord's; he descendeth. (That is: that very conception of the word I, which is elsewhere attributed to the supernal mother, forasmuch as in her agree the three letters of the word ANI, *Ani*, I; namely A, *Aleph*, is the highest crown; N, *Nun*, is the understanding itself, in its fifty celebrated gates; I, *Yod*, is the foundation or knowledge of the Father; but in this instance it is attributed to the lowest grade of the lower mother, and now is ADNI, *Adonaï*, without the D, *Daleth*, D, or poverty, but filled with the influx, and is ANI, *Ani*.) And all things are called BIDV, *Byodo* (that is, all these things are applied to IVD, *Yod*, concerning which this discourse is.) All things cohere by the tongue, which is concealed in the mother. (That is, through Daath, or knowledge, whereby wisdom is combined with the understanding, and the beautiful path with his bride the queen; and this is the concealed idea, or soul, pervading the whole emanation.) Since this is opened for that which proceedeth from itself (that is, Daath is itself the beautiful path, but also the inner, whereto Moses referreth; and that path lieth hid within the mother, and is the medium of its conjunction. But whensoever it is considered in the outer, when it hath come forth from the mother, then is it called Jacob.)

[The reader is referred to the Introduction for the names, &c., of the Sephiroth. *Nun* in its fifty gates refers to the numerica value of the letter N, which is 50. The "lower mother" is of course the final H of the word IHVH, the "bride." Daath generally symbolizes the conjunction of the second and third Sephiroth.]

41. (And herein IHV *Yod*, *He*, *Vau*, differeth from

the whole name and from all the four letters. Now, he turneth back to the other portion of the four—namely, IHV, *Yod, He, Vau*—and saith:) The Father resideth in the beginning (that is, that the letter I, *Yod*, which is the symbol of the wisdom and of the father, in that part holdeth the first place, like as in the whole system; since the crown nevertheless is hidden, and is only compared to the highest apex of the letter I, *Yod*). The mother in the middle (for the letter H, *He*, which is the symbol of the unformed understanding and the supernal mother, holdeth the middle place between I, *Yod*, and V, *Vau*, even as in the supernals she is comprehended by the Father from above, and by the Microprosopus, which is her son, she is covered from below, in whom she sendeth herself downward into the path of Hod, or of glory.) And she is covered on this side and on that (by the two, father and son). Woe, woe unto him who revealeth their nakedness! (Since this can be done by the faults of the inferiors, so that Microprosopus loseth this influx, whereby he is of so great power that he can seek to enshroud his mother; for that covering is the reception of the supernal influx, and the capability of transmitting the same to the inferiors, which cannot be done if the mother be uncovered and taken away from the Microprosopus, as the Israelites did when they committed the sin of the calf.

[IHV is of course the Tetragrammaton without the final H. It is interesting to note that in the qabalistical work called the "Sepher Yetzirah," this trigrammatic name is used instead of the Tetragrammaton. The crown which is hidden is Kether, the first ephira, or Macroprosopus, who is AHIH, and is therefore not openly shown in IHVH. The path of Hod is the eighth Sephira. The father and the son, by whom the mother is enclosed, are of ourse the letters I and V in the word IHV. With regard to what is said regarding the Israelites when they committed the sin of the alf, I imagine that it is intended to intimate—(*a*) That the calf as a symbol of ALHIM, Elohim, not of IHVH; for the Israelites had said, "Make us Elohim to go before us." (*b*) That this name "Elohim" is applied to the feminine portion of the Tetragrammaton HH. (*c*) That therefore the force was unbalanced which they adored, and that it would have been just as wrong to adore IV alone.]

42. And God said, let there be MARTH, *Maroth*, lights in the firmament of the heaven. (Now he hasteneth to the third part of that quadrilateral name, namely, to these two letters IH, *Yod*, *He*. But by lights are understood the sun and the moon, the beautiful path and the kingdom or bride. And herein the sense is this: although usually by these two letters are accustomed to be understood the Father and the Mother, or the wisdom and the understanding, yet in this place the supernal lights are wanting, like as the word MARTH, *Maroth*, is written in a defective form; and the meaning is proper to be applied unto the firmament of the heaven—that is, to the foundation, extended and prepared for marital conjunction; for the spouse is called the heaven, and the member of the treaty is the firmament, like, as, therefore, the two last paths in the whole name IHVI, *Yod*, *He*, *Vau*, *Yod* are designated by the letters V, *Vau*, and I, *Yod*, so likewise these in this portion of the square are designated by the letters, I, *Yod*, and H, *He*.) The husband hath dominion over the wife (since it is not written by V, *Vau*, but by I, *Yod*, which is the symbol of the member of the treaty, and herein denoteth the actual combination with the female): like as it is written (Prov. x. 25): "And the just man is the foundation of the world." (By this saying he illustrateth his meaning; because by the letter I, *Yod*, is understood the fundamental member by which the world is preserved in existence.)

[If the reader refers to the Introduction, he will there find in the Table showing the operation of the Sephiroth in the four worlds, &c., that in the world of Asiah the sun is referred to Tiphereth and the moon to Yesod. Furthermore, the circumstance of certain words being written defectively or redundantly is commented on in the Introduction, § 15. The term "square," or "square name," is sometimes applied to the Tetragrammaton. The phrase "member of the treaty" probably alludes to the symbolism of circumcision. In this sense, I, *Yod*, in the path of Yesod, the ninth Sephira, has a symbolical phallic signification.]

43. I, *Yod*, therefore irradiateth two. (That is, the letter I, *Yod*, in this square of the Tetragrammaton hath a double sense of influx, forasmuch as in the first instance it signifieth the father who illuminateth the mother; and forasmuch as in the second instance it signifieth the Microprosopus, or rather his treaty, which illuminateth the kingdom.) And (again in another manner) it shineth (that is, and also hath a third signification, whilst in the complete name it constituteth the last letter), and passeth on into the woman. That is, and denoteth the bride of Microprosopus, as is shown above, because it is put in the place of the last H, *He*, of the Tetragrammaton IHVH; like as also it hath the same power of signification in the connection of the names of existence and domination in this manner, IACHD, VNHI.)

44. (Now he turneth to the last part of this square, which is I, *Yod*, alone, and saith), I, *Yod*, remaineth one and alone (in order that it may show that all flow out from the one single letter I, *Yod*, which is in the form of a point, yet partaking of three parts, concerning which see elsewhere; yet in this place denoting only the woman, or the kingdom, wherein are contained all the supernals.)

[Yod at the end of the Tetragrammaton denotes the synthesis, the circular movement by which the end returns to the beginning. In the secret qabalistical alphabet known as the "celestial alphabet," Yod is represented by three circles at the angles of an equilateral triangle with the apex uppermost. Malkuth, the tenth Sephira, of course receives the influx of all the other Sephiroth (see Table showing the reception and transmission of the Sephiroth in the four worlds.]

45. And then (if now the Tetragrammaton be not considered in the manner just described, but in this manner of instituting the square, IHVI, IHV, IH, I,

then *Yod* also is in a certain sense solitary, but in a plainly contrary sense. For it ascendeth in its path upwards and upwards. (That is, it doth not so much receive the *higher* sense, in order that it may denote the beautiful path or the foundation; but the *highest*, that is, the father or the wisdom.) The woman is again hidden. (That is, in this instance, the former meaning by which it denoted the bride of Microprosopus, namely, the last letter of the above-written form of the Tetragrammaton, ceaseth in itself.)

[This is in the converse manner. The letter I no longer signifies the bride when it ceases to be the final letter of a Tetragrammaton.]

46. And the mother is illuminated (that is, in the second part of the ordinary averse Tetragrammaton, which consists of the letters IH, to the letter I, *Yod*, which hath the signification of the father, is added the letter H, *He*, which is the mother, and because these two are combined by themselves, hence that luminous influence is denoted wherewith the understanding is imbued by the supernal wisdom); and is opened out into her gates (that is, if these two letters be bound closely together, then out of the dead the pentad originateth the number 50, by which are denoted the fifty gates of the understanding; these are said to be opened because the letter H, *He*, is last and unprotected, not being shut in by any other succeeding letter.)

[This is taking the letters IH separate from the rest of the Tetragrammaton, but themselves conjoined. And as I=10 and H=5, these two conjoined (multiplied together) give N=50. And these are the fifty gates or properties of the understanding. These are opened, because in the word IH, *Yah*, the letter H is last, not being shut in, as by VH in the Tetragrammaton IHVH, or V in the trigram IHV.]

47. The key is added which containeth six, and closeth its gate. (That is, in the third part of this averse form, which is IHV, the letter H is not altogether

the last; but V, the third letter of the Tetragrammaton, closeth it in on the other side, whereby are denoted the six members of the Microprosopus, superinvesting the six members of the mother in such a manner that her last gate, which is the path of glory, HVD, *Hod*, is closed, and combined with the remainder, which are—Benignity, Severity, Beauty, Victory; drawing their existence singly out of the decad.)

[In the Trigram IHV, V may be called the key, because it closeth the fifty gates symbolized by IH, by coming next to H, so as to close or shut in that letter between itself and I. By "the decad" is meant the ten Sephiroth, which are symbolized by the numerical value of I, which is 10.]

48. And it applieth to the inferiors and to this part. (Or, as others read, "it applieth to this side and to that." Now, the discourse is concerning the fourth part of the square, where the name is complete, whether written as H or as I in the last path; so that, nevertheless, the bride of Microprosopus may be added. Therefore on either side hath Microprosopus a connecting link, for he superinvesteth the mother from the supernal part, so that he may receive her into himself as his soul; and he also again is covered by his bride from the inferior part, so that he in his turn may himself become her soul.)

[The bride, the inferior H, *He*, is said to be a reflection of the mother, the supernal H, *He*, in the Tetragrammaton; just as Microprosopus is said to be the reflection of Macroprosopus.]

49. Woe unto him who shall open her gate! (The gates are said to be paths through which influence rusheth forth; they are said to be closed, because, on the other hand, too much influence cannot be taken away from the inferiors; wherefore the members are said to be overshadowed by the members, so that the light may diminish in its transit. But when those very concatenations and cohibitions of the lights are separated by

the sins of the inferiors, no influx can come into the universe in a proper manner.)

[Following out the symbol of the equilibrium in the Sephiroth, the sin of the inferior paths would be the introduction of unbalanced force. The reader will at first find a little difficulty in following the reasoning of these last few sections, but after reading them over once or twice, their meaning will seem clearer to him.]

CHAPTER II.

1. The beard of truth. (That is, now followeth a description of the beard of Macroprosopus, and its thirteen parts, which are more fully described in the "Idra Rabba.")

[The beard is the influx which descends from the first Sephira through all the others. Macroprosopus is of course, as I have fully explained in the Introduction, the first Sephira, Kether, or the crown; also called the Ancient One.]

2. Of the beard mention hath not been made. (The correct Mantuan Codex hath this correction, so that the word DQNA, *Deqena*, is here inserted in the original text. The meaning is, that Solomon in the "Song of Songs" maketh mention of all the other members, but not of the beard.) Because this is the ornament of all. (It is called an ornament because it covereth the rest, just as a garment which ornamenteth the body covereth that. But this beard covereth not only the Macroprosopus, but also the father and the mother, and descendeth even unto Microprosopus. Whence, on account of the communication of so copious a light, it hath also itself been clothed as with a garment with the great reverence of silence.)

[By this beard, covering "not only Macroprosopus, but also the father and the mother," is meant that, while it is an important attribute of Macroprosopus (who is, be it carefully remembered by the reader *Eheieh*, AHIH, and *not* IHVH, in which latter name he is only alluded to as "the uppermost point of the letter I, *Yod*"), it also extends through the Sephiroth, for it covers the father and the mother (*i.e.*, the second Sephira, *Chokmah*, wisdom, and the third Sephira, *Binah*, understanding, the IH of IHVH). Thus, therefore, though properly speaking a part of AHIH, and *not* of IHVH, it extends through the Tetragrammaton IHVH, for it "descendeth even unto Microprosopus," the next six Sephiroth, the V of IHVH.]

3. From the ears it proceedeth about the circumference of the open space; the white locks ascend and descend. Into thirteen portions it is distributed in adornment. (Of all these see the explanation in the "Idra Rabba" and "Idra Zuta.")

[These thirteen divisions of the beard of Macroprosopus are all descanted upon at length in both the "Greater" and "Lesser Holy Assembly," in the first mentioned of which a chapter is devoted to the consideration of each division. I therefore shall not need to enter into the subject here, as the reader will find all the information he requires in the latter part of this volume. By Gematria (see Introduction), the word ACHD, *Achad*, one, unity = 13. The beard therefore is a glyph of the unity.]

4. Concerning that ornamentation it is written (Jer. ii. 6): "No man passed through it; and where no man dwelt." Man is without, man is not included therein; much less the male.

[The verse runs in the English version: "Through a land that no man passed through, and where no man dwelt."]

5. Through thirteen springs are the fountains distributed (by which there is an influx upon Microprosopus and the inferiors). Four are separately joined together, but nine flow upon the body (or, as others read, by advice of the correct Mantuan Codex), encircle the garden (that is, the Microprosopus).

[The four, separately joined, probably refer to the four letters of the Tetragrammaton, and the nine to the last nine Sephiroth—*i.e.*, exclusive of Kether. The Garden, or Paradise, is another term expressive of the whole Sephirotic system in Atziloth, the archetypal world.]

6. This ornamentation beginneth to be formed before the gate of the ears.

7. It descendeth in beauty into the beginning of the lips; from this beginning into that beginning.

8. There existeth a path which goeth out beneath the two galleries of the nostrils, in order that he may seek to pass over transgression; like as it is written, Prov. xix. 11: "And it is glory to pass over a transgression."

[The parting of the moustache on the centre of the upper lip. "It is his glory to pass over a transgression."]

9. Beneath the lips the beard goeth about into another beginning.

10. Beneath that another path goeth forth.

11. It covereth the approaches to the aromatic beginning which is above.

12. Two apples are beheld, to illuminate the lights.

[The two "apples," or "apple-trees," are the cheeks. Compare with this the imagery of the Song of Solomon.]

13. The influence of all floweth down as far as the heart (therein hang suspended the superiors and the inferiors).

14. Among those locks which hang down, none shineth forth above another.

15. The lesser cover the throat like an ornament; the greater are restored to perfect proportion.

16. The lips are free on every side. Blessed is he who shall become the receiver of their kisses.

17. In that influence of all stream down thirteen drops of most pure balm.

18. In this influence all things exist and are concealed.

19. At that time, when the seventh month draweth nigh, those months shall be found to be thirteen (for in the Codex, so often said to be correct, this word THRISR, *Tharisar*, or twelve, is expunged; as if it were then shown to be a year of thirteen months, according to the

number of those thirteen divisions of the influence) in the supernal world, and the thirteen gates of mercy are opened. At that time (by which principally the day of expiation is meant, according to that passage of Isaiah, lv. 6): "Seek ye the Lord while He can be found."

[The "thirteen divisions of the influence in the supernal world" are of course these thirteen parts of the beard of Macroprosopus considered in the sense of Atziloth, the archetypal world, the habitation of the pure Sephiroth alone: "Seek ye the LORD while he may be found."]

20. It is written, Gen. i. 11.: "And the Lord said, Let the earth bring forth germination; (let there be) grass yielding seed." (If here the word IHI, *Yehi*, "let there be," be inserted, they make nine words.) This is that which is written: "And humble your bodies in the ninth of the month at even." (This is to be understood concerning that time concerning which we have spoken above, because then the Lord is to be sought out.)

[VIAMR ALHIM THDSHA HARTz DSHA OSHB MZRIO ZRO, eight words, to which if IHI be added, we have nine. The English version = "And God said, Let the earth bring forth grass, the herb yielding seed."]

21. (In that passage, Deut. iii. 24, where it is written): "Adonai Jehovah, thou hast begun to show unto Thy servant Thy greatness," the name, Tetragrammaton, IHVH existeth perfectly written in its sides. (So that the name ADNI, *Adonai*, denoteth the inferior H, *He*, from the one side; and the points of the name ALHIM, *Elohim*, denote the superior H, *He*, from the other side.)

["In its sides"—*i.e.*, in its aspects. The points are the vowel marks.]

22. But here in this progermination of the earth it is not perfect, because IHI, *Yehi* (let there be), is not written. (But we read it so that also these letters do not represent a perfect name.)

23. (But therein is represented to us) the superior I,

Yod (that is, the mark of supernal mercy, which is that most holy Ancient One, as the correct Mantuan Codex shows in a marginal note), and the inferior I, *Yod* (that is, the mark of inferior mercy, which is Microprosopus with the influence which he hath from Macroprosopus, which two II, *Yods*, are also represented in that passage, Gen. ii. 7): VIITzR IHVH, *Vayeyetsir*, *Yod*, *He*, *Vau*, *He*, and Tetragrammaton formed (the supernal I, *Yod*, (and the inferior I, *Yod*).

[The only way that I can possibly see that VIITzR IHVH will bear the construction put upon it here is this (in which an eminent Hebrew scholar, Mr. Mew, agrees with me): V, *Vau*, and I, *Yod*, the Yod, ITzR, *Yetzer*, be formed (namely, the) IHVH, Tetragrammaton. In this construction the first letter Yod in the word VIITzR is taken as the *object* of the verb ITzR, and *not* as a pronominal prefix. The most holy Ancient One is the origin of Kether in Ain Soph when in the condition of the Ain Soph Aur (see Introduction), while the inferior Yod is the symbol of Yesod.]

24. (But in) IHI (besides) the superior and inferior (also existeth) the H, *He*, between both (like as) a connexion of perfection (whereby the influx is derived from the Macroprosopus and passed on to the Microprosopus.)

25. (Wherefore) it is perfect (since it is this name without separation), but it is not turned to every side (because therein is no symbol of the bride of Microprosopus). (Therefore) this name is taken out from this place and planted in another (that is, those letters also receive another signification from the inferior paths).

26. (For) it is written, Gen. ii. 8: "And the Tetragrammaton Elohim planted." (Whereby is understood) that H, *He*, which is between the two II, *Yods*, of the word IHI, *Yehi*, which in the supernals is) the position of the nose of the more Ancient One over the Microprosopus (concerning which see further in the "Idra Rabba," § 175). (For this) existeth not without the spirit.

[For this H, *He*, symbolised in Elohim, is rather the supernal *He* alone, than either the inferior *He* alone, or both conjoined. The nose of Macroprosopus is said in the "Idra Rabba" to be life in every part—*i.e.*, it, the life, existeth not therefore without the influx of the spirit which rusheth forth therefrom (See *ante*, Chapter I. § 15.)

27. Through H, *He*, therefore, it is perfected (rather by reason of the mother than by reason of the bride, of whom it is the soul). For the one H, *He*, is above (namely, designating the first understanding of the Tetragrammaton; and the other is) the H, *He*, below (denoting the queen and the bride).

28. Like as it is written, Jer. xxxii. 17: AHH ADNI IHVH, *Ahah, Adonaï, Yod He Vau He*: "Ah, Lord Jehovah," &c., where there is a cohesion of the connecting links (that is, in the word AHH, *Ahah*, those two HH, *He's*, are combined which elsewhere are the media of the connecting path). For by the spirit is made the connection of the balanced equilibria (that is, of the combinations as well of the father and mother as of the Microprosopus and his bride).

29. (Now the author of the "Siphra Dtzenioutha" descendeth to the inferior paths, leaving out Macroprosopus, and examineth the name IHV, *Yod He Vau*. In this are represented father and mother and Microprosopus. And first occurreth) the supernal I, *Yod* (the symbol of the father), which is crowned with the crown of the more Ancient One (that is, whose highest apex denoteth the highest crown, or Macroprosopus; or, according to another reading of the passage, "which is surrounded by the secret things"—that is by the influence or beard of Macroprosopus, which covereth both the father and the mother). It is that membrane of the supernal brain which, on account of its excellency, both shineth and is concealed. (Concerning this matter further, see the "Idra Rabba," § 58.)

30. The supernal H, *He* (then presenteth itself), which is surrounded by the spirit which rusheth forth from the

entrances of the galleries (or the nostrils of Macroprosopus), that it may give life to all things.

31. The supernal V, *Vau*, is that tremendous flashing flame (which is the beginning of judgment, seeing that doubtless hitherto the Microprosopus existeth in the mother) which is surrounded by its crown (namely, the mother).

32. And after are the letters taken in extended form (so that this name is written at length, in this manner: VV, *Vau*, HH, *He*, IVD, *Yod*, which form, when it is perfect, is usually called BN, *Ben*, because its numeration is 52), and in Microprosopus are they comprehended (seeing that then he embraceth his bride).

[See Introduction, page 33, Table showing the writing of the Tetragrammaton in the four worlds.]

33. When (this form) beginneth, they are discovered in the cranium (namely, these letters, and therein are they distributed in the most supernal part of Macroprosopus).

["In the cranium" (or skull), BGVLGLTHA, *Begolgoltha*, or in Golgoltha. In the New Testament it is worthy of note that Jesus Christ (the Son) is said to be crucified at Golgotha (the skull); while here, in the Qabalah, Microprosopus (the Son), as the Tetragrammaton, is said to be extended in the form of a cross, thus—

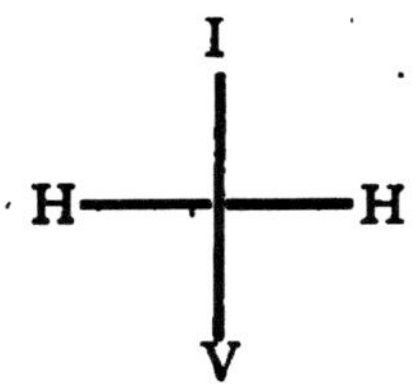

—in Golgotha (the skull). The text above says, at the end of section 33, "of Macroprosopus"; but I think this is a misprint for "of Microprosopus."

34. Thence are they extended throughout his whole form (from the original benignity), even to the foundation of all things (namely, as the soul of the inferiors).

35. When it is balanced in the pure equilibrium (that is, when the white locks of the most holy Ancient One send down the lights or names) then are those letters equilibrated. (That is, from their virtue cometh the light.)

[The "lights or names" are the ten Sephiroth and the Divine names associated with them (see Introduction), which are (with the exception of the first Sephira) comprehended in the Tetragrammaton IHVH.]

36. When he is manifested in Microprosopus (namely, Macroprosopus), in him are those letters, and by them is he named.

37. IVD, *Yod*, of the Ancient One, is hidden in its origin (that is, the father, who is usually symbolized by I, *Yod*, and is himself also called the Ancient One, is shrouded by the beard of Macroprosopus; or otherwise. Instead of that manner in which the other two letters duplicate their literal parts—*e.g.*, HH and VV—I, *Yod*, by reason of his very nature, cannot be expressed by this duplication, but remaineth one and alone), because the name is not found; that is, because if II be put, it can no longer be pronounced as I, *Yod*; therefore is it written IVD).

[The "Ancient One" is one of the titles of Macroprosopus, the first Sephira. But the letter I, *Yod*, of the Tetragrammaton is referred to the second Sephira, *Chokmah*, which is also called the Father. See Introduction, § 67.]

38. HA, *He*, is extended by another (*He*, as it is written HH in open and plain writing; but also it is sometimes written in another way, HI, also HA; the one in the name OB, *Aub*, the other in the name MH, *Mah*), and in the feminine symbol it denoteth the two females (namely, the supernal mother and the inferior mother; the understanding and the kingdom). And it is discovered through the forms. (That is, when the beard of Macroprosopus, and its forms or parts, send down his light into

Microprosopus; then herein is his bride produced in the light, and the supernal H, *He*, is reflected by another inferior H, *He*.)

[See introduction, wherein a table is given showing the writing of the Tetragrammaton in the four worlds.]

39. VV, *Vau*, is extended by another (*Vau*, as it is written VV, for likewise it is elsewhere written with I in the name OB, *Aub*, and by A in the names SG, *Seg*, and MH, *Mah*, in this manner VAV. So also in the name BN, *Ben*, it is thus written, VV. But to be disclosed it is fully written). Like as it is written, Cant. vii. 9, "Going down sweetly to my delight" (whereby "sweetly" are understood these two letters VV properly extended).

[The Authorised Version renders it: "And the roof of thy mouth like the best wine for my beloved, that goeth down sweetly, causing the lips of those that are asleep to speak."]

40. In that tremendous flashing flame (is he found —*i.e.*, in Microprosopus, seeing that in a lesser degree he hath in himself unmixed judgments), for the purpose of enshrouding that gate (that is, in order that he may be advanced to the condition of maturity, and may then superumbrate his mother, who is symbolised by the fifty gates).

["He," that is the letter V, *Vau*, of the Tetragrammaton. I have before noticed that the fifty gates of the understanding are equivalent to I and H, 10 and 5, multiplied together, which yield 50 = numerical value of the letter N, *Nun*.]

41. (He is therefore called) the supernal V, *Vau* (Daath or knowledge, and) the inferior V, *Vau* (that is, the external Microprosopus. And thus also) the supernal H, *He* (the mother), the inferior H, *He* (the bride). But I, *Yod*, is above all (symbolizing the father), and with him is none other associated; he is I, *Yod*, as at first; neither ascendeth he in himself (through the height of the numeration, like as with H, *He*, the

pentad, with *Vau*, the hexad, ascend to a similar height) except as a symbolic glyph. (That is, the decad, which is expressed not in that same letter I, *Yod*, but by a hexad and a tetrad).

[But *Vau*, V, is produced by *adding* the numerical values of I and H (the father and the mother of the Tetragrammaton), and then taking the *least number* of the result, thus: $I+H=10+5=15$, and by adding the digits of 15 together, $1+5$, we obtain $6=V$, *Vau*. By the phrase "with H, *He*, the pentad (5), with V, *Vau*, the hexad (6), ascend," is implied the numerical value of those letters *taken as symbolical sephirotic glyphs*. The decad is repeated in the word IVD, *Yod*, by the addition of the last two letters, V and D, which $=6+4=10$, I, *Yod*, again.]

42. For when the double forms are manifested (namely, the letters of the name in the above proposed form, as HH and VV) and are united in one path, in one combination, in order that they may be explained (that is, when they are fully written out in the above manner), then VD, *Vau*, *Daleth* (and *not* another I, *Yod*), are added unto I, *Yod* (so that also in it there may be a certain hidden analogy of the equilibrium).

43. Woe! woe! when this is taken away, and when the other two alone are manifested (that is, when from those two letters VD, in the word IVD, the letter I is taken away; seeing it representeth the abstraction of the father from the Microprosopus and his bride, who are as yet hidden in the mother, so that the disclosure of these two is vain and abortive, because the generative power of the father is absent * *) * * *. (Or, in another sense, if the influx be hindered and the supernal paths suffer disruption). Far, far from us be that effect!

44. (But that this may be done by the sins of the inferiors is clear from these words) Ezek. i. 14: "And the living creatures rush forth and return." Also Num. xxiv. 11: "Flee unto thy place." Also Obad. i. 4: "Though thou exalt thyself as the eagle, and though

thou set thy nest among the stars, thence will I cast thee down."

45. (Again it is said) Gen. i. 12: "And the earth brought forth germination." When? When the name is planted therein (that is, when Microprosopus receiveth his proper conformation, according to the requisite numbers—248 of the members, and 365 of the veins.)

[These numbers, 248 and 365, are formed by an elaborate combination of Gematria, too complicated to enter upon here.]

46. And then the wind bloweth (that is, the vital influx rusheth forth from Macroprosopus) and the spark of flame is prepared (that is, Microprosopus, who, great as he is, yet is in respect of the superiors only as a spark compared with fire, as he is produced from that terrific light.)

47. And amid the insupportable brilliance of that mighty light, as it were, the likeness of a head appeareth. (That is, the highest crown is found in Macroprosopus.)

48. And above him is the plenteous dew, diverse with two-fold colour. (Like as in Macroprosopus it is white alone, so here it is white and red, on account of the judgments. See "Idra Rabba," § 44.)

[Above Microprosopus, *not* Macroprosopus.]

49. Three hollow places are manifested, wherein the letters are expressed. (These are to be understood as symbolizing his three-fold brain, of wisdom, understanding, and knowledge, which here appear more plainly; whereas in the supernals they are more concealed.)

["The letters," that is, IHV, the first three letters of the Tetragrammaton.]

50. The black (locks issuing) from the four (sides of the head) float down over the curved openings of the ears, so that he may *not* hear.

["So that he may not hear." Remember, this is Microprosopus, or Zauir Anpin, not Macroprosopus, or Arikh Anpin.]

51. Right and left is here given (in all parts of the face and head).

["Right and left:" that is, Microprosopus is symbolized by a face in full; while in Macroprosopus "all is right"—*i.e.*, he is symbolized by a profile. This and the following sections are considered at length in the "Idra Rabba Qadisha" ("The Greater Holy Assembly"), and the "Idra Zuta Qadisha" ("The Lesser Holy Assembly"), to which the reader is referred.]

52. One slender higher path existeth. (The parting of the hair.)

53. His forehead, which shineth not, regulating the far distant future when it is his will to behold the same. (All the qualities, with their antitheses, which are found in Macroprosopus, are more fully described in the "Idra Rabba" and "Idra Zuta," which see).

54. His eyes are of triple colour (that is, red, black and gold) so that terror may go before them; and with glittering glory are they glazed.

55. It is written, Isa. xxxiii. 20: "Thine eyes shall behold Jerusalem at peace, even thy habitation."

56. Also it is written, Isa. i. 21: "Righteousness dwelled in it."

57. The "peaceful habitation" is the Ancient One, who is hidden and concealed. Wherefore "thine eyes" is written OINK, *Auinak* (without the letter *Yod.* All these things are explained in the "Idra Rabba.")

58. There is also the nose, to dignify the face of Microprosopus.

59. Through its nostrils three flames rush forth.

60. The profound path existeth in his ears for hearing both the good and the evil.

61. It is written, Isa. xlii. 8: "I am the Tetragrammaton, that is my name, and my glory I give not to another." (Now the author of the "Siphra Dtzenioutha" beginneth to explain the ulterior difference between Microprosopus and Macroprosopus, even as to their appellations; where the word ANI, *Ani*, "I," in the above passage referreth to

the Microprosopus, since it involveth the idea of the bride.) Also it is written, Deut. xxxii. 39: "I slay, and I make alive." Also it is written, Isa. xlvi. 4: "I will bear, and I will deliver you."

[In the word ANI, *Ani*, the idea of the bride (Malkuth, the H final of the Tetragrammaton) is implied by the letter I, *Yod*, being last, where it symbolizes the ninth Sephira, *Yesod*, which is the connecting link between Microprosopus and the queen. Also N, the second letter, symbolizes the conjunction of the father and the mother, I and H, as I have before observed.]

62. (Now, indeed, Macroprosopus is not so closely known by us as to address us in the first person; but he is called in the third person, HVA, *Hoa*, he.) Like as it is said, Ps. c. 3: "*He* hath made us, and not we ourselves." And again in Job xxiii. 13: "And *He* existeth in the unity, and who can turn *Him* aside?"

[For Macroprosopus is only the *commencement of manifested Deity.*]

63. (Therefore in the third person, HVA, *Hoa*, is He called who is the Concealed One, and is not found of any. He, who cometh not before the eyes of man; He, who is not called by the Name.

["He, who is not called by the Name;" for, as I have frequently before noticed, the first Sephira is *not* comprehended in the Tetragrammaton.]

64. (Hitherto hath the disquisition been concerning Microprosopus, to whom also was referred that fulness of form of the letter H, *He*, wherein it is written by the duplicated HH. But now another point is taken into consideration, namely, concerning the remaining two modes of writing that letter, when it is written with A, *Aleph*, and with I, *Yod*; of which the former is made in the name MH, *Mah*, and the latter in the names OB, *Aub*, and SG, *Seg*; which two forms are given conjoined in the name AHIH, *Eheieh* (translated "I am" in Exodus). Therefore are to be considered) HA and HI. (Whilst, therefore, it is written HA, this form can be resolved into HVA, *Hoa*, he, that pronoun of the third person concerning which mention

hath been made above: because A, *Aleph*, in itself containeth V, *Vau*; to which latter letter the middle line, in the form of the character of the letter *Aleph*, can be assimilated. And thus, while it is written HA, the word HVA can be symbolized; but not *vice versâ*. For although) V in itself containeth A (because the figure of the letter A may be said to be composed of VIV, if its middle line be divided; so that also, without taking the whole character A into consideration, it may be read HV: this HV) nevertheless doth not contain in itself any real form of writing H, so that it can be read HV or HI.

[The reader must remember that the argument in this section is concerning the *shape* of the Hebrew letters mentioned, alone, and that neither their numerical value nor articulate power is taken into consideration. The shape of the Hebrew letters can be seen in the Table of the Alphabet.]

65. (Moreover, in that same form of writing HA, like as A passeth into V, so that HVA, *Hoa*, may be read: so also) A is pronounced *Aleph* (and this is the second way of pronouncing the writing HA, which simply is referred unto MH, *Mah*. But, moreover, also) Aleph is pronounced as IVD, *Yod* (because the form of the letter A is usually resolved into these three letters, so that *Yod* may be above, *Vau* in the middle, and *Daleth* below. So that same written form HA in itself comprehendeth also that sublimer triune idea. But not *vice versâ*, from HI is HA to be understood, for I, *Yod*, is not pronounced Aleph; but IVD is pronounced as I, *Yod*, which is concealed with all concealments, and to which VD are not joined (like as that form is to be found in the shape of the letter *Aleph*.)

[H, *He*, in Hebrew is the definite article; so that H-A may be read *He-Aleph*, the Aleph.]

66. (But this form, which in itself includeth V, *Vau*, and D, *Daleth*, is usual in the inferior paths, and also in the father. And) Woe! when I, *Yod*, irradiateth not the letters V, *Vau*, and D, *Daleth*; (and much more) when I, *Yod*, is

taken away from V, *Vau*, D, *Daleth*, through the sins of the world; (because then) the nakedness of them all is discovered.

67. Therefore it is written, Lev. xviii. 7: "The nakedness of thy father thou shalt not uncover." (For VD, *Vau Daleth* are the same as H, *He*; and when it is written IVD, it is the same as if it were called IH (namely if V, *Vau*, be inserted in D, *Daleth*). Woe! when *Yod* is taken away from *He* (that is, wisdom from understanding, which is the conceiving mother) because it is written, Lev. xviii. 7: "And the nakedness of thy mother thou shalt not uncover; she is thy mother, thou shalt not uncover her nakedness." Revere her; she is thy mother; because it is written, Prov. ii. 3: "Because thou shalt call understanding thy mother." (This is arrived at by reading the word AM in this passage with the pointing *Tsere*, instead of with the usual *Chireq* pointing.)

["VD=H." This is again referring to the *shape* of the letter in question.]

[I have already stated in the Introduction, for the benefit of those of my readers who are not Hebrew or Chaldee scholars, that the Hebrew alphabet is chiefly consonantal, the vowels being supplied by small points or marks placed close to the letters.]

CHAPTER III.

1. NINE are said to be the conformations of the beard (of Microprosopus). For that which remaineth concealed (that is, the other four forms, which meanwhile are not found in Microprosopus), and which is not manifested, is supernal and venerable (that is, properly and of itself doth not refer to Microprosopus, but nevertheless descendeth upon him in another manner).

[It must be remembered that the beard of Macroprosopus had thirteen divisions, therefore the other four forms are the difference between the nine of Microprosopus and the thirteen of Macroprosopus.]

2. Thus, therefore, is this most excellent beard arranged. The hairs overhang the hairs from before the opening of the ears, even unto the beginning of the mouth. (This is the first conformation.)

3. From the one beginning even unto the other beginning (of the mouth. This is the second conformation—namely, the beard on the upper lip).

4. Beneath the two nostrils existeth a path filled with hairs, so that it appeareth not. (This is the third conformation.)

5. The cheeks extend on one side and on the other. (This is the fourth conformation.)

6. In them appear apples red as roses. (This is the fifth conformation.)

7. In one tress hang down those hairs strong and black, even unto the breast. (This is the sixth conformation.)

8. Red are the lips as roses, and bare. This is the seventh conformation.)

9. Short hairs descend through the place of the throat and cover the position of the neck. (This is the eighth conformation.)

10. Long and short descend alike. (This is the ninth conformation.)

11. Whosoever is found among them, is found strong and robust. (That is, he who directeth his meditations herein.)

12. It is written, Ps. cxviii. 4: "I called upon *Yah*, IH, in distress." (In this place) David commemorateth (these) nine (conformations) even unto (those words) "all nations compassed me about," in order that they (the nine above mentioned) might surround and protect him.

13. (It is written, Gen. i. 12): "And the earth brought forth germination, the herb yielding seed after its kind; and the tree bearing fruit, whose seed is therein, according to its kind."

14. Those nine (paths of Microprosopus) are evolved from the perfect name (that is, from the understanding or mother, in whom they were conceived; for unto her pertaineth the name IHVH, which is Tetragrammaton expressed and Elohim hidden, which form the nine in power). And thence are they planted into the perfect name, like as it is written, Gen. ii. 8: "And IHVH ALHIM planted" (that is, these nine letters of the perfect masculine and feminine name, so that they may be a garden—that is, Microprosopus in action).

[By the expression "Tetragrammaton expressed and Elohim hidden," is meant that the former is written with the vowel points of the latter. They "form nine in power," because the four letters IHVH together with the five letters ALHIM make nine.

15. The conformations of the beard (of Microprosopus) are found to be thirteen when that which is superior becometh inferior. (That is, whensoever the beard of Macroprosopus sendeth down its light. But in the inferior (that is, Microprosopus taken by himself), they are beheld in nine (parts of that form).

16. The twenty-two letters are figured forth in their

colour; not only when the law is given forth in black fire upon white fire, but also in ordinary writings, because this beard is black.)

[The number of the letters of the Hebrew alphabet is twenty-two. "Black fire" and "white fire" are the colours of the beards of Microprosopus and of Macroprosopus respectively.]

17. Concerning this (beard, that is understood which is said) concerning him who in his sleep beholdeth the beard. "When any one dreameth that he taketh the upper beard of a man in his hand, he hath peace with his Lord, and his enemies are subject unto him."

[By the "upper beard" is meant the moustache.]

18. Much more (if he seeketh to touch) the supernal beard. For the inferior light, taking its rise from the supernal light which existeth within the benignity (thus the beard of Macroprosopus is entitled), is called in Microprosopus the benignity in a more simple manner; but when it hath its action within the light, and it shineth; then is it called abounding in benignity. (Others read this passage thus:—He who dreameth that he toucheth the moustache of a man with his hand, he may be sure that he hath peace with his Lord, and that his enemies are subject unto him. If that happeneth because he beholdeth in sleep such a thing as this only, much more shall it occur if he be found sufficiently worthy to behold what the supernal beard may be. For this, seeing that it is the superior, and is called the benignity, irradiateth the inferior. But in Microprosopus, &c.)

19. It is written, Gen. I. 20: "Let the waters bring forth the reptile of a living soul" (CH-IH, *Chiah,* living creature is to be here noted).

(To this section belongs the annotation which is placed at the end of this chapter; which see.)

20. Like as it is said IH, *Yah* (CH-IH, *Ch-iah,* the corrected Mantuan Codex hath it, so that it may explain the word CHIH, *Chiah,* living creature, out of the eighth

path of the understanding, which is that water of the name *Yah*, which denoteth father and mother. For when) the light of the former is extended unto the latter (which is the moving of the water) all things reproduce their kind at one and the same time—the waters of good and the waters of evil. (That is, there is reproduction as well in divinity and sanctity as among terrestrial living creatures and man; for by the reptile form souls are symbolized.)

21. (For) while it saith: ISʜRTᴢV, *Yeshratzu*, "Let them bring forth abundantly," they have vital motion; and the one form is at once included in the other form; the living superior, the living inferior; the living good, the living evil.

22. (So also it is written, Gen. i. 26): "And Elohim said, Let us make man." (Where) it is not written HADM, *Ha-Adam*, "this man"; but *Adam*, man, simply, in antithesis of the Higher One who hath been made in the perfect name.

[Regarding the "form of the heavenly man," see Introduction, § 55.]

23. When that one was perfected, this one also was perfected; but perfected as male and female, for the perfecting of all things.

24. (When therefore it is said) IHVH, *Yod, He, Vau, He* (then is expressed), the nature of the male. (When) ALHIM, *Elohim* (is joined therewith, there is expressed), the nature of the female (who is called the kingdom).

["The female who is called the kingdom," *i.e.*, Malkuth, the tenth Sephira.]

25. (Therefore) was the male extended, and formed with his members (in order that he might have), as it were, regenerative power.

[The "members of the male" are the six Sephiroth which together form Microprosopus.]

26. By means of this regenerative power those kings,

who had been destroyed, were herein restored, and obtained stability. (For when the lights were sent down through narrow channels in less abundance, the inferior intelligences could take possession of them.)

[The "kings who had been destroyed" are the "Edomite kings," the "worlds of unbalanced force," who could not subsist because the "form of the heavenly man" was not as yet. See Introduction, §§ 41, 56.]

27. The rigours (of judgments, which are symbolized by those kings), which are masculine, are vehement in the beginning; but in the end they are slackened. In the female the contrary rule obtaineth.

28. (We have an example of this in this form of the name) VIH (where the male hath two letters, and the female one only; and the masculine also the letter in the beginning long, and afterwards short. But also in this form) the channels of connection are shrouded beneath His covering (that his, the supernal letters are doubtless connected in marital conjunction, but they are enshrouded in the letter *Vau*. And) *Yod* (is in this place) small, (a symbol of the foundation; because) in the very form (of the female, that is, even as he is hidden within H, *He*, which also is not the supernal but the inferior H, *He*) he is found. (And all are judgments, because the supernal influx is wanting.)

29. But if (these) judgments are to be mitigated, necessarily the Ancient One is required (that is, the first letters of the Tetragrammaton, denoting, IH *Yah*, the father together with the crown, which is the apex of the primal letter, and is called Macroprosopus.)

30. The same species of rigours and judgments occurred in the inferiors. For like as to the *He* of the bride, are added the two letters *Yod* and *Vau*, under the idea of the leviathan; (so) the serpent came upon the woman, and formed in her a nucleus of impurity, in order that he might make the habitation evil.

31. Like as it is written, Gen. iv. 1: "And she conceived and brought forth ATH QIN, *Ath Qain*, Cain, (that is) the nucleus QINA, *Qaina*, of the abode of evil spirits, and turbulence, and evil occurrences." (See further in the "Treatise of the Revolutions of the Soul.")

[The "Treatise of the Revolutions of the Soul" is not published in this volume.]

32. (But this name VIH) is restored (if it be written IHV; and thus) in that man (the supernal, concerning whom it hath been spoken above; and also) in those two (namely, the father and the mother, also in the androgynous Microprosopus; and also partly) in genus (seeing that *Vau* alone symbolizeth both the Microprosopus and his bride) and in species (seeing that *Yod* and *He* are placed separately as father and mother).

33. (But just as much) are they contained in the special (representation of those spouses, as) also in the general (that is, as much in father and mother as in Microprosopus with his bride); legs and arms right and left (that is, the remaining numerations, collected together in two lateral lines, with the middle line representing *Vau* and *Yod.*)

34. (But) this (that is, the supreme equality) is divided in its sides, because *Yod* and *He* are placed expressly as the father and the mother; but in another equality) the male is conformed with the female (like an androgyn, because the last *He* is not added. Whence are made) IHV.

35. I, *Yod*, is male (namely, the father); H, *He*, is female (namely, the mother); V, *Vau* (however, is androgynous, like as) it is written, Gen. v. 2: "Male and female created He them, and blessed them, and called their name Adam."

36. (Thus also) the form and person of a man was seated upon the throne; and it is written, Ezek. I. 26: "And upon the likeness of the throne was the likeness as the appearance of a man above it."

[This piece alludes to the Tetragrammaton itself, showing the hieroglyphic form of a man: the I=head, H=arms, V=body, and H=legs. See Introduction and Table of Alphabet.]

ANNOTATION.

(*Belonging to* § 19, *foregoing*.)

1. Another explanation. "Let waters bring forth abundantly." In this place, in the Chaldee paraphrase, it is said IRCHSHVN, which hath a general meaning of movement. As if it should be said: "When his lips by moving themselves and murmuring, produced the words, like a prayer from a righteous heart and pure mind, the water produced the living soul." (The meaning is concerning the act of generating life.)

2. And when a man wishes to utter his prayers rightly before the Lord, and his lips move themselves in this manner, (his invocations) rising upward from him, for the purpose of magnifying the majesty of his Lord unto the place of abundance of the water where the depth of that fountain riseth and floweth forth (that is, understanding emanating from wisdom); then (that fountain floweth forth plentifully, and) spreadeth abroad so as to send down the influx from the Highest, downwards from that place of abundance of water, into the paths singly and conjointly, even unto the last path; in order that her bountiful grace may be derived into all from the highest downwards.

[H, *He*, the supernal mother.]

3. Then indeed is such a man held to intertwine the connecting links of (them) all, namely, those connecting links of true and righteous meditation; and all his petitions shall come to pass, whether his petition be made in a place of worship, whether in private prayer.

["Such a man"—*i.e.*, a righteous man, when praying sincerely. "Links of them"—*i.e.*, the paths.]

4. But the petition which a man wisheth to make unto his Lord can ordinarily be propounded in nine ways.

5. Either (1) by the alphabet, or (2) by commemorating the attributes of the most holy and blessed God, merciful and gracious, &c. (according to the passage in Exodus xxxiv. 6, &c.); or (3) by the venerable names of the most holy and blessed God; such are these: AHIH, *Eheieh* (in respect of the Crown), and IH, *Yah* (in respect of the Wisdom); IHV, *Yod He Vau* (in respect of the Understanding); AL, *El* (in respect of the Majesty); ALHIM, *Elohim* (in respect of the Severity); IHVH, *Yod He Vau He* (in respect of the Beauty); TzBAVTh, *Tzabaoth* (in respect of the Victory and the Glory); ShDI, *Shaddai* (in respect of the Foundation); and ADNI, *Adonaï* (in respect of the Kingdom). Or (4) by the ten Sephiroth or numerations, which are: MLKVTh, *Malkuth*, the Kingdom; ISVD, *Yesod*, the Foundation; HVD, *Hod*, the Glory; NTzCh, *Netzach*, the Victory; ThPARTh, *Tiphereth*, the Beauty; GBVRH, *Geburah*, the Severity; ChSD, *Chesed*, the Benignity; BINH, *Binah*, the Understanding; ChKMH, *Chokhmah*, the Wisdom; and KThR, *Kether*, the Crown. Or (5) by the commemoration of just men, such as are patriarchs, prophets, and kings. Or (6) by those canticles and psalms wherein is the true Qabalah. And (7), above all these, if any one should know how to declare the conformations of his Lord, according as it is honourable to do. Or (8) if he may know how to ascend from that which is below to that which is above. Or (9) those who know also how to derive the influx from the highest downward. And in all these nine ways there is need of very great concentration of attention; because if he doeth not that, it is written concerning him, 1 Sam. ii. 30: "And they that despise Me shall be lightly esteemed."

["(1) by the alphabet"—*i.e.*, according to the mystic qabalistico, theosophic values of the letters. (2) Exod. xxxiv. 6, 7: "And the LORD passed by before him, and proclaimed, The LORD, the LORD

God, merciful and gracious, long-suffering and abundant, in goodness and truth, keeping mercy for thousands, forgiving iniquity and transgression and sin, and that will by no means clear the guilty; visiting the iniquity of the fathers upon the children, and upon the children's children, unto the third and to the fourth generation." (3) By the Divine Names associated with the Sephiroth. (4) The ten Sephiroth. (5) Those analogous to his desire. (6) Phrases bearing on the subject. (7) The qabalistical development of Deity. (8) By the paths. (9) The converse of (8).]

6. Hereto also pertaineth the meditation of the word *Amen* AMN! which in itself containeth the two names IHVH, ADNI, *Yod He Vau He Adonaï* (the numeration of the former alone, and of these two together yielding the same, 91); of which the one concealeth its goodness and benediction in that treasury which is called HIKL, *Ha-yekal*, the palace. (Which word by equality of numeration is the same as ADNI, *Adonaï;* but this name is said to be the palace of Tetragrammaton, because, in the first place it is pronounced by its aid; also, in the second place, it is mingled with it alternately, letter by letter, in this way —IAHDVNHI.

[A + M + N = 1 + 40 + 50 = 91. I + H + V + H + A + D + N + I = 10 + 5 + 6 + 5 + 1 + 4 + 50 + 10 = 91. Again: H + I + K + L = 5 + 10 + 20 + 30 = 65. A + D + N + I = 1 + 4 + 50 + 10 = 65. The Jews, when they come to the word IHVH in reading the Scriptures, either do not pronounce it at all and make a slight pause, or else substitute for it the word *Adonaï*, ADNI.]

7. And this is pointed out in that saying, Hab. ii. 20: "But the Lord is in His holy temple; let all the earth keep silence before Him." (HIKL, *Ha-yekal*, "the temple, or palace;" HS, *Hes*, "keep silence;" and ADNI, *Adonaï*, "Lord;" all have the same numeration—namely, 65.)

[H + S = 5 + 60 = 65.]

8. For which reason our wise men of pious memory have said mystically, that every good thing of a man is in his house; according to that which is written, Num. xi.,

7: "He is faithful in all Mine house." Which is the same as if it were said "in all which is with Me."

9. But if any man attentively meditateth on the nine divisions of these forms (*see* § 5 *ante*), like as it is meet to do; that man is one who honoureth the Name of his Lord, even the Holy Name. And hereunto belongeth that which is written, 1 Sam. ii. 30: "Since those who honour Me will I honour; and they that despise Me shall be lightly esteemed." I will honour him in this world, that I may preserve him, and provide him with all things of which he hath need, in order that all nations of the earth may see that the Name of the Lord is called upon by him; and that they may fear him. And in the world to come he shall be found worthy to stand in the tabernacle of the righteous.

10. Wherefore such an one seeketh nothing of which he hath need, because he is kept under the special providence of his Lord, and can meditate concerning Him, as it is right to do.

11. But what is to be understood by that passage—"And they that despise Me shall be lightly esteemed?" Such an one is that man who can neither institute the union of the Holy Name, nor bind together the links of truth, nor derive the supernals into the position required, nor honour the Name of his Lord. Better were it for that man had he never been created, and much more for that man who doth not attentively meditate when he saith Amen!

12. For which reason, concerning that man especially who moveth his lips (in prayer), with a pure heart (meditating) on those purifying waters, in that passage expressly and clearly written, Gen. i. 26: "And the Elohim said, Let us make man." As if it were said concerning such a man who knew how to unite image and likeness, as it is right: "And they shall have dominion over the fish of the sea, &c."

Hereunto is the annotation.

CHAPTER IV.

1. THE Ancient One is hidden and concealed; the Microprosopus is manifested, and is not manifested.

[The "Ancient One" is Kether, Eheieh, Macroprosopus, the Vast Countenance. See Introduction, §§, 42, 77.]

2. When he is manifested, he is symbolized by the letters (in the ordinary form in which the Tetragrammaton is written).

3. When he is concealed, he is hidden by the letters which are not disposed according (to the proper order) of the letters, or (according to another reading of this passage) in their proper place; because also in him their superiors and inferiors are not rightly disposed (because of the disturbed transpositions).

4. In Gen. i. 24 it is written: "The earth brought forth the living creature after its kind, cattle and reptile," &c. Hereunto belongeth that which is written, Ps. xxxv. 7: "O Lord, thou shalt preserve both man and beast."

5. The one is contained under the general meaning of the other, and also the beast under the general idea of the man (on account of the mystery of the revolution of the soul).

6. (And hereunto pertaineth that passage) Levit. i. 2: "When a man shall bring *from among you* an offering unto the Lord, &c. Ye shall offer, &c." Because animals are included under the generic term man.

7. When the inferior man descendeth (into this world), like unto the supernal form (in himself), there are found two spirits. (So that) man is formed from two sides—from the right and from the left.

8. With respect unto the right side he had NSHMTHA QDISHA, *Neschamotha Qadisha*, the holy intelligences; with

respect unto the left side, NPSH CHIH, *Nephesh Chiah*, the animal soul.

[These answer to the right and left pillars of the Sephiroth. See Introduction.]

9. Man sinned and was expanded on the left side; and then they who are formless were expanded also. (That is those spirits of matter, who received dominion in the inferior paths of the soul of Adam, whence arose base concupiscence.) When (therefore) both were at once joined together (namely by base concupiscence, together with connexion, and the animal soul) generations took place, like as from some animal which generateth many lives in one connexion.

10. (There are given) twenty-two letters hidden and twenty-two letters manifested (which are the symbols of those sublime forms).

11. (The one) *Yod* is concealed; the other is manifested. (The one is the understanding or mother, the other is the kingdom or queen; so that at the same time it looketh back to the superior paths.) But that which is hidden and that which is manifest are balanced in the equilibrium of forms. (That is, masculine and feminine; the one, the father and the mother; the other, the foundation and the queen; meaning principally the female idea, which includeth form and receptacle.)

12. Out of *Yod* are produced male and female (if, namely, it be fully written as IVD, *Yod*, they are then its augment), *Vau* and *Daleth*. In this position *Vau* is male, and *Daleth* is female. And hence arise DV, the two letters which are the duad male and female; and not only the duad, but also the co-equal duads (of the superior and inferior conjunctions).

13. *Yod* by itself is male (the father); *He*, female (the mother).

14. H, *He*, at first was D, *Daleth*; but after it was impregnated by I, *Yod* (so that thence it might produce the

form H—namely, the I, *Yod*, placed at the left hand lower part of *Daleth*) it brought forth V, *Vau*. (That is, the mother impregnated by the father produced Microprosopus. But in the shape of the letter out of that minute I, *Yod*, which is hidden within the H, *He*, V, *Vau*, is said to be formed. Or from the upper horizontal line of the letter H, which is one V, *Vau*, and from the right-hand vertical line, which is another V, *Vau*, and from the inserted I, *Yod*, is made VIV, the full form of letter *Vau*.)

[This is again referring to the *shape* of the letter. See Table of the Alphabet for Hebrew form.]

15. Whence it is plain that in the letter H, *He*, are hidden the letters D, *Daleth*, V, *Vau*; and in IVD, *Yod*, is hidden H: whence are formed IHV. Therefore it appeareth that IVD in its own form containeth IHV, whensoever it is fully written by IVD, which are male and female (namely I, *Yod*, male, and V, *Vau*, D, *Daleth*, in the form, H, *He*, female); hence is compounded (the son, who is) V, *Vau*, and who overshadoweth his mother. (That is V placed after H, so that IHV may form the father, the mother, and Microprosopus.)

16. (Therefore in the letter IVD, *Yod*, and in the name IHI are hidden two males and two females, which is symbolized in that saying, Gen. vi. 2: "And the sons of the Elohim beheld (the plural in its least form denoteth two) the daughters of men" (and this also). This explaineth on this account that which is written, Josh. ii. 1: "Two men as spies, saying" (hence is revealed the mystery of the two men). But how (is it proved that two females are understood) by the words, "Daughters of men?" Because it is written, 1 Kings iii. 16: "Then came there two women unto the king."

17. Of these it is written, *ibid.* 28: "Because they saw that the wisdom of Elohim was in him." (Here are involved the two males, in the wisdom, the father; in

Solomon, Microprosopus. Therefore) then came they (even the two women, the understanding and the queen) and not before.

18. In the palace of the union of the fountains (that is, in the world of creation) there were two connexions by conjunctions among the supernals; these descended from above, and occupied the earth; but they rejected the good part, which in them was the crown of mercy; and were crowned with the cluster of grapes. (That is instead of benignity, they were surrounded with judgments and rigours. Which also can be explained concerning Microprosopus and his bride, first in the mother, and afterwards in the existences below, and in exile with surrounding rigours and severities.)

[Referring to the previous symbolical explanation of Joshua ii, 1.]

19. (Also we find these two equations in that saying) Exod. xiv. 15: "And the Lord said unto Moses (who is referred to the mother), Why criest thou unto Me?" (But also a cry is referred to the mother, just as a groan is to the beautiful path, and an exclamation to the kingdom. But) ALI, *Eli*, unto me (note this is the same as, "and unto I, *Yod*;" or the father). "Speak unto the children of Israel (the speech is the queen; Israel is the beautiful path) that they set forward." Wherein note well the word VISOV, *Vayesaau*, "that they set forward," wherein are VI masculine letters; SO feminine letters).

["But also a cry, &c." Meaning the three Sephiroth, *Binah*, *Tiphereth*, and *Malkuth*.]

20. From above the power of life flowed down in equilibrium, for he entreated the influence of the Venerable One.

["The Venerable One"—*i.e.*, the first Sephira, proceeding from the AIN SVP AVR, *Ain Soph Aur*. See Introduction.]

21. Hereunto also pertaineth that passage, Exod. xv. 26: "And if thou shalt do right in His eyes, and shalt hearken

unto His precepts, and shalt keep all His statutes." (Wherein the last word also two equations are placed.) "Because I am the Lord thy God who healeth thee." (Note this, because again here is hidden the mystery of the understanding and the wisdom, of the path of beauty and of the congregation of Israel.)

CHAPTER V.

1. (It is written) Isa. i. 4: "Woe unto the sinful nation, unto the people heavy with iniquity, unto the seed of evildoers, &c." (Here the author of the "Siphra Dtzenioutha" reasoneth concerning the small word HVI, "woe," which also is a form of the name. And this word is alone separated from the following portions of the sentence.)

2. Seven are the paths (if the Tetragrammaton be written in this way partially complete), IVD, HH, V, H, (where the father and mother are written in full, Microprosopus and his bride are written uncovered. If here the last and first letters be combined, and the penultimate and second, and therefore the paths at either extremity, so that they may form the letters) HI and VV (mother and son), then are produced (the three middle letters) HH, D (which are the symbols of the queen, heavy with judgments. But if mother and daughter be combined) HVI and HH, (then) is produced forth VV (or Microprosopus) as well as DV (or the androgyn, who also is a condition of judgments), for occultly Adam is denoted, or the male and female, who are that DV concerning whom it is written (in the place cited above) "corrupt children."

3. (When it is said) BRASHITH, BRA, *Berashith bera*, "In the beginning created," (the supernal paths are under-

stood. For) BRAShITh, *Berashith*, is the speech (one of the ten rules of Genesis), but BRA, *Bera*, is the speech halved. (But there are here understood) Father and Son, the hidden and the manifest. (And also)

4 The superior Eden is hidden and concealed. (That is, no mention is made of the crown.) The inferior Eden cometh forth so that it may be transferred (towards the inferiors) and manifested (through the voice of its original, which denoteth wisdom.)

["No mention made of the crown"—*i.e.*, Kether, the first Sephira, Macroprosopus.]

5. For the name (Tetragrammaton) IHVH, *Yod*, *He*, *Vau*, *He*, includeth the name IH, *Yah*, (which is of the father, and the name) ALHIM, *Elohim* (which here followeth in the text, and pertaineth unto the mother).

6. ATh, *Ath* (the fourth word of this text, which in another manner signifieth the name) ADNI, *Adonaï*, "Lord" (namely, the path of the kingdom; also the name) AHIH, *Eheieh* (that is, the path of the crown, and thus symbolizeth in itself the two extreme paths; here denoteth) the right and the left (that is, benignity and severity), which are united in one (equilibrium).

[*Ath*, ATh, means "the," "the very substance of." Qabalistically it signifies "the beginning and the end," and is like the term "Alpha and Omega" used in the Apocalypse. For as Alpha and Omega are respectively the first and last letters of the Greek alphabet, so are Aleph and Tau of the Hebrew. The "two extreme paths" are the crown, Kether, and the kingdom, Malkuth, the first and tenth Sephiroth, the highest and the lowest, Macroprosopus, and the queen. If the reader turn to the Introduction, to the Table showing the Sephiroth arranged in three pillars, he will see that Malkuth is, as it were, the antithesis of Kether; and hence it is said that "Malkuth is Kether after another manner." And this recalls the precept of Hermes in the Smaragdine Tablet: "That which is below is like that which is above, and that which is above is like that which is below."

7. HShMIM, *Ha-Shamaim*, "the heavens" (the fifth word of this text, and) VATh, *Vaath*, "and the substance

of" (the sixth word; they are referred unto the paths of beauty and victory) like as it is written, 1 Chron. xxix. 11: "And the beauty and the victory." These paths are joined together in one.

[The beauty and the victory" are Tiphereth and Netzach, the sixth and seventh Sephiroth.]

8. HARTz, *Haaretz*, "the earth" (the seventh word of this beginning denoteth the queen joined together with the glory and the foundation), like as it is written, Ps. viii. 2: "How magnificent (this is the path of glory) is Thy name in all the world" (whereby is symbolized the foundation); the earth which is the kingdom. Also) Isa. vi. 3: "The whole earth is full of His glory" (where these three paths again concur).

9. "Let there be a firmament in the midst of the waters," "to make a distinction between the Holy Place and between the Holy of Holies." (That is, between Microprosopus and Macroprosopus.)

10. The Most Ancient One is expanded into Microprosopus (or the Crown into the Beauty), and adhereth (unto it, so that it may receive increase. If) it be not perfectly expanded (so that Microprosopus as it were existeth by himself, but instead is retained in his mother's womb) the mouth speaking great things moveth in that place (that Microprosopus, so that he may be fully born), and he is crowned with the lesser crowns under the five divisions of the waters. (That is, Microprosopus receiveth the influx of the five benignities, which are called "crowns," because they descend from the crown, or Macroprosopus; but "lesser crowns," because they take their rise from benignity in the *Microprosopic path*; and they are called the five divisions of the waters, because the water belongeth unto the benignity, and in this verse, Gen. i. 6, 7, the word MIM, *Meim*, waters, filleth the fifth place).

11. Like as it is written, Num. xix. 17: "And shall pour upon him living waters in a vessel." (But the life looketh towards the mother; and it) is (understood to be that path which is called) ALHIM CHIIM, *Elohim Chiim*, "the Elohim of life;" and the king of the universe (that is, the understanding. Whereunto belong also the following sayings:—) Ps. cxvi. v. 9: "I will walk before the Lord in the lands of life." Also 1 Sam. 29: "And the soul of my Lord shall be bound in the quiver of life." Also Gen. ii. 9: "And the tree of life in the midst of the garden." (All these, I say, refer unto the understanding, from which the six members receive the influx. And to it also pertain the following names, namely, the name) IH, *Yah* (whensoever it is written in full with A in this manner:) IVD HA, *Yod Ha* (and containeth the number of the numeral powers of the letters of the Tetragrammaton, namely, 26; unto which also is referred that form of the name belonging unto the intelligence), AHII, *Eheii* (where in the place of the final *He*, *Yod* is put, as in a former instance. (See Chap. 1. § 32.)

[In the Hebrew, CHIIM, *Chiim*, "iving"; in our version of the Old Testament it is translated "running water." Chiim is plural.]

12. Between the waters and the waters. (Since there are the superior) perfect waters, and (those which are in Microprosopus) imperfect waters (or those mingled with severities; because in another manner it is said) perfect compassion, imperfect compassion. (Now followeth a mystical explanation of Gen. vi. 3.)

13. And the Tetragrammaton hath said: "My spirit shall not strive with man for ever, seeing that he also is in the flesh." (In this passage, when it is said:) "And the Tetragrammaton hath said," (it is to be noted that) after that there was formed (the supernal structure), in the last place concerning Microprosopus (this name is

understood). For when it is said, "He calleth this also by the name," the Ancient One speaketh occultly in a hidden manner.

[The Ancient One is symbolized by the pronoun He in the sentence, "He calleth this also by the name."]

14. "My spirit shall not strive with man." (Here is understood, not the spirit of Microprosopus, but) that which is from the supernals, because from that spirit which rusheth forth from the two nostrils of the nose of Macroprosopus the influx is sent down unto the inferiors.

15. And because it is written (in the same place) "And his days shall be a hundred and twenty years," I, *Yod*, is either perfect (whensoever its singular parts exist in the form of decads) or imperfect (when they are in monads or units). When (theretore *Yod* (is placed by itself) alone (it is understood to be perfect, because in itself it containeth) a hundred. (But if) two letters (are put, then are understood the ten units) twice reckoned; (hence are produced) the hundred and twenty years.

[The "singular parts" of Yod are the numbers from one to ten, for the number of Yod is ten. But when Yod is taken as its square $I \times I = 10 \times 10 = 100$. But $II = I \times I + I + I$ (or the two letters both multiplied and added together) $= 10 \times 10 + 10 + 10 = 120$. But when Yod $= 100$, its digits are tens and not units—namely, the numbers 10, 20, 30, &c., instead of 1, 2, 3, &c.

16. *Yod* is alone whensoever he is manifested in Microprosopus (that is when the lights of Macroprosopus descend into Him, then indeed the paths of the decads are increased, and this decad) is increased into ten thousands (by the paths joined with the four letters of the Tetragrammaton) of years. (But) hence (if it be conceived only according unto the power of Macroprosopus, it hath that position) which is written, Ps. cxxxix. 5; "And thou shalt place upon me thine hand:" KPKH, *Khephakha*. (Where this word KPKH, if it be written according to the usual

custom KPK, *Khephakh,* yieldeth the number 120. But now by adding the paragogic H of the female, there is given the number 125, on account of the five severities.)

["This decad is increased into ten thousand by the paths joined with the four letters of the Tetragrammaton "—*i.e.*, the paths are the Sephiroth = the numbers from one to ten; and they are said to be joined with the four letters by multiplying the decad to the fourth power, or 10^4. Hence for I, the first letter, we have $10 \times 1 = 10$; for H, the second letter, we have $10 \times 10 = 100$; for V, the third letter, $10 \times 10 \times 10 = 1{,}000$; and for H, the fourth letter, $10 \times 10 \times 10 \times 10 = 10{,}000$.

In the Shemitic languages, a paragogic letter is one which is added to a word to give it additional emphasis.]

17. "There were giants in the earth," Gen. vi. 4. (If this word HIV, *Hayu,* is considered, which also is a form of the often varied name, it taketh its rise from the kingdom.) This is that which is written, Gen. ii. 10: "And thence is it divided, and is in four heads." (Where is understood the end of that emanation which the separated universe followeth. Nevertheless) from the place where the body is divided, they are called those trees (or, as the Mantuan Codex correcteth the passage: Where the garden is divided, and the seven inferior emanations are understood; where then it divideth the universe into the inferior worlds and provideth a habitation for the shells or spirits of matter). Hence it is written: "And from hence is it divided."

["The shells" = elemental spirits. The Qabalah always calls the evil elemental spirits of matter "shells."]

18. They were in the earth in those days, but not in the following time, until Joshua came. (That is, they are applicable unto the path of the bride, which also is called the land of Canaan, wherein Joshua found the giants. For the word NPILIM, *Nephilim,* occurreth not fully, except when it is used in the incident of the spies, Num. xiii. 33.)

19. And the sons of the Elohim are guarded (nor is mention made of a similar case) until Solomon came and joined himself with the daughters of men; like as it is written, Eccles. ii. 8: VTHONVGVTH, *Ve-Thonogoth* "And the *delights* of the sons of men," &c. Where (in the feminine gender) he calleth the word THONVGVTH, *Thonogoth*, and not (as elsewhere in the masculine gender) THONVGIM, *Thonogim*, "sons of Adam;" so that it is intimated in an occult manner that the latter (the sons of the Elohim) are of those other spirits who are not contained under the supernal wisdom; concerning which it is written, 1 Kings v. 12: "And the Lord gave wisdom unto Solomon." (Concerning these matters, further see the "Treatise of the Revolutions)."

["The Treatise of the Revolutions" is not published in this volume.]

20. Also it is written, *ibid.* iv. 31: "And He was wise above every man." Because these are not classed with man.

21. (But when it is said) "And the Tetragrammaton gave him wisdom," then is understood the supernal *He*. (Because he gave unto him the influx of the wisdom of the queen.) "And he was wise before every man," because from her he received the wisdom here below (through the path to the kingdom).

22. Those (spirits) are powerful who exist from eternity. That is, from (eternity or) the supernal world (the understanding, namely, whence are excited severity and rigour). The men of the name (that is) who exercised themselves in the name.

23. In what name? In the Holy Name, wherein they exercised themselves (for the performing of various wonders), and not the holy inferiors. Yet (these) did not exercise themselves save in the name (and not in holiness).

24. It is said openly "the men of the name," and not

"the men of the Tetragrammaton." Not (therefore used they the name) with respect unto the mystery of the Arcanum, or in a diminutive form; nor yet with any diminution of the (name itself).

25. (And because) the men of the name (are) openly (spoken of, hence) are they shut out from the general conception of man.

26. It is written, Ps. xlix. 12: "Man being in honour, abideth not." (When it is said) "man being in honour" (the same is as if also it were said, a man such as was Solomon) shall not remain long in the honour of the King without the spirit. (That is, in the influx from the King, Microprosopus, to whom, or to the beautiful path, the spirit belongeth.)

27. Thirteen kings (that is, the twelve metatheses of the Tetragrammaton with its radix, which are the measures of mercies) wage war with seven (with the Edomite kings; because, while the lights of the former flowed down, these could not maintain themselves, and, besides, they are the classes of the most rigorous judgments which are opposed to the mercies. For) seven kings are seen in the land (Edom), and now after that their vessels are broken, they are called shells, who have fallen down among the inferiors. (These) nine vanquished in war (the measures of Microprosopus, concerning which see the "Idra Rabba"; through which David conquered his enemies), which ascend in the paths of those which pass downward, on account of His ruling power (that is, which make thirteen, as they are in Macroprosopus and his beard, which is called his influence, and freely floweth down), and there is none who can withhold their hand. (For whilst the supernal measures permit the increase in the inferiors, all judgments are subdued.)

[Concerning the "twelve banners of the sacred Name," the metatheses of the Tetragrammaton, see Introduction, § 62; also concerning the Edomite kings. I have before remarked that the demons are called Qliphoth, or "shells," by the Qabalists. The thirteen in Microprosopus is composed of nine manifest and four hidden.

28. Five kings (that is, the five letters MNTzPK, *Me, Nun, Tzaddi, Pe, Kaph;* which are the roots of the judgments), betake themselves into swift flight before four (the four letters of the Tetragrammaton which bear with them the influx of benignity. They cannot remain (since the judgments and rigours cease and flee).

[The letters of the Hebrew alphabet are divided into three classes, the three mothers as they are called, AMSh: the seven duplex letters, BGDKPRTh, so called because they are sometimes tenues and sometimes aspirates, according to whether they are written with or without the Daghesh point; and the twelve simple letters, HVZChTILNSOTzQ. They are also divided into the three categories of *Chesed, Din,* and *Rachmim,* or mercy, judgment, and mildness. Now these five letters MNTzPK denote the severest judgments, and their number = 280 = PR = the name of the angel *Sandalphon,* SNDLPVN, the angel IOR, or of the wood of the world of Asiah, since the greatest part of it are sterile trees.

29. Four kings slay four (that is, the four letters of the Tetragrammaton are bound together with the four letters ADNI, *Adonaï,* which) depend from them like grapes in a cluster (in the concatenation of these two names, thus, IAHDVNHI).

30. Among them are set apart (that is, among these paths of the Divine names a selection of holiness is made from these broken vessels) seven channels (that is, seven broken vessels, which now are like the shells, and contain in themselves a great part of the lights and souls); they testify testimony (that is, the souls thus selected, thence having been born into the universe, testify that they are freed from impurity) and they do not remain in their place (and are no longer detained under the shells).

31. The tree which is mitigated (that is, the path of the kingdom or Schechinah, which is the tree of the

knowledge of good and evil, which in itself existeth from the judgments, but is mitigated by the bridegroom through the influx of mercies) resideth within (within the shells; because the kingdom hath its dominion over all things, and its feet descend into death). In its branches (in the inferior worlds) the birds lodge and build their nests (the souls and the angels have their place). Beneath it those animals which have power seek the shade (that is, the shells, "for in it every beast of the forest doth walk forth," Ps. civ. 20).

[See the Introduction for the Sephiroth arranged in the three pillars, or tree of life.]

32. This is the tree which hath two paths (for thus is this passage restored in the corrected Codex) for the same end (namely, good and evil, because it is the tree of the knowledge of good and evil). And it hath around it seven columns (that is, the seven palaces), and the four splendours (that is, the four animals) whirl around it (in four wheels) on their four sides (after the fourfold description of the chariot of Yechesqiel (Ezekiel).

The seven palaces answer to the 3rd, 4th, 5th, 6th, 7th, 8th, and 9th Sephiroth, operating through the respective orders of the angels into the spheres of the seven planets, Saturn, Jupiter, Mars, Sol, Venus, Mercury, and Luna. The four animals, or *Chaioth Ha-Qadesch*, are the vivified powers of the four letters of the Tetragrammaton operating under the presidency of the first Sephira as the mainspring of *primum mobile* of creation. The four wheels are their correlatives under the second Sephira, on their four sides—namely, the four elements of the air, fire, water, and earth, which are the abodes of the spirits of the elements, the sylphs, salamanders, undines, and gnomes, under the presidency of the tenth Sephira.

33. The serpent (which was made from the rod of Moses—that is, the shell—NVOH, *Nogah*, or splendour) which rusheth forth with three hundred and seventy leaps (the thirty-two names together with the five letters of ALHIM, *Elohim*, which make 37, multiplied by the

decad 370, and the judgments of the bride are denoted, to which that shell directeth his springs, because he is of middle nature betwixt the holy and the profane). "He leapeth upon the mountains, and rusheth swiftly over the hills," like as it is written (Cant. ii. 8. That is, he leapeth high above the rest of the shells). He holdeth his tail in his mouth between his teeth (that is, his extremity, by which he is linked to the shells, turneth towards his other extremity wherewith he looketh towards holiness). He is pierced through on either side (so that he may seek to receive the superior and inferior nature). When the chief ariseth (who is Matatron) he is changed into three spirits (that, is, he assumeth the nature of three inferior shells).

["Nogah" is also the qabalistical title of the sphere of the planet Venus. MTTRVN, *Metatron*, or Methraton, is the particular intelligence of the first Sephira, and is called the "Prince of Faces;" he is said also to have been the "ruler of Moses." Methraton has the same numeration as SHDI, *Shaddai*, the Almighty.]

34. (But concerning Metatron) it is written, Gen. v. 22: "And Enoch walked with the Elohim" (because out of Enoch, Metatron is formed). And it is written, Prov. xxii. 6: "Enoch hath been made into a boy, according to his path." (That is, "hath been changed into") the boy (namely, Metatron, who is spoken of under his name NOR, *Nour*, which meaneth a "boy").

["Enoch hath been made into a boy," &c. This peculiar rendering of the passage, "Train up a child in the way," &c., arises from reading in the Hebrew text CHNVK, *Chanokh*, Enoch, instead of CHNK, *Chanekh*, "train up," or "instruct."]

35. With the Elohim, and not with the Tetragrammaton (because he himself is referred unto the path of the queen, to whom is attributed this name of Rigour). "And he existed not" (longer) under this name (Enoch), because the Elohim took him in order that he might be called by this name. (For this name is communicable unto the angels,

and in the first instance unto this chief among them, namely, Metatron.)

36. There are three houses of judgment given, which are four (that is, the three letters IHV, referred into the understanding, which yield the four letters of the Tetragrammaton, pointed with the vowel points of the name Elohim. For) there are four superior houses of judgment (the four said Tetragrammatic letters) and four inferior (which are the four letters ADNI, *Adonaï*, belonging unto the kingdom). For it is written, Lev. xix. 35: "Ye shall not do iniquity in judgment, in dimension, in weight, and in measure." (Where these four are mystically intimated.)

37. (There is one) rigorous judgment (of severity), another that is not rigorous (that is, of the kingdom). There is one judgment by balance (wherein are the two scales of merit and error), another judgment which is not made by balance; (and this is) the gentle judgment (whereby the Israelites are judged. But also there is given) the judgment which is neither of the one nature nor of the other. (Namely, the beautiful path.)

[Of course the "beautiful path" is Tiphereth, the sixth Sephira.]

38. (Further on it is written), Gen. vi. 1. "And it came to pass when man began to multiply upon the face of the earth." (Where by these words) ADM, *Adam*, began to multiply (there is understood Daath, or the knowledge, the soul of the beautiful path, to which Moses is referred; which sendeth down many lights into the bride, the earth, when the spouse ascendeth thither). This is that which is written (*ibid.* 3): BSHGM, *Beshegam*, "in that also, he is flesh" (which word *Beshegam*, "in that also," by equality of numeration equalleth MSHH, *Moses*) Adam (namely) the supernal (Daath, or knowledge). And it is written: "Upon the face of the earth" (which face of the earth is this, that the highest representation of the queen is the understanding, the mother, unto whose gates Moses ascended).

39. (Concerning this face, it is written) Exod. xxxiv. 29: "And Moses knew not that the skin of his face shone" where by the face the mother is understood; by the skin, the queen.) This is that which is said, Gen. iii. 21: "Tunics of skin" (because by itself the kingdom is wanting in light).

40. To shine (but when it is said "the face of Moses," the mother is understood), according to that passage, 1 Sam. xvi. 13: "And Samuel took the horn of oil" (where by the oil, the wisdom, by the horn, or the splendour of the oil, the understanding is denoted). For there is no anointing except by the horn (that is, every descent of unction is through the mother). Hence it is said, Ps. lxxxix. 18: "And in thy favour our horn shall be exalted." (Also) Ps. cxxxii. 17: "There shall the horn of David flourish" (that is, the queen shall receive the influx from the mother). This is the tenth of the kings (that is, the path of the kingdom), and originateth from jubilee, who is the mother.

41. For it is written, Josh. vi. 5: "And it shall be when the horn of jubilee is sounded." This is the splendour of the jubilee, and the tenth (path) is crowned by the mother.

42. (This is) the horn which receiveth the horn and the spirit, that it may restore the spirit of *Yod He* unto *Yod He*. (That is, when the spirit is to be given unto Microprosopus, his mother contributed as much, which is QRN, *Qaran*, "the horn,' the brilliancy, as the increase which he receiveth from the father.) And this is the horn of jubilee. And IVBL, *Yobel*, "jubilee," is H, *He* (the first *He* of the Tetragrammaton); and *He* is the spirit rushing forth over all (because the mother is the world to come, when in the resurrection all things will receive the spirit); and all things shall return unto their place (like as in the jubilee, so in the world to come).

43. For it is written, AHH, IHVH, ALHIM, *Ahah Tetragrammaton Elohim!* "Ah Tetragrammaton Elohim!"

When the H, *He*, appeareth (first), and H, *He* (in the second place); then is Tetragrammaton called Elohim (like as a judge; because in the world to come there will be work for much strength. This is) the full name. And it is written, Isa. ii. 11: "And Tetragrammaton alone shall be exalted in that day." When the one *He* is turned towards the other *He*, and *Yod* is taken away, then cometh vengeance into the universe; and except for that Adam who is called Tetragrammaton, the universe would not exist; but all things would be destroyed. Hence it is written: "And the Tetragrammaton alone," &c.

44. Hereunto is the hidden and involved Mystery of the King, that is "The Book of Concealed Mystery." Blessed is he who entereth into and departeth therefrom, and knoweth its paths and ways.

HADRA RBA QDISHA

(HA IDRA RABBA QADISHA);

OR.

THE GREATER HOLY ASSEMBLY.

CHAPTER I.

THE INGRESS AND THE PREFACE.

1. TRADITION.—Rabbi Schimeon spake unto his companions, and said: "How long shall we abide in the condition of one column by itself? when it is written, Psa. cxix. 126: 'It is time for Thee, Lord, to lay to Thine hand, for they have destroyed Thy law.'

2. "The days are few, and the creditor is urgent; the herald crieth aloud daily, and the reapers of the land are few; and those who are about the end of the vineyard attend not, and have not known where may be the lawful place. *(That is, do not study holiness, which is called the vineyard.)*

3. "Assemble yourselves, O my companions, in an open space, equipped with armour and spears; be ye ready in your preparations, in council, in wisdom, in understanding, in science, in care, with hands and with feet! Appoint as King over you, Him in whose power is life and death, so that the words of truth may be received: things unto

which the supernal holy ones attend, and rejoice to hear and to know them."

4. Rabbi Schimeon sat down and wept; then he said: "Woe! if I shall reveal it! Woe! if I shall not reveal it!"

5. His companions who were there were silent.

6. Rabbi Abba arose and said unto him: "With the favour of the Lord, also it is written, Psa. xxv. 14: 'The Arcanum of the Tetragrammaton is with them that fear Him.' And well do these companions fear that Holy and Blessed One; and now they have entered into the assembly of the tabernacle of his house, some of them have only entered, and some of them have departed also."

7. Moreover, it is said the companions who were with Rabbi Schimeon were numbered, and they were found to consist of Rabbi Eleazer, his son; and Rabbi Abba, and Rabbi Yehuda, and Rabbi Yosi the son of Jacob, and Rabbi Isaac, and Rabbi Chisqiah the son of Rav, and Rabbi Chiya, and Rabbi Yosi, and Rabbi Yisa.

8. They gave their hands unto Rabbi Schimeon, and raised their fingers on high, and entered into a field under the trees and sat down.

9. Rabbi Schimeon arose and offered up a prayer. He sat in the midst of them, and said: "Let whosoever will place his hand in my bosom." They placed their hands there, and he took them.

10. When he began, he said (*from Deut.* xxvii. 15): "Cursed be the man that maketh any graven or molten image, the work of the hands of the craftsman, and putteth it in a secret place. And all the people shall answer and say Amen!"

11. Rabbi Schimeon began, and said: "Time for Thee, O Tetragrammaton to lay to Thine hand." Why is it time for the Tetragrammaton to lay to His hand? Because they have perverted Thy law. What is this,

'they hath perverted Thy law?' The higher law, which is itself made void, if it be not carried out according to his commands. Wherefore is this? *(Or, as others read: Wherefore is this name Tetragrammaton here employed?)* This hath been said concerning the Ancient of Days.*

12. "For it is written, Deut. xxxiii. 29: 'Blessed art thou, O Israel: who is like unto thee?' Also it is written, Exod. xv. 11: 'Who is like unto thee among the gods, O Tetragrammaton?'" †

13. He called Rabbi Eleazer, his son, and commanded him to sit down before him, and Rabbi Abba on the other side, and said: "We are the type of all things" (that is, "we represent the three columns of the Sephiroth;") "thus far are the columns established."

14. They kept silence, and they heard a voice; and their knees knocked one against the other with fear. What was that voice? The voice of the Higher Assembly, which had assembled above. *(For out of Paradise came the souls of the just thither, that they might hearken, together with the Schechinah of the Presence Divine.)*

15. Rabbi Schimeon rejoiced, and said: "O Tetragrammaton! I have heard Thy speech, and was afraid! (Hab. iii. 1). He hath said: 'It is therefore rightly done, seeing that fear hath followed; but for us the matter rather dependeth upon love.' Like as it is written,

* *I.e.*, one of the names of Macroprosopus, the first emanation, the crown, Kether. (See Introduction.)

† In the above verse it is well to note that by Notariqon, the second division of the Literal Qabalah, the initial letters of the first quotation give the word AIMK, *Aimakh*, "Thy terror," the addition of the numeration of which by Gematra, the first division of the Literal Qabalah, is 71; and that in a similar manner from the second quotation, the word MKBI, *Maccabee*, is obtained, whose numeration is 72. Now, 72 is the number of the Schemhamphorasch, or "divided name," to which Maccabee is always referred. And if to the 71 of the first quotation we add A, expressing thus the hidden unity, we obtain 72 again. Furthermore, it is well to note that each quotation consists of four words, thus answering to the letters of the Tetragrammaton.—TRANS.

Deut. vi. 5: 'And thou shalt delight in Tetragrammaton thy God.' Also it is written, Mal. i. 2: 'I have loved you.'"

16. Rabbi Schimeon said further: "'He who walketh, going up and down *(from one house unto another)* revealeth the secret; but the faithful in spirit concealeth the word' (Prov. xi. 13).

17. "'He who walketh going up and down.' This saying meriteth question, because it is said, 'going up and down.' Wherefore then 'walketh?' The man is already said to be going up and down: what is this word 'walketh?'

18. "For truly it is true concerning that man who is not stable in his spirit nor truthful, that the word which he hath heard is moved hither and thither, like a straw in the water, until it cometh forth from him.

19. "For what reason? Because his spirit is not a firm spirit.

20. "But concerning him who is firm in spirit it is written: 'But the faithful in spirit concealeth the word.' *(But this phrase)* 'faithful in spirit' denoteth firmness of spirit; like as it is said, Isa. xxii. 23: 'And I will fasten him as a nail in a sure place.' Matter dependeth upon Spirit.

21. "And it is written, Eccles. v. 6: 'Suffer not thy mouth to cause thy flesh to sin.'

22. "For neither doth the world remain firm, except through secresy. And if in worldly affairs there be so great need of secresy, how much more in the things of the most secret of secrets, and in the meditation of the Ancient of Days,* which matters are not even revealed unto the highest of the angels."

23. Rabbi Schimeon said, moreover: "I will not say it unto the heavens, that they may hear; I will not declare it unto the earth, that it may hear; for certainly we are (the symbols of) the pillars of the Universe."

* Macroprosopus, the first Sephira.

24. It is said in the Arcanum of Arcana, that when Rabbi Schimeon opened his mouth, the whole place was shaken, and his companions also were shaken.

CHAPTER II.

OF THE CONDITION OF THE WORLD OF VACANCY.

25. HE manifested the Arcanum, and commencing, said, Gen. xxxvi. 29: "And those are the kings which reigned in the land of Edom before that a king could rule over the children of Israel."

26. Blessed are ye, O just men! because unto you is manifested the Arcanum of the Arcana of the law, which hath not been manifested unto the holy superior ones.

27. Who can follow out this matter? and who is worthy to do so? For it is the testimony of the truth of truths. Therefore let all our prayers be undertaken with devotion, lest it be imputed *(to me)* as a sin, that I am making this matter manifest.

28. And perchance my companions may speak unto me, because some objection may arise against these words. For truly this work is not such a one as may be easily written down, so that by it may appear how many kings there were before the children of Israel came, and before there was a king over the children of Israel: how therefore doth this matter agree? And for this reason my companions have moved the question.

29. Therefore the Arcanum of Arcana is what men can neither know nor comprehend, nor can they apply their rules of science to it.

30. It is said that before the Ancient of the Ancient Ones, the Concealed One of the Concealed Ones, instituted the formations of the King *(under certain members and paths*

of Microprosopus) and the diadems of the diadems *(that is, the varied coverings whereby the superfluity of the Lights is circumscribed)*; beginning and end existed not *(that is, there was neither communication nor reception)*.

31. Therefore He carved out (*that is, hollowed out a space by which he might flow in*) and instituted proportions in Himself (*in as many ways as the Lights of His Understanding could be received, whence arose the paths of the worlds*), and spread out before Him a certain veil (*that is, produced a certain nature, by which His infinite light could be modified, which was the first Adam*); and therein carved out and distributed the kings and their forms by a certain proportion (*that is, all creatures under a condition of proper activity; by which He Himself might be known and loved*); but they did not subsist. (*Here is intimated the fall of the creatures, partly into a condition of quiet, such as matter; partly into a state of inordinate motion, such as that of the evil spirits*).

32. That is the same thing which is said, Gen. xxxvi. 29: "And these are the kings which reigned in the land of Edom, before that there reigned a king over the children of Israel." The first king in respect of the children of Israel (*by the children of Israel are understood the paths of the restored world*) is the first.

33. And all those things which were carved out, but subsisted not, are called by their names (*that is, were divided into certain classes*), neither yet did they subsist, until He forsook them (*so that they could receive the lights from the receptacles above themselves*), and hid Himself before them (in diminished light).

CHAPTER III.

CONCERNING THE ANCIENT ONE, OR MACROPROSOPUS, AND CONCERNING HIS PARTS, AND ESPECIALLY CONCERNING HIS SKULL.

34. AND after a certain time was that veil entirely disunited in formless separation, and recomposed according to its conformation.

35. And this is the tradition: The Absolute desired within Himself to create the essence of light (*the law—that is, the letters of the alphabet, from whose transpositions the law was formed*), hidden for two thousand years, and produced Her. And She answered thus unto Him: "He who wisheth to dispose and to constitute other things, let Him first be disposed according unto a proper conformation."

36. This is the tradition described in the "Concealed Book of the King," * that the Ancient of the Ancient Ones, the Concealed of the Concealed Ones, hath been constituted and prepared as in various members (*for future knowledge*).

37. Like as if it were said, "He is found (that is, He may in some way to a certain extent be known), and He is not found;" for He cannot be clearly comprehended; but He hath as it were been formed; neither yet is He to be known of any, since He is the Ancient of the Ancient Ones.

38. But in his conformation is He known; as also He is the Eternal of the Eternal Ones, the Ancient of the Ancient Ones, the Concealed of the Concealed Ones; and in His symbols is He knowable and unknowable.

39. White are His garments, and His appearance is the likeness of a Face vast and terrible.

* The "Siphra Dtzenioutha," cap. i. § 16.

40. Upon the throne of flaming light is He seated, so that He may direct its (flashes).

41. Into forty thousand superior worlds the brightness of the skull of His head is extended, and from the light of this brightness the just shall receive four hundred worlds in the world to come.

42. This is that which is written, Gen. xxiii. 16: "Four hundred skekels of silver, current money with the merchant."

43. Within His skull exist daily thirteen thousand myriads of worlds, which draw their existence from Him, and by Him are upheld.

CHAPTER IV.

CONCERNING THE DEW, OR MOISTURE OF THE BRAIN, OF THE ANCIENT ONE, OR MACROPROSOPUS.

44. AND from that skull distilleth a dew upon Him which is external, and filleth His head daily.

45. And from that dew which floweth down from His head, that (*namely*) which is external, the dead are raised up in the world to come.

46. Concerning which it is written, Cant. v. 2: "My head is filled with dew." It is not written: "It is full with dew;" but NMLA, *Nimla*, "it is filled."

47. And it is written, Isa. xxvi. 19: "The dew of the lights is Thy dew." Of the lights—that is, from the brightness of the Ancient One.

48. And by that dew are nourished the holy supernal ones.

49. And this is that manna which is prepared for the just in the world to come.

50. And that dew distilleth upon the ground of the holy

apple trees. This is that which is written, Exod. xvi. 14: "And when the dew was gone up, behold upon the face of the desert a small round thing."

51. And the appearance of this dew is white, like unto the colour of the crystal stone, whose appearance hath all colours in itself. This is that which is written, Num. xi. 7: "And its varieties as the varieties of crystal."

CHAPTER V.

FURTHER CONCERNING THE SKULL OF MACROPROSOPUS.

52. The whiteness of this skull shineth in thirteen carved out sides: in four sides from one portion; in four sides from the part of His countenance; and in four sides from another part of the periphery; and in one above the skull, as if this last might be called the supernal side.*

53. And thence is the Vastness of His Countenance extended into three hundred and seventy myriads of worlds; and hence ARK APIM,† *Arikh Aphim*, Vastness of Countenance is His name.

54. And He Himself, the Most Ancient of the Most Ancient Ones, is called ARIK DANPIN, *Arikh Da-Anpin*, the Vast Countenance, or Macroprosopus; and He Who is more external is called ZOIR ANPIN, *Zauir Anpin*, or

* The hidden sense of this somewhat obscure passage is, that the brightness arises from the skull, *which it conceals*, which latter is therefore the emblem of the Concealed One. The thirteen parts are three tetragrammatic forms, which give twelve letters, and symbolize thus the Trinity of the Tetragram; and the one supernal part is the unity. The meaning therefore is, the Trinity in Unity, proceeding from the Concealed Unity, which also proceedeth from the Negatively Existent. Thirteen, moreover, occultly points out unity, for ACHD, *Achad*, Unity, adds up for thirteen.

† Or, AVRKA DANPIN, *Aurikha Da-Anpin*, the Vast Countenance.

Him Who hath the Lesser Countenance (*Microprosopus*), in opposition to the Ancient Eternal Holy One, the Holy of the Holy Ones.

55. And when Microprosopus looketh back upon Him, all the inferiors are restored in order, and His Countenance is extended, and is made more vast at that time, but not for all time (*then only is it*), vast like unto the (*countenance*) of the More Ancient one.

56. And from that skull issueth a certain white shining emanation, towards the skull of Microprosopus, for the purpose of fashioning His head; and thence towards the other inferior skulls, which are innumerable.

57. And all the skulls reflect this shining whiteness towards the Ancient of Days,* when they are numbered out of their mingled confusion. And by reason of this there existeth herein an opening towards the skull below, when they proceed to numeration.

CHAPTER VI.

CONCERNING THE MEMBRANE OF THE BRAIN OF MACROPROSOPUS.

58. In the hollow of the skull is the aërial membrane of the supreme hidden Wisdom, which is nowhere disclosed; and it is not found, and it is not opened.

59. And that membrane enshroudeth the brain of the hidden Wisdom, and therefore is that Wisdom covered, because it is not opened through that membrane.

60. And that brain, which is itself the hidden Wisdom, is silent and remaineth tranquil in its place, like good wine upon its lees.

61. And this is that which they say:—Hidden is the

* Macroprosopus.

science of the Ancient One, and His brain is calm and concealed.

62. And that membrane hath an outlet towards Microprosopus, and on that account is His brain extended, and goeth forth by thirty and two paths.*

63. This is that same thing which is written: "And a river went forth out of Eden" (Gen ii. 7). But for what reason? Because the membrane is (*then*) opened, neither doth it (*completely*) enshroud the brain.

64. Nevertheless the membrane is opened from below. And this is that which we have said: Among the signatures of the letters (*is*) THV, *Tau*, TH; nevertheless He impresseth it as the sign of the Ancient of Days, from Whom dependeth the perfection of knowledge, because He is perfect on every side, and hidden, and tranquil, and silent, like as good wine upon its lees.

CHAPTER VII.

CONCERNING THE HAIR OF MACROPROSOPUS.

65. THIS is the tradition. From the skull of His head hang down a thousand thousand myriads; seven thousand and five hundred curling hairs, white and pure, like as wool when it is pure; which have not been mingled confusedly together less inordinate disorder should be shown in His conformation; but all are in order, so that no one lock may go beyond another lock, nor one hair before another.

66. And in single curls are four hundred and ten locks

*Which are the thirty-two paths of the *Sepher Yetzirah*; or Book of Formation; symbolised by the ten numbers; and twenty-two letters of the Hebrew alphabet.

of hair, according unto the number of the word, QDVSH, *Qadosch*, Holy.*

67. But these hairs, all and singular, radiate into four hundred and ten worlds.

68. But these worlds alone are hidden and concealed, and no man knoweth them, save himself.

69. And he radiateth in seven hundred and twenty directions (*others say four hundred and twenty*).

70. And in all the hairs is a fountain, which issueth from the hidden brain behind the wall of the skull.

71. And it shineth and goeth forth through that hair unto the hair of Microprosopus, and from it is His brain formed; and thence that brain goeth forth into thirty and two paths.

72. And each curl radiateth and hangeth down arranged in beautiful form, and adorned with ornament, and they enshroud the skull.

73. But the curls of the hair are disposed on each side of the skull.

74. Also we have said: Each hair is said to be the breaking of the hidden fountains, issuing from the concealed brain.

75. Also this is the tradition: From the hair of a man it is known what he is, whether rigorous or merciful, when he passeth over forty years; thus also when he is perfect in hair, in beard, and in the eyebrows of his eyes.

76. The curls of His hair hang down in order, and pure like unto (*pure*) wool, even unto his shoulders. Say we unto His shoulders? Nevertheless, even unto the rise of His shoulders, so that His neck may not be seen, because of that which is written, Jer. ii. 27: "Because they have turned away from Me the neck and not the face."

77. And the hair is less close to the ears, lest it should cover them; because it is written, Ps. cxxx. 2: "As Thine ears are open."

*For by Gematria Q + D + V + SH = 100 + 4 + 6 + 300 = 410.

78. From hence His hair stretcheth out behind His ears. The whole is in equilibrium; one hair doth not go beyond another hair, (*they are*) in perfect disposition, and beautiful arrangement, and orderly condition.

79. It is the delight and joy of the just, who are in Microprosopus, to desire to behold and to conform unto that conformation which is in the Ancient One, the Most Concealed of all.

80. Thirteen curls of hair exist on the one side and on the other of the skull; (*they are*) about His face, and through them commenceth the division of the hair.

81. There is no left in that Ancient Concealed One, but all is right.*

82. He appeareth, and He appeareth not; He is concealed, and He is not concealed; and that is in His conformation much more so than in Himself.

83. And concerning this the children of Israel wished to inquire in their heart, like as it is written, Exod. xvii. 7: "Is the Tetragrammaton in the midst of us, or the Negatively Existent One?" (*Where they distinguished*) between Microprosopus, who is called Tetragrammaton, and between Macroprosopus, who is called AIN, *Ain*, the Negatively Existent?

84. But why, then, were they punished? Because they did it not in love, but in temptation; like as it is written (*ibid*): "Because they tempted the Tetragrammaton, saying, Is it the Tetragrammaton in the midst of us, or is it the Negatively Existent One?"

85. In the parting of the hair proceedeth a certain path, which shineth into two hundred and seventy worlds, and from that (*again*) shineth a path wherein the just of the world to come shall shine.

86. That is what is written, Prov. iv. 18: "And the

*Meaning there is no evil in Him, but all is good. So that, in the symbolic language of the Zohar, Macroprosopus is represented by a profile countenance, wherein one side is not seen, rather than by a full face, as in Microprosopus.

path of the just shall shine as the light, going forth, and shining more and more unto the perfect day."

87. And out of that is the path divided into six hundred and thirteen paths, which are distributed in Microprosopus.

88. As it is written concerning Him, Ps. xxv. 6: "All the paths of the Tetragrammaton are mercy and truth," &c.

CHAPTER VIII.

CONCERNING THE FOREHEAD OF MACROPROSOPUS.

87. The forehead of His skull is the acceptation of acceptations, whereunto is opposed the acceptation of Microprosopus, like as it is written, Exod. xxviii. 38: "And it shall be upon His forehead alway for acceptation," &c.

90. And that forehead is called RTzVN, *Ratzon*, Will-power, because it is the ruler of the whole head and of the skull, which is covered by four hundred and twenty worlds.

91. And when it is uncovered, the prayers of the Israelites ascend.

92. "When is it uncovered?" Rabbi Schimeon was silent. He asked again a second time, "When?" Rabbi Schimeon said unto Rabbi Eleazar, his son, "When is it uncovered:"

93. He answered unto him: "In the time of the offering of the evening prayer on the Sabbath."

94. He said unto him: "For what reason?" He answered unto him: "Because at that time the lower judgment threateneth through Microprosopus; but that forehead is uncovered which is called 'Acceptation,' and then wrath is assuaged, and the prayer ascendeth.

95. "This is that which is written, Ps. lxix. 14: 'And I have prayed unto Thee, O Tetragrammaton! in an acceptable time.'

96. "And the time of acceptance by the Ancient of Days* is here to be understood, and of the unveiling of the forehead; and because it is thus disposed at the offering of the evening prayer on the Sabbath."

97. Rabbi Schimeon spake unto Rabbi Eleazar, his son, and said: Blessed be thou, O my son! by the Ancient of Days; for thou hast found in that time in which thou hast need the acceptation of His forehead.

98. Come and behold! in these inferiors, when the forehead is uncovered, there is found fixed shamelessness.

99. This is the same which is written, Jer. iii. 3: "Yet thou hadst the forehead of a shameless woman, thou refusedst to be ashamed."

100. But when this forehead † is uncovered, inclination and acceptation are found in perfect form, and all wrath is quieted and subdued before Him.

101. From that forehead shine forth four hundred habitations of judgments, when it is uncovered during that period of acceptation, and all things are at peace before it.

102. This is the same which is written, Dan. vii. 10: "The judgment was set"—that is, subsideth in its place, and the judgment is not exercised.

103. And this is the tradition: There is no hair found on that part, because it is opened and not covered.

104. It is covered, I say, and the executors of judgment behold this, and are pacified, and (*judgment*) is not exercised.

105. This is the tradition: This forehead hath been extended into two hundred and seventy thousand lights of the luminaries of the superior Eden.

*Macroprosopus. †That of Macroprosopus.

106. This is the tradition: There existeth an Eden which shineth in Eden. The superior Eden, which is not uncovered, and is hidden in concealment, and is not distributed into the paths, like as it hath been said.

107. The inferior Eden is distributed into its paths; (*namely*) into thirty-two directions of its paths.

108. And although this Eden is distributed into its path, yet is it not known unto any, save unto Microprosopus.

109. But no man hath known the superior Eden, nor its paths, except Macroprosopus Himself.

110. Like as it is written, Job xxviii. 23: "God understandeth the way thereof, and He knoweth the place thereof."

111. "The Elohim understand the way thereof:" this is the inferior Eden, known unto Microprosopus. "And He hath known the place thereof:" this is the superior Eden, which the Ancient of Days hath known, the most abstruse of all.

CHAPTER IX.

CONCERNING THE EYES OF MACROPROSOPUS.

112. The eyes of the White Head* are diverse from all other eyes. Above the eye is no eyelid, neither is there an eyebrow over it.

113. Wherefore? Because it is written, Ps. cxxi. 4: "Behold, He that keepeth Israël shall neither slumber nor sleep;" that is, the superior Israel.

114. Also it is written, Jer. xxxii. v. 19: "Whose eyes are open."

*This, like Macroprosopus, is a title of Kether, the first Sephira. (See introduction.)

115. And this is the tradition. Seeing that all is operated through mercies, He hath not covering unto His eye, nor eyebrow above His eye; how little, then, doth the White Head require such.

116. Rabbi Schimeon spake unto Rabbi Abba, and said: "To what is this like?" He answered unto him: "To the whales and fishes of the sea, which have no coverings for their eyes, nor eyebrows above their eyes; who sleep not, and require not a protection for the eye.

117. "How much less doth the Ancient of the Ancient Ones require a protection, seeing that He far above His creatures watcheth over all things, and all things are nourished by Him, and He Himself sleepeth not.

118. "This is that which is written, Ps. cxxi. 4: 'Behold! He that keepeth Israel shall neither slumber nor sleep.' That is, the superior Israel.

119. "It is written, Ps. xxxiii. 18: 'Behold the eye of the Lord is upon them that fear Him;' and it is written, Zech. iv. 10: 'They are the eyes of the Lord, running to and fro throughout the whole earth.

120. "There is no contrariety (*between these sayings*); one is concerning Microprosopus, and the other concerning Macroprosopus.

121. "And further, although there be two eyes, yet they are converted into one eye.

122. "This is pure in its whiteness, and so white that it includeth all whiteness.

123. "The first whiteness shineth, and ascendeth and descendeth for the purpose of combining with that which is connected (*with it*) in connection.

124. "This is the tradition: That whiteness darteth forth its rays, and igniteth three lights, which are called HVD, *Hod*, Glory, VHDR, *Vehedar*, and Majesty, VCHDVH, *Vachedoah*, and Joy; and they radiate in gladness and in perfection.

125. "The second whiteness shineth and ascendeth and

descendeth, and darteth forth its rays, and igniteth three other lights, which are called NTzCh, *Netzach*, Victory, ChSD, *Chesed*, and Benignity, ThPARTh, *Tiphereth*, and Beauty; and they radiate in perfection and in gladness.

126. "The third whiteness radiateth and shineth, and descendeth and ascendeth, and goeth forth from the part enclosing the brain, and darteth forth its rays toward the seventh middle light.

127. "And it formeth a path to the inferior brain, and formeth a path to the inferior, and all the inferior lights are thereby ignited."

128. Rabbi Schimeon said: Thou hast well spoken, and the Ancient of Days will open this eye upon thee in the time of thy necessity.

129. Another tradition runneth thus: Whiteness in whiteness, and whiteness which includeth all other whiteness.

130. The first whiteness shineth and ascendeth and descendeth in three lights on the left-hand side, and they radiate and are bathed in that whiteness, like as when a man batheth his body in good unguents and odours, in better than he at first possessed.

131. The second whiteness descendeth and ascendeth and shineth in three lights on the right-hand side, and they radiate and are bathed in that whiteness, like as when a man batheth in good ungeants and odours, in better than he at first possessed.

132. The third whiteness shineth and ascendeth and descendeth, and goeth forth the light of the inner whiteness of the brain, and darteth forth its rays when necessary unto the black hair, and unto the head, and unto the brain of the head.

133. And it irradiateth the three crowns which remain, when it is needful, so that it may be uncovered,

* Netzach, Chesed, and Tiphereth, are respectively the seventh, fourth, and sixth Sephiroth.

if that be pleasing unto the Most Ancient One hidden from all.

134. And this is the tradition: This eye is never closed; and there are two, and they are converted into one.

135. All is right; there is no left there. He sleepeth not and slumbereth not, and He requireth not protection. He is not such an one as hath need to defend Himself, for He defendeth all things, and He Himself waited upon all things, and in the sight of His eye are all things established.

136. This is the tradition: Were that eye closed even for one moment, no thing could subsist.

137. Therefore it is called the open eye, the holy eye, the excellent eye, the eye of Providence, the eye which sleepeth not neither slumbereth, the eye which is the guardian of all things, the eye which is the subsistence of all things.

138. And concerning it is it written, Prov. xxii. 9, "The bountiful eye;" thou shalt not read "the blessed eye," but "it blesseth," for it is called "the bountiful eye," and by it are all things blessed.

139. And this is the tradition: There is no light in the inferior eye, so that it can be bathed in redness and blackness; except when it is beheld by that white brilliance of the superior eye which is called "the bountiful eye."

140. And to no man is it known when this superior holy eye may shine and may bathe the inferior; and when the just and the supernal blessed ones are about to be beheld in that Wisdom.

141. This is that which is written, Isa. lii. 8: "For they shall see eye to eye;" When? "When the Lord shall bring again Zion." Also, it is written, Num. xiv. 14: "That Thou Tetragrammaton, art seen eye to eye."

142. And unless the bountiful superior eye were to look down upon and bathe the inferior eye, the universe could not exist even a single moment.

143. This is the tradition in the "Book of Concealed Mystery;" Providence ariseth from the inferior eye when the highest splendour shineth down upon it, and that highest splendour goeth forth into the inferior; for from it are all things illuminated.

144. This is that which is written, Num. xiv. 14: "That Thou, O Tetragrammaton! art seen eye to eye." Also it is written, Ps. xxxiii. 18: "Behold the eye of the Lord is upon them that fear Him." And it is written, Zech. iv. 10: "The eyes of the Lord running to and fro throughout the whole earth."

145. "The eye of the Lord is upon them that fear Him," if they be upright. This is the superior eye. On the contrary, when it is said, "The eyes of the Lord run to and fro," this is the eye which is below.

146. This is the tradition: On what account was Joseph worthy, so that the evil eye had no dominion over him? Because that he was worthy of being beheld by the superior benign eye.

147. This is what is written, Gen. xlix. 22: "Joseph is the son of a fruitful bough; the son of a fruitful bough above Ayin." Why "the son of a fruitful bough above Ayin?"* As though to imply, "because of that eye which beheld him."

148. Also it is written, Prov. xxii. 9: "The bountiful eye shall be blessed." Why? Because it giveth its bread unto the poor.

149. Why is it said in the singular number? Come and see. In the eyes which are inferior are a right eye and a left eye, and they are of two diverse colours.

150. But in this instance there is no left eye, and they both ascend in one path, and all are right. And on that account is one eye mentioned, and not two.

151. And this is the tradition: This eye, which is the eye of observation, is ever open, ever smiling, ever glad.

152. Such are not the inferiors, who in themselves have

* The word Ayin means eye.—TRANS.

redness, and blackness, and whiteness—three colours; and are not always open, for there are eyelids as a protection over these eyes.

153. And concerning this matter it is written, Ps. xliv. 23: "Awake, O Lord: why sleepest Thou?" And, 2 Kings xix. 16: "Open Thine eyes, O Lord."

154. When they are opened, for some are they opened for good, and on some are they opened for evil.

155. Woe unto him upon whom it is opened, so that the eye is mingled with redness, and unto whom the redness appeareth, spreading across that eye. Who can escape from it?

156. But the Ancient of Days is blessed, presiding over that eye the white brilliance of whiteness, seeing that also it is of such whiteness that it endureth all whiteness.

157. Blessed also is his portion whom that brilliance of all whiteness irradiateth.

158. And concerning this certainly it is written, Prov. xxii. 9: "The good eye is to be blessed." And it is written, Isa. ii. 5: "Be ye present, O house of Jacob, and let us walk in the light of Tetragrammaton!"

159. This is the tradition: Save in all these instances, the name of the Ancient One is concealed from all, and is not mentioned in the law, save in one place, where Microprosopus sware unto Abraham.

160. Like as it is written, Gen. xxii. 16: "By Myself have I sworn, saith Tetragrammaton." (*Understand*) that this is said concerning Microprosopus.

161. Also it is written, Gen. xlviii. 20: "In thee shall Israel bless." That is, the superior Israel.

162. Also it is written, Isa. xlix. 3: "Israel, in whom I will be glorified." In these passages the Ancient of Days is called Israel.

163. But we have also stated that the Ancient of Days is called by His name, yet both this (*statement*) and the other are correct.

164. This is the tradition: It is written, Dan. vii. 9: "I beheld until the thrones were cast down, and the Ancient of Days did sit."

165. "The thrones were cast down." What is this? He spake unto Rabbi Yehuda, and said: "Stand in thy place and explain these thrones."

166. Rabbi Yehuda answered: "It is written (*ibid*) 'His throne is of fiery flame;' and upon that throne sat the Ancient of Days."

167. "For what reason? Because thus is the tradition: If the Ancient of Days were not seated upon that throne, the universe could no longer exist before that throne.

168. "When the Ancient of Days sitteth upon that throne, it is subject unto Him. For He who sitteth upon it ruleth over it.

169. "But at that time when He departeth from that throne, and sitteth upon another throne, the first throne is overturned, lest any should rule over it save the Ancient One, who alone can sit upon it."

170. Rabbi Schimeon spake unto Rabbi Yehuda, and said: "May thy way be ordained for thee, and may it be pointed out (unto thee) by the Ancient of Days!"

CHAPTER X.

CONCERNING THE NOSE OF MACROPROSOPUS.

171. AND come, behold, lo! it is written, Isaiah xli. 4: "I, Tetragrammaton, (*am*) first and with the last. I am HE HIMSELF" (*Hoa*).

172. All things are HVA, *Hoa*, He Himself, and He Himself is hidden on every side. So also is His nose.

173. From the nose is the face known.

174. And come—see! What is the (*difference*) between the Ancient One and Microprosopus? Over these nostrils He ruleth; one of which is life, and the other is the life of life.

175. This nose is as a mighty gallery, whence His spirit rusheth forth upon Microprosopus, and they call it the Giver.

176. And it is thus: The Spirit descendeth; and again the Spirit from hence proceedeth through those nostrils.

177. One is the Spirit; She goeth forth unto Microprosopus, so that he may be aroused in the Garden of Eden.

178. And one is She the Spirit of Life, through Whom in process of time the sons of David hope to know Wisdom.

179. And from that gallery ariseth the Spirit, and proceedeth from the concealed brain, and at length resteth upon King Messiach.

180. Like as it is written, Isaiah xi. 2: "And the Spirit of Tetragrammaton shall rest upon him, the Spirit of Wisdom and Understanding, the Spirit of Counsel and Might, the Spirit of Knowledge, and of the Fear of Tetragrammaton."

181. Apparently four spirits (*are described*) here. But we have already said that the Spirit is one; why, then, are three (*others added unto it?*). Arise, Rabbi Yosi, in thy place.

182. Rabbi Yosi arose and said: "In the days of King Messiach, one shall not say unto the other, 'Teach me this Wisdom.'

183. "Because it is thus written, Jer. xxxi. 34: 'A man shall no more teach his neighbour, &c., because all shall know Me, from the least of them even unto the greatest of them.'

184. "And in that time shall the Ancient of Days arouse His Spirit which proceedeth from His brain, the most concealed of all.

185. "And when that cometh forth all the inferior spirits are aroused with Her.

186. "And who are they? They are the holy crowns of Microprosopus.

187. "And there are six other spirits which are given. They are those of whom it is written: 'The Spirit of Wisdom and Intelligence, the Spirit of Counsel and Might, the Spirit of Knowledge and of the Fear of the Lord.'

188. "For thus is the tradition: It is written, 1 Kings ii. 12: 'And Solomon sat upon the throne of David.' Also it is written, 1 Kings x. 19: 'The throne had six steps.'

189. "And King Messiach will be seated on those seven (steps). These are those six, and the Spirit of the Ancient of Days, Who is above them, is the seventh.

190. "Like as it is said, 'There are three spirits which comprehend three others.'"

191. Rabbi Schimeon said unto him: "Thy spirit shall rest in the world to come."

192. Come—behold! It is written, Ezek. xxxvii. 9: "Thus saith the Lord, 'Come from the four winds, O Spirit!' But what have the four winds of the world to do with this?

193. Nevertheless, the four winds are aroused; those three, namely, and the Spirit of the Concealed Ancient One; whence there are four.

194. And thus is the matter; because when that one is produced, three others are produced with it, who in themselves comprehend three others.

195. But it is the will of that Holy and Blessed One to produce the one Spirit, Who in Herself includeth all others.

196. Because it is written, Ezek. xxxvii. 9: "From the four spirits, come, O spirit!" It is not written thus: "Ye four spirits, come!" but "From the four spirits, come!"

197. And in the days of King Messiach there shall be no need that one should teach another; for that one Spirit Who in Herself includeth all spirits, knoweth all Wisdom and Understanding, Counsel and Might, (*and is*) the Spirit of Science and of the Fear of the Lord; because She is the Spirit comprehending all spirits.

198. Therefore is it written, "From the four spirits;" which are those four comprehended in the seven steps of which we have just spoken, § 189.

199. And this is the tradition: All things are comprehended in this Spirit of the Ancient of the Ancient Ones,* Who proceedeth from the concealed brain, into the gallery of the nostrils.

200. And come—see! Wherein is the difference between the nose (*of Macroprosopus*), and the nose (*of Microprosopus*).

201. The nose of the Ancient of Days is life in every part. Concerning the nose of Microprosopus it is written, Ps. xviii. 8: "There went up smoke out of His nostrils, and fire out of His mouth devoured," &c.

202. There goeth up a smoke through His nostrils, and out of that smoke is a fire kindled.

203. When that smoke goeth up, what afterwards followeth? Coals are kindled by it. What is the meaning of this "by it?" By that smoke, out of that nose, out of that fire.

204. This is the tradition: When Rav Hammenuna the elder wished to offer up his prayer, he said, "I pray unto the Lord of the nostrils, unto the Lord of the nostrils do I pray."

205. And this is that which is written, Isa. xlviii. 9: "In my praise (that is, My nose) will I refrain My nostrils for thee." In which place the sentence is concerning the Ancient of Days.

206. This is the tradition. The size of this nose is so

* *I.e.*, The Spirit.

vast that three hundred and seventy-five worlds are supported by it, which all adhere unto Microprosopus.

207. This is the praise of the conformation of the nose.

208. And this, and all forms of the Ancient of Days, are seen, and are not seen; they are seen by the lords of lords—viz., by pious men—and they are not seen by any others.

CHAPTER XI.

CONCERNING THE BEARD OF MACROPROSOPUS IN GENERAL.

209. RABBI SCHIMEON began, and said: Woe unto him who extendeth his hand unto that most glorious supernal beard of the Holy Ancient One, the concealed of all.

210. This is the praise of that beard; the beard which is concealed and most precious in all its dispositions; the beard which neither the superiors nor the inferiors have known; * the beard which is the praise of all praise; the beard to which neither man, nor prophet, nor saint hath approached so as to behold it.

211. The beard, whose hairs hang down even unto the breast, white as snow; the adornment of adornments, the concealment of concealments, the truth of all truths.

212. It is said in the "Book of Concealed Mystery": That beard, the truth of all (*truths*), proceedeth from the place of the ears, and descendeth around the mouth of the Holy One; and descendeth and ascendeth, covering (*the cheeks which it calleth*) the places of copious fragrance; (*it is*) white with ornament: and it descend-

* Because it is the beard of Macroprosopus, the Concealed Ancient One.

eth in the equilibrium (*of balanced power*), and furnisheth a covering even unto the midst of the breast.

213. That is the beard of adornment, true and perfect, from the which flow down thirteen fountains, scattering the most precious balm of splendour.

214. This is disposed in thirteen forms.

215. In the first disposition are classed the hairs from above, and it commenceth from that portion of the hair of His head which is above His ears; and descendeth in one tress before the apertures of the ears in the most perfect equilibrium, even unto the corner of the mouth.

216. In the second disposition are classed the hairs from the corner of the mouth, and they ascend even unto the other corner of the mouth in perfectly equated order.

217. The third disposition is from midway between the nostrils; beneath those two apertures there goeth forth a certain path, and the hair is wanting in that path; but on either side of and bordering that path it is fuller and in perfect order.

218. The hairs which are classed under the fourth disposition descend below the mouth from the one corner even unto the other corner, in perfect order.

219. The fifth disposition. Beneath the mouth proceedeth another path, from the region of the superior path, and those two paths are impressed on His mouth on this side and on that.

220. The hairs which are classed in the sixth disposition ascend and come from beneath upwards unto the corner of the mouth, and cover the places of copious fragrance, even unto the upper corner of the mouth, and the hair descendeth at the corner of the opening, and across below the mouth.

221. In the seventh disposition the hair terminateth, and there are seen two apples in the places of copious fragrance, beautiful and joyful in aspect, because (*in that aspect*) is the universe maintained. And this is that which is said, Prov.

xvi. 16: "In the light of the king's countenance is life."

222. In the eighth disposition a certain tress of hair proceedeth round about the beard, and (*the hairs*) hang down equilibrated even unto the chest.

223. In the ninth disposition the hairs of the beard are interwoven and mingled with those hairs which hang in equilibrium; which hang even thus, so that none is pre-eminent over another.

224. In the tenth disposition the hairs descend beneath the beard, and cover the throat beneath the beard.

225. The eleventh disposition is, that no hairs are pre-eminent over other hairs, and they are restored into perfect proportion.

226. The twelfth disposition is that the hairs do not hang over the mouth, and that the mouth is uncovered in every part, and that the hair surrounding it is beautiful.

227. The thirteenth disposition is that the hairs hang down on this side and on that beneath the beard, furnishing a covering in beautiful adornment, even unto the chest.

228. Nothing is seen of the whole countenance and of the places of fragrance, except those beautiful white apples which produce the life of the universe; and they radiate gladness upon Microprosopus.

229. Through those thirteen dispositions do they flow down, and the thirteen fountains of precious oil issue forth, and they flow down through all those inferiors, and in that oil do they shine, and with that oil are they anointed.

230. The beard of ornament of the Ancient of the Ancient Ones, the most concealed of all things, is configurated in thirteen dispositions.

231. From the two beautiful apples* of His countenance is the face of Macroprosopus illuminated; and whatsoever

* The cheeks.

is white and rosy is found below; * it shineth and radiateth from that light.

232. Those thirteen dispositions are found in the beard. And in proportion to the purity of his beard,† according to its dispositions, is a man said to be true; for also whosoever (*in sleep*) beholdeth his beard, that man is very desirous of truth.

233. We have taught in the "Book of Concealed Mystery," that certain (*dispositions*) are found in the universe, according to those thirteen (*dispositions*) which depend from that venerable beard, and they are opened out into the thirteen gates of mercies.

234. And he who extendeth his hand in swearing, also doth the same if he swear by the thirteen‡ dispositions of the beard: these are in Arikh Anpin, or Macroprosopus.

235. In Zauir Anpin, or Microprosopus, how many are there? He said unto Rabbi Isaac: "Arise in thy place, and describe the beard of the Holy King according unto the arrangement of its parts. How are these arranged?

236. Rabbi Isaac arose; he commenced and said, Micah vii. 18: "What god is like unto Thee," &c.; "Thou shalt give truth unto Jacob," &c.

237. "We have learned by tradition that herein are thirteen sections seen, and they all proceed from the thirteen fountains of excellent oil, of the parts of the holy beard of the Ancient of the Ancient Ones.

238. "Tradition: A most secret thing is this disposition of the beard. Secret is it and hidden; hidden, yet not

* That is, the lower Sephiroth reflect and partake of the properties of the superior emanations.

† By the beard is of course symbolically meant the atmosphere of good or bad deeds with which a man surrounds himself during his life. Concerning dreaming of the beard, see the "Book of Concealed Mystery," c. iii. §§17, 18.

‡ Thirteen is by Gematria the number of ACHD, *Achad*, Unity. For A+CH+D=1+8+4=13.

hidden; concealed, yet not concealed in its dispositions; known, yet unknown.

239. "The first disposition. We have learned that the single locks and the single hairs do not mutually adhere unto each other; and that the hairs of the beard take their rise from the disposition of the hair (of the head).

240. "This matter is worthy of examination. If all the hairs of the head and the hairs of the venerable supernal beard are balanced in one equilibrium, wherefore are some long, and others not so long?

241. "Wherefore are not the hairs of the beard constant in the same proportion of length? These also are firm; while those which are on the head are not firm, but soft.

242. "Therefore is it said that (in Macroprosopus) all the hairs descend equally from the head and beard; for the hair of the head is prolonged even unto the shoulders, so that it may reach unto the head of Microprosopus, from that flux of the one brain unto the other.

243. "And because they are not firm (also it is necessary that they be soft.*

244. "We have learned by tradition. What is that which is written, Prov. i. 20: 'Wisdom (*plural in Hebrew,* CHKMVTH, *not* CHKMH) will cry without; and at the end of the verse it is written, 'She (*singular*) will utter Her voice in the streets.' In this text the beginning doth neither agree with the end, nor the end with the beginning.

245. "Therefore is it said: Wisdom will cry without when She passeth from the concealed brain of Macroprosopus unto the brain of Microprosopus, through those longer hairs; and thus as it were extrinsically those two brains are connected and become in this way one brain.

246. "Since there is not subsistence in the inferior brain except by the preservation of the supernal brain.

* *I.e.* If they be not the one, they must be the other.

247. "And when this proflux is instituted from the one, namely, into the other, this hath place which is written, 'She will utter Her voice;' namely, in the singular number.

248. "And because She passeth over from brain unto brain through those long hairs, these same (hairs) are not found to be firm.

249. "Wherefore? Because if they were firm, Wisdom could not be conducted by them unto the brain.

250. "Because Wisdom cometh not from man, who is stern and wrathful, like as it is written, Eccles. ix. 17: 'The words of wise men are heard in quiet.'

251. "And thence we learn that in him whose hair is firm, wisdom dwelleth not*

252. "But because these are long (the others are soft) in order that they may bring assistance to all.

253. "How, unto all? So that it may have entrance into the marrow of the spine of the back, which is connected with the brain.

254. "And because the hair of the head doth not hang over the hairs of the beard, since the hair of the head hangeth down, and is drawn back behind the ears, and doth not overhang the beard; because it is not necessary to mingle these with those, but all are separated in their own paths.

255. "We have learned by tradition. All the hairs, as well of the head as of the beard, are white as snow.

256. "And we have learned. Those which are in the beard are all firm. Wherefore? Because those are firm accordingly, that they may firmly mark out their thirteen measurements from the Ancient of the Ancient Ones. †

257. "And those measurements take their beginning from before the ears.

* *I.e.*, Meaning symbolically, "in him who is hardened."

† I have before remarked that this refers to the unity of the Deity: ACHD, *Achad*, One; which by Gematria yields 13.

258. "And those measurements have been included within certain limitations, in order that they should not be confounded with each other. (Others read the passage thus: Because they are communicated unto the inferiors. For this have we been taught. The hairs commence before the ears, because they have been separated, and are not to be mingled with the others," &c.)

259. "But if thou sayest that other (sacred passages) are not given, analogous to these (measurements), thou art in error. For thus is the tradition: "The thirteen measurements of the mercies of the Most Holy Ancient One (are symbolized by these clauses of) Mic. vii. 18: 'What God is like unto Thee?' the first.

260. "'Pardoning iniquity;' the second.

261. "'And passeth by the transgression;' the third.

262. "'Of the remnant of His heritage;' the fourth.

263. "'He retaineth not His anger for ever;' the fifth.

264. "'Because He delighteth in mercy;' the sixth.

265. "'Again, He will have compassion on us;' the seventh.

266. "'He will subdue our iniquities;' the eighth.

267. "'And Thou wilt cast all their iniquities into the depths of the sea;' the ninth.

268 "'Thou wilt give truth unto Jacob;' the tenth.

269. "'Mercy unto Abraham;' the eleventh.

270. "'Which Thou hast sworn unto our fathers;' the twelfth.

271. "'From the days of old;' the thirteenth.

272. "'Unto these correspond in the law, Exod. xxxiv. 6: 'God merciful and gracious,' &c. And those are the Inferiors.

273. "And if thou sayest, 'Why did not Moses pronounce those majestic words?* It shall be answered unto thee: 'Moses hath no duty to perform save in the place

* Apparently meaning that, as the words of the text denote, it was the LORD and not Moses that proclaimed the titles of Tetragrammaton aloud.

where judgment is found; and in the place where judgment is found it is not necessary to speak thus.*

274. "And Moses spake not, save in that time when the Israelites had sinned and judgment was impending; hence Moses spake only in that place wherein judgment is found.

275. "But in another place the prophet hath instituted the order of the praise of the Ancient of Days.†

276. "And those thirteen forms of the supreme holy beard, concealed with many concealments, are most powerful to subdue and mitigate all the stern decrees of the judgments.

277. "What man is he who looketh back upon that most secret, holy supernal beard, who is not confounded before it?

278. "Because also all the hairs are hard and firm in their disposition.

279. "But if thou sayest, 'What if they be so? Surely the lower hairs are black: why are these not as those?'

280. "Nevertheless, thus is the tradition: It is written, Cant. v. 11: 'His locks are bushy and black as a raven.'

281. "Also it is written, Dan. vii. 18: 'The hair of His head like pure wool.'

282. "There is no contradiction here, for the one is said of the supernal beard, but the other of the inferior beard.‡

283. "Also because when the law was given forth unto the Israelites, it was written in black fire upon white fire.

284. "Also the foundation of the matter cometh from

* *I.e.*, Mentioning the merciful characteristics of the Deity, who is represented as the equilibrium of justice and mercy.

† That is, of AHIH, as distinct from IHVH. (See Introduction.)

‡ The hair and beard of Macroprosopus, as distinct from that of Microprosopus. (See the "Book of Concealed Mystery," ch. iii. § 16.)

those hairs; because they are found (arising) out of the (supernal) brain, and stretching down unto the inferior brain.

285. "Also because these are above the beard. Hence the beard is distinct, and all its forms are found separated (each from the other); so that the beard is alone, and its hairs are also distinct.

CHAPTER XII.

CONCERNING THE BEARD OF MACROPROSOPUS IN PARTICULAR; AND, IN THE FIRST PLACE, CONCERNING ITS FIRST PART.

286. "THE first disposition is that which commenceth almost at the beginning of the hair.

287. "Also we have learned: No beard (*i.e.*, no part of this beard) is found which doth not (virtually) arise from the brain of the head (or from the heart).*

288. "But in this (last section) this (first part of the beard) is not considered as distinct (from the others). For in this chapter only this first form (*or portion of the beard*) is to be considered, which descendeth from the beginning of the hair, and it hath this peculiarity (*namely, that it riseth directly from the brain, which cannot altogether be said concerning the other parts of the beard*).

289. "And this is to be kept perfectly distinct from this beard—namely, that which exists from the head (formed into), one thousand worlds, sealed with a most pure seal, with a seal which includeth all seals.

290. "The length of that portion of hair descending before the ears is not equal to the length (of the beard

* The heart being considered as the central motor of the body.

itself); neither doth it twine together, nor hang down far.

291. "But those hairs, when they flow down, are extended, and depend.

292. "And the beginning of the first disposition consists of thirty and one equal locks, extended even unto the beginning of the mouth.

293. "Also three hundred and ninety hairs are found in each lock.

294. "Those thirty and one equal locks, which exist in the first disposition (of the beard) are strong, in order that they may dispose the inferiors according to the number of AL, *El.**

295. "What is this AL, *El?* Mighty and Powerful One.

296. "And among those single locks are distributed one and thirty dominating worlds, so that they may be extended† (correctly) neither on this side nor on that.

297. "And out of each one of these worlds a partition is made into a thousand worlds of desires and of great pleasures.

298. "And they are all concealed in the commencement of the beard, which representeth strength; and they are included in that (name) AL.

299. "And notwithstanding is AL Himself disposed towards mercies, because in Him the Ancient of Days is mitigated and included and extended.

300. "Wherefore even unto the mouth? Because it is written, Dan. vii. 9: 'The judgment was set, and the books were opened.'

301. "What is this? 'And the judgment was set.' It was set in that place, so that it might not have dominion.

* AL, *El*, God, the Mighty One, is equivalent by Gematria to the number 31; for A+L=1+30=31.

† For were they extended, the number would be altered, and it would consequently no longer = AL.

302. "This is that which is written, Isa. ix. 15: "Wonderful, Counsellor, God the Mighty One.' That is, AL, *El*, such a one who also is mighty, but is rendered mild through the holy beard of the Ancient of Days.

303. "And an Arcanum is concealed in that place wherein it is written, Mic. vii. 18: 'What AL, *El*, like unto Thee?' Because of the Ancient of Days it is spoken in the form of the configuration of the holy supernal beard.

304. "The first world, which proceedeth from the first disposition, hath dominion over, and descendeth and ascendeth in a thousand times a thousand myraids of myriads of shield-bearers, and by it are they comprehended under a great seal.

305. "The second world, which proceedeth from that disposition, hath dominion over and descendeth and ascendeth in fifty-seven thousand bodyguards, who are the lords of lamentations; and these are connected with it for the purpose of disposing the neck of the spine.*

306. "The third world, which goeth forth from that arrangement, hath dominion over and descendeth and ascendeth in sixty-nine thousand authors of grief, who are upheld by it, like as metal (is upheld) by the tongs (of the smith).

307. "And by that conformation all those are subjected, and mitigated in the bitterness of tears, which become sweet in the great sea.†

308. "Who is he who beholdeth this conformation of the holy beard, excellent and venerable, who is not overcome with shame thereby?

309. "Who can comprehend the mystery of those locks of hair which hang down from Him, the Ancient One?

* This is of course simply pursuing the symbolism involved in the idea of Macroprosopus, being typified by a vast countenance or head.

† By the great sea, Binah, the third Sephira, is probably meant. (See the "Book of Concealed Mystery," ch. i. § 28).

310. "He is set on the crown of crowns, which are the crowns of all crowns, and the crowns which are not comprehended in the other crowns; I say, of those crowns which are not as the other crowns, for the inferior crowns are comprehended by them.*

311. "And therefore are those forms (arranged in) such conformations, whereunto the inferior forms adhere; and they are the dispositions in which He† is disposed Who hath need that He may be blessed by Him,‡ and Who desireth blessing.

312. "For whensoever the dispositions take the form of these, blessings are found beneath them; and It Is that which It Is.§

313. "All things are comprehended in those dispositions; all things raise themselves up in order that they may receive these dispositions of the Mighty King, of the Ancient One, the most concealed of all. And all those are mitigated by those ordinations of the King, the Ancient One.

314. "We have learned: Unless the Ancient of the Ancient Ones, the Holy of the Holy Ones, were disposed in those conformations, neither the superiors nor the inferiors would be found, and all things would be as though they existed not.

315. "Also we have learned by tradition: how far do those conformations of the beard radiate splendour? Even unto the thirteen inferiors; and whensoever those thirteen are found, those shine.||

* To comprehend the real meaning of section 310, the reader should have carefully studied that part of the Introduction which refers to the Sephiroth, which are symbolized by crowns. In this sense the "crown of crowns" is Kether, the first Sephira, the Ancient One; the crowns of all crowns will be the first three Sephiroth; and the inferiors will be the lower Sephiroth, and those other forms which are dependent on them, symbolized by the crowns of the twenty-four elders in the Apocalypse, which latter is a purely qabalistical work, and is unintelligible without the qabalistical keys.

† Microprosopus. ‡ Macroprosopus. § Cf. Exodus iii. 14.

|| This section refers to the statement that Macroprosopus pours forth His splendour upon Microprosopus, so that the latter shines by reflected light.

316. "And all of them are found in the number thirteen.

317. "Therefore is the beard of the King, the Ancient One, most venerable among all, at once in its entirety concealed, and most excellent.

318. "And because it is most excellent before all things, and concealed, there is no mention made concerning it in any place in the law, and it is not manifested.

319. "But what beard is manifested? The beard of the Great High Priest, and from that beard descendeth the influx unto the inferior beard of the inferior high priest.*

320. "How is the beard of the high priest disposed? The beard of the high priest is disposed in eight conformations. Because also the high priest hath eight vestments, when the ointment descendeth upon his beard.

321. "This is that which is written, Ps. cxxxiii. 2: 'Like the precious oil upon the head descending upon the beard, the beard of Aaron, which descendeth according to the proportion of his attributes,' &c.

322. "And whence is this to us? Because it is written in the same place: 'Also for brethren to dwell together in equality.' The word 'also' increaseth the signification of the inferior high priest.

323. "Seeing that in the same way as the inferior high priest ministereth in the high priesthood, so also, if it be permitted to say so, doth the High Priest above minister in His high priesthood.

324. "This is the first ordination of the beard of the Ancient One, the most concealed of all."

325. Rabbi Schimeon said unto him: "It is justly thy due, Rabbi Isaac, that thou shouldest be under the ornament of the conformation of the beard, and that

* The Great High Priest is the son, Microprosopus, symbolized on earth by the High Priest. Compare what St. Paul says about Christ being our Great High Priest.

thou shouldest receive the light of the countenance of the Ancient of Days, the Ancient of the Ancient Ones. Blessed is thy portion, and blessed be my lot with thee in the world to come."

CHAPTER XIII.

CONCERNING THE SECOND PART OF THE BEARD OF MACROPROSOPUS.

326. "ARISE, Rabbi Chisqiah, and stand in thy place, and declare the worthiness of this part of the holy beard."

327. Rabbi Chisqiah arose, and began his speech and said, Cant. vii. 10: "I am my beloved's and his desire is towards me."

328. "Who is under consideration here, that 'I am my beloved's?' and because that 'his desire is toward me?'

329. "I have meditated, and lo! I have beheld the most excellent light of the supernal lights.

330. "It shone forth, and ascended on three hundred and twenty-five sides.

331. "And in that light was a certain obscurity washed away, like as when a man batheth in a deep river, whose divided waters flow round him on every side from that part which is above.

332. "And that light ascendeth unto the shore of the deep superior sea,* for all good openings and dignities are disclosed in that opening.

333. "I asked of them what might be the interpretation of that which I beheld; and, commencing they replied,

* Binah, the third Sephira, which is called the "sea" in the "Book of Concealed Mystery." It answers to the first letter H, *He* in the Tetragrammaton. (See Introduction.)

'NVSHA OVN, *Nosha Auan*, Thou hast beheld iniquity being taken away.'"

334. He said: "This is the second disposition," and sat down.

335. Rabbi Schimeon said: Now is the universe united together (*or mitigated*). Blessed be thou, Rabbi Chisqiah, of the Ancient of the Ancient Ones!

336. Rabbi Schimeon said: All the lights are congregated together which come under this holy seal.

337. I bear witness that the highest heavens from the highest (powers) are above me, and the highest holy earth from the supernals, because now I can see what man hath not beheld from that time, when Moses for the second time ascended the mountain of Sinai.

338. For I see that my countenance shineth like the vehement splendour of the sun, who is about to issue forth for the healing of the universe.*

339. Like as it is written, Mal. iv. 2: "But unto you that fear my name shall the sun of righteousness arise, and healing in his wings."

340. Furthermore, I know that my countenance shineth; Moses neither knew nor perceived (the fact).

341. Like as it is written, Exod. xxxiv. 29: "And Moses knew not that the skin of his face shone."

342. Furthermore, I behold before me with mine eyes those thirteen sculptured (forms of the beard of Macroprosopus), and like flaming light did they shine.

343. And when the second of those (dispositions) was explained by thy mouth, that same at once was raised, and conformed, and crowned, and concealed in the concealment of the forms of the beard, but all the others were reinstated (in outward form).†

* This phrase "splendour of the sun, who is," &c., evidently refers to the sixth Sephira, Tiphereth, or beauty, the splendour of the countenance of Microprosopus, while the "universe" refers to Malkuth.

† While Rabbi Chisqiah was speaking Rabbi Schimeon had this vision of the conformations of the beard.

344. And what is more, that one (formation), whilst it was explained by thy mouth, flamed forth in splendour, and was crowned with a crown, and seated upon a throne, like a king in the midst of his army.

345. And when the explanation ceased it ascended, and was crowned with a holy crown, and ordained, and concealed, and again placed among the forms of the holy beard; and thus with (the forms) all and singular.

346. Be ye glad, O my holy companions! for surely (*the universe*) shall not be in such a condition until King Messiach shall come.

CHAPTER XIV.

CONCERNING THE THIRD PART OF THE BEARD OF MACROPROSOPUS.

347. "ARISE, Rabbi Chisqiah, for the second time."

348. We have learned that before Rabbi Chisqiah arose, a voice came forth and said: "One angel doth not undertake two messages."

349. Rabbi Schimeon was disturbed, and said; "Assuredly, let each (*of you*) speak singly in his place (*in respect of the symbolism of the seven inferiors*); but as for myself, and Rabbi Eleazar my son, and Rabbi Abba, we (*three*) refer unto the highest and complete perfection (*of the whole decad*). Arise, Rabbi Chiya."*

* On a little consideration it will be seen that this meeting of ten of the principal Rabbis—viz., Schimeon, Eleazar, Abba, Yehuda, Yosi Ben Jacob, Isaac, Chisqiah Ben Rav, Chiya, Yosi, and Yisa—was intended to be symbolical of the ten Sephiroth, wherein, furthermore, the three first-named were also representative of the great trinity of the crown, the king and the queen. In other words, to speak plainly, the whole arrangement of this assembly was closely

350. Rabbi Chiya arose, and, commencing, said, Jer. i. 6: "AHH ADNI IHVH.* *Ahah Adonai Tetragrammaton!* 'Ah, Lord Tetragrammaton! behold I cannot speak, for I am a child.'

351. "Therefore, why was it that Jeremiah could not speak, seeing that many sayings had passed from his lips prior to his saying this? Did he not therefore lie (*when he said*) that which is written (*in the text*): 'Behold, I cannot DBR, *Deber*, speak'?

352. "But we have learned that God influenced him so that he should speak to this end. For this is the tradition: "What is the difference between DBVR, *Debur*, and AMIRH, *Amirah?* 'Amirah' is, as it were (*simple*) speech, wherein is required no especial uplifting of the voice; 'Debur' is public speaking, wherein is indeed necessary (*considerable*) elevation of voice and (*loud*) proclamation of words.

353. "Since it is written, Exod. xx. 1: 'And God spake all these words, saying.'

354. "And according to what we have learned (*by tradition*), 'The whole earth heard this DBVR, *Debur*, speech, and the whole earth trembled.' Because also it is written: 'VIDBR, *Vayedeber*, and He spoke forth.' And it is not written: 'VIAMR, *Vayomar*, and He said.'

355. "So also in this place: 'Behold! I cannot speak, DBR, *Deber*;' that is, as a herald, by declaring

similar to the constitution of a masonic lodge. Confer also § 13 of this book, wherein these three Rabbis further symbolize the "Three Pillars" of the Sephiroth—this assembly of the ten forms of the Greater Holy Assembly. But on reference to the "Idra Zuta" we shall find that the Lesser Assembly consists of only seven Rabbis, of which the seventh, Rabbi Isaac, came in later than the others. These seven were Schimeon, Eleazar, Abba, Yehuda, Yosi Ben Jacob, Chiya, and Isaac. (Conf. "Idra Zuta," § 13.)

* This is the Hebrew text of the Polyglot Bible, but in that of the "Idra Rabba," "AHH IHVH ALHIM, *Ahah Tetragrammaton Elohim*," is substituted for "*Adonai Tetragrammaton*."

an address, and convincing the world through the Holy Spirit.

356. "If thus be the matter, this is also to be noted which is written: 'VIDBR IHVH, *Vayedeber Tetragrammaton*; and Tetragrammaton spake forth unto Moses, saying.' Nevertheless, what one of the prophets was so great as Moses? For never was any man so worthy as he; for he heard the DBVR, *Debur*, loud voice, like the proclamation of a herald, and he feared not, neither did he tremble; while the other prophets trembled even at AMIRH, *Amirah*, the speech, and were greatly afraid.

357. "Also we have learned that through the first and second dispositions of the beard it is necessary to pass on to the third; like as it is written, Job xxxiii. 29: 'Behold, God worketh all this with man by three paths.'*

358. "And come, behold! it is necessary through the two first conformations that thou pass on unto the third, because the third form is in the midst.

359. "For, under the nose,† beneath the two nostrils, there issueth a certain path, and from that path the hairs are wanting.

360. "Wherefore are they wanting? Because it is written, Mic. vii. 18: 'VOVBR OL PSHO, *Va-Ghober Ghal Peshang*, and passing over transgression.' Therefore is that path prepared (*namely*) for the purpose of passing over (*transgression*).

361. "And therefore that path resideth beneath the nostrils of the nose; and the hairs do not grow in that path, because it subdueth iniquities.

362. "For it is written: 'Passing over transgression,' for the purpose of passing over unto the sacred mouth, in order that it may say, 'I HAVE PARDONED.'

* The same word which is here rendered thus is translated in the ordinary version of the Bible, "oftentimes."

† See § 217 of this book, and also the "Book of Concealed Mystery," ii. § 8.

363. "We have learned that many threatened vials of wrath look for this mouth, and to none among them is it manifested; for it is withdrawn and guarded around; it is known, and it is not known.

364. "We have learned in the 'Book of Concealed Mystery': What is this which is written (*in this disposition of the letters in this*) word, PSHO, *Peshang*? If they be first, the word 'OVBR, *Ghober*, passing over,' hath place; if, on the other hand, not so, the word 'PSHO, *Peshang*, transgression,' hath place.

365. "What doth this phrase teach, 'passing over transgression'? SHPO, *Shephau*, influence, (*it teacheth*) if SH (*in PSHO*) be placed before the P.*

366. "If they are not just, it remaineth (*i.e., the influence*), and passeth not over into Microprosopus.

367. 'What is the difference between the one and the other? In Microprosopus (*the matter standeth thus*): this path descendeth beneath the nostrils of His nose. It is written, Num. xii. 9: 'And the anger of Tetragrammaton was kindled against him, and He departed.'

368. "What is this, 'And He departed'? Because the spirit of anger departed from those nostrils, and if he found any man before him, he was taken away, and was no more found.

369. "Which is intimated in these words, Isa. xl. 7:

* This is simply a transposition of the first two letters of the word in question. Of course, the same letters being retained, though their relative places are changed, the numeration of the two words by Gematria will be identical. But it is worth our while to notice what the numeration of this word is, especially as Rabbi Chiya has not examined it. P+SH+O=80+300+70=450=THN, *Than*, the dragon. Ergo, according to the exegetical rule of Gematria, the dragon will be the symbol of transgression. But 450 is also the numeration of SHPO, influence: therefore is the dragon a symbol also of influence and of power. But "this influence passeth over into Microprosopus;" now one of the qabalistical axioms given by Pistorius is: "Paradise is the sephirotic tree. In the midst thereof the great Adam is Tiphereth." (See Introduction.) Therefore the influence passing over into Microprosopus is also the serpent entering into the garden of Eden.

'Because the Spirit of Tetragrammaton bloweth upon it.'

370. "But concerning Macroprosopus it is written: 'Passing over transgression.'

371. "Also it is written, Job. xxxvii. 21: 'And the spirit (*wind*) passeth over and hath cleansed them.'

372. "Also we have learned that on this account it is thus written: 'Passing over transgression' in that path. Also concerning that (*passage*), Exod. xii. 23: 'And He passeth over to smite the Egyptians.'

373. "Blessed is his portion who is worthy in this matter. And this is the third conformation of the path of the venerable, holy, and excellent beard of the Ancient of the Ancient Ones."

374. Rabbi Schimeon said unto him: "May God, the Holy One, blessed be He, be gracious unto thee, and protect thee most abundantly.

375. "Also we have learned: What is this which is written, 'With rejoicing will I rejoice in Tetragrammaton?' Concerning the Ancient of Days, is it said: 'For He is the praise of all things.'

376. "We have learned, whensoever that path of the beard of the Ancient of Days is manifested, all the authors of lamentation and mourning, and all the executors of judgment, are silent and hidden; nor is there one of them who openeth his mouth to do harm, because that path is manifested in due form.

377. "Hence also he who toucheth that mouth, and adviseth it to keep silence,* pointeth out this path with his finger; and that is the symbol denoting the Holy Ancient One." (Others read: Because that path is the symbol of silence; hence he who looked at another, and adviseth him to be silent, toucheth this path, which is the symbol, &c.)

* Meaning symbolically the idea of judgment.

CHAPTER XV.

CONCERNING THE FOURTH PART OF THE BEARD OF MACROPROSOPUS.

378. THE hair is disposed in the fourth conformation, and it descendeth beneath the mouth from the one side even unto the other side.

379. That is intimated (*in the saying of Micah*) in these words: "Of the remnant of his heritage:" LSHAIRITH NCHLTHV, *Lishairith Nachalatho.*

380. Like as it is said in 2 Kings xix. 4: "And thou shalt lift up thy prayer for the remnant that is left." Where every part that is found truly remaining is called the remnant.

381. For it is written, Zeph. iii. 13: "The remnant of Israel, SHARITH ISHRAL, *Sharith Israel,* shall not do iniquity."

CHAPTER XVI.

CONCERNING THE FIFTH PART OF THE BEARD OF MACROPROSOPUS.

382. The fifth conformation. Another path goeth forth beneath the mouth. This is that which is written in the saying of Micah: "LA HCHZIQ LOD APV, *Lo Hecheziq Lead Apo,* He hath not kept his anger for ever." Arise! Rabbi Yosi!"

383. Rabbi Yosi arose, and commencing said, Ps. cxliv. 15: "'Blessed is the people that is in such a case; blessed is the people whose God is Tetragrammaton.'

384. "'Blessed is the people that is in such a case.' What is this 'SHKKH LV, *Shekakah Lo,* That is in such

a case?' Like as it is said in Est. vii. 10: 'And the wrath of the king was appeased,' SHKKH, ***Shekakah***; that is, 'Became quiet from his wrathfulness.'

385. "Another exposition: He was appeased through his wrath, which is intimated in these words, Num. xi. 15: 'And if Thou dealest thus with me, kill me, I pray Thee, out of hand, if I have found grace in thy sight.'

"'Kill me, I pray Thee, out of hand;' this is judgment of judgments. But 'Blessed is the people whose God is Tetragrammaton;' this is mercies of mercies.

387. "Another exposition: SHKKH, ***Shekakah***, is the name which includeth all names,* in consequence of which that Holy Blessed One maketh His wrath to pass away, and caused Microprosopus to be at peace, and taketh away all those extraneous (*matters*) from the midst.

388. "We have learned through Barietha (*or the tradition given forth without the holy city*), that that path of the conformation of the holy superior Ancient of the Ancient Ones, which descendeth in the beard beneath the nostrils of the nose, and this inferior path, are equal in every way, in such a manner that that which is below is like that which is above.† The superior (*path*) is called 'passing over transgression'; the inferior, 'He hath not kept his anger for ever.'

* It is not at first sight evident why this word should be the "name which includeth all names." But if we examine it by Gematria we shall soon see the reason. SHKKH, SH+K+K+H=300+20+20+5=345= SHMH, *Shemah*=*Ha Shem*, The Name. This title Shemah is applied to the Tetragrammaton frequently as being *the* name of all names, and therefore SHKKH is taken as concealing Tetragrammaton.

† Compare the precept in the Smaragdine tablet of Hermes Trismegistus: "That which is below is like that which is above, and that which is above is like that which is below, for the performance of the miracles of the one substance." This is the fundamental principle of all the ancient mystic doctrines, whether qabalistical, mythological, alchemical, or magical; and in this formula all are contained. As is God, so is the universe; as is the Creator the Supernal Man, so is the created the inferior man; as Macrocosm, so Microcosm; as eternity, so life!

389. "Also we have learned this: 'He hath not kept,' *i.e.*, there is no place *wherein anger* can remain. Like as in the superior there is opportunity given for taking away (*anger*), so also in the inferior is the (same opportunity) afforded.

390. "We have learned this: whensoever in this Ancient One, the most concealed of all, this path is uncovered, it is well for all the inferior (*paths*);* for then appeareth counsel for doing good to them all.

391. "But when it is withdrawn, and is not uncovered, there is no counsel, neither is there any who knoweth Him, save Himself.†

392. "Like as also none knoweth the superior Eden, save Himself, save Him, the Ancient of the Ancient Ones.

393. "And concerning this it is written, Ps. xcii. 6: 'O Lord, how excellent are Thy works! Thy thoughts are very deep!"

394. Rabbi Schimeon said unto him: "May thy works be reckoned in order in the world to come by the Ancient of the Ancient Ones!"

CHAPTER XVII.

CONCERNING THE SIXTH PART OF THE BEARD OF MACROPROSOPUS.

395. The hair is arranged in the sixth conformation, and ascendeth from below upwards, and toucheth the circles

* That is, the lower forms of the Sephiroth.

† Himself, HVA, *Hoa*, whom we can only symbolize by this pronoun; HE, Who is the Absolute; HE, Who is beyond us; that awful and unknowable Crown, Who hath said, I AM; in Whom is neither past nor future, He who is the ETERNAL PRESENT. Therefore is HE, *Hoa*, the Father, known of none save the Son, IHVH, and him to whom the Son will reveal Him. For none can see *Hoa* and live, for they would be absorbed in Him.

of most excellent fragrance, even unto the beginning of the mouth above; and the hair descendeth from the beginning (*of the mouth above*) unto the beginning of the opening of the mouth below. "Arise thou! Rabbi Yisa, and expound this conformation."

396. Rabbi Yisa arose, and commenced, and said, Is. liv. 10: "'And thy blessing shall not depart from thee!'

397. "Also it is written: 'And in everlasting compassion have I had mercy upon thee.'

398. "Do not these verses contradict one another? They do not. For this is what we have learned: there is given a compassion (*of one kind*), and again there is given a compassion of another kind. For the one is the interior compassion, and the other is the external compassion.

399. "The interior compassion is that of which we have spoken concerning the Ancient of Days, and that is concealed in this part of the beard, which is called the angle of the beard.

400. "Neither is it advisable for a man to destroy this part (*of his beard*) because of this interior compassion of the Ancient of Days.

401. "And therefore is it written concerning the inferior priesthood, Lev. xxi. 5: 'They shall not make baldness upon their head, neither shall they shave off the angle of their beard.'

402. "Wherefore? Lest they should destroy the path of the Mercy of the Ancient One. For also the priesthood is (*symbolically*) referred unto this path.

403. "Also we have learned in the 'Book of Concealed Mystery' that every work existeth in order that it may procure increase for Mercy, and that it may establish the same; also that this is not to be cut off nor removed from the world.

404. "This is that which is written: "And My Compassion shall not depart from thee.' Namely, the Compassion of the Ancient of Days.

405. "*(But when it is said in another text)*, 'And in Mercy, OVLM, *Olahm*, for ever *(this is the sense)*, the mercy which is called 'mercy for ever' is the second form concerning which it is written, Ps. lxxxix. 2: 'I have said, Mercy shall be built up for ever.'

406. "And this compassion of the Ancient of Days is the mercy of truth. And *(this phrase)* 'mercy of truth' is not said concerning the life of the body, but concerning the life of the soul.

407. "And therefore is it written, Mic. vii. 18: 'Since He Himself wisheth Mercy.' This is the sixth conformation of the venerable beard of the Ancient of the Ancient Ones."

CHAPTER XVIII.

CONCERNING THE SEVENTH PART OF THE BEARD OF MACROPROSOPUS.

408. THE seventh conformation is that wherein the hair is wanting, and there appear two apples in the circles of fragrance, fair and beautiful of aspect.

409. Rabbi Schimeon commenced, and said, Cant. ii. 3: "'Like as the apple-tree among the trees of the wood, so is my beloved among the sons.'

410. "What is the apple-tree? Like as this in itself hath three colours, so do the two apples of the holy blessed one contain six colours.

411. "And those two apples which are the seventh conformation include all the six conformations before mentioned.

412. "And concerning them is that passage *(to be taken in)*, Prov. xvi. 15: 'In the light of the countenance of the King is life.'

413. "Also we have learned that from those apples goeth forth the life of the universe, and it giveth joy unto Microprosopus; like as it is written, Num. vi. 24: 'The Lord maketh His countenance to shine upon thee.'

414. "And it is written: 'In the light of the countenance of the King is life.' 'In the light of the countenance of the King.' Those are the two apples of the circles of fragrance of which we have spoken.

415. "'The Lord make His countenance to shine upon thee.' Here is understood the exterior countenance which when it shineth blesseth the universe.

416. "And we have learned that whensoever those external lights shine He blesseth the whole world, and wrath is no longer found in the universe.

417. "And if these externals (*do this*), how much more do these two apples, which ever shine, which ever are joyful!

418. "This is a tradition, given forth without the city.* 'When those two apples are disclosed, Microprosopus appeareth in joy; for all those inferior lights are joyful; and all those inferiors shine; and all the worlds rejoice, and are perfected in all perfection; and all things rejoice and shine, and no good thing is wanting; all things are satisfied at once; all things rejoice together at the same time.

419. "Come, behold! The external countenance at times shineth, at times is obscured; and therefore is it written: 'The Lord make His face to shine upon thee.' And, Ps. i.: 'And cause His face to shine upon us. Selah.'

420. "Whence (*we learn*), that it is not always (*luminous*), but only when those superior apples are uncovered.

421. "This have we learned by tradition. 'Those hidden apples shine, and are ever brilliant; and from them

* I suppose this means later than the Captivity.

proceed rays in three hundred and seventy* directions; and in them all the six (*preceding*) conformations of the beard are included.'

422. "This is that which is said, Mic. vii. 18: 'May He return and have mercy upon us!" May He return, that is, again; † whence it is to be noticed that sometimes they are concealed and sometimes uncovered; wherefore it is said: 'May He return and have mercy upon us!"

423. "And in that which is inferior (*correspondeth to this form*) the name, AMTH, *Amath*, Truth. This is the seventh conformation, which includeth the six first, in the two apples of the Ancient of the Ancient Ones."

CHAPTER XIX.

CONCERNING THE EIGHTH PART OF THE BEARD OF MACROPROSOPUS.

424. The eight conformation. There goeth forth a certain tress of hairs surrounding the beard, and they hang down evenly into the heart. "Arise thou, Eleazar, my son, and expound this conformation."

425. Rabbi Eleazar, his son, arose, and commenced, and said: "All things depend from the influx, even the Book of the Law in the Temple. This have we understood from the 'Book of Concealed Mystery,' and it speaketh thus.

426. "Therefore do not then all things depend from the influx? Also we have learned that the Book of the Law must be holy, and its covering holy, and the Temple holy.

* 370=OSH, *Aush*=formation, action, creation. And the least number of 3+70=73=10=Malkuth, the decad of the Sephiroth.

† Expressed by the *re* in *re*turn.

427. "Also it is written, Isa. vi. 4: 'And they called one unto another and said: Holy, holy, holy!' Behold these three (*repetitions of the word 'holy'*), unto which the Book of the Law correspondeth, for its covering is holy, and the Temple is holy, and the book itself is holy.

428. "And thus the law hath been constructed in triple holiness, in three degrees, in three days, (*but*) the Schechinah (*is*) in the three (*following*) which are the Table, the Ark, and the Temple; and in the same manner it dependeth from the Book of the Law, and that dependeth from the Influx.

429. "Also it is written, Jer. x. 2: 'Be ye not dismayed at the signs (*or influences*) of the heavens.' Because if they exist in holiness, in the same way they must depend from the Influx.

430. But thus have we read in the "Book of Concealed Mystery" that this venerable holy tress of hair, wherein all the locks of the beard hang down, is called the Influx. Wherefore? Because that all the holinesses of the holinesses of all holinesses depend from that Influx.

431. "And in the Book of the Law, although it is holy, the ten holinesses* do not descend, until it be brought into the Temple. But after that it is brought into the Temple it is called holy with the ten holinesses.

432. "As in the above instance mention is not made of the Temple save when the ten holinesses are associated with it.

433. "Also we have learned that all things depend from

* This of course refers to the ten Sephiroth. In the *Sepher Yetsirah*, SPR ITzIRH, a very ancient and mystical qabalistical book attributed to Abraham the Patriarch, which treats of the creation of the universe through the symbolism of the ten numbers (*Sephiroth*), and the twenty-two letters, together called the thirty-two paths of wisdom, where the ten numbers are derived into a tetrad and a hexad (the latter consisting of the four cardinal points of the compass, together with height and depth), this phrase is employed: "And in the midst of the hexad is the Holy Temple." This book "Yetzirah" is not included in the present volume.

that Influx which is (*symbolised by*) that tress of (hair of the beard) from which all (*the other*) hairs depend.

434. "Why is this called the Influx (*or influence*)? Because from it depend the influences and the influences of the influences, and from it come forth those which are above and those which are below.

435. "And because it dependeth, and that in it all the things of the universe depend, superiors and inferiors; also in the last place the Book of the Law, which is in the Temple, and is crowned with the ten holinesses, is not excepted hence with the other holinesses. All things depend from it (*this conformation, namely*).

436. "And he who beholdeth that form, before him are they subjected and inflected (others read: '*all sins are subjected, &c.*') according to that which is written: 'IKBVSH OVNVTHINV, *Yekebosh Auonothino*, He hath pardoned our iniquities' (*or He hath subjected, &c.*)."

437. Rabbi Schimeon said unto him: "O my son! blessed be thou by the Holy of the Holy Ones, the One Ancient before all."

CHAPTER XX.

CONCERNING THE NINTH PART OF THE BEARD OF MACROPROSOPUS.

438. The ninth conformation. The hairs are mingled with those hairs that hang down, neither is one pre-eminent above another. "Arise, Rabbi Abba!"

439. Rabbi Abba arose and said: "These are the hairs which are mingled with these which hang down, and they are called 'the deep places of the sea,' because they depart from above in the fluid places of the brain.

440. "And from that place are cast out all the lords who

are the exactors of the debts (*of the trespasses*) of mankind, and they are subjugated."

441. Rabbi Schimeon said unto him: "Blessed be thou of the Ancient of Days!"

CHAPTER XXI.

CONCERNING THE TENTH AND ELEVENTH PARTS OF THE BEARD OF MACROPROSOPUS.

442. THE tenth conformation. The hairs descend beneath the beard, and cover the throat beneath the beard. "Arise, Rabbi Yehuda."

443. Rabbi Yehuda arose, and commenced, and said, Isa. ii. 19: "'And they shall enter into the holes of the rocks, and into the caves of the earth, from the countenance of the terror of the Lord of Hosts, and from the glory of His Majesty, when he shall arise to shake terribly the earth.'

444. "'From the countenance of the Terror* of the Lord.' It is to be carefully noted that that which is exterior is called the Terror of Tetragrammaton.

445. "'And from the Glory of His Majesty.' These are the hairs beneath the beard, and they are called the Glory of His Majesty.

446. "(*But*) these two (*conformations agree with*) §§ 268, 269, *ante*); the tenth with 'Thou shalt give truth unto Jacob.'

* PCHD, *Pachad*, Terror, is a title of the fifth Sephira, Geburah, Strength, to which the divine name of Elohim Gibor, the Elohim of Strength, is referred. It is likewise to be remembered that from this Sephira the Pillar of Justice takes its title, which includes the third, fifth, and eighth Sephiroth; Binah, Geburah, and Hod; Understanding, Strength or Terror, and Splendour. Mars, "the star of the unconquered will," is also referred to this fifth Sephira.

447. "And the eleventh, because one hair is not pre-eminent over another hair, with 'mercy unto Abraham.'"

CHAPTER XXII.

CONCERNING THE TWELFTH PART OF THE BEARD OF MACROPROSOPUS.

448. The twelfth conformation is that the hairs do not hang over the mouth, and that the mouth is bare on every part, and that beautiful are the hairs surrounding it, so that there may be no molestation there, as is fit.

449. But wherein consisteth the molestation? Doubtless it is frequently said, "If judgment exist in the place of judgment (or, "If judgment follow after judgment"), molestation ariseth."

450. Therefore are the hairs of the beard either (*symbolical of*) molestation or judgment, while the other parts appear to (symbolise) mercy.

451. Surely it is said for this reason, because the breathings forth of the Spirit upon Microprosopus are not molestations.

452. For we have learned that from that holy and excellent mouth of the Holy of the Holy Ones the Spirit breaketh forth.

453. What spirit? The Spirit which floweth forth upon Microprosopus, that it may enshroud Him.

454. And with that Spirit are all those* veiled which are inferior. And when that Spirit goeth forth, then is it divided into 37,000 aspects,† of which each one is expanded, but only in its proper place.

* That is, the fourth, fifth, sixth, seventh, eighth, and ninth Sephiroth which form Microprosopus; and the tenth, which is the Bride.

† That is, 37 in the material, or Asiah = ZL, *Zal* = profession, or LZ, *Laz* = diversion of force.

455. And he who is worthy to be enshrouded is enshrouded by (*the Spirit*).

456. And therefore hairs are not found upon the holy mouth, because thence the Spirit rusheth forth; neither is it necessary that any (*extraneous things*) whatsoever should be mingled therewith or approach thereto.

457. And that (*mouth*) is very secret, because to it nothing adhereth, nor doth anything touch upon it from above or below; and it is concealed in the secret of secrets, so that it cannot be known.

458. In fact, it is not formed, nor doth it exist* (properly speaking) in this conformation.

459. And because that Spirit which proceedeth unto the exteriors, and wherewith the true prophets have been overshadowed, is called the mouth of Tetragrammaton.

460. But herein, in the Ancient of the Ancient Ones, is it not made manifest, nor is there any who knoweth His Spirit save Himself.

461. And therefore are the hairs of (*the beard*) of equal length around the mouth; and this latter is bare in every part.

462. And herein have our fathers put their trust, that they might be overshadowed by that Spirit which is developed in multitudinous aspects, each in its proper place, wherewith all the equal hairs are surrounded.

463. This is that which is written in that passage of Micah: "Which thou has sworn unto our fathers."

464. And this is the holy and excellent twelfth conformation, from which, linked together, depend twelve limitations above and twelve limitations below; even twelve limitations, according unto the twelve tribes of our fathers.

465. This is that which is written: "Which Thou hast sworn unto our fathers."

* Meaning that in this place it is the conformations of the *beard* and not the *mouth* that are being described.

CHAPTER XXIII.

CONCERNING THE THIRTEENTH PART OF THE BEARD OF MACROPROSOPUS.

466. THE thirteenth conformation. The hairs which are beneath the beard hang down on this side and on that in beautiful and excellent dignity, and form a covering even unto the chest, and nothing is seen of the countenance and of the places of fragrance save those two brilliant and beautiful apples.

467. Rabbi Schimeon spake and said: "O how blessed is his portion who is found in this excellent holy assembly,* wherein we are (*assembled*)! Blessed is his portion in this world and in the world to come.

468. "For we are seated in that excellent holiness which surroundeth us.

469. "And all those excellent conformations are coordinated, and crowned, and placed round about, each in its own (*proper*) position, in the holy form of the beard.

470. "And this thirteenth disposition is the beautiful disposition which exciteth in itself so great desire that the head† ariseth towards it.

471. "From it depend all those which are comprehended in Microprosopus; from it depend alike those which are supernal, those which are inferior.

472. "This is the form of perfection which con-

* Because this assembly of ten Rabbis, as I have before remarked, was intended to typify the ten Sephiroth and their grouping.

† This somewhat obscure text means this: The number of the parts of the beard are 13, which are now completed in this disposition. But 13 = ACHD, *Achad*, Unity, and also AHBH, *Ahebah*, Love. Hence love of unity ariseth when the 13 are complete. And the head of Macroprosopus ariseth, because that is Kether, the first Sephira, the number one, unity.

summateth all the dispositions, and which perfecteth all things.

473. "We have learned by tradition. Those parts* are called QDM, *Qadam*,† ancient days, days first of the first. But those which are found in Microprosopus are called OVLM, *Olahm*, everlasting days, or days of the ages.

474. "Also we have learned that those QDM, *Qadam*, ancient days, are all conformed in the conformations of the beard, wherein is composed the Ancient of the Ancient Ones, the Concealed of the Concealed Ones. But this thirteenth (*conformation*) comprehendeth them.‡

475. "And all the concealed superiors and inferiors are concealed in it, and they are comprehended in that Influx from which all things emanate; like as it is said:

476. "And that day is not comprehended in them, seeing it comprehendeth all things.

477. "And in that time wherein is stirred up the Ancient of Days in the superior conformations, that is called one day wherein He ariseth to magnify His beard.

478. "Which is intimated in those words, Zech. xiv. 7: 'One day which is known to the Lord.'

479. "That alone prevaileth over all, that includeth all things that is called by the known name.

480. "For thus we have learned. In that place where there is day there is also night, seeing that day cannot exist without night.

481. "But because in that time shall be the time of the dignity of the beard, that day is found alone.

482. "It is called neither day nor night, for it is not

* That is, the thirteen conformations of the beard.

† And hence is Macroprosopus called the "Ancient of Days." Qadam also means the east, eastward. "Tetragrammaton Elohim planted a garden, MQDM, *Miqedem*, eastward (or of ancient time), in Eden. It is worthy of notice that the Gematria of QDM and OVLM are 144 and 146 respectively; the least numbers of which are 9 and 2—Yesod and Chokmah, foundation and wisdom.

‡ By way of synthesis, as if it were a repetition of the rest conjointly.

called day except for our (*better understanding of the symbolism involved*), neither is it called night except for the same reason.

483. "And because that form includeth all things, hence nothing whatsoever is known or seen concerning it.

484. "And from it streameth down the oil of magnificence in thirteen directions, which flow down upon all the inferiors in order that they may shine forth.

485. "In that oil are consummated the thirteen parts of the holy and excellent beard.

486. "And those forms which are in that beard are disposed and descend in many directions, neither can it be seen how they are extended nor how they arise.

487. "They are hidden in all things, and they are concealed in all things; and no man knoweth their place, except Him, the Ancient One.

488. "In their expansion are they all included, like as it is said:

489. "He is known, and He is not known; He is concealed, and He is manifest.

490. "Concerning Him it is written. Isa. xlii. 8: 'ANI IHVH HVA*, *Ani Tetragrammaton Hoa*, This is My name, and My glory I give not unto another.'

491. "Also it is written, Ps. c. 2: 'HVA, *Hoa*, He, hath made us, and not we ourselves.'

492. "Also it is written, Dan. vii. 9: 'The Ancient of Days did sit,' that is, He remained in His place, and Him hath no man known. He sitteth, but He is not found.

493. "Also it is written, Ps. cxxxix. 14: 'I will praise Thee, for I am fearfully and wonderfully made.'"

* "Ani Tetragrammaton Hoa, This is my name;" for in this are contained Macroprosopus, Microprosopus, and the Tetragrammaton. ANI represents Microprosopus; HVA, Macroprosopus; and IHVH is between them. Ani is 53 and Hoa is 12, which together give 65, which is ADNI, *Adonai*, Lord; and IHVH = 26, which added hereunto is 91 = AMN, *Amen*. Now, apart from the sacred ideas we attach to amen, it it well to know that the ancient Egyptians called their greatest Deity *Amen*, AMN, Amen-Ra, and Ra = Light, AVR in Hebrew; Amen our Light, the light of the two countenances.

CHAPTER XXIV.

CONCLUSION OF THE MATTER CONCERNING MACROPROSOPUS.

494. RABBI SCHIMEON spake unto his companions, and said: "When that veil is expanded (*by which is to be understood the representation of the beard of Macroprosopus*) which ye behold above us,* I see that all the conformations have descended therein, and that they shine forth in that place. (*Now like as if he intended to say, AMN, Amen, the discourse concerning Macroprosopus being finished, he describeth this particular symbolism, which is contained in the ensuing symbols.*)

495. "And a certain covering, even the splendour of the most holy and blessed God (*otherwise the opening of holiness; but by this is understood the Tetragrammaton, which, together with the name, ADNI, Adonai, maketh the number of the word AMN, Amen, that is* 91): is expanded through four columns on four sides (*which are the four letters of the holy name, by which he saith that space is surrounded*).

496. "One column is so placed that it reacheth from the lowest unto the highest. (*This is the Kingdom of the emanations,*† *the base and lowest part of the whole system*‡ *of emanation, because it is said to ascend from the lowest part of the middle column*§ *even unto the summit of the Crown.*||)

497. "And therein is a certain MGRVPIA,¶ *Megerophia*, vessel containing fire (*for like as the fire on the altar could not be touched with bare hands, so that*

* Again alluding to their symbolical representation of the ten Sephiroth.

† Malkuth, the tenth Sephira. ‡ The Sephiroth.

§ Or Pillar of Mildness, consisting of the first, sixth, ninth, and tenth Sephiroth.

|| Kether. "Malkuth is Kether after another manner," says one of the qabalistic axioms of Pistorius.

¶ I believe the best translation of Megerophia is a "fire shovel." Knorr de Rosenroth makes it "uncus focarius."

name, Tetragrammaton, cannot be touched and pronounced by the mouth, but it is touched and produced by ADNI, Adonai, which is SHM, Sham, His name; for SHM and MGRVPIA both yield 340 *by Gematria*); and in the fire-containing vessel are four keys,* sharp on every side (*for such was the form of the keys, in order that they might draw aside the veil, as a lock is shot back by a key. But the four letters of the name ADNI, Adonai, are hereby to be understood, which are inserted into and united with the four letters IHVH, in this manner, IAHDVNHI*); which seize upon that veil, and withdraw it from the superiors.

498. "And thus in the second column,† and the third column and the fourth column (*that is, the four letters are applied to the other four letters, as hath just been said*).

499. "And between one column and another column are contained eighteen ‡ bases of columns (*here is to be understood the name expounded through the seventy-two* § *names or numbers; for either pertain unto Macroprosopus, and four times eighteen yieldeth seventy-two*): and they shine forth with brilliancy in the openings carved out in

* Quatuor claves traditæ sunt in manu Domini mundi, quas non tradidit neque ulli Angelo, neque seraphino: clavis pluviæ: clavis sustentationis: clavis sepulchorum: clavis sterilitatis, &c. (Zanolini: "Lexicon Chaldæo-Rabbinicum," art. MPTHCH, root PTHCH.)

† These four columns also refer to the four worlds of Atziloth, Briah, Yetzirah, and Asiah. (See Introduction.)

‡ 18 = CHI = Life.

§ In Exodus xiv. are three verses (19, 20, and 21), which each consist of 72 letters. Now, if these three verses be written at length one above another, the first from right to left, the second from left to right, and the third from right to left (or, as the Greeks would say, *boustrophedon*), they will give 72 columns of three letters each. Then each column will be a word of three letters, and as there are 72 columns, there will be 72 words of three letters, each of which will be the 72 names of the Deity alluded to in the text. And these are called the Schemahamphorasch, or the divided name. By writing the verses all from right to left, instead of *boustrophedon*, &c., there will be other sets of 72 names obtainable. (See annexed Table of the Schemahamphorasch.)

THE SCHEMAHAMPHORASCH.

I	K	L	H	H	M	I	H	L	A	H	K	A	L	M	O	S	I	V
	L	A	Q	R	B	Z	H	A	L	Z	H	K	L	H	L	I	L	H
	I	V	M	I	H	L	O	V	D	I	Th	A	H	Sh	M	T	I	V
	18	17	16	15	14	13	12	11	10	9	8	7	6	5	4	3	2	1
H	M	K	L	I	V	L	A	R	Sh	I	H	N	Ch	M	I	N	P	L
	N	V	H	Ch	Sh	K	V	I	A	R	A	Th	H	L	I	L	H	V
	D	Q	Ch	V	R	B	M	I	H	Th	A	H	V	H	I	K	L	V
	36	35	34	33	32	31	30	29	28	27	26	25	24	23	22	21	20	19
V	N	N	O	H	D	V	M	O	O	S	I	V	M	H	I	R	Ch	A
	I	N	M	Ch	N	H	I	Sh	R	A	L	V	I	H	I	H	O	N
	Th	A	M	Sh	I	V	H	L	I	L	H	L	K	H	Z	O	M	I
	54	53	52	51	50	49	48	47	46	45	44	43	42	41	40	39	38	37
H	M	H	I	R	Ch	A	M	D	M	O	I	V	M	H	I	N	P	M
	V	I	B	A	B	I	N	M	Ch	N	H	M	Tz	R	I	M	V	B
	M	I	M	H	V	O	Q	B	I	V	H	B	R	Ch	L	M	I	H
	72	71	70	69	68	67	66	65	64	63	62	61	60	59	58	57	56	55

(If to each of these triliteral names AL or IH, El or Yah, be added, the names of 72 Angels are obtained, who rule over the 72 quinaries of the degrees of the Zodiac.)

1. Vehu; 2. Yeli; 3. Sit; 4. Aulem; 5. Mahash; 6. Lelah; 7. Aka; 8. Kahath; 9. Hezi; 10. Elad; 11. Lav; 12. Hahau; 13. Yezel; 14. Mebah; 15. Heri; 16. Haqem; 17. Lau; 18. Keli; 19. Levo; 20. Pahel; 21. Nelak; 22. Yiai; 23. Melah; 24. Chaho; 25. Nethah; 26. Haa; 27. Yereth; 28. Shaah; 29. Riyi; 30. Aum; 31. Lekab; 32. Vesher; 33. Yecho; 34. Lehach; 35. Keveq; 36. Menad; 37. Ani; 38. Chaum; 39. Rehau; 40. Yeiz; 41. Hahah; 42. Mik; 43. Veval; 44. Yelah; 45. Sael; 46. Auri; 47. Aushal; 48. Miah; 49. Vaho; 50. Doni; 51. Hachash; 52. Aumem; 53. Nena; 54. Neith; 55. Mabeh; 56. Poï; 57. Nemem; 58. Yeil; 59. Harach; 60. Metzer; 61. Vamet; 62. Yehah; 63. Aunu; 64. Mechi; 65. Dameb; 66. Menaq; 67. Aiau; 68. Chebo; 69. Raah; 70. Yebem; 71. Haiai; 72. Möum.

that veil, and so on all four sides. (*By the "openings carved out" is to be understood the exposition of the name, Tetragrammaton.*)

500. "I beheld those forms which shine above it, and await the words of our lips, that they may be crowned and raised each in its own place.

501. "And when they are expounded by our lips, they ascend singly and are crowned, and are disposed in that order which is here given forth by the mouth of whosoever amongst us (*happeneth to be expounding them*).

502. "And whensoever anyone amongst us openeth his mouth, so that he may speak concerning any conformation, that form is localized and awaiteth the voice which goeth forth from our lips, and then it ascendeth in its place and is crowned.

503. "And all the columns on this side and on that side rejoice (*here are understood the holy living creatures, the cherubim, which were before the columns, and the chiefs of the angelic guards, and they are said to have come hither*); because they hear that which before they knew not.* And in the sound of your voices are heard the rushing of countless chariots (*the noise of the wings of the hosts of the angelic chariots of God, rushing onwards*); and they stand here around you in multitudes, awaiting the speeeh of your voice.

504. "O blessed are ye in the world to come! because all the words which go forth from your mouth are all holy, all true, which err not, neither on the right nor yet on the left (*seeing they are the holy names of God*).

* I must again remind the reader that Rabbi Schimeon and his companions are speaking as symbolizing the action of the Sephiroth in the creation, and that when it is said the angels, &c., wait for the words from their lips, it signifies symbolically the way in which the angels, &c., were created by the word of the Deity in his Sephirotic form. And when it is said that "they hear that which before they knew not," it signifies the creation of forms, powers, and attributes which at the beginning of time existed not.

505. "God, the holy and blessed one, rejoiceth to hear these things, and He listeneth unto these words until He himself shall give sentence, for in the world to come all these holy words shall be enumerated for the second time.

506. "Concerning you is it written, Cant. vii. 9: 'And the roof of thy mouth, like the best wine for my beloved, that goeth down sweetly, causing the lips of those that are asleep to speak.'

507. "What is this? 'Causing the lips of those that are asleep to speak.' Because even in the world to come shall your lips utter the words of the law before Him."

CHAPTER XXV.

THE INGRESS OF MICROPROSOPUS.

508. "Now take ye your places, and apply the science (*the Qabalah*) to describe how the parts of Microprosopus are conformed, and how He is clothed with His conformations, from the forms of the Ancient of Days, the Holy of the Holy Ones, the Withdrawn of the Withdrawn ones, the Concealed one of All.

509. "For now wisdom requireth that ye judge a true judgment, becoming and honourable; so that ye may dispose all the conformations as accurately as possible.

510. "But the conformations of Microprosopus are disposed from the forms of Macroprosopus; and his constituent parts are expanded on this side and on that under a human form, so that there may be manifest in Him the Spirit of the Concealed One in every part.

511. "So that He may be placed upon His throne, because it is written, Ezek. i. 26: 'And above the likeness

of a throne, the appearance as the likeness of a man upon it above.'

512. "'Like as the appearance of a man;' because that (form) includeth all forms. 'Like as the appearance of a man;' because He includeth all names. 'Like as the appearance of a man.' Because He includeth all secret things which have been said or propounded before the world was created, even although they have not been substituted herein." *

CHAPTER XXVI.

CONCERNING THE EDOMITE KINGS.

513. Behold! this have we learned in the "Book of Concealed Mystery": that the Ancient of the Ancient Ones before that He prepared His conformations † (*in the equilibrium of balance*) formed certain kings, collected certain kings, and gave due proportion unto certain kings; but they only subsisted (*for a time*) until He could expel them; and in that time hath He concealed them.

514. This is intimated in those words, Gen. xxxvi. 31: "And these are the kings which have reigned in ADVM,‡

* This brings in the subject of the worlds of unbalanced force which are said by the Zohar to have been created and destroyed prior to the creation of the present world. These worlds of unbalanced force are typified by the Edomite kings. (See Introduction.)

† As the Sephiroth proceed each from the preceding one in the series, it is evident that before the counterbalancing Sephira is formed, the force in the preceding Sephira is unbalanced; *e.g.*, the fourth Sephira is Gedulah or Chesed, Mercy; and the fifth Sephira is Geburah or Pachad, Sternness; therefore, till Geburah appears, Gedulah is unbalanced, and this condition is the reign of one of the Edomite kings; but when Geburah appears, his reign is over.

‡ ADVM = 1+4+6+40 = 51 = NA = Failure. AN = also 51, and means pain. *Ergo*, also unbalanced force is the source alike of failure and of pain.

Edom." In the land of Edom; that is, in the place wherein all judgments exist.

515. But all these subsisted not until the White Head* of the Ancient of the Ancient Ones was disposed (*in its ordination*).

516. When this was conformed, He disposed all the inferior conformations, and all the superior and inferior forms were thus arranged.

517. Thence we learn that unless the head (*or ruling power, or government*) of a nation, whatever form of government it may happen to be, be first properly constituted, that nation cannot be properly ruled. For if the head be first disposed aright, then all things can be ordained, but if that be not first disposed aright, neither can the nation be governed aright.

518. The ordering of all things is from the Ancient of Days. For before that He was disposed in His conformation, nothing could be ordained, because as yet it was first necessary that Himself † should be ordained; and all the worlds were desolate.

519. Which these words intimate, *ibid.* 32: "And there reigned in Edom Bela, the son of Beor."

520. "And there reigned in Edom." Here is a certain venerable Arcanum hidden; for herein is that place intimated wherein all the judgments are collected together, and whence they depend.

521. "Bela, the son of Beor." This is the tradition. This denoteth the most rigorous judicial decree, for whose cause there are collected together a thousand times a thousand authors of mourning and woe.

522. "And the name of his city is Dinhabah." What is DNHBH, *Dinhabah?* As if it were to be said, "Give forth judgment. Like as it is written, Prov. xxx. 15: "The horse-leech hath two daughters, crying, 'Give, give.'"

* This is another title of the Crown, Kether, the first Sephira. (See Introduction.)

† Because He is the Absolute One, the Eheieh Asher Eheieh.

523. But when he ascendeth, so that he may be conformed therein, he cannot subsist and he cannot consist. Wherefore? Because the form of the man is not as yet constituted.

524. What is the reason of this? Because the constitution of man containeth all things under this form, and in that form are all things disposed.

525. And because that constitution of Adam was not as yet found, they (*the Edomite Kings*) could not subsist, nor be conformed, and they were destroyed.

526. Have they then been abolished, and are all these included in (*the supernal*) man? For truly they were abolished that they might be withdrawn from form, until there should come forth the representation of Adam.

527. But when that form is configurated, they all exist, and have been restored in another condition.

528. Some among them are mitigated, and (*some*) are not mitigated; but evidently there are certain of them which have not been mitigated.

529. And if thou shalt say: "Also it is written, 'and he died,' surely that denoteth that they were altogether abolished." I answer that it is not so; but whosoever descendeth from his former position wherein he was before, concerning such an one is it said in Scripture that he died.

530. Like as it is written, Exod. ii. 23: "And the King of Egypt died." Because he descended from the former condition wherein he was.

531. But after that Adam was constituted they are called by other names, and are mitigated in a permanent condition through him; and they exist in their place, and are all called by other names and not by their former (*appellations*).

532. Excepting that one* concerning whom it is written, Gen. xxxvi. 39: "And the name of his wife

*Hadar, HDR.

was Mehetabel, the daughter of Matred, the daughter of Mezahab.

533. For what reason? Because they were not abolished like the others. Wherefore? Because they were male and female, like as the palm-tree, which groweth not unless there be both male and female.

534. And because now they are found male and female, and it is not written concerning them that they died like as the others, but remained in a fixed condition.

535. But they were not (*definitely composed*) until the form of the man was composed (*that is, the supernal man*). But after that the form of the supernal Adam was constituted, they were restored in another condition, and came in proper order.

CHAPTER XXVII.

CONCERNING THE SKULL OF MICROPROSOPUS AND ITS APPURTENANCES; NAMELY, CONCERNING THE SUBTLE AIR, AND THE FIRE, AND THE DEW.

536. This is the tradition. When the White Head* propounded unto Himself to superadd ornament unto His own adornment, He constituted, prepared, and produced one single spark from His intense splendour of light. He fanned it and condensed it (or conformed it).

537. And He developed His thought, and extended it in three hundred and seventy directions.

538. And the spark subsisted, and waited until the pure air went forth which involved it around; and an ultimate extension having been made, He produced a certain hard skull (*bounded*) on four sides.†

* Another title for the crown, Kether. (See Introduction.)

† By the letters of the Tetragram.

539. And in that pure subtle air was the spark absorbed and comprehended and included therein.

540. Dost thou not think therein? Truly it is hidden therein.

541. And therefore is that skull expanded in its sides; and that air is the most concealed attribute of the Ancient of Days.

542. In the spirit which is hidden in that skull there are expanded fire on the one side and air on the other. And the subtle air is whirled about it from this side, and the subtle fire is whirled about it from that side.

543. What is the fire in this place? But verily it is not fire, but that splendour which is included in the subtle air, and it shineth in two hundred and seventy worlds.

544. And rigour or judgment is found therefrom; and therefore it is called the hard skull.

545. Within that skull are nine thousand myriads of worlds, which receive the influx from it, and are at peace above it.

546. In that skull distilleth the dew* from the White Head, which is ever filled therewith; and from that dew are the dead raised unto life.

547. And that dew hath in itself two colours. From the White Head there is a whiteness in it, which entirely comprehendeth all whiteness.

548. But whensoever it remaineth in that head of Microprosopus, there appeareth in it a redness, like as in crystal, which is white, and there appeareth a red colour in the white colour.

549. And therefore is it written, Dan. xii. 2: "And many of them that sleep in the dust of the earth shall awake, some to everlasting life, and some to shame and everlasting contempt."

* This subtle air, fire, and dew are analogous to the three "mother letters" of the "Sepher Yetzirah," A, M, and SH; the letter A symbolising air, the medium between M the water, and SH the fire.

550. "To everlasting life." Because they are worthy of that whiteness which cometh from Macroprosopus, even from the Ancient of Days.

551. "To shame and everlasting contempt." Because they are worthy of that redness of Microprosopus.

552. And all things are contained in that dew as is intimated in these words, Isa. xxvi. 19: "Because the dew of lights is thy dew"—where there is a duality of expression.

553. And that dew, which distilleth, distilleth daily upon the field of apples, in colour white and red.

554. This skull shineth in two colours toward this side and toward that.

555. And from that subtle air, from the skull, there are expanded in His countenance one hundred and fifty myriads of worlds; and therefore is He called Zauir Aphin (or Anpin), Microprosopus, the Lesser Countenance.

556. But in that time, when there is need, is His countenance expanded and made vast, because He looketh back upon the countenance of the Ancient of the Ancient Ones, from whom is the life of the universe.

557. And from that skull there is a place of exit in one place unto those which are below; and they reflect His light towards the Ancient of Days, when they ascend in numeration beneath the wand.*

558. Therefore is His skull cleft beneath, when (the inferiors) ascend in numeration, and from this cleavage a reflection of light ariseth toward the Ancient of Days.

* This statement will be utterly unintelligible to the ordinary reader, unless he is told that there are four secret qabalistical symbols attached to the four letters of Tetragrammaton—viz., the wand to I, the cup of libation to H, the sword to V and the shekel of gold to H final. The wand in the text refers to the I, *Yod*, of the Ancient One, hidden and concealed in the I of IHVH, and at the head of the Sephiroth.

CHAPTER XXVIII.

CONCERNING THE BRAIN AND MEMBRANE OF THE BRAIN OF MICROPROSOPUS.

559. In the cavities of the skull three hollow places are found wherein is located the brain.

560. And a thin membrane is placed therein, but not a thick membrane, hidden also as that of the Ancient of Days.

561. And therefore is this brain expanded, and it shineth (or proceedeth) in thirty-two* paths. The same is that which is written, Gen. ii. 7: "And a river went forth out of Eden."

562. Also we have learned that in the three hollow places of the skull the brain is contained.

563. Out of the first cavity proceedeth a certain fountain of the brain in four directions, and it goeth forth from the skull, in whose cavity are contained those thirty-two paths which are the spirits of wisdom.

564. Out of the second cavity there goeth forth and expandeth a second certain fountain, and the fifty gates (*of the Understanding*) are opened.

565. In those fifty gates are contained the fifty days of the law; the fifty years of the jubilee; and the fifty thousand generations wherein the most holy God—blessed be He!—intendeth to restore and commemorate His Spirit in them.

566. From the third cavity there go forth a thousand times a thousand conclaves and assemblies, wherein DOTH,† *Daath*, Knowledge, is contained and dwelleth.

* These are the thirty-two paths of the "Sepher Yetzirah," symbolised by the ten numbers of the decad, and the twenty-two letters of the Hebrew alphabet.

† It is to be remembered that, according to the "Book of Concealed Mystery," Daath is the conjunction of the second and third Sephiroth, Wisdom and Understanding, the I and H of IHVH, the Supernal Father and Mother.

567. And the hollow place of this cavity is placed between the other two cavities;* and all those conclaves are filled from either side.

568. This is that which is written, Prov. ii. 4: "And in knowledge shall the conclaves be filled."

569. And those three are expanded over the whole body, on this side and on that, and with them doth the whole body cohere, and the body is contained by them on every side, and through the whole body are they expanded and diffused.

CHAPTER XXIX.

CONCERNING THE HAIR OF MICROPROSOPUS.

570. WE have learned that from the skull of His head (*i.e., of Microprosopus*) hang one thousand times a thousand myriad myriads of locks of black hair, and they are intertwined together each to the other, and they are mingled together.

571. But there is no classification made of the locks of hair separately, because pure and impure alike adhere to each other therein, and here (*the description above given*) mentions both pure and impure together.

572. In all those sides which are pure, and in all those which are impure, there are intricate and dense locks of hair, some of which are soft, some hard.

573. And in single locks doth the hair hang down, curls upon curls, which emit flames, and hang down in beautiful and strong array, like those of a brave hero victorious in war.

574. They are excellent as the great and foliated cedars. This is that which is written, Cant. v. 15: "Excellent as the cedars."

* As the mediating path between them.

575. The curling locks are parted on this side and on that above the head.

576. Also we have learned that they remain in curls because they proceed from many fountains of the three canals of the brain.

577. For from the fountain of one cavity of the skull proceedeth the hair, and it becomes curls upon curls (*formed*), from the fountains proceeding from that cavity.

578. From the second cavity there go forth fifty fountains, and from those fountains the hair issueth, and it becometh curls upon curls, and they are mingled with the other locks.

579. From the third cavity there go forth a thousand times a thousand conclaves and assemblies, and from them all the hair issueth; and it becometh curls upon curls, and they are mingled with the other locks.

580. And therefore are those locks so curling, and all the progeny of them is produced from the three cavities of the brain of the skull.

581. And all those curls hang down and are spread over the sides of the ears.

582. And therefore is it written, Dan. ix. 18: "Incline thine ear, O my God, and hear."

583. And in those curls there are found alike right and left,* light and dark, mercy and judgment, and everything (*that hath in itself the qualities of*) right and left dependeth thence (*from Microprosopus*), and not from the Ancient One.†

584. In the parting of the hair appeareth a certain slender path, which hath a certain connection with that path of the Ancient of Days, and from that path are divided six hundred and thirteen paths,‡ which are

* Whereas Macroprosopus is symbolized only by the right side of the profile.

† For the reason I have given in the preceding note.

‡ The precepts of the law are said to be 613 in number, which is also expressed by Gematria in the words "Moses our Rabbi"; MSHH RBINV, *Mosheh Rabbino* = 40+300+5+200+2+10+50+6=613.

distributed among the paths of the precepts of the law.

585. Like as it is written, Ps. xxv. 6: 'All the paths of Tetragrammaton are mercy and truth unto such as keep His covenant and His testimony."

586. We have learned that in the single locks a thousand times a thousand utterances of the speech of Tetragrammaton are found, which depend from the single locks.

587. Among them some are hard (*rigorous*) and some soft (*merciful*), as (*belonging unto*) the Lord of the equilibrium (or, the Lord of mercy, who is an equilibrium between these); and therefore is He (*Microprosopus*) said to include right and left.

CHAPTER XXX.

CONCERNING THE FOREHEAD OF MICROPROSOPUS.

588. THE forehead of the skull is the inspection of inspection, and it is not uncovered, except in that time when it is necessary to visit sinners for the purpose of examining their deeds.

589. Also we have learned that when that forehead is uncovered, all the lords of judgment are stirred up, and the whole universe is brought under judgment.

590. Save in that time when the prayers of the Israelites ascend before the Ancient of Days, and entreat mercy for His children; then is uncovered the forehead of the benevolence of benevolences,* and it shineth down upon this (*forehead*) of Microprosopus, and judgment is quieted.

591. Over this forehead there goeth forth a certain

* Namely, that of Macroprosopus.

portion of hair, which is extended over it from the brain, which produceth the fifty gates (*of understanding*).

592. And when it is expanded, that brow glows with anger; it is the inspector of the sinners of the world—namely, of those who are shameless in their deeds.

593. Like as it is written, Jer. iii. 3: "And thou hadst the forehead of a woman who is a whore, thou refusedst to be ashamed."

594. And we have learned that that hair subsisteth not in that part of the forehead; so that it may be uncovered against those who remain steadfast in their iniquities.

595. And when the Holy One — blessed be He! — is awakened, that He may be pleased with the just, the Countenance of the Ancient of Days shineth upon the Countenance of Microprosopus, and His forehead (*that of Macroprosopus*) is uncovered, and illuminateth that forehead (that of Macroprosopus), and then is called the time of benevolence.

596. But as often as judgment threateneth, and that forehead of Microprosopus is uncovered, there is uncovered the forehead of the Ancient of the Ancient Ones, and judgment is mitigated and is not exercised.

597. We have learned that that forehead is expanded into two hundred thousand rednesses of rednesses, which are contained therein, and are included therein.

598. And when the forehead of Microprosopus is uncovered, licence is given unto all those to destroy. But when the forehead of the benevolence of benevolences is uncovered, so that it may shine upon that forehead (*of Microprosopus*) and upon all those (*rednesses*), then are they quieted.

599. Also we have learned by tradition: Twenty-four superior judgments are found, and they are all called NTzCHIM, *Netzachim*, or Victories; howsoever, while (*in the arrangement of letters, NTzCHIM, the singular*) NTzCH, *Netzach*, is called Victory (*i.e., means that*), the neighbouring

letters * (*M and N in NTzCHIM*), being permuted, (*we obtain MTzCHIN singular*), MTzCH, *Metzach* (*meaning*) forehead.

600. Therefore (*the same word signifieth*) forehead and Victory, which is in the plural victories. And this is that which is given by tradition: The Victory of victories. And they are in the forehead, but certain among them are extended in the body in (*certain*) known parts.

601. This is the exotic tradition: What is that which is written, 1 Sam. xv. 29: "Also the Netzach of Israel doth not lie nor repent, for He is not man that He should repent."

602. Now have we declared that Arcanum according to its constitution. All that Victory which is expanded in the body, at that time when the world is to be judged and converted, admitteth repentance, neither executeth judgment if they be converted.

603. For what reason? Because the matter resteth in that place which is called Adam, and He may repent.

604. But if that Victory be seen and uncovered in that part of the head just spoken of — namely, the forehead—there is neither time nor opportunity for repentance.

605. Wherefore? Because it is not that place which is called Adam, for the countenance and the nose are not uncovered, but the forehead alone.

606. And in that part—(*i.e., the forehead*) the whole countenance is not found, for that (*forehead*) is not called Adam, and therefore is it said: "He is not a man that He may repent" (*i.e., He, HOA VA, H, is not Adam*), *&c.*). So also is it as regardeth the (*proportion of*) Victory in the other parts of the body (*of Macroprosopus*).

* *I.e.*, in their usual place in the order of the alphabet.

CHAPTER XXXI.

CONCERNING THE EYES OF MICROPROSOPUS.

607. THE eyes of the head (*of Microprosopus*) are diverse from all other eyes. There is a shadowy darkness cast by the eyebrows which is (*as if it were*) painted above the eyes, whence all eyes are overshadowed with a dark shade.

608. Curling hairs hang down from the curls of the hair which is above them, and mark the form of the eyebrows above the eyes, at the commencement of the forehead.

609. And in both (*the eyebrows*) are contained seven hundred times a thousand lords of inspection who reside above the eyelids.

610. In the eyelids radiate one thousand four hundred myriads (*of hairs*), which adhere to the edges and form the eyelashes; and far above these is the inspection of the eye of the Ancient of Days.*

611. And as often as those eyelids (*of Microprosopus*) are raised, the same eye (*i.e., that of Macroprosopus*) appeareth, just as when the eyes of any man are opened when he awaketh from sleep.

612. And (*the eyes of Microprosopus*) behold the open eye (*of Macroprosopus shining down upon them*), and they are rendered brilliant with a certain brilliant whiteness of the good eye (*i.e., that of Macroprosopus, because in Him "all is right"—i.e., good—and there is no left*).

613. Like as it is written, Cant. v. 12: "Washed with milk." What is "with milk?" With this excellent primal whiteness.

* True to all the previous symbolism, the eye of the Ancient of Days, Macroprosopus, is here spoken of, instead of eyes in the plural number, seeing that, as I have before remarked, he is rather to be symbolized by a profile than by a full face.

614. And in that time is there found with Him (*i.e.*, *Microprosopus*) an intuition of mercy, and therefore the prayer of the Israelites ascendeth, because His eyes are opened (*i.e.*, *those of Microprosopus*), and are whitened with that whiteness (*of the eye of Macroprosopus*).

615. Like as it is written, Ps. xliv. 23: "Awake; why sleepest Thou, O Tetragrammaton? Arise."

616. And truly as often as His eyes are not open, all the lords of judgment subdue the Israelites, and the other nations have dominion over them.

617. But whensoever He openeth His eyes, these are illuminated from the good eye (*of Macroprosopus*), and mercy is over Israel; and His eye turneth around and executeth vengeance upon the other nations.

618. This is that same which is written, Ps. xxxv. 23: "Awake, and arise." "Awake!" and (*Thine eye*) shall be illuminated with that whiteness. "Arise!" so that it may exercise judgment upon those who have overcome them.

619. When his eyes are opened they appear beautiful as those of doves; in colour, white, red, and black, and golden yellow.

620. And this eye (otherwise, this whiteness) is not uncovered except when it is looked upon by the good eye, and then all those colours are covered (otherwise, bathed) with this whiteness of the rays.

621. From those colours, when they are uncovered, go forth seven eyes of Providence, which issue from the black of the eye.

622. This is that which is said, Zac. iii. 9: "Upon one stone seven eyes."

623. What is the "one stone?" The black of the eye

624. From the red go forth seven emissaries, who deflect towards the left side, and they flame with fire, which is toward the north side, and they are combined, so that they may be expanded into the world for the purpose of uncovering the ways of sinners.

625. This is that which is written, Zach. iv. 10: "Those seven are the eyes of Tetragrammaton going forth throughout the whole earth."

626. From the yellow go forth seven pure splendours (otherwise lights), which are turned towards the south side, and they are combined so that they may be extended into the world, towards those ways which are necessary to be uncovered (otherwise towards those deeds, &c.).

627. Like as it is written, Job xxxiv. 21: "Because His eyes are upon the ways of man." And when they are illuminated with that whiteness, then they behold all the lords of truth, in order to do good unto the world because of them; and every glance (*of those eyes*) is benevolent towards Israel.

628. But with the red colour He beholded those who are bound; which is intimated in these words, Exod. iii. 7: "In seeing have I seen;" "In seeing," for the purpose of doing good unto them; "I have seen," that by vindicating them I may deliver them from their afflictors.

629. And therefore is it written, Ps. xliv. 24: "Awake: wherefore sleepest Thou, O Tetragrammaton? Arise! forsake us not for ever." "Awake and arise." There are two inspections, two openings, two good things; there is mercy, there is also vengeance.

630. The first colour is red, hidden and inclosed within red; in comparison with it, all other reds do not seem to be (*red*).*

631. Around this red goeth a certain black thread (*of colour*), and surroundeth it.

632. This second colour is black, like that stone which goeth forth from the abyss once in a thousand years into the great sea.

* Meaning that it is so brilliant that all other red colours seem poor and pale in comparison with it.

633. And when that stone* goeth forth there cometh a tempest and a storm upon the great sea,† and its waters are troubled, and (*their motion soundeth as*) a voice, and they are heard by the great fish which is called Leviathan.

634. And this stone goeth forth, and is whirled onward in the current of the sea, and goeth forth thence; and this is so great a blackness‡ that beside it all other blacknesses are as nought (otherwise, now it is withdrawn because all the other paths are hidden and enshrouded by it).

635. And such is the blackness of the black (*part of*) the eye, which includeth and concealeth all the remaining blacknesses; and about that blackness there is found a certain red thread (of colour) which surroundeth that blackness.

636. The third colour is the yellow of all yellows, which includeth and concealeth all other yellows, and in the circumference of that yellow there whirl around two threads (*of colour*), a red thread on the one direction, and a black thread in another direction; and they surround that yellow colour.

637. But when that white brilliance whirleth around it, and the eye flameth with that white brilliance, all those other colours are not at rest, and are submerged in the lowest depths thereof; the red, the yellow, and the black are not seen, only that white brilliance alone; which receiveth its light from Him, even from the Ancient of Days.

638. And from that (*white brilliance*) all the inferiors shine, neither is any colour seen save that white brilliance alone. And therefore are all the lords of red-

* Cf. Rev. viii. 8. This also suggests alchemical symbolism.

† The great sea is Binah, and the great fish is Leviathan, "whose head is broken by the waters of the great sea." (See the Introduction, "Book of Concealed Mystery," i. § 28; Ps. lxxiv. 13; and Rev. xiii.)

‡ Cf. the "blackest of the black" of Hermes Trismegistus.

ness and blackness, which are as it were twin (*colours*), displaced.

639. This is the same which is written, Cant. iv. 2: "Which go up from the washing, which are all twins."

640. What is this, "From the washing?" From that white brilliance of the excellent holy eye; for all are twins, the one (*colour*) is as the other.*

641. But truly doth not he (the author of the Canticles) say that the teeth are each in turn like a shorn flock; and thou sayest that all these are twins?

642. Nevertheless, the sense is that this whiteness of them is as that whiteness of the eyes (*of Microprosopus*) when they are made brilliant by the white brilliance of the supernal eye (*of Macroprosopus*).

643. And the just are about to understand and behold that thing in the Spirit of Wisdom.

644. Like as it is written, Isa. lii. 3: "Because they shall see eye to eye." When? "When Tetragrammaton shall bring again Zion."

645. Also it is written, Num. xiv. 14: "By whom Thou, O Tetragrammaton! art seen eye to eye:"† and then the opening of the eyes is toward good.

646. For there is an opening of the eyes toward good, and there is also another (*opening of the eyes*) toward evil.

647. Toward good, like as it is written, Dan. ix. 18: "Open Thine eyes and behold our desolations, and the city over which Thy name hath been pronounced." Here it is toward good.

648. But toward evil, like as it is written, Isa. xxxiii. 20: "Thine eyes shall see Jerusalem a quiet habitation, a tabernacle that shall not be taken down; not one of the stakes thereof shall ever be removed." Here truly it is toward good and toward evil, because the one existeth not without the other.

* *I.e.*, the black and the red, which are here represented as simultaneously involving each other.

† In our version it is translated "face to face," and not "eye to eye"; but in the original Hebrew it is OIN BOIN, *Ayin Be-Ayin*, "eye to eye."

649. We have learned it in the "Book of Concealed Mystery." What is this? "Thine eyes shall see Jerusalem a quiet habitation." Is not Jerusalem therefore a quiet habitation? Also it is written, Isa. i. 21: "Justice dwelt therein." But in the place wherein justice is found there is not rest, neither is it at peace (otherwise: In the place wherein judgment dwelleth and is found, this justice is not rest, &c.).

650. For verily this is the true interpretation: "Thine eyes shall see Jerusalem a quiet habitation" (is thus to be explained). The habitation is said to be quiet, in respect of the Ancient of Days, who looketh upon those eyes (*of Microprosopus*).

651. For truly His eye is quiet and tranquil; the eye of mercy the eye which altereth not from this aspect unto any other aspect.

652. And therefore is it written OINK* (*instead of* OINIK) "They shall behold Thine eye:" not Thine eyes, (*seeing* OINK *is written*) without the second I, *Yod.*

653. But how cometh it that it is said Jerusalem, and not Zion? It is properly thus said for the purpose of subjugating judgment which was found therein, and for exciting mercy upon it.

654. Also have we learned this. It is written, Deut. xi. 12: "The eyes of Tetragrammaton thy God are upon it, from the beginning of the year even unto the end of the year." This is that which is written: "Justice dwelt therein;" because therein are found many most severe judgments, as in all other instances.

655. But in the time to come there shall be found therein one eye of mercy (*namely*) the eye of the Ancient of Days.

656. This is that which is intimated, Isa. liv. 7: "But with great mercies will I gather thee."

657. Where, because it is said "with mercies," what is

* OINK signifies "thine eye," in the singular.

(*the meaning of the adjective*) "great" (*used herewith*): Assuredly because mercy is duplicated, (*namely*) the mercy of the Ancient of Days (*Macroprosopus*), which is called "great mercies."

658. And the mercy of Microprosopus, which is called mercies plain and unqualified, seeing that in Him there are right and left,* (*symbolizing the balance of*) Justice and Mercy. And therefore is it said: "And in great mercies will I gather thee;" those, namely, of the Ancient of Days.

659. This have we learned. In those eyes (*of Microprosopus*), and in the two colours of them—namely, in the red and in the black—there are said to abide two tears, and when He, even the Holy of the Holy Ones, desireth to have mercy upon the Israelites, then He sendeth down those two tears so that they may grow sweet in the (*waters of the*) great sea.

660. The great sea, which is that of excellent wisdom, so that in that stream (otherwise, white brilliance) and in that fountain they may be cleansed; and they go forth from the great sea, and there is mercy upon the Israelites.

CHAPTER XXXII.

CONCERNING THE NOSE OF MICROPROSOPUS.

661. We have learned it in the "Book of Concealed Mystery." The nose of Microprosopus. From the nose is the countenance known. In this nose is diverse symbolism.

662. For it is written, Ps. xviii. 8: "There went up

* Right and left exist in Microprosopus, while in Macroprosopus all is right. The latter is rather to be symbolised by a profile, as I have before remarked, than by a full face, as in the case of the former.

a smoke out of His nose,* and fire out of His mouth devoured; coals were kindled by it."

663. "There went up a smoke out of His nose." In this smoke are included both the fire and the burning coals; for there is no smoke without fire, neither fire without smoke. Truly all things result (*herefrom:* otherwise, are kindled *herein*) and go forth from His nose.

664. Also we have learned that when these three things are associated together which are included in that smoke which issueth from the nose, the nose† is lengthened.

665. And therein are two colours, for the smoke bloweth and rusheth forth black and red; and they call it AP,‡ *Aph,* wrath; and CHIMH, *Chimah,* fervour; and MSHCHITH, *Meshachith,* perdition.

666. And if thou sayest wrath and fervour, it is well, since it is written, Deut. ix. 19: "Since I have feared because of wrath and fervour." For these are the black and red smoke. But whence is added MSHCHITH, *Meshachith,* perdition?

667. Because it is written, Gen. xiii. 10: "Before that Tetragrammaton destroyed Sodom and Gomorrah." But the word SHCHTH, *Shachith,* denoted perdition brought about by burning, kindled fire.

668. Also we have learned that there are five § GBVRAN, *Geboran,* severities in this conformation of Microprosopus, and they ascend in one thousand and four hundred severities, GBVRAN; and they are extended in

* The ordinary English version renders it "nostrils" and not "nose," but in the Hebrew the word is singular.

† Isa. xlviii. 9 is translated in the ordinary English version: "For my name's sake will I defer mine anger;" but Parkhurst in his Hebrew and Chaldee Lexicon, art. CHTM, says the correct rendering is "for my name's sake will I lengthen my nose." Knorr de Rosenroth, in his Latin version of § 664, renders it by "corrugatur," which is hardly correct.

‡ The word AP, *Aph,* stands alike for the words "nose" and "anger."

§ If we carefully examine this obscure passage, I think we shall find that the number five is the key to unlock its symbolism; for five is the fifth Sephira, *Geburah,* GBVRH, Strength or Severity, which operates

His nose, and in His mouth, and in His arms, and in His hands, and in His fingers.

669. And therefore is it written, Ps. cvi. 2: "Who can declare the GBVRVTH, *Geburoth*, powers of Tetragrammaton?"

670. Hence it is written, "powers," Geburoth (*in the plural number*); and it is written, 1 Chron. xxix. 11: "Thine! O Tetragrammaton, are Gedulah and Geburah,"* in the singular (*number*).

671. Assuredly thus have we learned. When all those severities are amalgamated into one, then are they called one Geburah, GBVRH.

672. And all those powers, Geboran, commence to descend from the nose. And from it depend a thousand times a thousand and four hundred myriads in their single (*forms*).†

673. And from that smoke which issueth from his nose depend a thousand times a thousand myriads, and four hundred and five which belong to this (*idea of*) Severity.‡ For all the severities depend from this nose.

674. For it is written, Ps. cxlv. 4: "From generation unto generation shall they praise thy works, and announce thy GBVRVTH, *Geburoth*."

675. And when that GBVRH, *Geburah*, Strength, commenceth (*to be manifested*), all the severities radiate thence, and are sharpened, until they descend in the form of a swift-whirling fire-flaming sword (Gen. iii. 24.)

through Judgment, and ultimately through the numbers and intelligences of the planet Mars. Now, the 1,400 severities are the fivefold form of RP, *Raph*, which = the idea of terror, and RP = 280, which × 5 = 1,400. And the least number of 1,400 is 1 + 4 + 0 + 0 = 5. Also 1,400 = ATH = chaos, or substance of anything. Finally, these are extended into five parts of Macroprosopus—viz., nose, mouth, arms, hands, fingers. And the number 5 = H.

* See Introduction. GBVR (the root being GBR) = 211 = IAR, a flood. This is of course by Gematria.

† This formidable sounding arrangement is only our previous 1,400, considered on another plane of operation, in the material world.

‡ This is 1,400 again in its most material forms in Asiah; the number five at the end is simply the number of the Sephira of Severity added to the other.

676. It is written, Gen. xix. 13: "For we will destroy this place." Also it is written, Gen. xiii. 10: "Before that Tetragrammaton destroyed Sodom and Gomorrah?" And again, Gen. xix. 24: "Tetragrammaton rained upon Sodom and Gomorrha."

677. Assuredly thus have we learned: There is no judge over the wicked, but they themselves convert the measure of Mercy into a measure of Judgment.

678. But how do they convert it thus? Also it is written, Mal. iii. 6: "I, Tetgrammaton, change not."

679. Assuredly as many times as the Ancient of the Ancient Ones and that White Head uncovereth the benevolence of benevolences, great mercies are found everywhere.

680. But when that is not uncovered, all the judgments of Microprosopus are prepared; and in this manner, if it be permitted us to say so, Mercy becometh Judgment; that is, the most Ancient One of all.

681. We have learned in Barietha*: "When the Ancient of the Ancient Ones uncovereth the benevolence of benevolences, all those lights which are called by a similar name shine, and Mercy is found in all things.

682. But when that Concealed One of the Concealed Ones is not uncovered, and those lights shine not, judgments are stirred up, and Judgment is exercised.

683. Who therefore is the cause of that Judgment? The benevolence of the benevolences, because it is not uncovered, and therefore do sinners change Mercy into Judgment (*as regardeth themselves*).

684. But because this is said, Gen. xix. 24: "From Tetragrammaton out of heaven," it is said concerning Zauir Anpin, Microprosopus.

685. And whence is this obtained? Because it is written (*in the preceding passage*): MN HSHMIM, *Men Ha-Shamayim*, out of heaven. (*But the word*

* See *ante*, § 388 of this book.

HShMIM, Ha-Shamayim, is equivalent to) ASh VMIM,* *Ash Ve-Mim*, fire and water, Mercy and Judgment, in the antithesis of that (*condition*) wherein no Judgment is found at all.

686. We have learned that this nose (*of Microprosopus*) is short,† and when the smoke commenceth to issue therefrom, it departeth thence swiftly, and Judgment is exercised.

687. But what hindereth that nose that it may not produce smoke? The nose of the Ancient and Holy One; for He is also called before all others ARK APIM, *Arikh Aphim*, Long of Nose.

688. And this is the Arcanum which we have learned: Between the two words, IHVH, IHVH, Tetragrammaton, Tetragrammaton, an accent is interpolated ‡ (*whensoever these two are found in juxtaposition in Scripture*).

689. For wheresoever any name is repeated twice over, a distinction is made (*between them*), as when it is said, Gen. xxii. 11, "Abraham, Abraham;" also, Gen. xlvi. 2, "Jacob, Jacob;" also, 1 Sam. iii. 10, "Samuel, Samuel;" where, by the *Psiq* accent, these pairs of names are distinguished; excepting that place, Exod. iii. 4, "Moses, Moses," where no accent interveneth.

690. For what reason? "Abraham, Abraham," Gen. xxii. 11 (*herein therefore is an accent introduced because*

* In the "Sepher Yetzirah," to which work I have already had occasion to refer more than once, the letter Sh is said to symbolize fire, and therefore ShMIM may be said to be fire and water.

† In contradistinction to that of Macroprosopus, who is called also Arikh Aphim, Long of Nose, as well as Arikh Anpin, Vast of Countenance.

‡ This accent is called *Psiq*, and in the grammar of Gesenius is classed as the twentieth accent, or the fifth of the third series known as the "lesser distinctives." It is represented by a vertical line placed between the two words to which it applies. An example of its use is to be found in Exod. xxxiv. 6: "Tetragrammaton, Tetragrammaton (*between these two words a Psiq accent is introduced*), merciful and gracious, longsuffering and abundant in goodness and truth." It is worthy of note that the word here translated "long-suffering" is ARK APIM, *Arikh Aphim*, Long of Nose.

that) the latter (*of these two names*) denoteth that which is perfect, but the former that which is not as yet perfect; for at this time he is perfected with ten temptations, and therefore is the (*Psiq*) accent interpolated, for at this time he can hardly be said to be the same man as he was before.

691. (*When it is said*) "Jacob, Jacob" (Gen. xlvi. 2), the latter denoteth that which is perfect, the former that which is not as yet perfect; for now the messenger had come to him from his son Joseph, and over him was the Schechinah at rest.

692. Also, now at this time was perfected in the earth the holy tree, similar unto the Supernal One, in having twelve limitations and seventy branches,* which were not hitherto completed; and therefore the latter denoteth that which is perfect, and the former that which is not as yet perfect; whence the accent falleth between them.

693. In the passage, "Samuel, Samuel" (1 Sam. iii. 10), an accent is also interpolated: wherefore? The latter name denoteth that which is perfect; the former that which is not as yet perfect; for now he is a prophet, whereas before this he was not as yet a prophet.

694. But when it is said, Exod. iii. 4: "Moses, Moses," no accent is interpolated, because he was perfect from the very day of his birth, seeing it is written, Exod. ii. 2: "And she saw him, that he was good."

695. So also here between these two names of Tetragrammaton, Exod. xxxiv. 6, the *Psiq* accent is interpolated; for the first is indeed a perfect name, but the latter is thoroughly and completely perfect.

696. But Moses speaketh thus in the place of Judgment, in order that for them he may cause Mercy to

* That is, the *Auts Chaiim*, or tree of life, composed of the Sephiroth and the Schemhamphorasch, the former being ten and the latter seventy-two. The twelve limitations are the twelve sons of Jacob, and the seventy ranches the total number of the combined families.

descend upon Microprosopus from the Most Holy Ancient One.

697. For thus is the tradition. So great was the virtue of Moses that he could make the measures of Mercy descend.

698. And when the Ancient One is uncovered toward Microprosopus all things are beheld in the light of Mercy, and the nose is appeased, and fire and smoke issue not therefrom.

699. Like as it is written, Isa. xlviii. 9: "And with my praise will I defer mine anger for thee."

700. Also we have learned: The nose hath two nostrils. From the one issueth a flaming smoke, and it entereth into the opening of the Great Abyss.

701. And from the other nostril issueth a fire which is kindled by its flame; and it floweth into four thousand worlds, which are upon His left side.

702. Truly, he who is the cause of war is called the fire of Tetragrammaton, the consuming fire, the fire which consumeth all other fires.

703. And that fire is not mitigated save by the fire of the altar.

704. And that smoke which issueth forth from the other nostril is not mitigated unless by the smoke of the sacrifice of the altar. But all things depend from the nose.

705. Therefore is it written, Gen. viii. 12: "And Tetragrammaton smelled a sweet savour." For all these are attributed unto the nose, to smell a savour, and to emit smoke and fire, and red colour, and therefore is it opposed unto the benevolence (*namely, the forehead*).

706. And for that cause is it written, Exod. iv. 14: "And the anger of Tetragrammaton was kindled." Deut. vii. 4: "And the anger of Tetragrammaton will be kindled." Exod. xxii. 24: "And My wrath is kindled." Deut. vi. 15: "Lest the wrath of Tetragrammaton be kindled." Which are all to be understood concerning Zauir Anpin, or Microprosopus.

CHAPTER XXXIII.

CONCERNING THE EARS OF MICROPROSOPUS.

707. THIS have we learned. It is written, 2 Kings xix. 16: "Incline, O God, Thine ear and hear;" namely, that ear which is hidden beneath the hair, and the hair hangeth down over it, and yet the ear is there for the purpose of hearing.

708. And from the inner part of the ear, elaborated with strongly marked concave formations, like a winding spiral ladder, with incurvation on every side.

709. But wherefore with curvings? So that He may hear both good and evil.

710. Also we have learned: From that curving part within the ears depend all those Lords of Wings concerning whom it is written, Eccles. x. 20: "For a bird of the air shall carry the voice, and the Lord of the Wings shall tell the matter."

711. Within that ear, (*the Spirit*) floweth from the three hollow places of the brain into this opening of the ears. And from that afflux (*the Spirit*) the voice departeth into that profound depth (otherwise, incurvation) and is conjoined with (*the Spirit*) in that distillation, as well good as evil.

712. In good: as it is written, Psa. lxix. 33: "For Tetragrammaton heareth the poor." In evil; as it is written, Num. xi. i.: "And Tetragrammaton heard, and His wrath arose, and the fire of Tetragrammaton was kindled against them."

713. And that ear is closed from without, and a depth otherwise an incurvation) proceedeth within that gallery of inspiration from the brain.

714. So that the voice may be collected together within, neither issue forth thence, and that it may be guarded and

shut in on every side; hence it is in the nature of an Arcanum.*

715. Woe unto Him who discloseth secrets! For he who revealeth secrets doth the same thing as if he should deny the superior formation, which is so arranged that the secrets may be collected together, and that they may not issue forth without.

716. Also we have learned in Barietha †: At that time when they call aloud in their troubles, and the hairs are moved from before the ears, the voice entereth into the ears through that channel, and the spirit of distillation from the brain (*entereth into that channel likewise*).

717. And in the brain is it collected (otherwise, and it slideth on into the brain), and departeth through the nostrils of the nose, and is bound, and the nose becometh shorter (*that of Microprosopus, namely*) and gloweth with fire, and fire and smoke issue forth; and from those nostrils are excited all the severities, and vengeance is exercised.

718. Truly before that from those nostrils the fire and smoke issue forth, that voice ascendeth upwards, and slideth into the beginning of the brain; and the two tears flow down from the eyes.

719. And by means of that voice the smoke goeth forth, and the fire from the brightness which openeth those gates; for through that voice which entereth into the ears all these things are excited and urged forth (otherwise, are mingled together).

720. And therefore is it written, Num. xi. 1: "And Tetragrammaton heard, and His wrath was kindled, and the fire of Tetragrammaton was kindled against them." For through that hearing of that voice the whole brain is stirred up.

721. We have learned. It is written, 2 Kings xix. 16: "Incline, O my God, Thine ear;" like as if it should be

* Because in a similar manner a secret is guarded and shut in.

† See *ante*, § 388. Barietha is "Traditio extra urbem."

said, "Let six hundred thousand myriads of those wings which depend from those ears be elongated;" and they are all called the ears of Tetragrammaton.

722. When therefore it is said, "Incline, O Tetragrammaton, Thine ear," (*this phrase*) "Thine ear," is that of Microprosopus.

723. From one cavity of the brain do those ears depend; and from the fifty gates * which proceed from that cavity, this is one gate, which extendeth and goeth forth and openeth into that channel of the ear.

724. Like as it is written, Job xxxiv. 3: "Because the ear trieth words." Also it is written, Ps. vii. 10: "And He trieth the heart and reins."

725. And in proportion to the expansion of that cavity of fifty gates which proceedeth into the body, so is the latter expanded even in that place wherein the heart resideth.

726. Therefore concerning the ear it is said that in it is made probation; and also concerning the heart it is said that in it is made probation; because that they proceed (*alike*) from one place.

727. We have learned in the "Book of Concealed Mystery" that, like as this ear proveth as well the good as the evil, so all things which are in Microprosopus have part good and part evil, right and left, Mercy and Judgment.

728. And this ear is contiguous unto the brain; and because it is contiguous unto the brain, hence that voice is directed into a cavity which entereth into the ear.

729. Therefore concerning the ear it is called hearing; but in this hearing, Binah, the Understanding (*the third Sephira*) is comprehended; for, also, to hear, is the same as to understand, because that thereby all examinations are examined together.

730. And those words of the Lord of Lords are given

* This refers to the "fifty gates of the Understanding"—alluding to the third Sephira.

forth so that they may be heard, so that they may be meditated upon and be understood.

731. Come, behold! it is written, Hab. iii. 1: "O Tetragrammaton! I have heard Thy voice, and was afraid."

732. This passage hath this meaning: When that holy prophet heard and understood and knew, and was occupied with those conformations, it is written: "I was afraid." Rightly was it (*so written*) that he should be afraid and be broken before Him, for these words are said concerning Microprosopus.

733. When further he understood and knew, what is then written? "O Tetragrammaton! revive Thy work in the midst of the years." But concerning the Ancient of Days is this said.

734. And in every passage wherein is found Tetragrammaton, Tetragrammaton, with Yod He twice, or with Aleph Daleth and Yod He, the one belongeth unto Microprosopus, and the other unto the Ancient of the Ancient Ones. For because all these things are one certain thing, hence by one name are they called.

735. Also we have learned. When is the full name expressed? When it is written, IHVH ALHIM, *Tetragrammaton Elohim*. For that is the full name of the Most Ancient of all, and of Microprosopus; and when joined together they are called the full name. But other forms are not called the full name, like as we have established.

736. When it is said, Gen. ii. 8: "And Tetragrammaton Elohim planted," &c., the name is given in full, where the discourse is concerning the planting of the garden; and whensoever Tetragrammaton Elohim occurreth the full name is expressed.

737. In IHVH IHVH all things generally are comprehended, and then mercies are stirred up over all things.

738. (*When it is said*) "O Tetragrammaton! revive Thy work in the midst of the years," concerning the Ancient of Days is it said.

739. What is "Thy work"? Zauir Anpin, Microprosopus.

740. "In the midst of years." These are the former years, which are called IMI QDM, *Yemi Qedem*, former days; and not years, OVLM, *Olahm*, or of the world.

741. The former years are the former days; the years of the world are the days of the world.*

742. And here (*it is said*): "In the midst of the years." What years? The former years.

743. "Revive it." Concerning whom is it said, "Revive it"? Concerning Microprosopus. For all His splendour is preserved by those years, and therefore is it said, "Revive it."

744. "In wrath remember mercy." He looketh to that supernal benignity wherein mercies are excited over all; (*those mercies*) who desire compassion, and to whom mercy is owing.

745. We have learned, Rabbi Schimeon said: "I call to witness the heavens which are above me, towards all those who stand around, that great joy ariseth in all the worlds because of these words.

746. "Also these words excite joy in my heart; and in the veil of excellent expansion are they hidden and do they ascend; and He, the Most Ancient One of all, preserveth them, He, the Concealed and Hidden of all.

747. "And when we began to speak my companions knew not that all these words therein were worthy hereof in any degree.

748. "O how blessed is your portion, companions of this conclave! and blessed is my portion with you in this world, and in the world to come!"

* In connection with § 741, note Ps. lxxvii. 5: "CHSHBTHI IMIM MQDM SHNVTH OVLMIM, I have considered the days of old, the years of ancient times."

CHAPTER XXXIV.

CONCERNING THE BEARD OF MICROPROSOPUS.

749. RABBI SCHIMEON commenced and said, Deut. iv. 4: "And ye shall cleave unto Tetragrammaton your God," &c.

750. What nation is so holy as Israel? for it is written concerning them, Deut. xxxiii. 29: Blessed art thou, O Israel!* who is like unto thee?" Because that they are applied unto God in this world through the holy name.

751. And in the world to come more than here, for therein shall we never be separated from that conclave wherein the just are assembled.

752. And this is that which is written: "And ye shall cleave *in* Tetragrammaton;" for it is not written "CHDBQIM LIHVH, *Chedebeqim Le Tetragrammaton*, Ye shall cleave *unto* Tetragrammaton;" but "BIHVH, *Be Tetragrammaton*, *in* Tetragrammaton," properly.

753. We have learned this. There is a descent from the beard which is venerable, holy, excellent, hidden and concealed in all (*the beard, namely, of Macroprosopus*), through the holy magnificent oil, into the beard of Microprosopus.

754. And if thou shalt say that this beard is not to be found, for that even Solomon only spake of the cheeks,† but not at all of the beard.

755. Truly thus have we learned (*we make answer*) in the "Book of Concealed Mystery." It is that which is hidden and recondite, and of which mention is not made,

* It must not be forgotten that Israel is a mystical name which was substituted for Jacob.

† Namely, in the description in the Song of Solomon, ch. v.

neither is it uncovered; it is that which is venerable and excellent before all things, seeing that it is concealed and hidden.

756. And since the beard is the praise and perfection and dignity of the whole countenance, in these sacred things it is found to be hidden, neither is it discerned.

757. And that beard is the perfection and beauty of the countenance in Microprosopus. In nine conformations is it disposed.

758. But when the venerable beard of the Ancient of the Ancient Ones shineth upon this beard of Microprosopus, then the thirteen fountains of excellent oil flow down upon this beard.

759. And therein are found twenty-two parts, and thence extend the twenty-two letters of the holy law.

760. Also we have learned that this beard departeth from His ears, and descendeth and ascendeth, and toucheth upon the places of fragrance.

761. What are the places of fragrance? Like as it is said, Cant. v. 13: "Like a bed (*singular*) of spices," and not "beds" (*plural*).

762. But this beard of Microprosopus is disposed in nine conformations.

763. And also the hairs being black, and in careful order, like a handsome man, as it is written, Cant. v. 15: "Excellent as the cedars."

764. The first conformation. The hair is conformed from the portion which is above, and there goeth forth therefrom a spark which is of most intense brilliance; and it goeth forth from the Absolute of the pure ether, and passeth beneath the hair of the head, even beneath those locks which are above the ears; and it descendeth in front of the opening of the ears, hair above hair, even unto the beginning of the mouth.

765. The second conformation. The hair goeth forth, and ascendeth from the one part of the mouth even unto the

other part of the opening of the mouth; and it descendeth beneath the mouth unto the other side, hair above hair, in beautiful arrangement.

766. The third conformation. From the midst, beneath the nose, and beneath the two nostrils, there goeth forth a certain path, and short and coarse hairs fill up that path; and the remaining hairs fill up the place from this side unto that, around this path.

767. But this path is not clearly seen (*to be continued*) below (*the mouth*), but only the upper part of it which descendeth even unto the beginning of the lips, and there is this path applied.

768. The fourth conformation. The hair goeth forth and is disposed in order, and ascendeth, and is spread over His cheeks, which are the place of fragrance of the Ancient One.

769. The fifth conformation. The hair is wanting, and there are seen two apples on this side and on that, red as a red rose, and they radiate into two hundred and seventy worlds, which are enkindled thereby.

770. The sixth conformation. The hair goeth forth as in a tress about (*the border of*) the beard, and hangeth down even unto the commencement of the vital organs, but it descendeth not unto the parts about the heart.

771. The seventh conformation. That the hairs do not hang over the mouth, but that the mouth is uncovered on every side, and that the hairs are disposed in order about it.

772. The eighth conformation. That the hairs descend beneath the beard, and cover the throat, so that it cannot be seen; all those hairs are slender, hairs above hairs, plentiful in every part.

773. The ninth conformation. That the hairs are mingled together with those which are joined unto them; and that they all are in equality from the cheeks even unto those hairs which hang down; all are in fair

equality, like a brave man, and like a hero victorious in war.

774. Through these nine conformations there proceed and flow down nine fountains of magnificent oil, and these indeed flow down from that magnificent supernal oil (*of the beard of Macroprosopus* into all those inferiors.

775. Those nine conformations are found in form herein (otherwise, in this beard); and in the perfection of the conformation of this beard is the inferior son of man called the brave man.*

776. For whosoever seeth (*in sleep*) that his beard existeth in proper form,† in him is found courage and strength.

777. Rabbi Schimeon spake unto Rabbi Eleazar, his son, and said: "Arise, O my Son, and expound the parts of the holy beard in its conformations."

778. Rabbi Eleazar arose, and commenced and said, Ps. cxviii. 5: "'I called upon IH, *Yah*, in my distress; *Yah* heard me at large. Tetragrammaton is on my side, I will not fear; what can man do unto me? Tetragrammaton taketh my part with them that help me, and I shall see my desire upon mine enemies. It is better to trust in Tetragrammaton than to put any confidence in man; it is better to trust in Tetragrammaton than to put any confidence in princes.'

779. "Herein are delineated the nine conformations of this beard. For King David had need of these dispositions, that he might vanquish other kings and other nations.

780. "Come, behold! After that he had said these nine conformations, he added (verse 10): 'All nations compassed me about, but in the name of Tetragrammaton I will destroy them.'

781. "Therefore did he rehearse those conformations

* Meaning, that as is the Supernal Man so is the earthly man.

† Meaning, if he dreams that his beard is arranged like that of Microprosopus.

which we have repeated. But what was the necessity for so doing? Because that he said: 'All nations compassed me about.' For in this disposition of those nine conformations which are the name of IHVH, *Tetragrammaton*, are they cut off from the earth.

782. "This is that same which is written: 'In the name of IHVH will I destroy them.'

783. "Also this have we learned in the 'Book of Concealed Mystery.' David hath here enumerated the nine conformations; of which six consist in the holy name, for there are six names;* and there are three in the word ADM, *Adam*, or man.

784. "And if thou shalt say that there are only two (*in the word Adam*), assuredly there are three, because also the princes pertain unto the idea of the word Adam.†

785. "This have we learned. These are the six names, because it is thus written: 'I called upon Yah in my distress.' The first.

786. "'Yah heard me at large.' The second.

787. "'Tetragrammaton is on my side, I will not fear.' The third.

788. "'Tetragrammaton taketh my part with them that help me.' The fourth.

789. "'It is better to trust in Tetragrammaton.' The fifth.

790. "'It is better to trust in Tetragrammaton.' The sixth.

791. "But in the word ADM, *Adam*, Man, are three; for it is written: 'Tetragrammaton is on my side, I will not fear; what can ADM, *Adam*, Man, do unto me?' The first.

792. "'It is better to trust in Tetragrammaton than to put any confidence in princes.' The second.

* *I.e.*, there are six repetitions of the name of the Deity in the verses under consideration.

† Meaning, that the word princes, in the verse "than to put any confidence in princes," refers also to man.

793. "'It is better to trust in Tetragrammaton than to put any confidence in ADM, *Adam*, Man.' The third.

794. "And come, behold! There is an Arcanum hidden in this thing; and wheresoever in this passage mention is made of the word ADM, *Adam*, thereunto the Holy name is joined; and truly for a reason, seeing that man subsisteth only through that which is analogous unto himself.

795. "But what is it which is analogous unto him? The Holy Name; because it is written, Gen. ii. 7: 'And IHVH ALHIM, *Tetragrammaton Elohim*, created ADM, *Adam*, Man,' with the full Name, which is IHVH ALHIM, analogous to him (*Adam*), seeing that IHVH, Tetragrammaton, denoteth the masculine, and ALHIM, *Elohim*, the feminine.*

796. "And therefore in this passage there is no mention made of ADM, *Adam*, Man, without the Holy Name.

797. "Also we have learned this. It is written: 'I called upon IH, *Yah*, in my distress; IH, *Yah*, heard me at large.' IH is here twice repeated, IH, IH, in reference to the two jaws unto which the hairs (*of the beard*) adhere, and from which it is seen that the hairs issue and depend.

798. "He hasteneth and saith (*i.e.*, *King David*): 'IHVH, *Tetragrammaton*, is on my side; I will not fear; IHVH taketh my part with them that help me; wherein the Name is not written defectively (*IH as before, but IHVH*) which is the Holy Name, and with this Name mention is also made of man.

799. "And what is this thing which is said, 'What can ADM, *Adam*, Man, do unto me?' It is thus, as we have

* For Elohim is from the *feminine* root ALH, and is really a FEMININE PLURAL, for while many masculines form their plural in VTH, many feminines conversely form theirs in IM. In both these cases, however, the gender of the singular is retained in the plural. (See Gesenius' Hebrew Grammar, § 86, art 4.

learned by tradition: All those sacred diadems of the King,* when He is conformed in his dispositions (*that is, when the letters of Tetragrammaton are all conjoined together*), are called ADM, *Adam*, Man, which is the Form † which comprehendeth all things.

800. "But when any portion is taken away therefrom (*that is to say, when it is said IH, and not IHVH*), then is understood (*Microprosopus*) the Holy Name (*by the letter I, Yod*) and THORA, *Tauara*, or the Gate (*that is, the Bride, to whom is attributed the name ADNI, Adonai, whose number when written in its plenitude is* 671,‡ *as the word THORA or THROA exhibiteth it, summed up in the letter H, He, of the name IH*), and that which is therein.

801. "When therefore it is called Tetragrammaton, man is mentioned, with the Gate Tauara included, and those which are therein [otherwise, concerning the inferior worlds. And when it is taken away from the gate (*that is, when the letters Vau and He are not joined hereunto, of which the latter denoteth the inferior gate*), then is understood the Holy Name (*by the Yod*), and the Gate and those which are therein (*by the He in the name IH*). But when it is called IHVH, it is called the man, ADM, and all the rest (*conjoined therewith*), namely, the gate and those (*paths*) which are therein.] §

802. "And therefore did David enumerate those nine conformations; because he unto whom it is allowed

* The King—*i.e.*, Microprosopus. (See Introduction.)

† For it is said that the Tetragrammaton, written thus in the Hebrew letters, gives the figure of a man. For *Yod* = the head, *He* = the arms, *Vau* = the body, and *He* final = the legs. (See Table of Hebrew letters in Introduction.)

I
H
V
H

‡ That is to say, when the letters of ADNI are spelt thus: ALP, DLTH, NVN, IVD, *Aleph, Daleth, Nun, Yod*; for A + L + P + D + L + TH + N + V + N + I + V + D = 1 + 30 + 80 + 4 + 30 + 400 + 50 + 6 + 50 + 10 + 6 + 4 = 671. And THORA or THROA = 400 + 70 + 200 + 1 = 671 also.

§ The long piece above in brackets, but in ordinary type, is from the Cremona Codex.

to touch the beard of the King can do all which he desireth.

803. "Wherefore then the beard, and not the body? Because the body is hidden behind the beard, but the beard hath no place (*of concealment*) behind the body.

804. "But he in reckoning it proceedeth in a duplex manner*—once as we have given it; and next thus, when he saith: 'I called upon Yah in my distress.' The first.

805. "'Yah heard me at large.' The second.

806. "'Tetragrammaton is on my side; I will not fear. The third.

807. "'What can man do unto me?' The fourth.

808. "'Tetragrammaton taketh my part with them that help me.' The fifth.

809. "'And I shall see my desire upon mine enemies.' The sixth.

810. "'It is better to trust in Tetragrammaton.' The seventh.

811. "'Than to put any confidence in man.' The eighth.

812. "'It is better to trust in Tetragrammaton.' The ninth.

813. "'Than to put any confidence in princes.' The tenth.† (Otherwise: 'It is better to trust in Tetragrammaton than to put any confidence in man.' The seventh. 'It is better to trust in Tetragrammaton.' The eighth. 'Than to put any confidence in princes.' The ninth.)

814. "'I called upon Yah in my distress.' What is this which he saith? Assuredly doth David say all these things which are here said concerning the form of the beard."

* Referring to the order of the conformations, and the way in which in the passage those referring to IHVH and ADM are conjoined.

† The reader will of course also observe that these answer to the ten Sephiroth.

815. Rabbi Yehudah answered and said: "'I called upon Yah in my distress.' From the part where the beard beginneth to extend, which is from the more remote part (*is one*), before the ears, beneath the hair (*is the second*). And therefore is it twice said, IH, IH.

816. "But in that place wherein the beard is expanded, and descendeth before the ears, in wider extension, the name of ADM, *Adam*, Man, hath place (that is to say, the complete Tetragrammaton). Also this expansion was necessary to David when he wished to subject to himself the kings and nations through the dignity of this beard. (Otherwise, when therefore he saith, 'Tetragrammaton is on my side, I will not fear;' for this is such a one who spareth not the wicked, and this was altogether necessary, &c.)

817. "Also we have learned this in the 'Book of Concealed Mystery'*: Whosoever seeth in his sleep that he toucheth the beard or moustache of the supernal man with his hand, or extendeth his hand unto it, let him know that he is at peace with the supernals, and that those who afflict him are about to be subjected unto him."†

818. "We have learned that the supernal beard is disposed in nine conformations, and that it is the beard of Microprosopus.

* See *ante*, "Book of Concealed Mystery," ch. iii. § 17.

† This is apparently the end of Rabbi Yehudah's short interpolation regarding the duplicated IH. Rabbi Eleazar now apparently resumes the discourse.

CHAPTER XXXV.

CONCERNING THE FIRST PART OF THE BEARD OF MICROPROSOPUS.

819. "In the first conformation the hair is disposed from above, and goeth forth before the opening of the ears, beneath the locks which hang down over the ears; and the hairs descend, hairs above hairs, even unto the beginning of the mouth.

820. "This have we learned. All those hairs which are in the beard are harder than all the hairs of the locks of the hair of the head. But the hair of the head is longer and bendeth more easily, while these hairs (*of the beard*) are not so long.

821. "Of the hairs of the head some are hard and some are soft.

822. "And whensoever the white locks of the Ancient of Days reach forward into Microprosopus, it is written that, Prov. i. 20: 'Wisdom crieth without.'

823. "What is this (*word*) 'without'? In this (*instance*) in Microprosopus, wherein are conjoined the two (*forms of the*) brain. Two forms of the brain, sayest thou? But it should rather be said, four forms of the brain.

824. (*Assuredly*) "there are three (*forms of the*) brain in Microprosopus, and they are found in the three cavities of the skull of His head.

825. "And there is one calm and tranquil brain residing in its own clear brilliancy, which comprehendeth all the three (*forms of the*) brain, and from it are brought forth the productions of the hairs which are produced and continued in equilibrium in the white hair into that part of Microprosopus, into His three (forms of) brain (*namely*), so that therein in Him are found four (*forms of the*) brain.

826. "And hence are perfected the four texts which are written on the phylacteries, because in them is contained the Holy Name of the Ancient of Days, the Ancient of the Ancient Ones, and that of Microprosopus.

827. "For this is the perfection of the Holy Name, concerning which it is written, Deut. xxviii. 10: 'And all the people of the earth shall see that the name of Tetragrammaton have been invoked over thee, and they shall be afraid of thee.'

828. "The Name of the Lord is this very Name of Tetragrammaton, which formeth the canals and hollows of the phylacteries.

829. "And therefore is it said: 'Wisdom crieth without,' Prov. i. 20, because it is herein found (*i.e.*, *in Microprosopus*).

830. "For truly the Ancient of the Ancient Ones, even He who is concealed with all concealments, is not found, neither doth His wisdom come forth (*openly*); seeing that His wisdom is concealed in all, and doth not make itself manifest.

831. "And since there are four (*forms of the*) brain associated together, and that herefrom, even from Microprosopus, there flow down four fountains in four directions, and that they are all distributed from one fountain, which proceedeth from them all, therefore are there four.*

832. "Also we have learned: From the Wisdom which is comprehended in the Quaternary the hairs flow down,

* This four proceeding from one, and containing all things, is precisely the Pythagorean doctrine of the Tetractys, which Pythagoras probably obtained from qabalistic sources, though indeed most religions of antiquity attached considerable importance to this number four. Four is said to contain the whole Decad, because the sum of the first four numbers = ten; $1+2+3+4=10$. But eight is the reflection of four, and eight is IHVH ADNI (see Introduction). And $1+2+3+4+5+6+7+8 = 36$, the number of the Decans (or groups of ten degrees) in the Zodiac. But $5+6+7+8 = 26$, the number of the IHVH. Therefore thirty-six represents the sum of the letters of the Tetragrammaton, and the number of the Sephiroth.

which hang in curls upon curls, and all are strong and close, and they extend and flow down singly each in its own direction.

833. "And so many thousand thousand myriads of myriads depend from them that they are innumerable.

834. "This is that same which is written, Cant. v. 11: 'His locks are bushy, ThLThLIM, *Teltelim*,' as if it were ThLI ThLIM, curls heaped upon curls.

835. "And all are strong and close (*fit*) for breaking (*whatsoever is opposed to them*), hard as the rock, and as hardest stone.

836. "Until they can make openings in the skull, and the fountains can flow down beneath the locks, those strong fountains flow forth in separate directions, and in separate ways.

837. "And because those locks are black and obscure, it is written, Job xii. 22: 'He discovereth deep things out of darkness, and bringeth out to light the shadow of death.'

838. "Also we have learned that those hairs of the beard are so much harder than those hairs of the head, because these alone make themselves so prominent, and are easily found, and are hard in their paths.*

839. "Wherefore sayest thou that they are hard? Is it because they all symbolize Judgment? By no means; for truly in those dispositions Mercy as well as Judgment is found.

840. "When the thirteen fountains of the rivers of oil descend, all these are mercies.

841. "But yet we have learned that all those hairs of the beard are hard. Wherefore? Those which symbolize mercies necessarily must be hard in order to divert the course of Judgment.

842. "And all those which denote Judgment, are also firm; and therefore it is necessary in every instance that they should both be hard.

* See definition of term "path" in Introduction.

843. "When the Universe hath need of Mercy, mercies are strong, and prevail over Judgment; but when it requireth Judgment, Judgment is strong, and prevaileth over Mercy; and therefore is it necessary that in each instance they should be firm and strong.

844. "And whensoever Mercy is required, those hairs which symbolize Mercy stand forth, and the beard is evident in those hairs only (otherwise, is contained by those hairs only), and all are abundant mercies.

845. "But when Judgment is required the beard is evident in those hairs only (*which denote judgment*), and all consist in judgments.

846. "But when that holy white beard* is uncovered, all these (*hairs denoting Mercy*) and all those (hairs denoting Judgment) are alike illuminated and made brilliant, like as when a man cleanseth himself in a deep river from his uncleanness.

847. "And all consist together in Mercy, and there is no Judgment to be found at all.

848. "And when all those† nine forms shine together, all are made white with Mercy.

849. "And therefore Moses saith in another place, Num. xiv. 18: 'Tetragrammaton is ARK APIM, *Arikh Aphim*, long-suffering (*literally long of nose*), and of great mercy.'

850. "And that which he had said concerning truth,‡

* Which is of course that of Macroprosopus, the Ancient of Days.

† The nine conformations into which the beard of Microprosopus is divided.

‡ I give these two passages side by side for the reader's benefit.

Exod. xxxiv. 6 and 7: "The LORD, the LORD God, merciful and gracious, long-suffering, and abundant in goodness and truth.

"Keeping mercy for thousands, forgiving iniquity and transgression and sin, and that will by no means clear the guilty; visiting the iniquity of the fathers upon the children, and upon the children's children, unto the third and to the fourth generation."

Num. xiv. 18: "The LORD is long-suffering, and of great mercy, forgiving iniquity and transgression, and by no means clearing the guilty, visiting the iniquity of the fathers upon the children unto the third and fourth generation."

Exod. xxxiv. 6, he addeth not (*in this passage*), because the Arcanum of the matter is these nine measurements which shine down from the Ancient of Days into Microprosopus.

851. "For when Moses in the second passage rehearseth these praises of God, Num. xxiv. 18, he enumereth the nine conformations; and these are the conformations of the beard, even those which are found in Microprosopus, and descend from the Ancient of Days and shine down into Him.

852. "The word AMTH, *Emeth*, Truth, therefore dependeth from the Ancient One; whence in this passage Moses saith not: 'And in truth.'

853. "We have learned that the hairs of the head of Microprosopus are all hard and curling, and not soft.*

854. "For we see that in Him three forms of the brain are found in the three cavities (*of the skull*), which shine forth from the hidden and concealed brain.

855. "And because the brain of the Ancient of Days is tranquil and quiet, like good wine upon the lees, hence all His hairs are soft, and anointed with excellent oil.

856. "And therefore is it written, Dan. vii. 9: 'His head like pure wool.'

857. "But those which are in Microprosopus are partly hard, and partly not hard, because they all hang down, and are not diverted from their course.

858. "And therefore Wisdom† floweth forth and proceedeth (*therefrom*); but it is not the Wisdom of Wisdom, for that is quiet and tranquil.

859. "For we have learned that no one knoweth the brain of the Ancient of Days save Himself alone.

* It appears to read thus in the Chaldee and in the Latin alike, though this statement is contradicted distinctly both in § 587 and in § 857. I should think the word "LA, not," before "soft," is a mistake, or else that the passage refers to the hair of the *beard*, and not that of the *head*.

† That is, Chokmah of the second Sephira, and not that Chokmah which is its root concealed in Kether; for in Kether are all the other Sephiroth contained.

860. "This is that very thing which is said, Job xxviii. 23: 'God understandeth the way thereof,' &c.; which (*words*) are spoken concerning Microprosopus."

861. Rabbi Schimeon said (*unto him*): "Blessed be thou, O my son! in that Holy and Blessed One, in this world and in the world to come!"

CHAPTER XXXVI.

CONCERNING THE SECOND PART OF THE BEARD OF MICROPROSOPUS.

862. "THE second conformation. The hair goeth forth and ascendeth from the beginning of (*the one side of*) the mouth even unto the beginning of the other side of the mouth; and descendeth beneath the mouth unto the other side, hair above hair, in beautiful arrangement. Arise, Rabbi Abba!"

863. Rabbi Abba arose, and commenced and said: "When the disposition of this beard is instituted in the formation of the King, then is He Himself like a brave hero, strong and beautiful in appearance, valiant and conquering.

864. "This is that same which is written, Ps. cxlvii. 5: 'Great is our Lord and great is His power.'

865. "And whilst He is mitigated by the disposition of the venerable and holy beard (*of Macroprosopus*), and this (*beard of Microprosopus*) reflected that, then through its light is He called 'God merciful,' Exod. xxxiv. 6: 'and gracious, long-suffering, and abundant in goodness and in truth.' And thus is the second disposition instituted.

866. "When He shineth in the light of the Ancient

of Days, then is He called 'abundant in Mercy,' and when another of the other forms is considered, in that form is He called 'and in truth,' for this is the light of His countenance."

CHAPTER XXXVII.

CONCERNING THE THIRD PART OF THE BEARD OF MICROPROSOPUS.

867. "Also we have learned. Bearing iniquity is this second conformation called, like as in the Holy Ancient One.

868. "But because that path which goeth forth in the third disposition beneath the two nostrils is filled with short and rigid hairs; hence because of that path these conformations are not called 'bearing iniquity and passing over trangression;' but these are collected together in another place.

869. "Also we have learned in Barietha that three hundred and seventy-five mercies are comprehended in the benignity of the Ancient of Days; which are all called primal benignities.

870. "Like as it is said, Psalm lxxxix. 50: 'Where are thy former mercies?' And they are all comprehended in the benignity of the Most Holy Ancient One, the most concealed of all.

871. "But the benignity of Microprosopus is called ChSD OVLM, *Chesed Olahm*, the benignity of time.

872. "And in the 'Book of Concealed Mystery' (*have we learned*) that on account of the former benignity of the Ancient of Days is he called 'Abundant in Benignity.' But in Microprosopus (*the word*) 'mercy' is placed alone and absolutely.

873. "And therefore is it here written: 'And abundant in benignity;' and again it is written: 'Keeping mercy for thousands;' plain and without addition.

874. "And now we have taught concerning this Name, 'And abundant in benignity,' because therefrom is mitigated the (*interior*) benignity, so that it may shine into all the lights (otherwise, this Name, 'Abundant in mercy,' stretcheth down even unto the 'mercy' which is so called absolutely, so that it may illuminate it, and kindle the lights).

875. "For we have learned that that path which descendeth beneath the two nostrils of the nose is filled with short hairs; and concerning this path, that it is written: 'Passing over transgression' (otherwise, and the shorter hairs fill that path. But that path is not called 'Passing over transgression'); because there is therein no occasion for passing over; for a double reason.

876. "Firstly, because that path is a hard place for passing over. (Otherwise, because the hairs which are found therein are hard.)

877. "Secondly, because the passing over of that path descendeth even unto the commencement of the mouth.

878. "But concerning this it is written, Cant. v. 13: 'His lips like roses * (that is, red as roses), dropping sweet-smelling myrrh while passing over;' which denoteth notable redness.

879. "And this path of that place is a duplex form, and is not mitigated, whence he who wisheth to threaten toucheth that path twice with his hand."

* The English version of this passage renders it, "His lips like lilies, dropping sweet-smelling myrrh." The word here translated roses by Knorr de Rosenroth is SHVSHNIM, *Shoshanim*, which I think should undoubtedly be translated "lilies," as in the ordinary version. The symbology of this chapter is very difficult and obscure.

CHAPTER XXXVIII.

CONCERNING THE SEVEN LAST PORTIONS OF THE BEARD OF MICROPROSOPUS.

880. "THE fourth conformation. This path of hairs is disposed, and ascendeth and descendeth in His cheeks into the place of fragrance.

881. "This disposition is fair and beautiful in appearance, and it is Glory and Honour; and it is taught in Barietha that the Supernal Honour, HVD, *Hod*, goeth forth and is crowned, and floweth down, so that it may be comprehended in His cheeks, and is called the Honour of the Beard.

882. "And thence depend Glory and Honour, which are as vestments, and as very precious purple, so that He may be clothed therewith.

883. "For it is written, Ps. civ. 1: 'Thou art clothed with Honour and Majesty.' (Otherwise: In the fourth conformation the hair goeth forth, and is disposed, and ascendeth and descendeth in the cheeks, in the places of fragrance. This conformation is elegant and beautiful in appearance, and it is the supernal glory. And this is the tradition: The supernal glory goeth forth, and is crowned, and floweth down in the beauty of the cheeks. And this glory is called the glory of the beard; and from it depend honour and glory, the vestments of adornment, those magnificent purple garments wherewith he is clothed. Concerning which it is written: 'Thou art clothed with honour and majesty, which are the forms of clothing. In this form of man is he formed, rather than in any other form.)

884. "These are the dispositions denoting the clothing (*of the divine form*), and he is more fitly sym-

bolized under this figure of man than under any other forms.

885. "Also we have learned, that when this glory (*of Microprosopus*) is illuminated by the light of the excellent beard,* and emitteth light into the other dispositions, then it is called 'Bearing Iniquity' on the one side, and 'Passing over Transgression' on the other side.

886. "And therefore in Scripture is it called by the name of his jawbones.

887. "And in the 'Book of Concealed Mystery' is the same called Glory, HVD,† *Hod*, and Honour, HDR, *Hadar*, and ThPARTh, ‡ *Tiphereth*, Beauty.

888. "And unto *Tiphereth*, Beauty, appertaineth the title 'Passing over Transgression,' since it is said, Prov. xix. 15: 'And it is His Beauty (*Tiphereth*) to pass over transgression.'

889. "Also we have learned that we should only refer that *Tiphereth*, Beauty, unto the ninth conformation (*of the beard of Microprosopus*); as it is said, Prov. xx. 29: 'And the beauty of young men is their strength.' And therefore also is it (the ninth conformation) called Beauty; and when they are weighed together in the balance they are as one."

890. Rabbi Schimeon said unto him: "Worthy art thou, O Rabbi Abba! for which reason mayest thou be blessed by the Most Holy Ancient One, from whom all blessings proceed.

891. "The fifth conformation. The hair is wanting, and there appear two apples, on this side and on that, red as red roses, and they radiate into two hundred and seventy worlds.

892. "As to those two apples, when they shine on either side, from the light of the two supernal apples (*the cheeks of Macroprosopus*), redness is removed therefrom, and a white brilliance cometh upon them.

* Namely, that of Macroprosopus.

† The eighth Sephira. ‡ The sixth Sephira.

893. "Concerning this is it written, Num. vi. 25: 'Tetragrammaton make His face shine upon thee, and be gracious unto thee.' Seeing that when they shine he is blessed by the world.

894. "But when that redness is stirred up (*in them*), it is written, *ibid.* 26: 'Tetragrammaton take away His wrath from thee;' as if it were said: 'It is taken away, and wrath is no longer found in the world.'

895. "We have learned that all the lights which shine from the Most Holy Ancient One are called the former benignities, because all those lights are the benignities of time.

896. The sixth conformation. The hair goeth forth as it were in a certain tress, among the hairs in the circumference of the beard; and this is called one of the five angles which depend from the CHSD, *Chesed*, Mercy and Compassions.

897. "And it is not permitted to lose this benignity, as it is said.

898. Therefore is it written, Lev. xix. 27: 'Thou shalt not lose the angle of thy beard.'

899. "The seventh conformation is that the hairs hang not over the mouth, and that the mouth is uncovered on every side. Arise thou, Rabbi Yehudah."

900. Rabbi Yehudah arose, and commenced, and said, Dan. iv. 17: "'This matter is by the decree of the Watchers.'

901. "Many thousands of myriads stand around, and are preserved by this mouth, and depend therefrom, and all those are called (*by the general title of*) the mouth.

902. "As it is written, Ps. xxxiii. 6: 'And all the host of them by the Spirit of His mouth.'

903. "And by this Spirit which goeth forth from the mouth are all those exteriors clothed who depend from that mouth.

904. "And by that mouth, when that path is opened, are

clothed many true prophets; and they are all called the mouth of Tetragrammaton.

905. "And in that place where the Spirit goeth forth no other thing is mingled therewith; for all things wait upon that mouth, that they may be clothed with the Spirit going forth therefrom.

906. "And this disposition ruleth over the six (*foregoing conformations*), because herein are all things established and comprehended.

907. "And therefore are the hairs (*of this conformation*) equal around the mouth, and this itself is uncovered on every side."

908. Rabbi Schimeon said (*unto him*): "Blessed be thou, by the Most Holy Ancient One.

909. "The eighth conformation is that the hairs descend beneath the beard, covering the throat, that it cannot be seen.

910. "For we have learned in the exotic tradition that neither the throat nor any of its parts (*are apparent*) through (*the hair*). And if in the time of contest (otherwise of Victory, NTzCh, *Netzach**), during such contest any portion of (*the throat*) be visible, then it appeareth like Strength (*Geburah*).†

911. "For we have learned that a thousand worlds are contained thereby.

912. "This is that which is said, Cant. iv. 4: 'Wherein there hang a thousand bucklers, all shields of mighty men.' And this 'thousand shields' is an Arcanum.

913. "It is related in the 'Book of Concealed Mystery' that 'all the shields of the mighty men,' which come from the side of the rigours,‡ are derived from those severities (*Geboran*, GBVRAN).

914. "The ninth conformation is that the hairs flow

* The seventh Sephira. † The fifth Sephira.

‡ We must not forget that in Microprosopus are "right and left," Mercy and Justice.

down in perfect equilibrium even unto those hairs which hang down beneath, and all of them in beautiful arrangement, like (*that of*) a brave hero, (*of*) a chief victorious in war.

915. "Because all the hairs follow those which hang down, and all are joined unto those which hang down, and each holdeth its own course.

916. "Concerning this it is written, Prov. xx. 29: 'The beauty of a young man is his strength.'

917. "And He appeareth upon the (*Red*) Sea,* like a beautiful youth, which is written in Cant. v. 16: 'Excellent (or young) as the cedars.'

918. "Like a hero hath He exhibited His valour, and this is that THPARTH, CHILA, VGBVRTHA, VRCHMI, *Tiphereth, Chila, Ve Geburatha, Ve Rechmi,* Beauty, Strength, and Valour, and Mercy."

CHAPTER XXXIX.

CONCERNING THE BODY OF MICROPROSOPUS IN GENERAL, UNDER THE CONDITION OF AN ANDROGYN.

919. THIS have we learned. Rabbi Schimeon said: All those dispositions and all those words ought to be revealed by those who are weighed in the balance, and not by those who have not entered therein, but by those who have both entered therein and departed therefrom. For he who entereth therein and goeth not out therefrom, better were it for that man that he had never been born.

920. The sum of all is this: The Ancient of the Ancient Ones existeth in Microprosopus; He is the all-existent One; He was all, He is all, He will be all; He will not be changed, neither is He changed, neither hath He been changed.

* Microprosopus, the *Vau*, V, of IHVH. The sea is Binah, the Supernal Mother, the third Sephira, and the first H of IHVH.

921. But by means of those conformations hath He conformed Himself in that form which comprehendeth all forms, in that form which comprehendeth all names.

922. But this form wherein He Himself only appeareth is in the similitude of this form; and is not that form, but is analogous unto this form*—namely, when there are associated therewith the crowns and the diadems and the perfection of all things.

923. And therefore is the form of the man the form of the superiors and inferiors which are included therein.

924. And because that form comprehendeth the superiors and the inferiors, therefore by such a disposition is the Most Holy Ancient One conformed; and thus also is Microprosopus configurated in this disposition.

925. And if thou sayest: What, then, is the difference between the one and the other?

926. Assuredly all things are equally (*balanced in the*) Unity. But yet from our point of view (*ie., from our plane*) His paths are divided, and from our point of view (*on our plane*) is judgment found, and from the side which is turned towards us are (*His attributes*) by turns duplicated.†

927. And these Arcana are not revealed save unto the reapers of the Sacred Land.‡

928. For it is written, Ps. xxv. 14: "The secret of Tetragrammaton is with them that fear Him."

929. Also it is written, Gen. ii. 7: "VIITzR IHVH ALHIM ATH HADM, *Va-Yeyetzer Tetragrammaton Elohim Ath Ha-Adam.*§ And Tetragrammaton Elohim formed the

* I take the sense of this second clause to be that He is not really in the outward and visible form of a material man; but that he can be best expressed hereby in a symbolic spiritual form. Cf. Ezek. i. 26; "And upon the LIKENESS of the throne was the LIKENESS as the APPEARANCE of a man above it."

† In connection with this section read ch. i. §§ 5, 6, 7, and 8, of the "Book of Concealed Mystery."

‡ *I.e.*, to the students of the Qabalah.

§ See also "Book of Concealed Mystery," ch. ii. § 23.

substance of man, completed (*him*) formation by formation from the most ethereal (*portion*) of the refined (*element of*) earth (otherwise formation within formation from the best, &c.)

930. And this is *Va-Yeyetzer* VIITzR, written with two *Yods*, I's *instead of VITzR, Va-Yetzer, with one Yod*, I).

931. Wherefore? There is an Arcanum of the Most Holy Ancient One, and an Arcanum of Microprosopus.

932. VIITzR, *Va-Yeyetzer*, and formed. What did (*Tetragrammaton Elohim*) form? Form in form. And this is VIITzR.

933. And what is form in form? The two names, which are called the full name, IHVH ALHIM, *Tetragrammaton Elohim.*

934. And this is the Arcanum of the two I's, *Yods*, in VIITzR; and of how it hath been conformed form within form; namely, in the disposition of the perfect name, Tetragrammaton Elohim.

935. And in what are they comprehended? In the supernal beard (otherwise, in this supernal form which is called (*the supernal*) man; the man who comprehendeth Male and Female equally).

936. And therefore is it written: "ATH HADM, *Ath Ha-Adam* (τὸν ἄνθρωπον), the substance of man," because it comprehendeth equally the Male and the Female, for to the word ADM, ATH is subjoined, so as to extend and exaggerate the species which is here produced. Most assuredly here therefore is it as Male and as Female.

937. "OPR MN HADMH, *Ophir Men Ha-Adamah*, from the dust of the ground," dust, form within form (otherwise, from the most ethereal portion of the refined element of earth, one within the other).

938. But wherefore are all these things so? Because that from the supernals there was sent down into him (*Man*) the Arcanum of the supernal Arcana, even the end of all Arcana.

939. This is that which is herein written: "VIPCH BAPIV NSHMTHCHIIM, *Ve-Yepech Be-Ephaiu Neschamath Chiim*, and breathed into his nostrils the Neschamath* of (*their*) lives.

940. Their souls, from which all things living, superiors and inferiors, alike depend, and wherein they have their existence.

941. "VIHI HADM LNPSH CHIH, *Va-Yehi Ha-Adam Le-Nephesch Chiah*, and the Adam was formed into a living Nephesch," so that it (*the physical Nephesch form*) might be attached to himself (otherwise, so that it might be developed in him), and that he might form himself into similar conformations; † and that he might project himself in that Neschamah from path into path,‡ even unto the end and completion of all the paths.

942. So that in all this Neschamah might be found, and that it might be extended into all, and that it itself might be still one.

943. Whence he who taketh this away from the universe doth the same thing as if he should take away this Neschamah for the purpose of setting in its place another Neschamah beside it.§

944. And therefore shall such a man and his remembrance be cut off from generations unto generations.

* Neschamath is either the plural of Neschamah, *defectively written*, or else shows that Neschamah is *in regimine* to Chiim, and evidently means the united higher souls of *both Adam and Eve conjoined in one body*. (For explanation of Neschamah, &c., see Introduction.)

† That is into conformations similar to those of the Supernal Man.

‡ That is, into forms, conditions, and qualities analogous to the Sephiroth. (See Introduction regarding the soul, and Plate showing the analogy between the soul, the letters of Tetragrammaton, and the four worlds, where the Sephiroth are shown reflected in Nephesch.)

§ Apparently the sense of this passage is intended to combat Atheism, and to show that it is logically absurd to deny the existence of a Spirit of God which works in the universe; inasmuch that if this be denied, at all events something analogous in its general properties will have to be substituted for it.

CHAPTER XL.

CONCERNING THE FEMININE PORTION OF MICROPROSOPUS; AND CONCERNING THE REMAINING PARTS OF THE BODY OF EACH.

945. THUS in this Adam androgyneity hath commenced to be disposed when it hath been formed in its disposition. It hath commenced from His back. (Otherwise, from His breast.)

946. Between the two arms, in that part whereunto the beard hangeth down, which is called Tiphereth, the Beauty.

947. And this Beauty is expanded and disposeth two breasts.

948. And it is separated from the back, and produceth the Head of a Woman completely covered on every side by Her hair as far as to (*the limits of*) the face of Her head.

949. Insomuch that through that Tiphereth, Beauty, Adam becometh in one body, Male and Female.

950. This is that which is written, Isa. xliv. 13: "According to the beauty of a man, KTHPARTH ADM, *Ke-Tiphereth Adam*, that it may remain in the house."

951. When the countenance of the Female Head is created, one curled lock of hair at the back of Microprosopus hangeth over the head of the Woman.

952. And all hairs red gold are produced in Her head; yet so that other colours are intermixed therewith.

953. This is that which is written, Cant. vii. 5: "The hair of Thy head like ARGMN, *Argaman*, purple."

954. What is Argaman? Colours intermixed with other colours.

955. This Tiphereth, Beauty, hath been extended from the heart, and penetrateth it, and passeth through unto the other side, and instituteth the formations from the Countenance of the Woman even unto Her heart; so that from the parts about the heart it taketh its rise on this side, and in the parts about the heart it terminateth on that side.

956. Moreover, this Tiphereth is extended, and it formeth the internal parts of a Man.

957. And it entereth into and disposeth therein all mercies and aspects of mercies.

958. Also we have learned that in those internal parts are comprehended six hundred thousand Lords of Mercies, and that they are called the Lords of the Internal Parts.

959. Whence it is written, Jer. xxxi. 20: "Therefore My bowels are troubled for him, I will surely have mercy upon him, saith Tetragrammaton."

960. We have learned that this Tiphereth, Beauty, embraceth Mercies and Judgment, and that Mercy is extended in the Male.

961. And it passeth over and goeth through unto (otherwise, shineth on) the other side, and formeth the internal parts of a Woman on the side of Judgment; and thus also are Her internal parts disposed.

962. We have learned that the Male hath been conformed on His side (otherwise, from His heart), in 248* members; of which some are within, some without; some Mercies, some Judgments.

963. All which pertain unto Judgment, cohere in Judgment around the hinder part, where the Woman is extended; and they coalesce and are extended round about on that side.

964. Also we have learned that five nakednesses can be revealed on that side, which are the five judgments;

* The number of 248 = RCHM, *Rechem* = Mercy + 248; thus conveying this idea in the number.

and these five judgments are extended into 248 paths.*

965. And thus have we learned: the voice in the Woman is uncovered; the hair in the Woman is uncovered; the leg † in the Woman is uncovered; the hand in the Woman is uncovered; the foot in the Woman is uncovered.

966. And also, furthermore, concerning these two our companions have not inquired, yet these two have more nakedness.

967. Also, we have learned in the "Book of Concealed Mystery" that the Male is extended and conformed with His parts, and there is formed in Him forma partis tegendæ puræ, et illud est membrum purum.

968. Longitudo autem membri hujus est 248 mundorum, et omnes illi pendent in orificio membri hujus quad dicitur, I, *Yod*.

969. Et cum detegitur Yod, orificium membri; detegitur Benignitas superna.‡

970. And this member is the Benignity, quo nomine

* For five is H, *He*, the number of the feminine letter in the Tetragrammaton, the number also of the Microcosm or Lesser World, the symbol or sign of which is the Pentragram. The 248 paths into which the five judgments are extended are the correlates of those of mercy.

† This word is SHVQ, *Shoq*, in the original. Fuerst translates it Leg, especially the part from knee to ankle. So does Gesenius in his Lexicon; but in his large Hebrew and Chaldee Thesaurus it is, apparently by an oversight, omitted. Zanolini translates it "Armus, Crus," and adds: "In BRKVTH, *Berachoth*, fol. 24, SHVQA BASHH ORVH, Crura in muliere res pudenda sunt, scilicet crura nuda. Hinc in more positum apud Judæos est, ut ipsorum mulieres, et puellæ demissis ad talos vestibus verecundiæ caussa utantur, ne viros ad libidinem excitent.'" ("Lexicon Chaldæo-Rabbinicum," art. SHVQ.)

‡ I have thought it advisable to retain this piece in the Latin, as it will be equally intelligible in that language to the ordinary student; and it is not so well fitted for expression in English. It contains the symbolism of the *genitalia*.

tamen proprie vocatur orificium membri; neither is it called Benignity until I, *Yod*, orificii membri, is uncovered.

971. And come, behold, Abraham is not called perfect in that Benignity, until I, *Yod*, of the member is uncovered; but when that is uncovered he is called perfect.*

972. This is that which is written: "Walk before Me and be thou perfect; really and truly perfect," Gen. xvii. 1.

973. Also it is written, Ps. xviii. 24: "I will be upright before Him, and will keep myself from the sinner."

974. Who is he concerning whom the discourse is both in the first and second instance (*in this passage*)? Assuredly, he who uncovereth that Yod; et cavet, ne Yod istud introducat in potestatem adversam; so that he may have part in the world to come, and that he may be bound together in the sheaf of life.

975. What is this, "in potestatem adversam"? Even that which is written, Mal. ii. 11: "And hath married the daughter of a strange god."

976. And therefore is it written: "I will be upright before Him," because he hath become perfect in the uncovering of *Yod*," and I will keep myself from the sinner."

977. Et dum extenditur membrum hoc, etiam extenditur latus rigoris de illis rigoribus sinistræ in fæmina.

978. Et inseritur in fæminam, in loco quodam, et signatioram facit in nuditate, seu parte maxime contegenda in toto corpore fæminino.

* This apparently refers to the qabalistical symbolism of the changing of the names of Abram and Sarai into Abraham and Sarah; ABRM and SHRI into ABRHM and SHRH; ABRM = 243 is made into ABRHM = 248 by addition of the number 5, the letter H, *He*; and SHRI = 510 is made SHRH = 505 by the subtraction of five from the final I, *Yod*; 248 is the number of the members of Microprosopus, and 5 is that of the five judgments. Hence the united numbers of Abram and Sarai, 243 + 510 = 753, which number is also obtained by the addition of Abraham and Sarah, 248 + 505 = 753; so that the total numeration of the two names remains unchanged.

979. Et ille locus dicitur nuditas ab omnibus occultanda, locus scilicet pro membro illo, quod dicitur Benignitas, ut scilicet mitigetur rigor iste, qui continet quinque rigores.

980. And that Benignity comprehendeth in itself five Benignities (otherwise, and herein existeth the Benignity from the other Benignities). And Benignity is from those on the right, but Severity from those on the left.

981. And when the latter is mitigated by the former He is called man, consisting in both aspects.

982. And therefore in all the crowns (*the former state of things*) was not permanent, before that the conformations of the King* were prepared by the Ancient of the Ancient Ones, so that He might construct the worlds, and form (*their*) conformations, for the purpose of establishing that Woman, † so that She might be mitigated.

983. Until the supernal Benignity could descend, and then the conformations of the Woman became permanent, and were mitigated by this member (of Microprosopus), which is called the Benignity.

984. This is that which is written, Gen. xxxvi.: "And these are the kings which reigned in the land of Edom;" which is the place where all the judgments are found, and they are the constitutions of the Woman.

985. For it is not written, "Who were," but "Who reigned," because they were not mitigated until all were formed, and that Benignity went forth.

986. Therefore is it said, "And he died," because they were not permanent, neither was Judgment mitigated through Judgment ‡

987. But, and if thou sayest: "That if it be thus that all are judgments, wherefore is it written, Gen. xxxvi. 37:

* Microprosopus.

† Malkuth, the tenth Sephira, the Kingdom, the Queen, the Bride of Microprosopus; the Isis, Rhea, Ceridwen, Hertha, &c., of other religions; Nature, the Great Mother of us all.

‡ Compare with this the meaning of the names of the two Pillars at the entrance to King Solomon's Temple.

'And Saul of Rechoboth * by the waters reigned in his stead,' for this man truly doth not appear (*to symbolize*) a judgment ?"

988. We have learned that all denote judgment, excepting one, which last remaineth.

989. But this Saul of Rechoboth by the waters is one order (otherwise, one side or aspect), an order which is expanded, and goeth forth from Rechoboth by the waters.

990. And this is Binah, wherefrom are opened the fifty gates † in the aspects of the world of lights and luminaries.

991. This is what is said concerning Rechoboth by the waters. And they were not all permanent. Thou shalt not say that they were abolished, but that they were not permanent in that kingdom which is from the side of the Woman.

992. Until there was excited and extended that Last One of them all concerning whom it is said: "And *Hadar*, HDR, reigned after him."

993. Who is Hadar ? The Supernal Benignity. ‡

994. "And the name of his city was POV, *Paau* (*crying aloud*)." What is Paau ? Through this the man prayeth who is worthy of the Holy Spirit.

995. "And the name of his wife was *Mechetabel*, MCHITBAL," herein are they mitigated together, and his (*Hadar's*) wife is named, which is not written concerning any other of them. MCHITBAL, *Mechetabel* (*which bears the*

* It is not at first sight clear why Saul of Rechoboth should be taken exception to as symbolizing judgment. But if we examine the word RCHVBVTH, *Rechoboth*, by Gematria, we shall find a reason. For R + CH + V + B + V + TH = 200 + 8 + 6 + 2 + 6 + 400 + 622 = BRKTH, *Berachoth*, Blessings, and also "pools of water," which is also "Rechoboth by the waters." And "the waters" are Binah, the third Sephira.

† *Vide ante* in the "Book of Concealed Mystery."

‡ For HDR = 213, which = CHSD OLAH DAL, *Chesed Aulaeh Da-El*, the Supernal Mercy of El = 213 also. And Chesed is the fourth Sephira, which succeeds Binah the third, as Hadar succeeds Saul of Rechoboth by the waters.

signification of "as if were made better by the name of Benignity, AL, EL, MCHI TB AL") mitigation of the one by the other.

996. "The daughter of MTRD, *Matred*," the elaborations, on the side of Severity: "the daughter of MIZHB, *Mezahab*;" that is they have been firmly contempered and intertwined together—namely MI, *Me*, Mercury,* and ZHB, *Zahab*, Gold, Mercy, and Judgment.

CHAPTER XLI.

CONCERNING THE SEPARATE MEMBERS OF EACH PERSONIFICATION, AND ESPECIALLY CONCERNING THE ARMS OF MICROPROSOPUS.

997. HEREUNTO have adhered together both the Woman and the Man; now in Their condition are They separated in arms and limbs.

998. Of the Male, one arm is right and the other left.

999. In the first arm (otherwise in the holy arm) three members † (or divisions) are bound together.

1000. And the two arms are completed. And they are perfected in three members in the right arm, and in three members in the left arm.

1001. The three members of the right arm correspond to the three members of the left arm.

1002. And therefore is mention only made of the one

* This partakes of alchemical symbolism — Mezahab, the philosophical Mercury.

† As in the arm there are three natural divisions, from shoulder to elbow, from elbow to wrist, and from wrist to the tips of the fingers. The word QSHRIN, here translated "members," means, properly speaking, "zones."

arm. For of the arms there is only made mention of that on the right side; but in Exod. xv. 6 it is called, "Thy right hand, O Tetragrammaton!"

1003. Therefore it is said "the right hand of Tetragrammaton," with reference to the three divisions of the Patriarchs * who have occupied those parts.

1004. And if thou shalt say: "Also these are found (*symbolized*) in the three cavities of the skull."

1005. We have learned that all these three (*as to their conceptions*) are expanded through and connected with the whole body (*of Microprosopus*) through those three which are bound together in the right arm.

1006. And therefore David desired Him, and said, Ps. cx. 1: "Sit thou with those on my right hand," that he might be associated with the Patriarchs, and sit there in the perfect throne.

1007. And therefore it is written, Ps. cxviii. 22: "The stone which the builders rejected," because that he sat on the right hand.

1008. This is that which is written, Dan. xii. 13: "And thou shalt rest, and rise again in thy lot at the limit of My right hand." †

1009. Like as if it were said: "Even as he who is worthy of the friendship of the King is happy when the King extendeth His right hand, and placeth him at His right hand.

1010. But when He sitteth, certain members are extended as to this right hand, but the arm extendeth not the hand (otherwise, when He sitteth, also the members are not extended, and the arm is not stretched

* This word in the original is ABHTHA, *Ebahatha*, which, according to the context, may mean simply "Fathers"; or in a more emphatic sense, "Patriarchs"; this latter is the sense in which it is employed in this passage. The three Patriarchs are Abraham, Isaac, and Jacob, for this word Ebahatha is *not* employed to denote the twelve sons of the latter.

† This is usually translated "at the end of the days." This translation is simply due to a difference in the *pointing*, the words being the same in orthography—thus, IMIN.

forth but remaineth still), with its three members, of which mention hath been made before.

1011. But when sinners are stirred up and spread abroad in the world, three other members are excited, which are severe judgment, and His arm is stretched forth.

1012. And when that arm is stretched forth, it is as it were the right hand (*also*); but it is called "the arm of Tetragrammaton": "O Tetragrammaton! Thine arm hath been stretched forth" (1 Kings viii. 42).

1013. When these three members are contained in those three, all are called the right hand, and judgment is exercised and mercy.

1014. This is that which is said, Exod. xv. 6: "Thy right hand, O Tetragrammaton, is marvellous in power; with Thy right hand, O Tetragrammaton, wilt Thou dash in pieces the enemy;" seeing that therein are stirred up the mercies.

1015. Also, we have learned that unto this right hand adhere three hundred and fifty thousand myriads (otherwise, which are called the right hand, and one hundred and eighty-five thousand myriads) from the arm, which is called the arm of Tetragrammaton.

1016. Therefore, from either side is the arm (*i.e., it is either the right arm or the left arm*), because that it is said (*to be*) on either side of Tiphereth.*

1017. For it is written, Isa. lxiii. 12: "That led Moses to his right hand, by the arm of his Tiphereth."

1018. The first expression denoteth the right; but the "arm" denoteth the left; for it is written, "by the arm of his Tiphereth," one (*side*) with the other (*i.e., right and left*).

1019. Moreover, we have learned that to that which is on the left side there adhere four hundred and fifty†

* See table of the Sephiroth, &c., in the Introduction, where it will be seen that Tiphereth is as it were the centre.

† 450 = THN, *Than*, which is the root of Serpent or Dragon. Compare Leviathan, which is probably formed from this root.

Lords of Shields, and that they adhere unto those separate fingers.

1020. And in the single fingers there are found ten thousand Lords of the Shields. Go thou then forth, and number how many of them there are in the hand.

1021. And this right hand is called the Holy Aid, which cometh forth from the right arm, from the three members (*thereof*).

1022. And although it be called the hand, yet is it Aid, since it is written, 2 Sam. iii. 12: "And behold, My Hand is with thee."

1023. And in it are contained one thousand and four myriads and five hundred and eight thousand lords, the aiders in every world,* who are called the supernal hand of the Tetragrammaton, the inferior hand of the Tetragrammaton.

1024. And although everywhere it be called the hand of Tetragrammaton, it is understood (*that sometimes*) the left hand† (*is intended to be spoken of*). For if they be benevolent, it is called the right hand of Tetragrammaton, and the hand is included in the arm, and is for aid, and is called the hand; and if, on the other hand, it be not so, the inferior hand of Tetragrammaton is (*to be understood*).

1025. We have learned that when the severe judgments are excited so that they may descend into the world, that then it is written, Ps. xxv. 14: "The Arcanum of Tetragrammaton is over those who fear Him."

* That is, on every qabalistical plane. (See Introduction regarding the Four Worlds, &c.)

† For in Microprosopus there is always right and left, Mercy and Justice; while in Macroprosopus all is said to be "right." But Microprosopus is manifest, and Macroprosopus is hidden.

CHAPTER XLII.

CONCERNING THE SEPARATION OF THE MASCULINE AND THE FEMININE, AND CONCERNING THEIR CONJUNCTION.

1026. ALSO we have learned in the "Book of Concealed Mystery"* that all the judgments which arise from the Masculine are vehement in the commencement, and relax in the termination; but that those which are found to arise from the Feminine are relax in commencement, and vehement in termination.

1027. And were it not that they could be conjoined, the world could not suffer them; whence the Ancient of the Ancient Ones, the Concealed by all things, separateth the one from the other, and associateth them together so that at once they may be mitigated.

1028. And when He wisheth to separate them He causeth an ecstasy (*or trance*, cf. Gen. ii. 21) to fall upon Microprosopus, and separateth the Woman from His back.

1029. And He conformeth all Her conformations, and hideth Her even unto Her day, on which She is ready to be brought before the Male.

1030. This is that which is said, Gen. ii. 21: "And Tetragrammaton Elohim caused a deep sleep to fall upon Adam, and he slept."

1031. What is this, "And he slept?" This is that which is written, Ps. xliv. 24: "Awake! wherefore sleepest thou, O Tetragrammaton?"

1032. And He taketh away one of his sides. What is this one? This is the Woman.

1033. And She is taken away and conformed; and in Her place is inserted Mercy and Benignity.

* See "Book of Concealed Mystery," *ante*, ch. iii. § 27.

1034. Like as it is said: "And he hath shut up flesh before her." Ezek. xxxvi. 26: "And I will take away from you the stony heart out of your flesh, and I will give you a heart of flesh."

1035. And when He wisheth to introduce the Sabbath, then did He create the spirits, and the malignant demons, and the authors of disturbance; neither at first did He finish them, until the Mother could come into Her formation, and could sit before Him.

1036. When She could sit before Him, He ceased from those creatures, and they were not completed because the Mother sat before the King, and they were associated together face to face.

1037. Who shall enter between Them? Who shall stir up war between Them mutually?

1038. Because the Arcanum of the matter is hidden in the time of the disciples of wisdom, who know our Arcanum, from Sabbath unto Sabbath.

1039. And when they are associated together, then are They mutually mitigated in that day on which all things are mitigated. And therefore are the judgments mitigated mutually and restored into order, both superiors and inferiors.

CHAPTER XLIII.

CONCERNING THE JUDGMENTS.

1040. ALSO, we have learned in the "Book of Concealed Mystery" that when the Most Holy Ancient One desired to see whether the judgments could be mitigated, and whether these two could adhere together, that then from the side of the Woman there went forth a vehement judgment, which the world could not bear.

* See "Book of Concealed Mystery," ch. iii. §§ 27-31.

1041. Whence it is written: "And Adam knew Eve his wife" (Gen. iv. 1). And she conceived and brought forth QIN, *Qain*, and said: "I have acquired a man with Tetragrammaton."

1042. And She was not perfect, because She had not been mitigated, and the powerful serpent had transmitted unto Her the pollution of severe judgment; and therefore She could not be mitigated.

1043. When therefore this man Qain proceeded from the side of the Woman, he went forth vigorous and severe; severe in his judgment, rigorous in his judgment.

1044. But when he had gone forth, She Herself became thereafter weaker and more gentle. And there went forth another and gentler birth.

1045. And the former one was removed, which was so vehement and rigorous that all the judgments could not be mingled together before Her.

1046. Come and see. What is written? "And it came to pass when they were both in the field." "In the field," which is known to be the supernal (*field*); "in the field," which is called the field of the apple-trees.

1047. And this judgment hath conquered his brother because he is stronger than he, and hath subdued him, and hath concealed him in his own power.

1048. Then therefore, that Holy God was stirred up regarding this—may His Name be blessed!—and took him away from the midst before him, and placed him in the mouth of the Great Abyss.

1049. And enclosed his brother by immersion in the Great Sea, so that he might temperate the supernal tears.

1050. And from them men descend in the world according to their path.

1051. And although they are concealed, yet are they extended mutually in themselves and from one body.

1052. And from that body descend the souls, NSHMTHHVN, of the impious, of the sinners, and of the hardened in spirit.

1053. From them both at once, dost thou think? No; but one floweth down from the one side, and another from the other.

1054. Blessed are the just, whose NSHMTHHVN, souls, are drawn from that Holy Body which is called Adam, which includeth all things; the place, as it were, wherein all the Crowns and Holy Diadems are associated together, arrayed in the equilibrium of balance.

1055. Blessed are the just, because all these are holy words which are sent forth through the Supernal Holy Spirit, the spirit wherein all the Holy Ones are comprehended; the spirit in whom the supernals and inferiors are collected together (otherwise, whom the supernals and inferiors hear).

1056. Blessed are ye, O Lords of Lords, Reapers of the Field, who know and contemplate those words, and know well your Lord, face to face, and eye to eye; and through those words worthy in the world to come.

1057. This is that very thing which is written, Deut. iv. 38: "Know therefore this day, and consider it in thine heart, that Tetragrammaton, *He* is Elohim (HVA HALHIM), in the heavens above, and upon the earth beneath: there is none other."

1058. Where Tetragrammaton is the Ancient of Days. *Hoa Ha-Elohim*, that is the One, blessed be His Name for ever, and unto the Ages of the Ages.

CHAPTER XLIV.

FURTHER REMARKS CONCERNING THE SUPERNAL MAN.

1059. RABBI SCHIMEON spake, and said: Let us behold. The superiors are below, and the inferiors are above.*

* Which is equivalent to the great magical precept of Hermes Trismegistus in the second clause of the Smaragdine Tablet: "That which is

1060. The superiors are below. That is the form of the Man which is the Universal Superior Conformation.

1061. We have learned this which is written, "And the just man is the foundation, ISVD, *Yesod*, of the world," Prov. x. 25, because He comprehendeth the Hexad in one enumeration.*

1062. And this is that which is written, Cant. v. 15: "His legs are as columns, SHSH, *Shesh*, of the Number Six." †

1063. We have learned in the "Book of Concealed Mystery" that in man are comprehended the Superior Crowns in general and in special; and that in man are comprehended the Inferior Crowns in special and in general.

1064. The Superior Crowns in general (*are comprehended in*) the figure of all those conformations, as hath been already said.

1065. (*The Superior Crowns*) in special (*are comprehended*) in the fingers of the hands, which are CHMSH KNGD CHMSH, *Chamesh Ke-Neged Chamesh*, Five over against (or opposed to, or chief above) Five.‡

1066. The Inferior Crowns (*are comprehended in*) the toes of the feet, which are special and general.

1067. For the body is not seen with them, seeing they are extraneous to the body. And therefore they

below is like that which is above, and that which is above is like that which is below, for the performance of the miracles of the one substance."

* It is not at first sight clear what is meant by this statement. But if we examine the passage closely, we shall see that the "just man" is taken for Microprosopus, who is the son, the "form of the man"; "comprehending the Hexad," because he is composed of the six Sephiroth—*Chesed, Geburah, Tiphereth, Netzach, Hod*, and *Yesod*.

† The ordinary translation of this passage is: "His legs are as pillars of marble." SHSH may be translated either "marble" or "the Number Six," according to the pointing.

‡ Compare "Sepher Yetzirah," ch. i. § 3: "Ten are the restricting numerations (*Sephiroth*). The Number Ten (is that of the) fingers—Five as chief above (or over against, or opposed to) Five, CHMSH KNGD CHMSH, and the pure Unity enthroned in Her strength in the Word of Renewal, and in the Word of Might."

are not in the body, seeing the body hath receded from them.

1068. For if so, what is this, Zach. xiv. 4: "And His feet shall stand in that day?" Truly the feet of the body, the Lords of Judgments to exercise vengeance.

1069. And they are called the Lords of the Feet; and certain of them are powerful, and the Lords of the Judgments, who are below, adhere unto the inferior crowns.

1070. We have learned that all those superior conformations which are in the Holy Body, in the Male and in the Female, which (*arrangement of Male and Female*) is the proper ordering (*of the Form*) of the man, are deduced from themselves by turns, and that by turns they adhere each to its (*order of deviation*): and that by turns they flow down into themselves (*i.e., the duplicate Male and Female form*).

1071. Like as the blood floweth through the passages of the veins—now through one, now through another; now hither, now thither; from one place into another place.

1072. And those interior portions of the Body bind themselves together by turns until all the worlds are illuminated, and receive benediction because of them.

1073. We have learned that all those Crowns which are not comprehended in the Body are all far distant and impure, and pollute whom they are permitted—whosoever, namely, cometh near unto them so that he may learn anything from them.

1074.* This have we learned. Wherefore, then, is there so great a desire for them among the Disciples of Wisdom? For no other reason than that they (*the Crowns which are impure*) should approach that Holy Body, and that thus perchance through them (*the Disciples of Wisdom*) they (the *impure Crowns*) may seek to be comprehended in that Body.

* This section apparently intends to inculcate the doctrine that it is the duty of the righteous to endeavour to improve not only the ungodly but even the demons themselves.

1075. But if thou sayest that if it be so, surely the Holy Angels also are not included in the comprehension of the Body.

1076. Most assuredly it is not so in the least. For if, He being absent from them, there were Holy Ones without the conformative arrangement of the Body, surely (*He being absent from them*) they could neither (*continue to*) be holy, nor to subsist.

1077. And nevertheless it is written, Dan. x. 6: "And his body like as THRSHISH, *Tarshish*;" also, Ezek. x. 12: "And their backs full of eyes;" also, Dan. ix. 21: "The man Gabriel." All these passages refer to the analogy of the Man.

1078. Those being accepted which exist not in the ordered arrangement of the Body; for those are impure, and pollute him—namely, whosoever shall approach unto them.

1079. Also, we have learned that these are found to proceed from the spirit of the left side, which is not mitigated in human form; and they have gone out from the ordered arrangement of the Holy Body, neither do they adhere unto it.

1080. And therefore are they all impure, and they wander to and fro, and fly through the world.

1081. And they are entered into the mouth of the Great Abyss, so that they may adhere unto that former Judgment which had gone forth from the ordered arrangement of the Body, and which is called the Inferior Qain.

1082. And they wander to and fro, and fly up and down, through the whole world, being carried abroad hither and thither; and they adhere not in the Syntagma of the Body.

1083. And therefore are they without, and impure, among all the hosts above and below; like as it is written, Lev. xiii. 46: "And his habitation shall be without the camp."

1084. But from the Spirit which is called Abel, which hath been more mitigated in the Syntagma of the Holy Body, others go forth who have been more mitigated, and can *ad*here *unto* the body, but cannot completely be *in*herent *within* it.

1085. They all hang in the air, and go forth from this genus of those Impure Ones, and hear whatsoever may be said above and below; and concerning them they have knowledge who have spoken concerning them.

1086. Also, this is the tradition in the "Book of Concealed Mystery." When the Syntagma of the Supernal Man had been mitigated as to the Holy Body, in Male and Female form, these two were conjoined together again for the third time.*

1087. And the temperation of all things proceeded therefrom, and the superior and inferior worlds were mitigated.

1088. And thenceforth the superior and inferior worlds are bound together under the form of the Holy Body, and the worlds are associated together, and cohere together, and have been made one Body.†

1089. And since all things are one Body, the Schechinah Superior, the Schechinah Inferior—that Holy One, may He be blessed above! that Holy One, may He be blessed below!—hence is His Spirit drawn forth, and She entereth into the One Body, and in all things there appeareth nothing but the Unity.

1090. QDVSH, QDVSH, QDVSH, IHVH TZBAVTH; *Qadosh, Qadosh, Qadosh, Yod He Vau He Tzabaoth*; Holy, holy, holy, Tetragrammaton of the Hosts! the whole earth is full of Thy glory, for all things are Thy One Body.

1091. We have learned that because the one hath

* For their first conjunction produced Qain, the severe and evil judgment; their second, Abel, the milder and weaker form whom Qain absorbs; but their third produces Seth, the equilibrium of the supernals and inferiors.

† "And they twain shall be one flesh."

been tempered by the other, hence it is written, Cant. i. 11: "We will make thee borders of gold with studs of silver." For judgment and mercy are connected together (otherwise, judgment is tempered through mercy), and She is mitigated by Him.

1092. And therefore She ascendeth not without Him, like as with the palms; one sex ariseth not without the other.

1093. And therefore have we learned by tradition that if any one in this world cutteth himself off from the race of mankind, he hereafter, when he quitteth this world, shall not enter into the Syntagma of mankind, which is called the Holy Body; but (*shall enter*) among those who are not called mankind, so that he shall go forth from the Syntagma of the Body.

1094. We have learned in exotic tradition that this is the sense of "We will make the borders of gold with studs of silver" (Cant. i. 11), that judgment is mitigated through mercy, so that there can be no judgment in which mercy is not found.

1095. And therefore it is written, *ibid.* 10: "Thy cheeks are beautiful in their outlines, and thy neck in pearls."

1096. "In outlines (or borders)," as it is written: "He will make thee borders of gold."

1097. "In pearls" answering to that which is written: "With studs of silver."

1098. "Thy neck" involveth the perfection of the Woman. This is found to be the habitation of the Sanctuary above, but the Jerusalem below.

1099. And all this is after that She is mitigated through the Male, and They twain are become one being, even the Syntagma of Truth.

1100. What is this Truth? Wherein is found all Truth?

1101. Thus have we learned. If any one be called Adam, and his soul (*Neschamah*) goeth from him, and he dieth, it is forbidden to leave him in his abode so that he should abide upon the earth.

1102. On account of the honour of that Body wherein no corruption can appear.

1103. For it is written, Ps. xlix. 13: "Man (*Adam*) shall not abide in honour;" that is, Adam, who is more worthy that all honour, shall not abide.

1104. Wherefore? Because if it were thus, he would be like unto the beasts (BHMVTH, *Behemoth*) which perish.

1105. In what manner is it with the beast? He is not in the race of Adam, neither is he able to receive the Holy Spirit (RVCHA QDISHA), for thus also would he be like unto the beast were his body without the Spirit, when at the same time that body (*of his*), which is the most honourable of all (*bodies, seeing it is the image of the Supernal*), is not meet to be associated with those things which are ignominious.

1106. Also we have learned in the "Book of Concealed Mystery," that were any one permitted to remain in such (*image of the*) Holy Body, and yet without the Spirit (*Ruacha*), there would be a void in the Body of the World.

1107. For assuredly, therefore, it could not be permitted unto him that he should abide in the holy place, in that earth wherein justice abideth. (Otherwise: Under the command of the Holy Crown, *Kether*, of the King, *Microprosopus*, in the earth, concerning which it is written, Isa. i. 21, "Justice abideth in Her.")

1108.* Since that venerable Body is the Form of the King; but if it were thus permitted to remain, then it would be counted as one of the beasts. (Otherwise: Since this venerable Body is called the Form of the King, and if it were thus left abiding, it would be like as the

* These sections are going on the idea of the Body remaining alive when the Divine Spirit has been withdrawn therefrom; that is, were it possible for it to be so.

beast.) Therefore is it said, "Like unto the beasts which perish."

1109. We have learned this which is written, Gen. vi. 2: "And the sons of the Elohim beheld the daughters of Adam." These (*sons of the Elohim*) are they who were withdrawn, and who fell into the mouth of the Great Abyss.*

1110 "The daughters of Adam." (*Here it is to be noted that it is written HADM, Ha-Adam, the initial being demonstrative and emphatic, signifying*) of that especial Adam.

1111. And it is written: "And they came in unto them . . . the same were mighty men, who were from the Earth," &c. From that place, namely, which is called the earth, like as the tradition is concerning the phrase IMI OVLM, *Yemi Olahm*, the day of the world.

1112. The impurities † of the Name. From them have gone forth the Spirits, RVCHIN, *Ruachin*, and the Demons, SHDIN, *Shedin*, into the world, so that they may adhere unto the wicked.

1113. "There were HNPILIM, *Ha-Nephilim*, Giants, BARTZ, *Be-Aretz*, in the earth;" for the restraining of those who were left, who existed not in the earth.

1114. Those giants are OZA, *Auza*, and OZAL, *Auzael*, who were in the earth, the sons of the Elohim were not in the earth. And this is an Arcanum, and all these things are said.

1115. It is written, Gen. vi. 6: "And it repented Tetragrammaton that He had formed Adam in the earth;" *i.e.*, for the restriction of the Supernal Adam, who is not in the earth.

1116. "And it repented Tetragrammaton;" this is said concerning Microprosopus.

1117. "And He was grieved about His heart;" it is

* See *ante*, § 1048

† Knorr Von Rosenroth translates this word ANSHI, *Anshi*; Viri, "men;" but I think "impurities" preferable.

not written, VIOTzB, *Va-Yautzeb*, and He affected with grief; but VITHOTzB, *Va-Yethautzeb*, and He was touched with grief; *i.e.*, He was affected with grief from whom the matter depended, for the restriction of Him who was not touched with grief.

1118. "About His heart." It is not written, "within His heart," but "about His heart"; like as when any man is afflicted with grief, and mourneth before his Lord; for herein it is referred unto the heart of all hearts.

1119. And Tetragrammaton said: "I will destroy the Adam whom I have created, from off the face of HADMH, *Ha-Adamah*, the Earth," &c., for the restriction* of the Adam, who is supernal.

1120. And if thou sayest that the Inferior Adam is alone to be understood, it is to be known that these cannot altogether be opposed, seeing that the one existeth not without the other.

1121. And unless *Chokmah*, Wisdom, could be hidden from all, all things could be conformed like as from the beginning.

1122. Hence it is said, Prov. viii. 12: "ANI CHKMH, *Ani Chokmah*, I, Wisdom, have dwelt with Prudence;" read it not SHKNTHI, *Shekenethi*, I have dwelt; but SHIKNTHI, *Shikeneth-i*, My Shechinah or my Presence.

1123. And unless Adam were thus, the world could not consist; like as it is written, Prov. iii. 19: "Tetragrammaton in Chokmah hath founded the earth, IHVH BCHKMH ISD ARTz, *Tetragrammaton Be-Chokmah Yesed Aretz*.

1124. Also it is written, Gen. vi. 8: "And Noah found grace in the eyes of Tetragrammaton."

1125. Also we have learned that all brains depend from this brain (*supernal*).

1126. And *Chokmah*, Wisdom, also is a general name, but this concealed Wisdom corroborateth and con-

*Or counterbalancing.

formeth the form of the Man, so that He may abide in his place.

1127. Like as it is written, Eccl. vii. 19: "Wisdom is a strength to a wise man more than ten rulers which are in a city;" which (*ten*) are the integral conformation of the man.

1128. Adam, truly, is the interior conformation, wherein consisteth the RVCH, *Ruach*, Spirit; like as it is said, 1 Sam. xvi. 6: "Because Adam seeth according to the eyes, but Tetragrammaton seeth according to the heart," which is within the interior parts.

1129. And in that formation appeareth the true perfection of all things, which existeth above the Throne. Like as it is written: "And the appearance as the likeness of Adam upon it from above" (Ezek. i. 26).

1130. Also it is written, Dan. vii. 13: "And, behold, there came with the clouds of heaven one like unto a son of man, and even unto the Ancient of Days he came, and they made Him approach unto Him."

CHAPTER XLV.*

CONCLUSION.

1131. HEREUNTO are the concealed words, and the more secret meaning (*of them hath been set forth in many places*). Blessed is his portion who hath known and beheld them, and who erreth not therein.

1132. Because these words are not given forth save unto the Lords of Lords and the Reapers of the Field, who have both entered into and departed therefrom.

* It is worthy of note that the total number of chapters in the "Idra Rabba Qadisha" is 45, which is equal to MH, *Mah*, the concealed name of Yetzirah. (See Introduction concerning the Four Worlds.)

1133. Like as it is written, Hosea xiv. 9: "For the paths of Tetragrammaton are right, and the just shall walk in them, but transgressors shall fall therein."

1134. This have we learned. Rabbi Schimeon wept, and lifted up his voice and said: "If on account of our words which be here revealed, the Companions are to be concealed in the Conclave of the world to come, and are to be taken away from this world, it is justly and rightly done, in order that they may not reveal (*these secrets*) unto one of the children of this world."

1135. Again he said: "I return unto myself. For truly I have revealed (*these secrets*) before the Ancient of the Ancient Ones, the Concealed One with all Concealments; but not for mine own glory, not for the glory of the house of my father, not for the glory of these my Companions, have I done (*this thing*).

1136. "But in order that they might not err in His paths, nor that they might enter into the portals of His Palace to be made ashamed, nor that they might be destroyed for their error. Blessed be my portion with them in the world to come."

1137. We have learned that before the companions departed from this Assembly, Rabbi Yosi, Rabbi Chizqiah, and Rabbi Yisa died.

1138. And the companions beheld that the holy angels carried them away into that veil expanded above. And Rabbi Schimeon spake a certain word, and fell upon his face.

1139. Rabbi Schimeon cried aloud and said: "Wherefore is this? Because a certain decree hath been decreed against us to punish us, seeing that through us that hath been revealed which had not been revealed hitherto, from that day wherein Moses stood upon the mountain of Sinai.

1140. "Like as it is written, Exod. xxxiv. 28: 'And he was there with Tetragrammaton forty days and forty nights.' Why then do I tarry here, if therefor I am to be punished?"

1141. And a Voice was heard which spake, and said: "Blessed art thou, Rabbi Schimeon, and blessed is thy portion, and that of those companions who are with thee; for unto ye hath that been revealed which is not revealed unto the whole supernal host.

1142. "But come, behold. It is written, Josh. vi. 26: 'And in his first-born son shall he establish it, and in his youngest son shall he set up the gates thereof;' much more than in this instance also are these taken away, seeing that with most severe and vehement study have they applied their souls (NPSHTHHVN, *Nepheschethhun*) hereunto at this time.

1143. "Blessed is their portion, for assuredly they have been taken away in perfection; and such were not those who were before them."

1144. Wherefore died they? We have learned this. When thus far these words were revealed, the Supernals and Inferiors of those Chariots were disturbed, and the Voice which revealed the Ancient Word below resounded through two hundred and fifty worlds.

1145. And before that those (three *Rabbis*) could recollect their souls, NSHMTHIIHV, *Neschamathiyehu*, among those words (*of that Voice*) their souls had gone forth with a kiss *; and were joined unto that expanded veil, and the Supernal Angels carried them away.

1146. But wherefore those? Because they had entered in, and had not gone forth alternately, before this time. But all the others had entered in, and had gone forth.

1147. Rabbi Schimeon spake and said: "How blessed

* The palace which is situate in the secret and most elevated part of heaven is called the Palace of Love. There dwells the Heavenly King—blessed be He!—with the holy souls, and is united with them with a loving kiss. This kiss is the union of the soul with the substance from which it emanated.

is the portion of those three, and therefore also blessed is our portion!"

1148. And a second time that Voice pealed forth and said, Deut. iv. 4: "But ye that did cleave unto Tetragrammaton, your God, are alive every one of you this day."

1149. They arose, and behold there was no place whence a fragrance went not forth.

1150. Rabbi Schimeon spake and said: "From this I perceive that the world receiveth blessing on account of us."

1151. And the faces of them all shone, so that men could not look upon them.

1152. We have learned that there were ten (*Rabbis*) entered into (*the Assembly*), and that seven came forth.

1153. And Rabbi Schimeon rejoiced, and Rabbi Abba was sad.

1154. On a certain day Rabbi Schimeon sat, and Rabbi Abba with him. Rabbi Schimeon spake a certain word.

1155. And they saw those three (*Rabbis*) who had died, and with them were most beautiful angels, who were showing unto them the supernal treasures and conclaves, on account of their great dignity.

1156. And they were entering into a mountain of pure balm; and the soul of Rabbi Abba was comforted.

1157. We have learned that after that day the companions did not quit the house of Rabbi Schimeon.

1158. And when Rabbi Schimeon revealed the Arcana, there were found none present there save those (*companions*).

1159. And Rabbi Schimeon called them the seven eyes of Tetragrammaton, like as it is written, Zach. iii. 9: "These are the seven eyes of Tetragrammaton." And this was said concerning us.*

* Meaning, I suppose, that Rabbi Abba adds this by way of note to the text.

1160. Rabbi Abba spake and said: "We six are lights which shine forth from a seventh (*light*); thou art the seventh light (*the origin of*) us all.

1161. "For assuredly there is no stability in those six, save (*what they derive*) from the seventh. For all things depend from the seventh."

1162. Rabbi Yehudah called him * the Sabbath of all the six (*Rabbi*).

1163. Like as it is written: "The Sabbath for Tetragrammaton, holy unto Tetragrammaton."

1164. What is the Sabbath? Holy unto Tetragrammaton; so also Rabbi Schimeon is, like the Sabbath, holy unto Tetragrammaton.

1165. Rabbi Schimeon said: "It is strange that he † who is girded about the loins, and clothed with a heavy garment, was not found in the place of our conclave when those holy matters were revealed!"

1166. Meanwhile Elihu entered, and three beams of light shone in his countenance.

1167. Rabbi Schimeon said unto him: "Why was it that he was not present (otherwise, Why was not my lord present) in the sculptured square of his Lord in the nuptial day?"

1168. He answered unto him: "Through thy life, Rabbi, seven were chosen before Him, the Holy One—may He be blessed!—(otherwise, seven days are prostrate before the blessed God) all those who could come and abide with Him, before that ye could enter into the House of Conclave.

1169. "And I prayed that I might come among the others, and I wished to adhere unto His shoulders (otherwise, And I asked Him, that it might be permitted me to enter in, but He constrained my shoulders), and I could not.

* Him: *i.e.*, Rabbi Schimeon Ben Yochai, who was chief among the seven surviving Rabbis, like the Sabbath among the days of the week.

† Elihu, who now enters.

1170. "For in that day was I sent that I might perform miracles for Rav Hamenuna the elder and his companions, who had been taken away into the palace (otherwise: into the prison) of the King.

1171. "And I performed a miracle for them, and cast down the King's rampart (otherwise: I cast down the wall of the royal palace for them), with whose chains they were bound; so that (*their*) forty-five warders were kept back.

1172. "And I led forth Rav. Hamenuna and his companions, and brought them up unto the valley of Aunu; and they have been set free.

1173. "And I have given unto them bread and water, seeing they had not eaten for three days.

1174. "And all the day I quitted them not.

1175. "And when I returned (*hither*), I found the Veil expanded, which all these Columns * upheld; and three of the Companions (*had ascended*) above it.

1176. "And I spake unto them, and they answered: 'This is the portion of God the most Holy One—may He be blessed!—from the nuptials † of Rabbi Schimeon and his companions.'

1177. "Blessed art thou, Rabbi Schimeon, and blessed is thy portion, and that of those companions who are sitting in thy presence.

1178. "How many paths are prepared for ye in the world to come! how many lights of lights are prepared that they may enlighten ye!

1179. "And come, behold! Therefore on this day there are bound together for thee fifty crowns for Rabbi Benchas Ben Yair, thy father-in-law, and I walk with him.

1180. "And all those are rivers of the mountains of pure balm, for assuredly his place and lot is chosen (otherwise: and I saw that he had, &c.).

* The columns of the Sephiroth.

† This term is occasionally used in a mystical sense to signify the acquisition of divine wisdom.

1181. (*Rabbi Schimeon*) said unto him: "Are therefore the just united by the Union of the Diadems more on the days of the New Moon, of the feasts, and of the Sabbaths, than on any other days?"

1182. He answered unto him: "Most certainly; also all those who are without. Like as it is written, Isa. lxvi. 23: 'And it shall come to pass that from one new moon to another, and from one sabbath unto another, shall all flesh come to worship before me, saith Tetragrammaton.'

1183. "If those come, how much more the just!

1184. "Wherefore from one new moon unto another? Because the patriarchs surround the Holy Chariot.

1185. "And from one Sabbath unto another Sabbath, because the seventh day is surrounded by all the other six days.

1186. "Like as it is written: 'And the Elohim blessed the seventh day,' &c.

1187. "And thou, Rabbi Schimeon, art the seventh: thou shalt be the chief; and thou shalt be more crowned and sanctified than all.

1188. "And with three most delicious feasts of the seventh day shall the just be entertained because of thee in the world to come.

1189. "Also it is written, Isa. lviii. 13: 'Thou shalt call the sabbath a delight, the holy of Tetragrammaton, honourable.'

1190. "Who is He, the Holy One of Tetragrammaton? This is Rabbi Schimeon Ben Yochai, who is called very glorious (*both*) in this world and in (*the world*) to come."

Hereunto is the Greater Holy Assembly.

HADRA ZVTA QDISHA

(HA IDRA ZUTA QADISHA);

OR,

THE LESSER HOLY ASSEMBLY.

CHAPTER I.

WHICH CONTAINETH THE INTRODUCTION.

1. TRADITION.—On that day on which the Companions were assembled together in the house of Rabbi Schimeon, and on which he had arranged his affairs because he was about to depart from the world, before him were Rabbi Eleazar his son, and Rabbi Abba, and the rest of the Companions; and the house was full.

2. Therefore lifting up his eyes, Rabbi Schimeon saw that the house was full. And Rabbi Schimeon wept, saying: "The second time when I was sick, and Rabbi Benchas Ben Yair was in my presence, and until I had chosen my place, life hath been prolonged unto me even until now.

3. "When I was restored, fire surrounded (*my habitation*) which hitherto hath never ceased, neither did any man enter in unto me without permission.

4. "But now I see that it is taken away, and that the house is filled."

5. Whilst they were sitting down, Rabbi Schimeon,

opening his eyes, beheld a certain vision, and lo! fire surrounded the house!

6. Therefore all (*the others*) went forth, and Rabbi Eleazar his son, and Rabbi Abba remained; but the other Companions sat without.

7. Rabbi Schimeon said unto Rabbi Eleazar his son: "Go forth, and see whether Rabbi Yitzchaq be present, for whom I have made myself surety.

8. "And say thou unto him that he dispose his affairs, and that he may sit down with me. Blessed is his portion."

9. Rabbi Schimeon arose and again sat down; and he laughed aloud, and rejoicing, said: "Where are the Companions?"

10. Rabbi Eleazar arose and introduced them, and they sat down in his presence.

11. Rabbi Schimeon lifted up his hands and prayed a prayer, and was joyful.

12. And he said: "Let those Companions who were in the former Conclave* assemble here."

13. Therefore, all the others having gone forth, there remained Rabbi Eleazar his son, and Rabbi Abba, and Rabbi Yehudah, and Rabbi Yosi Bar Yoqeb, and Rabbi Chiya.

14. In the meantime Rabbi Yitzchaq entered, to whom Rabbi Schimeon said: "How excellent is thy lot! How much joy is this day stored up for thee!"

15. Rabbi Abba sat down behind his (*i.e., Rabbi Schimeon's*) back, and Rabbi Eleazar before him (*i.e., Rabbi Schimeon*).

16. Rabbi Schimeon spake and said: "Surely now is the time of benevolence, and I desire to enter without confusion into the world to come.

17. "And verily these sacred things, which hereunto have never been revealed, I desire to reveal before the Schekhinah;

* That is, who had formed part of the Greater Holy Assembly.

18. "Lest they should say that I have kept back anything, and that I have been taken away from the world; for even until now these things have been concealed in my heart, so that having entered into these very matters I may be with them in the world to come.

19. "But this is my arrangement of you; let Rabbi Abba write, and let Rabbi Eleazar my son speak openly; but let the rest of the Companions in silence meditate in their heart."

20. Rabbi Abba arose from his seat behind him, and Rabbi Eleazar his son sat down.

21. He said unto him, "Arise, O my son, for another shall sit in that seat;" and Rabbi Eleazar arose.

22. Rabbi Schimeon covered himself and sat down; and he commenced, and said Ps. cxv. 17: "'The dead shall not praise IH, *Yah*, nor all they who go down into silence!

23. "'The dead shall not praise Yah;' so it is certain that it is assuredly those who are called dead; for He, God, the most Holy One—may He be blessed!—is called the Living One, and is Himself commemorated among those who are called living, and not with those who are called dead.

24. "And the end of this text runneth thus: 'Nor all they who go down into silence;' for all they who go down into silence remain in Gehenna.

25. "There is another reason appertaining to those who are called living, for God the most Holy One—may He be blessed!—desireth their glory."

26. Rabbi Schimeon said: "How different is this occasion from that of the former conclave! For into a certain conclave* came He, the most Holy and Blessed God, and His Chariot.

27. "Now verily He, the Holy One, is here—may He

* Meaning that the Greater Holy Assembly had been as it were the reflection of the conclave of the Sephiroth above. The word used for "chariot" is not *Mercavah*, but *Kthikh*.

be blessed—and He hath approached with those Just who are in the Garden of Eden,* which did not occur in the former conclave.

28. "And God, the Most Holy One—may He be blessed—more promoteth the glory of the Just than His own glory.

29. "As it is written concerning Jeroboam, who sacrificed unto and served other gods, and yet God, the Most Holy One—may He be blessed!—waited for him.

30. "But because he stretched forth his hand against Iddo the prophet, his hand became withered.

31. "For it is written, 1 Kings xiii. 4: 'And his hand became withered, &c.' Here it is not written that it was because he served other gods, but because he extended his hand against Iddo the prophet, &c.

32. "Now, therefore, God the Most Holy One—may He be blessed!—promoteth their glory (*i.e.*, that of the Just), and they all come with Him."

33. He said: "Verily, Rav Hamenuna the elder is here, and around him are seventy Just represented in his circle, of whom certain shine with the splendour of the Ancient and Most Holy One, the Concealed with all Concealments.

33.† "He, I say, cometh, in order that with joy he may hear those words which I shall speak."

34. And when he had sat down he said: "Assuredly here a seat hath been set aside for Rabbi Benchas Ben Yair."

35. The companions who were there trembled greatly, and they arose, and sat down in the lower part of the house; but Rabbi Eleazar and Rabbi Abba (*still sat*) before Rabbi Schimeon.

36. Rabbi Schimeon said: "In the former Assembly we acted thus, namely, that all the companions spoke, and I also with them, by turns.

* *I.e.*, The Paradise above.

† In the original both this and the foregoing section, apparently by an oversight, have the number 33 attached to them.

37. "Now I shall speak alone, and let all hear my words superiors and inferiors; blessed be my portion this day!"

38. Rabbi Schimeon commenced, and said, Cant. vii. 10: "'I am my beloved's, and his desire is towards me.'

39. "As long as I have been bound unto this world in one link with God, the Most Holy One—may he be blessed! —have I been bound, and therefore now is His desire towards me.

40. "For He Himself and His whole holy company come, so that with joy they may hear the concealed words, and the praise of Him, the Most Holy Ancient One, the Concealed with all Concealments.

41. "And He separateth Himself ever more and more; He is separated from all things, neither yet doth He altogether separate Himself, seeing that unto Himself all things adhere, and that He Himself adhereth unto all; HVA, *Hoa*, He Himself is all; He the Most Holy Ancient of all Ancients, the Concealed with all Concealments.

42. "He hath been formed, and yet as it were He hath not been formed. He hath been conformed, so that He may sustain all things; yet is He not formed, seeing that He is not discovered.

43. "When He is conformed He produceth nine Lights, which shine forth from Him, from His conformation.

44. "And from Himself those Lights shine forth, and they emit flames, and they rush forth and are extended on every side, like as from an elevated lantern the rays of light stream down on every side.

45. "And those rays of light,* which are extended, when anyone draweth near unto them, so that they may be examined, are not found, and there is only the lantern alone.

46. "So also is He the Most Holy and Ancient One: He is that highest Light concealed with all concealments,

* Carrying on the simile of the lantern and its rays.

and He is not found; those rays* (*proceeding from Him*) being excepted, which are extended, which are revealed, and which are hidden.

47. "And they are called the Holy Name, and therefore are all things One.

48. "Which truly our companions have said in former books, that certain paths have been created by the Most Holy Ancient One, who is revealed through them collectively and severally; since they are the conformations of the Most Holy Ancient One, concerning them now there is not time for examination.

49. "I have spoken concerning them in the Holy Assembly, and I have beheld that which before I did not understand in such a manner, and I have hidden the matter in my heart.

50. "But now I alone will describe these things before the Holy King, and all those assuredly just men who have assembled to hear these words."

CHAPTER II.

CONCERNING THE SKULL OF THE ANCIENT ONE, AND CONCERNING HIS BRAIN; AND CONCERNING THE THREE HEADS, AND THE HAIR, AND THE DISCRIMINATORY PATHS.

51. THE skull of the White Head hath not beginning, but its end is the convexity of its joining together, which is extended, and shineth.

52. And from it the just shall inherit four hundred† desirable worlds in the world to come.

53. And from this convexity of the joining together

* The Sephiroth.

† Which is the number of TH, the last letter of the Hebrew Alphabet, which includes the symbology of the cross.

of this White Skull daily distilleth a dew into Microprosopus, into that place which is called Heaven; and in that very place shall the dead be raised to life in the time to come.

54. Like as it is written, Gen. xxvii. 27: "And Elohim shall give thee from the dew of heaven."

55. And His head is filled with that dew, and all the place of the apple-trees distilleth therewith.

56. He, the Most Holy Ancient One, is hidden and concealed, and in that Skull is the Supernal Wisdom concealed, who is found and who is not found.

57. For assuredly in Him, the Ancient One, nothing is revealed save the Head alone, seeing that that Head is itself the Head of all heads.

58. The beginning of that Supernal Wisdom which also is itself the Head, is hidden therein, and is called the Supernal Brain, the Hidden Brain, the Tranquil and Calm Brain; neither doth any man know it save He Himself.

59. Three Heads have been formed forth, one within the other, and the other above the other.

60. One Head is the Concealed Wisdom, which is covered and is not disclosed.

61. And this Hidden Wisdom is the Head of all things, and the Head of the remaining wisdoms.

62. The Supernal Head is the Most Holy Ancient One, the Concealed with all Concealments.

63. The Head of all Heads, the Head which is not a Head*—namely, that which is *in* that Head—neither knows nor is known, because it cannot be comprehended either by Wisdom or Understanding.

64. And therefore is it read, Num. xxiv. 11: "Fly thee in thy place;" and Ezek. i. 14. The *Chaioth*, living creatures, are said to run forth and return.

* That is to say, which will hardly admit even of so vague a definition, seeing it is the Indefinite Absolute in Kether.

65. And therefore is the Most Holy Ancient One called AIN, *Ain*, the Negatively Existent; seeing that back from Him dependeth the AIN, the Negative Existence.*

66. But all these hairs and all those locks depend from the Hidden Brain.

67. And all are calm (otherwise, are disposed) in the Equilibrium; neither in any manner is the neck seen (i.e., *because of the locks which overshadow it*).

68. Because He the Most Holy Ancient One is in an unvarying condition of joy, neither changeth He from mercy for ever.

69. But in the thirteen measurements† of mercies is He found, because that Wisdom hidden in Him is divided into three‡ paths in a quarternary, and He Himself the Ancient One comprehendeth them, and through them doth He reign over all things.

70. One (*path*) which shineth in the midst of the hairs going forth from the Skull, is that path by whose light the just are led into the world to come.

71. Like as it is written, Prov. iv. 18: "And the path of the just shineth as the light."

72. And concerning this it is written, Isa. lviii. 14: "Then shalt thou delight thyself in Tetragrammaton."

* We must be most careful not to misapprehend the meaning intended to be conveyed in this passage. Kether, the Ancient One, Macroprosopus, is *not* in the more restricted sense of the first Sephira, the AIN, but that that idea links back from Him must be manifest on consideration. Yet even He, the Vast Countenance, is hidden and concealed; how much more, then, the AIN! From Negative to Positive, through Potential Existence, eternally vibrates the Divine Absolute of the Hidden Unity of processional form masked in the Eternal Abyss of the Unknowable, the synthetical hieroglyph of an illimitable pastless futureless PRESENT. To the uttermost bounds of space rushes the Voice of Ages, unheard save in the concentrated unity of the thought-formulated Abstract, and eternally that Voice formulates a Word which is glyphed in the vast ocean of limitless life.

† The thirteen conformations of the beard of Macroprosopus.

‡ The Trinity completed by the Quaternary.

73. And from that path* are all the other paths illuminated which depend from Microprosopus.

74. He the Eternal Ancient of the Ancient Ones is the highest Crown among the Supernals, wherewith all Diadems and Crowns are crowned.

75. And from Him are all the Lights illuminated, and they flash forth flames and shine.

76. But He verily is the Supreme Light, which is hidden, which is not known.

77. And all the other Lights are kindled by Him, and derive (*their*) splendour (*from him*).

78. He the Most Holy Ancient One is found to have three heads, which are contained in the one Head.†

79. And He Himself is that only highest supreme Head.

80. And since He the Most Holy Ancient One is thus symbolized in the Triad, hence all the other Lights which shine are included in Triads.‡

81. Moreover, the Most Holy Ancient One is also symbolized by the Duad.

82. And the division of the Ancient One in the Duad

* Kether, the first Sephira, from which all the other Sephiroth, proceed, namely, those which are summed up in the Tetragrammaton.

† *I.e.*, His manifestation is triune.

‡ This refers to the Triads in the Sephiroth, when the Autz Chaiim is formed. (See Introduction.) It will be found that in this arrangement of the ten Sephiroth there are ten Triads, viz:

(1) Kether, Chokmah, Binah.
(2) Chesed, Geburah, Tiphereth.
(3) Netzach, Hod, Yesod.
(4) Chokmah, Chesed, Netzach.
(5) Tephereth, Yesod, Malkuth.
(6) Binah, Geburah, Hod.
(7) Chokmah, Tiphereth, Hod.
(8) Binah, Tiphereth, Netzach.
(9) Chesed, Tiphereth, Hod
(10) Geburah, Tiphereth, Netzach.

Wherein Kether and Malkuth are each repeated once; Chokmah, Binah, Chesed, and Geburah thrice; Tiphereth, six times; Netzach and Hod each four times; and Yesod twice.

is so that the (*one form is*) the Highest Crown of all the Supernals, the Head of all Heads.

83. And (*the other is*) that superior Head, and It is not known.

84. So also all the remaining Lights are mystically divided into Duads.

85. Furthermore, the Most Holy Ancient One is symbolized and concealed under the conception of the Unity, for He himself is One, and all things are One.

86. And thus all the other Lights are sanctified, are restricted, and are bound together in the Unity or Monad, and are One; and all things are HVA, *Hoa*, Himself.

CHAPTER III.

CONCERNING THE FOREHEAD OF THE MOST HOLY ANCIENT ONE.

87. THE Forehead, which is uncovered in the Most Holy Ancient One, is called Grace.

88. For that Supernal Head concealed in the Higher, which no man hath known, expandeth a certain external manifestation, beautiful and gracious, which is comprehended in the Forehead.

89. And since He Himself is the grace of all graciousness; hence He assumeth the conformation of the Forehead, which is disclosed in the most intense light (otherwise, hath a formation in the figure of a leaf).

90. And when It is disclosed, the grace of all graciousness is found in all worlds.

91. And all the prayers of the Inferiors are accepted; and the countenance of Microprosopus is illuminated, and all things are found to exist in mercy.

92. And since (*through this*) all judgments are hidden

and subjected, hence in the Sabbath, in the time of the afternoon prayers, in which all judgments are excited, that Forehead is disclosed.

93. And all the judgments are turned aside, and mercies are found.

94. And therefore is the Sabbath found without judgment, as well that which is above as that which is below; also the fire of Gehenna is restrained in its place, and the transgressors are at rest.

95. And therefore is the Spirit, NSHMTH, of Joy added on the Sabbath.

96. And it behoveth man to rejoice with three feasts on the Sabbath; for all truth, and the whole system of true faith, is found therein (*i.e., in the Sabbath*).

97. And it behoveth man to prepare the table, that he may eat in the three feasts of true faith, and rejoice in them.*

98. Rabbi Schimeon said: "I attest concerning myself, before all these who are here present, that through all my days I have not omitted these three feasts, and that because of them I have not been compelled to fast on the Sabbath.

99. "Furthermore, also on other days I have not been compelled (*to fast*), much less on the Sabbath, for he who rightly acteth concerning these (*feasts*) is the adept of perfect truth.

100. "The first feast is that of the Great Mother; the second that of the Holy King; and the third that of the Most Holy Ancient One, the Concealed with all Concealments.†

101. "And in this world, who can thoroughly follow out, through them, those paths?

* In many of the ancient mysteries *a feast* was part of the ceremony, analogous to our Eucharist. *Verbum sapientibus.*

† That is, the greatest triad of the Sephiroth, the Crown, King, and Queen; which finds a parallel in the Osiris, Isis, and Horus; the Axieros, Axiochersos, and Axiochersa of Lemnos and Samothrace, &c., &c.

102. "If this RTzVN, *Ratzon*, Grace, be revealed, all those judgments are enlightened, and are diverted from their concentrated rigour.

103. "The conformation of Him, the Most Holy Ancient One, is instituted through one form, which is the ideal Syntagma of all forms.

104. "The same is the Concealed Supernal Wisdom, the synthesis of all the rest.

105. "And this is called ODN, *Eden*, or the supernal Paradise, concealed with all occultations.

106. "And it is the Brain of the Most Holy Ancient One, and that Brain is expanded on every side.

107. "Therefore is it extended into Eden, or another Paradise,* and from this is Eden or Paradise formed forth.

108. "And when this Head, which is concealed in the Head of the Ancient One, which is not known, extendeth a certain frontal formation, which is formed for brilliance, then flasheth forth the Lightning of His Brain.

109. "And it is formed forth and illuminated with many Lights.

110. "And it produceth and designeth (*a certain effect*) in this Light (otherwise, in this opening), in this Forehead, whereon is inscribed a certain Light, which is called RTzVN, *Ratzon*, Grace.

111. "And that Grace is extended backward into the beard, even unto that place where it can remain in the beard, and it is called the Supernal, CHSD, *Chesed*, Mercy.

112. "And when this Grace is uncovered, all the Lords of Judgment behold It, and are turned aside."

*Described in other places as the Supernal Eden and the Inferior Eden.

CHAPTER IV.

CONCERNING THE EYES OF THE MOST HOLY ANCIENT ONE.

113. The eyes of the Head of the Most Holy Ancient One are two in one,* equal, which ever watch, and sleep not.

114. Like as it is written, Ps. cxxi. 4: "The Keeper of Israel neither slumbereth nor sleepeth," &c.—namely, of Israel the holy.

115. And therefore are there no eyebrows nor eyelashes unto His eyes.

116. This Brain is conformed and illuminated with three supernal white brilliances.

117. With this white brilliance are the eyes of Microprosopus bathed.

118. As it is written, Cant. v. 12: "Washed with milk," flowing down from the fulness of that primal white brilliance.

119. And with the remaining white brilliances are the other lights cleansed and purified.

120. The Brain is called the fountain of Benevolence, the fountain wherein all blessings are found.

121. And since this Brain radiateth into the three white brilliances of the eye (*of Microprosopus*), hence is that called the "good eye," concerning which it is said, Prov. xxii. 9: "It shall be blessed," or rather that from it dependeth blessing.

122. For through the Brain are manifested the white brilliances of the eye.

123. And when this eye looketh upon Microprosopus, all the worlds are (*in a state of*) happiness.

* The Duad equated in the Monad. Compare what I have previously remarked concerning the profile symbolism of Macroprosopus.

124. This is the right eye. The inferior eyes are right and left, two in duplicate colour.

125. In the "Book of Concealed Mystery" have we taught that there is a Superior Yod, an Inferior Yod; a Superior He, an Inferior He; a Superior Vau, an Inferior Vau.

126. Unto the Ancient One pertain all the Superiors, and unto Microprosopus the Inferiors.

127. They depend not in another manner, but only thus; for from the Most Holy Ancient One do they depend.

128. For the Name of the Ancient One is concealed in all things, neither is it found.

129. But those letters which depend from the Ancient One, so that they may be established, are all inferiors. For were it not so, they could not be established.

130. And therefore is the Holy Name* *alike* concealed and manifest.

131. For that which is concealed pertaineth unto the Most Holy Ancient One, the Concealed in all things.

132. But that, indeed, which is manifested, because it dependeth, belongeth unto Microprosopus. (Otherwise, that which is manifested, is so for this reason—that it is manifested because it dependeth, &c.)

133. And therefore do all the blessings require both concealment and manifestation.

134. Those concealed letters which hang behind depend from the Most Holy Ancient One.

135. Wherefore do they hang behind? For the purpose of establishing the Inferior Yod. (Otherwise, assuredly from the Skull, from the Forehead, from the Eyes, do they depend. And the Yod Maternal† dependeth towards the Inferior Yod.)

* The student will observe throughout the Qabalah that great stress is laid on the power of names, which arises from the fact that each qabalistical name is the synthesis of a power. Hence to "pronounce that name" is to use that power.

† The word I have translated "Maternal" is AMH, *Amah*, with a double *Kamets* point. Rosenroth renders it "*Yod Membri.*"

CHAPTER V.

CONCERNING THE NOSE OF THE MOST HOLY ANCIENT ONE.

136. THE NOSE. From this nose, from the openings of the nostrils, the Spirit of Life rusheth forth upon Microprosopus.

137. And from that opening of the nose, from those openings of the nostrils, dependeth the letter He, in order to establish the other and Inferior He.

138. And that Spirit proceedeth from the hidden brain, and She is called the Spirit of Life, and through that Spirit* will all men understand CHKMTHA, *Chokmatha*, Wisdom, in the time of King Messiah.

139. As it is written, Isa. xi. 2: "And the Spirit of Wisdom and Understanding, *RVCH CHKMH VBINH*, *Ruach Chokmah Va-Binah*, shall rest upon Him," &c.

140. This nose is life in every part; perfect joy, rest of spirit, and health.

141. The nose of Microprosopus is as we have (*before*) conformed it.

142. Since concerning Him it is said, Ps. xviii. 9: "There ascendeth a smoke in His nose," &c.

143. But concerning this it is written, Isa. xlviii. 9: "And for my name's sake will I defer mine anger (*literally, lengthen my nose*) for thee."

144. (But in the Book which is called "The Treatise of the School of Rav Yeyeva the Elder," the letter He is located in the mouth, and he doth not argue in the same manner as in the text, neither doth he bring about the

* Speaking of the unity, the "Sepher Yetzirah" says: "One is She, the Spirit of the Elohim of life (blessed and more than blessed be His name who is the life of ages), Voice, and Spirit, and Word—this is She the Spirit of holiness.

same combination, although the matter eventuateth in the same manner.)

145. But yet from the letter the judgment dependeth, and judgment pertaineth unto the nose (*of Microprosopus*). Like as it is written, Ps. xviii. 9: "Smoke ascendeth out of His nose."

146. And if thou sayest that behold also it is written, "And fire out of His mouth consumeth," surely the foundation of wrath dependeth from His nose.

147. All the conformations of the Most Holy Ancient One are formed forth from the calm and concealed brain.

148. And all the conformations of Microprosopus are formed through the Inferior *Chokmah*, Wisdom. Like as it is written, Ps. civ. 24: "All these hast thou made in Chokmah." And certainly it (*Wisdom*) is the epitome of all things.

149. Now what is the difference between H, *He*, and H, *He?* By the Inferior He is judgment stirred up; but in this instance, through the other *He*, mercy unto mercy is denoted.

CHAPTER VI.

CONCERNING THE BEARD OF THE MOST HOLY ANCIENT ONE.

150. From the Beard of the Most Holy Ancient One hangeth the whole ornament of all, and the Influence; for all things are called from that beard, Influence.

151. This is the Ornament of all Ornaments, and this influence do all the superiors and inferiors alike behold.

152. From this Influence dependeth the life of all things.

153. From this Influence heavens and earth depend, the rains of grace, and the nourishment of all things.

154. From this Influence cometh the providence of all things. From this Influence depend all the superior and inferior hosts.

155. Thirteen fountains of excellent and precious oil depend from this beard of most glorious Influence, and they all flow down into Microprosopus.

156. Say not thou, however, that all do so, but nine of them are found (*in Microprosopus*) for the purpose of diverting the judgments.

157. And whensoever this Influence hangeth down in equilibrium even unto the heart, all the Holinesses of the Holinesses of Holiness depend from it.

158. In that Influence is extended an expansion of the Supernal Emanation,* which is the Head of all Heads, which is not known nor perfected, and which neither superiors nor inferiors have known, because from that Influence all things depend.

159. In this beard the Three Heads concerning which we have spoken are expanded, and all things are associated together in this Influence, and are found therein.

160. And therefore every ornament of ornaments dependeth from that Influence.

161. Those letters which depend from this Ancient One all hang in that beard, and are associated together in that Influence.

162. And they hang therein for the purpose of establishing the other letters.

163. For unless those letters could ascend into the Ancient One, those other letters could not be established.

164. And therefore Moses saith when necessary IHVH,

* The word is QVTRA: Rosenroth translates it by "Aporrhea." It may also be translated "vapour," or "nebula."

IHVH, twice; and so that an accent distinguishes the one from the other.

165. For assuredly from the Influence all things depend.

166. By that Influence are both superiors and inferiors brought into reverence, and are prostrate before It.

167. Blessed is he who attaineth hereunto.

CHAPTER VII.

CONCERNING THE BRAIN AND THE WISDOM IN GENERAL.

168. Of this Most Holy Ancient One, Concealed with all Concealments, there is no mention made, neither is He found.

169. For since this Head is the supreme of all the supernals, hence He is only symbolized as a head alone without body, for the purpose of establishing all things.

170. And He Himself is concealed, and hidden, and kept recondite by all things.

171. His conformation is that He is formed forth in that brain, the most hidden of all things, which is expanded and formed forth, and hence proceedeth the superior and inferior ChSD, *Chesed*, Mercy.

172. And the superior Chesed is formed forth and expanded, and all things are comprehended in this concealed brain.

173. For when that White Brilliance is formed forth in that Light, it acteth upon that which acteth upon this brain, and it is enlightened.

174. And the second brain dependeth from that very glorious Influence, it is expanded into the thirty-two*

* The ten numbers and twenty-two letters.

paths, when it is illuminated, then it shineth from that very glorious Influence.*

175. Therefore are the Three Supernal Heads illuminated; Two Heads, and One which comprehendeth them; and they hang in that Influence, and by It are they comprehended.

176. Hence becometh the ornament of the beard to be manifested, which is the occult Influence.

177. And those inferiors are conformed, like as the Most Holy Ancient One.

178. The Three Heads surround Him; thus all things can appear in the Three Heads; and when they are illuminated all things depend together from Him in the Three Heads, whereof two are on the two sides, and one which includeth them.

179. And if thou sayest, "Who is the Most Holy Ancient One?" Come and see. The Supreme Head is that which is not known, nor comprehended, nor designated, and that (*Head*) comprehendeth all things.

180. And the Two Heads are contained in Itself. (Otherwise hang, &c.)

181. And then are all these things thus ordained; truly Himself existeth not in numeration, nor in system, nor in computation, but in the judgment of the heart.

182. Concerning this it is written, Ps. xxxix. 2: "I said I will take heed unto my ways, that I offend not with my tongue."

183. The place of commencement is found from the Most Holy Ancient One, and it is illuminated by the Influence. That is the Light of Wisdom.

184. And it is extended in thirty-two directions, and departeth from that hidden brain, from that Light which existeth in Itself.

185. And because the Most Holy Ancient One shineth in the beginning (otherwise, in the wisdom), this itself is

* MZL = 40 + 7 + 30 = 77, which is OZ, Strength or Vigour. This Gematria is worthy of note as giving the idea of foundational power.

this. And the same is that beginning from which manifestation is made.

186. And is conformed in the Three Heads, which One Head includeth.

187. And those three are extended into Microprosopus, and from them all things shine forth.

188. Thenceforth this Wisdom instituteth a formation, and produceth a certain river which floweth down and goeth forth to water the garden.

189. And it entereth into the head of Microprosopus, and formeth a certain other brain.

190. And thence it is extended and floweth forth into the whole body, and watereth all those plants (*of the garden of Eden*).

191. This is that which standeth written, Gen. ii. 9: "And a river went out of Eden to water the garden, &c."

192. But also this Wisdom instituteth another formation, and is extended and goeth into the head of Microprosopus, and formeth another brain.

193. That is the Light from which are produced those two rivulets which are associated together, carved out hollows in the One Head, which is called the depth of the fountain.*

194. Concerning which it is written, Prov. iii. 20: "In DOTH, *Daath*,† Knowledge, the depths are broken up."

195. And it entereth into the head of Microprosopus, and formeth another brain.

196. And thenceforth is it extended and goeth into the interior parts of His body, and filleth all those conclaves and assemblies of His body.‡

197. This is that same which is written, Prov. xxiv. 4: "In Daath shall the secret places be filled."

198. And those shine from the Light of that supernal

* *I.e.*, the containing power.

† Daath is the conjunction of Chokmah and Binah. (See "Book of Concealed Mystery," ch. i. § 40.)

‡ See "Greater Holy Assembly," ch. xxviii. § 566.

concealed brain which shineth in the Influence, MZL, of the Most Holy Ancient One.

199. And all things depend mutually from Himself, and mutually are bound together unto Himself, until He is known, because all things are one, and HVA, *Hoa*, He, the Ancient One, is all things, neither from Him can anything whatsoever be separated.

200. Into three other Lights, which are called the Fathers, do these three Lights shine, and these fathers shine into the children, and all things shine forth from the one place.*

201. When He, that Ancient One, who is the Grace of all Grace, is manifested, all things are found in light and in perfect happiness.

202. This Eden is derived from the superior Eden, the Concealed with all Concealments.

203. And therefore is that Eden called the beginning in the Ancient One; neither yet, however, is there beginning or end.†

204. And since in Him beginning and end exist not, hence He is not called ATHH, *Atah*, Thou; seeing that He is concealed and not revealed. But HVA, *Hoa*, He, is He called.

205. But in that aspect wherein the beginning is found, the name ATHH, *Atah*, Thou, hath place, and the name AB, *Ab*, Father. For it is written, Isa. lxiii. 16: "Since *Atah*, Thou, art *Ab*, our Father."

206. In the teaching of the school of Rav Yeyeva the Elder, the universal rule is that Microprosopus be called ATHH, *Atah*, Thou; but that the most Holy Ancient One, who is concealed, be called HVA, *Hoa*, He; and also with reason.

* This is analogous to the teaching of the "Sepher Yetzirah," that the Three Mothers A, M, SH, radiate into three paternal forms of the same. A, M, and SH, symbolize the potencies of Air, Water, and Fire.

† For commencement denotes end, and end denotes commencement; how, then, in the Absolute can there be either? Nevertheless, in the Absolute must we seek for the hypothetical starting-point of life.

207. Now truly in that place wherein beginning is found, is He thus called, although He is concealed.

208. And therefrom is the beginning, and it is called AThH, *Atha*, Thou; and He is the Father of the Fathers.

209. And that Father proceedeth from the Most Holy Ancient One, like as it is written, Job. xxviii. 12: "And ChKMH, *Chokmah*,* Wisdom, is found from AIN, *Ain*, the Negatively Existent One;" and therefore is He not known.

210. Come and see! It is written, *ibid.* 22: "The Elohim have known the path;" His path, properly speaking.

211. But again, further on: VHVA, *Va-Hoa*, and He Himself knoweth His place;" His place properly speaking; much more His path; and much more this Wisdom which is concealed in the Most Holy Ancient One.

212. This Wisdom is the beginning of all things. Thencefrom are expanded the thirty-two paths: ShBILIN, *Shebilin*, Paths, I say; and not ARChIN, *Archin*, By-ways.

213. And in them is the Law comprehended, in the twenty-two letters and in the ten utterances.†

214. This Chokmah is the Father of Fathers, and in this Chokmah is beginning and end discovered; and therefore is there one Chokmah supernal, and another Chokmah inferior.

215. When Chokmah is extended, then is He called the Father of Fathers, for in none else are all things comprehended save in Him. (Otherwise, when they are expanded all things are called Chokmoth,‡ and the Father of Fathers; all things are comprehended in no place, save herein.)

* Let the student carefully note that this is the second Sephira, the I of IHVH, the Father proceeding from Macroprosopus, Kether, as He proceedeth from Ain Soph.

† The Sephiroth, or numbers.

‡ Chokmoth is plural of Chokmah, Wisdom.

216. As it is written, Ps. civ. 25: "All things in Chokmah hast Thou formed."

217. Rabbi Schimeon lifted up his hands, and rejoiced, and said: Assuredly it is Eden or Paradise, and all things have their operation in this hour.

CHAPTER VIII.

CONCERNING THE FATHER AND THE MOTHER IN SPECIAL.

218. Come and behold. When the Most Holy Ancient One, the Concealed with all Concealments, desired to be formed forth, He conformed all things under the form of Male and Female; and in such place wherein Male and Female are comprehended.

219. For they could not permanently exist save in another aspect of the Male and the Female (their countenances being joined together).

220. And this Wisdom embracing all things, when it goeth forth and shineth forth from the Most Holy Ancient One, shineth not save under the form of Male and Female.

221. Therefore is this Wisdom extended, and it is found that it equally becometh Male and Female.

222. ChKMH AB BINH AM, *Chokmah Ab Binah Am*: Chokmah* is the Father, and Binah is the Mother, and therein are Chokmah, Wisdom, and Binah, Understanding, counterbalanced together in most perfect equality of Male and Female.

223. And therefore are all things established in the

* Chokmah is the second and Binah is the third of the Sephiroth. This section is a sufficient condemnation of all those who wish to make out that woman is inferior to man.

equality of Male and Female; for were it not so, how could they subsist!

224. This beginning is the Father of all things; the Father of all Fathers; and both are mutually bound together, and the one path shineth into the other—Chokmah, Wisdom, as the Father; Binah, Understanding, as the Mother.

225. It is written, Prov. ii. 3: "If thou callest Binah the Mother."

226. When They are associated together They generate, and are expanded in truth.

227. In the teaching of the school of Rav Yeyeva the Elder it is thus taught: "What is Binah the Mother of Understanding?" Truly when They are mutually associated together.

228. Assuredly *Yod*, I, impregnateth the letter *He*, H, and produceth a Son, and She herself bringeth Him forth.*

229. And therefore is it called BINH, as if (*it were a transposition of*) BN IH, *Ben Yah*, Son of IH (*or I, Yod, H, He, and BN, the Son*).

230. But They both are found to be the perfection of all things when They are associated together, and when the Son is in Them the Syntagma of all things findeth place.

231. For in Their conformations are They found to be the perfection of all things—Father and Mother, Son, and Daughter.

232. These things have not been revealed save unto the Holy Superiors who have entered therein and departed therefrom, and have known the paths of the Most Holy God (may He be blessed!), so that they have not erred in them either on the right hand or on the left.

* For Chokmah and Binah in the Sephiroth answer unto I and H in the name IHVH, as has been already shown in the Introduction; and these bring forth Microprosopus the Son, the letter *Vau*, V, answering in numerical value to the number 6, and to the fourth, fifth, sixth, seventh, eighth, and ninth Sephiroth.

233. For thus it is written, Hos. xiv. 9: "The paths of Tetragrammaton are true, and the just shall walk in them," &c.

235. For these things are concealed, and the Holy Highest Ones shine in them, like as light proceedeth from the shining of a lantern.

236. These things are not revealed save unto those who have entered therein and departed therefrom; for as for him who hath not entered therein and departed therefrom, better were it for him that he had never been born.

237. For it hath been manifested before the Most Holy Ancient One, the Concealed with all Concealments, because these things have shone into mine heart in the perfection of the love and fear of the Most Holy God, may He be blessed!

238. And these, my sons, who are here present, know these things; for into these matters have they entered and therefrom have they departed; but neither yet into all (*the secrets of them*).*

239. But now are these things illustrated in (*their*) perfection, even as it was necessary. Blessed be my portion with them in this world!

240. Rabbi Schimeon said: All which I have said concerning the Most Holy Ancient One, and all which I have said concerning Microprosopus, all are one, all are HVA, *Hoa*, Himself, all are Unity, neither herein hath separation place.

241. Blessed be HVA, *Hoa*, He, and blessed be His Name unto the Ages of the Ages.

242. Come, behold! This beginning which is called Father,† is comprehended in I, *Yod*,‡ which dependeth from the Holy Influence.

* This clause refers to the "Unwritten Qabalah."

† Chokmah, the second Sephira, which, however, is as it were the repetition of Kether.

‡ That is, the letter I, *Yod*, in IHVH, which is said in the "Book of Concealed Mystery" to symbolize Macroprosopus only in its highest point.

243. And therefore is I, *Yod*, the Most Concealed of all the other letters.*

244. For I, *Yod*, is the beginning and the end of all things.

245. And that river which floweth on and goeth forth is is called the World, which is ever to come and ceaseth never.

246. And this is the delight of the just, that they may be made worthy of that world which is to come, which ever watereth the garden of Eden, nor faileth.

247. Concerning this it is written, Isa. lviii. 11: "And like a fountain of water, whose waters fail not."

248. And that world to come is created through I, *Yod*.

249. As it is written, Gen. ii. 9: "And a river went forth out of Eden to water the garden."

250. For I, *Yod*, includeth two letters.

251. In the teaching of the school of Rav Yeyeva the Elder thus is the tradition. Wherefore are VD, *Vau Daleth*,† comprehended in IVD, *Yod?* Assuredly the planting of the garden is properly called V, *Vau;* and there is another garden which is D, *Daleth*, and by that Vau is Daleth watered, which is the symbol of the quaternary.‡

252. And an Arcanum is extended from this passage, where it is written: "And a river went forth out of Eden."

253. What is Eden? It is the supernal CHKMH, *Chokmah*, Wisdom, and that is I, *Yod* (*in I, V, D*).

* See "Book of Concealed Mystery," ch. ii. § 37; ch. iv. § 11.

† See "Book of Concealed Mystery," ch. ii. § 37.

‡ The amount of occult symbolism in this section is enormous, and the key of it is the name of the letter I, which is IVD, *Yod*. This is a trinity of letters, and their numerical value is I = 10, V = 6, D = 4, total 20, equivalent to double I; but for reasons given in the "Book of Concealed Mystery," the second I is reproduced by a Hexad and a Tetrad—namely, V and D. I = 10, the decimal scale of Sephirotic notation, the key of processional creation; V = 6 = Tiphereth, and Microprosopus the Son united to D = 4, the Cross. Here is the mystery of the crucifixion of the Son on the tree of life; and again the Qabalah agrees with Christian symbolism.

254. "To water the garden." That is V, *Vau*.

255. "And thence it is divided and goeth forth into four heads." That is D, *Daleth*.

256. And all things are included in IVD, *Yod*, and therefore is the Father called All, the Father of Fathers.

257. The beginning of all is called the Home of All. Whence IVD, *Yod*, is the beginning and the end of all; like as it is written, Ps. civ. 24: "All things in Chokmah hast Thou made."

258. In His place He is not manifested, neither is He known; when He is associated with the Mother, BAMA, *Be-Ama*, then is He made known (otherwise, symbolized) in the Mother, BAIMA, *Be-Aima*.*

259. And therefore is Aima known to be the consummation of all things, and She is signified to be the beginning and the end.

260. For all things are called Chokmah, and therein are all things concealed; and the Syntagma of all things is the Holy Name.

261. Thus far have we mystically described that which we have not said on all the other days. But now are the aspects shown forth.

262. (*As to the Sacred Name IHVH,*) I, *Yod*, is included in this Chokmah, Wisdom; H, *He*, is Aima, and is called Binah, Understanding; VH, *Vau He*, are those two Children who are produced from Aima, the Mother.

263. Also we have learned that the name BINH, Binah, comprehendeth all things. For in Her is I, *Yod*, which is associated with Aima, or the letter H, *He*, and together they produce BN, *Ben*, the Son, and this is the

* *Be Ama*, with the Mother. Here *Ama*, AMA, Mother = 42. *Be Aima*, in the Mother. Here *Aima*, AIMA = 52 = BN, *Ben*, Son. This Gematria is most important, because, be it noted, Aima, AIMA, is the letter I, *Yod*, which we have just been told represents Chokmah, joined to AMA, Mother, which is Binah, BINH, which again is BN IH, by Metathesis, *Ben Yod He*—*i.e.*, son of IH, eternally conjoined in Briah.

word Binah. Father and Mother, who are I, *Yod*, and H, *He*, with whom are interwoven the letters B, *Beth*, and N, *Nun*, which are BN, *Ben*; and thus far regarding Binah.

264. Also is She called THBVNH, *Thebunah*, the Special Intelligence. Wherefore is She sometimes called Thebunah, and not Binah?

265. Assuredly Thebunah is She called at that time in which Her two Children appear, the Son and the Daughter, BN VBTH, *Ben Va-Bath*, who are VH, *Vau He*; and at that time is She called THBVNH, *Thebunah*.

266. For all things are comprehended in those letters, VH, *Vau He*, which are BN VBTH, *Ben Va-Bath*, Son and Daughter; and all things are one system, and these are the letters THBVNH.

267. In the Book of Rav Hamenuna the Elder it is said that Solomon revealeth the primal conformation (that is, the Mother) when he saith, Cant. i. 15: "Behold, thou art fair, my love;" wherefore he followeth it out himself.

268. And he calleth the second conformation the Bride, which is called the Inferior Woman.

269. And there are some who apply both these names (those, namely, of Love and Bride) to this Inferior Woman, but these are not so.

270. For the first H, *He (of IHVH)*, is not called the Bride; but the last H, *He*, is called the Bride at certain times on account of many symbolic reasons.

271. For many are the times when the Male is not associated with Her, but is separated from Her.

272. Concerning this period it is said, Lev. xviii. 19: "Also thou shalt not approach unto a woman in the separation of her uncleanness."

273. But when the Female hath been purified, and the Male desireth to be united unto Her, then is she called the Bride—the Bride, properly so called.

274. But as to that which pertaineth unto the Mother, then the benevolence of Them both is not taken away for all eternity.

275. Together They (*Chokmah and Binah, IH*) go forth, together They are at rest; the one ceaseth not from the other, and the one is never taken away from the other.

276. And therefore is it written, Gen. ii. 10: "And a river went forth out of Eden"—*i.e.*, properly speaking, it continually goeth forth and never faileth.

277. As it is written, Isa. lviii. 11: "And like a fountain of waters, whose waters fail not."

278. And therefore is She called "My love," since from the grace of kindred association They rest in perfect unity.

279. But the other is called the Bride, for when the Male cometh that He may consort with Her, then is She the Bride, for She, properly speaking, cometh forth as the Bride.

280. And therefore doth Solomon expound those two forms of the Woman; and concerning the first form indeed he worketh hiddenly, seeing it is hidden.

281. But the second form is more fully explained, seeing that it is not so hidden as the other.

282. But at the end all his praise pertaineth unto Her who is supernal, as it is written, Cant. vi. 9: "She is the only one of Her Mother, She is the choice one of Her that bare Her."

283. And since this Mother, Aima, is crowned with the crown of the Bride, and the grace of the letter I, *Yod*, ceaseth not from Her for ever, hence unto Her arbitration is committed all the liberty of those inferior, and all the liberty of all things, and all the liberty of sinners, so that all things may be purified.

284. As it is written, Lev. xvi. 30: "Since in that day he shall atone for you."

285. Also it is written, Lev. xxv. 10: "And ye shall

hallow the fiftieth year."* This year is IVBL, *Yobel*, Jubilee.

286. What is Yobel? As it is written, Jer. xvii. 8: "VOL IVBL, *Va-El Yobel*, And spreadeth out her roots by the river;" therefore that river which ever goeth forth and floweth, and goeth forth and faileth not.

287. It is written, Prov. ii. 3: "If thou wilt call Binah the Mother, and wilt give thy voice unto Thebunah."

288. Seeing it is here said, "If thou wilt call Binah the Mother," wherefore is Thebunah added?

289. Assuredly, according as I have said, all things are supernal truth: Binah is higher than Thebunah. For in the word BINH, *Binah*, are shown Father, Mother, and Son; since by the letters IH, Father and Mother are denoted, and the letters BN, denoting the Son, are amalgamated with them.

290. THBVNH, *Thebunah*, is the whole completion of the children, since it containeth the letters BN, *Ben*, BTH, *Bath*, and VH, *Vau He*, by which are denoted the Son and Daughter.

291. Yet AB VAM, *Ab Ve-Am*, the Father and the Mother, are not found, save BAIMA, *Be-Aima*, in the Mother, for the venerable Aima broodeth over Them, neither is She uncovered.

292. Whence it cometh that that which embraceth the two Children is called THBVNH, *Thebunah*, and that which embraceth the Father, the Mother, and the Son is called BINH, *Binah*.

293. And when all things are comprehended, they are comprehended therein, and are called by that name of Father, Mother, and Son.

294. And these are CHKMH, *Wisdom*, Father; BINH, *Understanding*, Mother; and DOTH, *Däath*, Knowledge.

* The number answering to the "fifty gates of Binah." (See "Book of Concealed Mystery," ch. i. § 46.)

295. Since that Son* assumeth the symbols of His Father and of His Mother, and is called DOTH, *Däath*, Knowledge, since He is the testimony of Them both.

296. And that Son is called the first-born, as it is written, Exod. iv. 22: "Israel is my first-born son."

297. And since He is called first-born, therefore it implieth dual offspring.

298. And when He increaseth, in His Crown appear three divisions.†

299. But whether it be taken in this way or in that, there are as well two as three divisions herein, for all things are one; and so is it in this (*light*) or in that.‡

300. Nevertheless, He (*the Son*) receiveth the inheritance of His Father and of His Mother.

301. What is that inheritance? These two crowns, which are hidden within Them, which They pass on in succession to this Son.§

302. From the side of the Father (*Chokmah*) there is one Crown concealed therein, which is called Chesed.

303. And from the side of the Mother (*Binah*) there is one Crown, which is called Geburah.

304. And all those crown His head (*i.e.*, the Head of Microprosopus), and He taketh them.

305. And when that Father and Mother shine above Him, all (*these crowns*) are called the phylacteries of the

* Compare this with the Egyptian Horus, the son of Isis and Osiris. Also notice the interchange of symbols between Amen, Kneph, and Khem. The name of the great Egyptian God Amen is noticeable when we compare it with the qabalistic name AMN.

† Compare with this the alchemical symbolism of Duenech, the King of Earth, after being overwhelmed by the waters, rising again, glorified and crowned with the triple crown of silver, iron, and gold—Chesed, Geburah, and Tiphereth, in the alchemic Sephiroth of the metals.

‡ The meaning is, that Father and Mother are contained in the Son; for these are the second, third, and sixth Sephiroth—*i.e.*, 2, 3, and 6; and both 2 and 3 are contained in 6, for $2 \times 3 = 6$.

§ The reflexive essence of Kether, the Crown, which operates in Chokmah and Binah.

Head, and that Son taketh all things, and becometh the heir of all.

306. And He passeth on His inheritance unto the Daughter, and the Daughter is nourished by Him. But, properly speaking, henceforth (*from the parents*) doth the Son become the heir, and not the Daughter.

307. The Son becometh the heir of His Father and of His Mother, and not the Daughter, but by Him is the Daughter cherished.

308. As it is written, Dan. iv. 12: "And in that tree food for all."

309. And if thou sayest all, assuredly He as well as She are called TzDIQ, *Tzediq*, Just, and TzDQ, *Tzedeq*, Justice, which are in one and are one.

310. All things are thus. Father and Mother are mutually contained in and associated with themselves.

311. And the Father is the more concealed (*of the two*), and the whole adhereth unto the Most Holy Ancient One.

312. And dependeth from the Holy Influence, which is the Ornament of all Ornaments.

313. And they, the Father and the Mother, constitute the abode, as I have said.

314. As it is written, Prov. xxiv. 3, 4: "Through Chokmah is the abode constructed, and by Thebunah is it established, and in Däath shall the chambers be filled with all precious and pleasant riches.

315. Also it is written, Prov. xxii. 18: "For it is a pleasant thing if thou keep (*Däath*) within thee."

316. This is the system of all things, even as I have said, and (*all things*) depend from the Glorious Holy Influence.

317. Rabbi Schimeon said: In the (*former*) Assembly I revealed not all things, and all those things have been concealed even until now.

318. And I have wished to conceal them, even unto the world to come, because there also a certain question will be propounded unto me.

319. As it is written, Isa. xxxiii. 6: "And Chokmah and Däath shall be the stability of thy times, and strength of salvation; the fear of Tetragrammaton is His treasure," &c., and they shall seek out Wisdom, Chokmah.

320. Now truly thus is the will of the Most Holy and Blessed God, and without shame will I enter in before His palace.

321. It is written, 1 Sam. ii. 3: "Since AL DOVTH, *El Daoth*,* is Tetragrammaton." Daoth, or of Knowledges (plural), properly speaking, for He acquireth Daoth by Inheritance.

322. Through Daoth are all His palaces filled, as it is written, Prov. xxix.: "And in Däath shall the chambers be filled."

323. And therefore Däath is not furthermore revealed, for It occulty pervadeth Him inwardly.

324. And is comprehended in that brain and in the whole body, since "El Daoth is Tetragrammaton."

325. In the "Book of the Treatise" it is said concerning these words, "Since El Daoth is Tetragrammaton," read not DOVTH, *Daoth*, of knowledges, but ODVTH,† *Edoth*, of *testimony*.

326. For HVA, *Hoa*, He Himself, is the testimony of all things, the testimony of the two portions.

327. And it is said, Ps. lxxviii. 5: "And He established a testimony, ODVTH, in Jacob."

328. Moreover, also, although we have placed that matter in the "Book of Concealed Mystery," still also there what is mentioned of it is correct, and so all things are beautiful and all things are true.

329. When the matter is hidden, that Father and Mother contain all things, and all things are concealed in them.

330. And they themselves are hidden beneath the

* Plural of Däath. † By Metathesis.

Holy Influence of the Most Ancient of all Antiquity; in Him are they concealed, in Him are all things included.

331. HVA, *Hoa*, He Himself, is all things; blessed be Hoa, and blessed be His Name in eternity, and unto the ages of the ages.

332. All the words of the conclave of the Assembly are beautiful, and all are holy words—words which decline not either unto the right hand or unto the left.

333. All are words of hidden meaning for those who have entered in and departed thence, and so are they all.

334. And those words have hereunto been concealed; therefore have I feared to reveal the same, but now they are revealed.

335. And I reveal them in the presence of the Most Holy Ancient King, for not for mine own glory, nor for the glory of my Father's house, do I this; but I do this that I may not enter in ashamed before His palaces.

336. Henceforth I only see that He, God the Most Holy—may He be blessed!—and all these truly just men who are here found, can all consent (*hereunto*) with me.

337. For I see that all can rejoice in these my nuptials, and that they all can be admitted unto my nuptials in that world. Blessed be my portion!

338. Rabbi Abba saith that when (*Rabbi Schimeon*) had finished this discourse, the Holy Light (*i.e., Rabbi Schimeon*) lifted up his hands and wept, and shortly after smiled.

339. For he wished to reveal another matter, and said: I have been anxious concerning this matter all my days, and now they give me not leave.

340. But having recovered himself he sat down, and murmured with his lips and bowed himself thrice; neither could any other man behold the place where he was, much less him.

CHAPTER IX.

CONCERNING MICROPROSOPUS AND HIS BRIDE IN GENERAL.

341. He said: Mouth, mouth, which hath followed out all these things, they shall not dry up thy fountain.

342. Thy fountain goeth forth and faileth not: surely concerning thee may this be applied: "And a river went forth out of Eden;" also that which is written: "Like a fountain of waters whose waters fail not."

343. Now I testify concerning myself, that all the days which I have lived I have desired to behold this day, yet was it not the will (*of God*).

344. For with this crown is this day crowned, and now as yet I intend to reveal certain things before God the Most Holy—may He be blessed!—and all these things crown mine head.

345. And this day* suffereth not increase, neither can it pass on into the place of another day, for this whole day hath been yielded unto my power.

346. And now I begin to reveal these things, that I may not enter ashamed into the world to come. Therefore I begin and say:

347. "It is written, Ps. lxxxix. 14: 'TzDQ VMShPT, *Tzedeq Va-Meshephat*, Justice and Judgment are the abode of Thy throne; ChSD VAMTh, *Chesed Va-Emeth*, Mercy and Truth shall go before Thy countenance.'"

348. What wise man will examine this, so that he may behold His paths, (*those, namely,*) of the Most Holy Supernal One, the judgments of truth, the judgments which are crowned with His supernal crowns.

349. For I say that all the lights which shine from

* Meaning the period of revealing these matters, not exactly a day of twenty-four hours: day in the scriptural and qabalistical sense.

the Supreme Light, the Most Concealed of All, are all paths (*leading*) towards that Light.

350. And in that Light which existeth in those single paths, whatsoever is revealed is revealed.

351. And all those lights adhere mutually together, this light in that light, and that light in this light.

352. And they shine mutually into each other, neither are they divided separately from each other.

353. That Light, I say, of those lights, severally and conjointly, which are called the conformations of the King, or of the Crown of the King, that which shineth and adhereth to that Light, which is the innermost of all things, nor ever shineth without them.

354. And therefore do all things ascend in one path, and all things are crowned by one and the same thing, and one thing is not separated from another, since HVA, *Hoa*, Himself, and His Name, are one.

355. That Light which is manifested is called the Vestment; for He Himself, the King, is the Light of all the innermost.

356. In that Light is Hoa, Who is not separated nor manifested.

357. And all those lights and all those luminaries shine forth from the Most Holy Ancient One, the Concealed with all Concealments, who is the Highest Light.

358. And whensoever the matter is accurately examined all those lights which are expanded are no longer found, save only that Highest Light.

359. Who is hidden and not manifested, through those vestments of ornament which are the vestments of truth, QSHVT, *Qeshot*, the forms of truth, the lights of truth.

360. Two light-bearers are found, which are the conformation of the throne of the King; and they are called TzDQ, *Tzedeq*, Justice, and MSHPT, *Meshephat*, Judgment.

361. And they are the beginning and the consumma-

tion. And through them are all the Judgments crowned, as well superior as inferior.

362. And they all are concealed in Meshephat. And from that Meshephat is Tzedeq nourished.

363. And sometimes they call the same, MLKI TzDQ MLK ShLM, *Meleki Tzedeq Melek Shalem*, Melchizedek, King of Salem.

364. When the judgments are crowned by Meshephat, all things are mercy; and all things are in perfect peace, because the one temperateth the other.

365. Tzedeq and the Rigours are reduced into order, and all these descend into the world in peace and in mercy.

366. And then is the hour sanctified, so that the Male and the Female are united, and the worlds all and several exist in love and in joy.

367. But whensoever sins are multiplied in the world, and the sanctuary is polluted, and the Male and Female are separated.*

368. And when that strong Serpent beginneth to arise, Woe, then, unto thee, O World! who in that time art nourished by this Tzedeq. For then arise many slayers of men and executioners (*of judgment*) in thee, O World. Many just men are withdrawn from thee.

369. But wherefore is it thus? Because the Male is separated from the Female, and Judgment, Meshephat, is not united unto Justice, Tzedeq.

370. And concerning this time it is written, Prov. xiii. 23: "There is that is destroyed, because therein is not Meshephat." Since Meshephat is departed from this Tzedeq which is not therefore restrained; and Tzedeq hath operation after another manner.

371. And concerning this (*matter*) thus speaketh Solomon the king, Eccles. vii. 16: "All these things have I seen

* In other words, where there is unbalanced force, there is the origin of evil.

in the days of my HBL, *Hebel;* there is a just man who perisheth in his Tzedeq," &c.

372. Where by the word HBL, *Hebel* (*which is usually translated* "*vanity*"), is understood the breath from those supernal breathers forth which are called the nostrils of the King.

373. But when he saith HBLI, *Hebeli*, of my breath, Tzedeq, Justice, is to be understood, which is MLKVTHA QDISHA, *Malkutha Qadisha*, the holy Malkuth (*Sanctum Regnum, the Holy Kingdom*).

374. For when She is stirred up in Her judgments and severities, then hath this saying place: "There is a just man who perished in his Tzedeq."

375. For what reason? Because Judgment, Meshephat, is far from Justice, Tzedeq. And therefore is it said, Prov. xiii. 23: "And there is that is destroyed because therein is not Meshephat."

376. Come and see! When some sublimely just man is found in the world, who is dear unto God the Most Holy One—may He be blessed!—then even if Tzedeq, Justice, alone be stirred up, still on account of him the world can bear it.

377. And God the Most Holy—may He be blessed!—increaseth His glory so that He may not be destroyed by the severity (*of the judgments*).

378. But if that just man remaineth not in his place, then from the midst is he taken away for example by that Meshephat, Judgment, so that before it he cannot maintain his place, how much less before Tzedeq, Justice.

379. David the king said at first, Ps. xxvi. 2: "Try me, O Tetragrammaton, and prove me!" For I shall not be destroyed by all the severities, not even by Tzedeq, Justice Herself, seeing that I am joined thereunto.

380. For what is written, Ps. xvii. 15: "In Tzedeq, Justice, I will behold Thy countenance." Therefore, properly speaking, I cannot be destroyed through

Tzedeq, seeing that I can maintain myself in its severities.*

381. But after that he had sinned, he was even ready to be consumed by that Meshephat, Judgment. Whence it is written, Ps. cxliii. 2: "And enter not into Meshephat, Judgment, with Thy servant!"

382. Come and see! When that Tzedeq, Justice, is mitigated by that Meshephat, Judgment, then is it called TzDQH, *Tzedeqah*, Liberality.

383. And the world is tempered by Chesed, Mercy, and is filled therewith.

384. As it is written, Ps. xxxiii. 5: "Delighting in TzDQH, Liberality, and MShPT, Judgment; the earth is full of the ChSD, Mercy, of Tetragrammaton.

385. I testify concerning myself, that during my whole life I have been solicitous in the world, that I should not fall under the severities of Justice, nor that the world should be burned up with the flames thereof.

386. As it is written, Prov. xxx. 20: "She eateth and wipeth her mouth."

387. Thenceforward and afterwards all and singular are near unto the Abyss.

388. And verily in this generation certain just men are given (*upon earth*); but they are few who arise that they may defend the flock from the four angles (otherwise, but judgments arise against the world, and desire to rush upon us).

* Because in those severities, and behind them, he can see the Countenance of God.

CHAPTER X.

CONCERNING MICROPROSOPUS IN ESPECIAL, WITH CERTAIN DIGRESSIONS; AND CONCERNING THE EDOMITE KINGS.

389. HEREUNTO have I propounded how one thing agreeth with another; and I have expounded those things which have been concealed in the most Holy Ancient One, the Concealed with all Concealments; and how these are connected with those.

390. But now for a time I will discourse concerning the requisite parts of Microprosopus; especially concerning those which were not manifested in the Conclave of the Assembly, and which have been concealed in mine heart, and have not been given forth in order therefrom.

391. Hereunto have I mystically and in a subtle manner propounded all those matters. Blessed is his portion who entereth therein and departeth therefrom, and (*blessed the portion*) of those who shall be the heirs of that inheritance.

392. As it is written, Ps. cxliv. 15: "Blessed are the people with whom it is so," &c.

393. Now these be the matters which we have propounded. The Father* and the Mother† adhere unto the Ancient One, and also unto His conformation; since they depend from the Hidden Brain, Concealed with all Concealments, and are connected therewith.

394. And although the Most Holy Ancient One hath been conformed (*as it were*) alone (*i.e., apparently apart from all things at first sight*); yet when all things are accurately inspected, all things are HVA, *Hoa*, Himself, the Ancient One, alone.

395. Hoa is and Hoa shall be; and all those forms

* Chokmah. † Binah.

cohere with Himself, are concealed in Himself, and are not separated from Himself.

396. The Hidden Brain is not manifested, and *Microprosopus*) doth not depend immediately from it.

397. The Father and the Mother proceed from this Brain, and depend from It, and are connected with It.

398. (*Through Them*) Microprosopus dependeth from the Most Holy Ancient One, and is connected (*with Him*). And these things have we already revealed in the Conclave of the Assembly.

399. Blessed is his portion who entereth therein and departeth therefrom, and hath known the paths; so that he declineth not unto the right hand, or unto the left.

400. But if any man entereth not therein and departeth therefrom, better were it for that (*man*) that he had never been born. For thus it is written, Hos. xiv., 10: "True are Thy ways, O Tetragrammaton!"

401. Rabbi Schimeon spake and said: Through the whole day have I meditated on that saying where it is said, Ps. xxxiv. 2: "My Nephesch* shall rejoice in Tetragrammaton, the humble shall hear thereof and rejoice;" and now that whole text is confirmed (*in my mind*).

402. "My Nephesch shall rejoice in Tetragrammaton." This is true, for my Neschamah is connected therewith, radiateth therein, adhereth thereto, and is occupied thereabout, and in this same occupation is exalted in its place.

403. "The humble shall hear thereof and rejoice." All those just and blessed men who have come into communion with God, the most Holy—blessed be He!—all hear and rejoice.

404. Ah! now is the Holy One confessed; and therefore "magnify Tetragrammaton with me, and let us exalt His Name together!"

* See Introduction concerning the parts of the soul, Chiah, Neschamah, Ruach, and Nephesch.

405. Thus is it written, Gen. xxxvi. 31: "And those are the kings who reigned in the land of Edom." And also it is written thus, Ps. xlviii. 4: "Since, lo! the kings assembled, they passed away together."

406. "In the land of Edom." That is, in the place wherewith the judgments are connected."

407. "They passed away together." As it is written, "And he died, and there reigned in his stead."

408. "They themselves beheld, so were they astonished; they feared, and hasted away." Because they remained not in their place, since the conformations of the King had not as yet been formed, and the Holy City and its wall were not as yet prepared.

409. This is that which followeth in the text: "As we have heard, so have we seen, in the city," &c. For all did not endure.

410. But She (*the Bride*) now subsisteth beside the Male, with Whom She abideth.

411. This is that which is written, Gen. xxxvi. 39: "And Hadar reigned in his stead, and the name of his city was Pau, and the name of his wife was Mehetabel, the daughter of Matred, the daughter of Mizaheb."

412. Assuredly this have we before explained in the Assembly.*

413. Now, also, in the book of the teaching of Rav Hamenuna the Elder it is said: "And Hadar reigned in his stead." The word HDR, *Hadar*, is properly to be expounded according unto that which is said, Lev. xxiii. 40: "The fruit of trees which are HDR, *Hadar*, goodly."

414. "And the name of his wife Mehetabel," as it is written (*in the text just cited*), "branches of palm trees."

415. Also it is written, Ps. xcii. 3: "The just man shall flourish as the palm tree." For this is of the male and female sex.

416. She is called "the daughter of Matred;" that is,

* See "Greater Holy Assembly," ch. xlii. §§ 984-996; ch. xxvi. §§ 513-532.

the Daughter from that place wherein all things are bound together, which is called AB, Father.

417. Also it is written, Job. xxviii. 13: "Man knoweth not the price thereof, neither is it found in the land of the living."

418. She is the Daughter of Aima, the Mother; from Whose side the judgments are applied which strive against all things.

419. "The Daughter of Mizaheb;" because She hath nourishment from the two Countenances (*Chokmah and Binah, which are within Kether*); and shineth with two colours—namely from CHSD, *Chesed*, Mercy; and from DIN, *Din*, Judgment.

420. For before the world was established Countenance beheld not Countenance.*

421. And therefore were the Prior Worlds destroyed, for the Prior Worlds were formed without (*equilibrated*) conformation.

422. But these which existed not in conformation are called vibrating flames and sparks, like as when the worker in stone striketh sparks from the flint with his hammer, or as when the smith smiteth the iron and dasheth forth sparks on every side.

423. And these sparks which fly forth flame and scintillate, but shortly they are extinguished. And these are called the Prior Worlds.

424. And therefore have they been destroyed, and persist not, until the Most Holy Ancient One can be conformed, and the workman can proceed unto His work.

425. And therefore have we related in our discourse that that ray sendeth forth sparks upon sparks in three hundred and twenty directions.

426. And those sparks are called the Prior Worlds, and suddenly they perished.

427. Then proceeded the workman unto His work, and was conformed, namely as Male and Female.

* See "Book of Concealed Mystery," ch. i. §§ 2, 3, 4, *et. seq.*

428. And those sparks became extinct and died, but now all things subsist.

429. From a Light-Bearer of insupportable brightness proceeded a Radiating* Flame, dashing off like a vast and mighty hammer those sparks which were the Prior Worlds.

430. And with most subtle ether were these intermingled and bound mutually together, but only when they were conjoined together, even the Great Father and Great Mother.

431. From *Hoa*, Himself, is AB, the Father; and from *Hoa*, Himself, is Ruach, the Spirit; Who are hidden in the Ancient of Days, and therein is that ether concealed.

432. And It was connected with a light-bearer, which went forth from that Light-Bearer of insupportable brightness, which is hidden in the Bosom of Aima, the Great Mother.

CHAPTER XI.

CONCERNING THE BRAIN OF MICROPROSOPUS AND ITS CONNECTIONS.

433. And when both can be conjoined and bound together mutually (*i.e.*, the Father and the Mother), there proceedeth thenceforth a certain hard Skull.

434. And it is extended on its sides, so that there may be one part on one side, and another one on another side.

435. For as the Most Holy Ancient One is found to include equally in Himself the Three Heads,† so all things

* Compare this with Miölner, the hammer of Thor, of Scandinavian mythology.

† Chokmah and Binah, included in Kether.

are symbolized under the form of the Three Heads, as we have stated.

436. Into this skull (*of Microprosopus*) distilleth the dew from the White Head (*of Macroprosopus*), and covereth it.

437. And that dew appeareth to be of two colours, and by it is nourished the field of the holy apple trees.

438. And from this dew of this Skull is the manna prepared for the just in the world to come.*

439. And by it shall the dead be raised to life.

440. But that manna hath not at any other time been prepared so that it might descend from this dew, save at that time when the Israelites were wandering in the wilderness, and the Ancient One supplied them with food from this place; because that afterwards it did not fall out so more fully.

441. This is the same which is said, Exod. xvi. 4: "Behold I rain upon you bread from heaven." And also that passage where it is thus written, Gen. xxvii. 28: "And the Elohim shall give unto thee of the dew of heaven."

442. These things occur in that time. Concerning another time it is written: "The food of man is from God the Most Holy One—blessed be He!"—and that dependeth from MZLA, *Mezla*, the Influence; assuredly, from the Influence rightly so called.

443. And therefore is it customary to say: "Concerning children, life, and nourishment, the matter dependeth not from merit, but from the Influence." For all these things depend from this Influence, as we have already shown.

444. Nine thousand myriads of worlds receive influence from and are upheld by that GVLGLTHA, *Golgeltha*, Skull.

* It is to be noted that this word is MNA, *Manna*, and is a Metathesis of the letters AMN, *Amen*, which has been shown in the "Book of Concealed Mystery" to be equal by Gematria to IHVH ADNI.

445. And in all things is that subtle AVIRA, *Auira*, Ether,* contained, as It Itself containeth all things, and as in It all things are comprehended.

446. His countenance is extended in two sides,† in two lights, which in themselves contain all things.

447. And when His countenance (*i.e.*, *that of Microprosopus*) looketh back upon the countenance of the Most Holy Ancient One, all things are called ARK APIM, *Arikh Aphim*, Vastness of Countenance.

448. What is ARK APIM, or Vastness of Countenance? Also it should rather be called ARVK APIM, *Arokh Aphim*, Vast in Countenance.

449. Assuredly thus is the tradition, since also He prolongeth His wrath against the wicked. But the phrase ARK APIM, *Arikh Aphim*, also implies the same as "healing power of countenance."

450. Seeing that health is never found in the world save when the countenances (*of Macroprosopus and Microprosopus*) mutually behold each other.

451. In the hollow of the Skull (*of Microprosopus*) shine three lights. And although thou canst call them three, yet notwithstanding are there four,‡ as we have before said.

452. He (*Microprosopus*) is the heir of His Father and of his Mother, and there are two inheritances from Them; all which things are bound together under the symbol of the Crown of His Head. And they are the phylacteries of His Head.

453. After that these are united together after a

* ? Astral Light.

† Right and left; while in Macroprosopus "all is right."

‡ At first sight this seems a contradiction, but on careful examination the difficulty disappears. A triangle is a fit expression of the number 3. It has 3 angles, it has 3 sides; but there is the whole figure itself also, which is the synthesis of the sides and the angles. So there are the 3 angles and the whole figure itself which contains them, and thus completes the Trinity by the Quaternary: in the Tetragrammaton, IHV, and H final, which forms the synthesis.

certain manner they shine, and go forth into the Three Cavities of the Skull.

454. (*And then*) singly they are developed each after its own manner, and they are extended through the whole body.

455. But they are associated together in two Brains, and the third Brain containeth the others in itself.*

456. And it adhereth as well to the one side as to the other, and is expanded throughout the whole body.

457. And therefrom are formed two colours mixed together in one, and His countenance shineth.

458. And the colours of His countenance are symbols of Ab (*the Father*) and Aima (*the Mother*), and are called Däath (*Knowledge*) in Däath.

459. As it is written, 1 Sam. ii. 3: "Since El Däoth (*plural*) is Tetragrammaton," because in him there are two colours.

460. Unto Him (*Microprosopus*) are works ascribed diversely; but to the Most Holy Ancient One (*operations*) are not ascribed diversely.

461. For what reason doth He (*Microprosopus*) admit of variable disposition? Because He is the heir of two inheritances (*i.e., from Chokmah and Binah*).

462. Also it is written, Ps. xviii. 26: "With the merciful man thou shalt show thyself merciful."

463. But also truly and rightly have the Companions decided concerning that saying where it is written, Gen. xxix. 12: "And Jacob declared unto Rachel that he was her father's brother, and that he was Rebekah's son.

464. It is written, "Rebekah's son," and not "the son of Isaac." And all the mysteries are in Chokmah.†

* Thus rigidly following out the rule of the symbolism before given, that Chokmah and Binah are contained in Kether. In this is the key of all religions.

† BCHKMTHA, *Be-Chokmatha*; CHKMTHA is the emphatic Chaldee form of CHKMA, which is Chaldee for Hebrew CHKMH.

465. And therefore is (*Chokmah*) called the Perfection of all: and to it is ascribed the name of Truth.

466. And therefore is it written, "And Jacob declared:" and not written, "and Jacob said."

467. Those (*two*) colours are extended throughout the whole Body (*of Microprosopus*) and His Body cohereth with them.

468. In the Most Holy Ancient One, the Concealed with all Concealments, (*things*) are not ascribed diversely, and unto Him do they not tend (*diversely*), since the whole is the same (*with itself*) and (*thus is*) life unto all (*things*); and from Him judgment dependeth not (*directly*).

469. But concerning Him (*Microprosopus*) it is written, that unto Him are ascribed (*diverse*) works, properly speaking.

CHAPTER XII.

CONCERNING THE HAIR OF MICROPROSOPUS.

470. From the skull of the Head (*of Microprosopus*) depend all those chiefs and leaders (otherwise, all those thousands and tens of thousands), and also from the locks of the hair.

471. Which are black, and mutually bound together, and which mutually cohere.

472. But they adhere unto the Supernal Light from the Father, AB, *Ab*, which surroundeth His Head (*i.e.*, (*that of Microprosopus*); and unto the Brain, which is illuminated from the Father.

473. Thencefrom, even from the light which surroundeth His Head (*i.e., that of Microprosopus*) from the Mother, Aima, and from the second Brain, proceed long locks upon locks (*of hair*).

474. And all adhere unto and are bound together with those locks* which have their connection with the Father.

475. And because (these locks are) mutually intermingled with each other, and mutually intertwined with each other, hence all the Brains are connected with the Supernal Brain (*of Macroprosopus*).

476. And hence all the regions which proceed from the Three Cavities of the Skull are mingled mutually together, as well pure as impure, and all those accents and mysteries are as well hidden as manifest.

477. And since all the Brains have a secret connection with the ears of Tetragrammaton, in the same way as they shine in the crown of the Head, and enter into the hollow places of the Skull.

478. Hence all these locks hang over and cover the sides of the ears, as we have elsewhere said.

479. And therefore is it written, 2 Kings xix. 16: "Incline, O Tetragrammaton, Thine ear, and hear!"

480. Hence is the meaning of this passage, which is elsewhere given: "If any man wisheth the King to incline His ear unto him, let him raise† the head of the King and remove the hair from above the ears; then shall the King hear him in all things whatsoever he desireth."

481. In the parting of the hair a certain path is connected with the (*same*) path of the Ancient of Days, and therefrom are distributed all the paths of the precepts of the law.

482. And over these (*locks of hair*) are set all the Lords

* That is, the locks which have their origin in the influence of the Great Mother are interwoven mutually with those which originate from Chokmah.

†Meaning, let him supplicate Macroprosopus, developed in the forms of Chokmah and Binah, which are summed up in Aima the Great Mother, to incline Microprosopus to be favourable. This is identical with the Catholic custom of invoking the intercession of the Virgin with Her Son; for Mary = Mare = Sea; and the Great Sea is Binah.

of Lamentation and Wailing; and they depend from the single locks.

483. And these spread a net for sinners, so that they may not comprehend those paths.

484. This is that which is said, Prov. iv. 18: "The path of the wicked is as darkness."

485. And these all depend from the rigid locks; hence also these are entirely rigid, as we have before said.

486. In the softer (locks) adhere the Lords of Equilibrium, as it is written, Ps. xxv. 10: "All the paths of Tetragrammaton are CHSD, *Chesed*, and AMTH, *Emeth*, Mercy and Truth."

487. And thus when these developments of the Brain emanate from the Concealed Brain, hencefrom each singly deriveth its own nature.

488. From the one Brain the Lords of Equilibrium proceed through those softer locks, as it is written: Ps. xxv. 10: "All the paths of Tetragrammaton are Chesed and Emeth."

489. From the second Brain the Lords of Lamentation and Wailing proceed through those rigid locks and depend (from them). Concerning whom it is written: Prov. iv. 19: "The path of the wicked is as darkness; they know not wherein they stumble."

490. What is this passage intended to imply? Assuredly the sense of these words, "they know not," is this, "They do not know, and they do not wish to know."

491. "Wherein they stumble." Do not read "BMH, *Bameh*, wherein," but "BAIMA, *Be-Aima*, in Aima, the Mother," they stumble. That is, through those who are attributed unto the side of the Mother.

492. What is the side of the Mother? Severe Rigour, whereunto are attributed the Lords of Lamentation and Wailing.

493. From the third Brain the Lords of Lords proceed

through those locks arranged in the middle condition (*i.e. partly hard and partly soft*), and depend (*therefrom*); and they are called the Luminous and the Non-Luminous Countenances.

494. And concerning these it is written, Prov. iv. 26: "Ponder the path of thy feet."

495. And all these are found in those locks of the hair of the Head.

CHAPTER XIII.

CONCERNING THE FOREHEAD OF MICROPROSOPUS.

496. The forehead of the Skull (*of Microprosopus*) is the forehead for visiting sinners (otherwise, for rooting out sinners).

497. And when that forehead is uncovered there are excited the Lords of Judgments against those who are shameless in their deeds.

498. This forehead hath a rosy redness. But at that time when the forehead of the Ancient one is uncovered over against this forehead, the latter appeareth white as snow.

499. And that time is called the Time of Grace for all.

500. In the "Book of the Teaching of the School of Rav Yeyeva the Elder" it is said: The forehead is according as the forehead * of the Ancient One. Otherwise, the letter *Cheth*, CH, is placed between the other two letters, accord-

* The word translated forehead is MTzCH, *Metzach*; now if a metathesis be formed of this word by placing the last letter between the first and second letters, we get MCHTz, he shall smite. Hence the first form symbolizes Mercy, and the second, Severity.

ing to this passage, Num. xxiv. 17: "VMCHTz, *VeMachetz*, and shall smite the corners of Moab?"

501. And we have elsewhere said that it is also called NTzCH, *Netzach*, the neighbouring letters (*M and N; neighbouring letters in the alphabet that is, and allied in sense, for Mem = Water, and Nun = Fish, that which lives in the water*) being counterchanged. (*Netzach = Victory, and is the seventh Sephira*).

502. But many are the NTzCHIM, *Netzachim*, Victories;* so that another (development of) Netzach may be elevated into another path, and other Netzachim may be given which are extended throughout the whole body (*of Microprosopus*).

503. But on the day of the Sabbath, at the time of the afternoon prayers, the forehead of the Most Holy Ancient One is uncovered, so that the judgments may not be aroused.

504. And all the judgments are subjected; and although they be there, yet are they not called forth. (Otherwise, and they are appeased.)

505. From this forehead depend twenty-four tribunals, for all those who are shameless in their deeds.

506. And it is written, Ps. lxxiii. 11: "And they have said, 'How can El know? and is there knowledge in the Most High?'"

507. But truly (the tribunals) are only twenty; wherefore are four added? Assuredly, in respect of the punishments of the inferior tribunals which depend from the Supernals.

508. Therefore there remain twenty.† And therefore unto none do they adjudge capital punishment until

* And therefore is the divine name of Tzabaoth, or hosts, attributed both to Netzach and to Hod, the seventh and eighth Sephiroth, as may be seen by referring to the Introduction, and to the "Book of Concealed Mystery," ch. iii. § 5, annotation.

† And 20 is H, *He*, in the four worlds, for H = 5, which, multiplied by 4 = 20.

he shall have fulfilled and reached the age of twenty years in respect of these twenty tribunals.

509. But in our doctrine regarding our Arcana have we taught that the books which are contained in the Law refer back unto these twenty-four.

CHAPTER XIV.

CONCERNING THE EYES OF MICROPROSOPUS.

510. The Eyes of the Head (*of Microprosopus*) are those eyes from which sinners cannot guard themselves; the eyes which sleep, and yet which sleep not.

511. And therefore are they called "Eyes like unto doves, KIVNIM, *Ke-Ionim*." What is IVNIM, *Ionim?* Surely it is said, Lev. xxv. 17: "Ye shall not deceive any man his neighbour."

512. And therefore is it written, Psalm xciv. 7: "IH, *Yah*, shall not behold." And shortly after verse 9: "He that planteth the ear, shall He not hear? He that formeth the eye, shall He not see?"

513. The part which is above the eyes (*the eyebrows*) consisteth of the hairs, which are distributed in certain proportions.

514. From those hairs depend one thousand seven hundred Lords of Inspection for striving in battles. And then all their emissaries arise and unclose the eyes.

515. In the skin which is above the eyes (*the eyelids*) are the eyelashes, and there unto adhere thousand thousands Lords of Shields.

516. And these be called the covering of the eyes. And all those which are called (*under the classification of*) the eyes of IHVH, Tetragrammaton, are not unclosed, nor awake, save in that time when these coverings of the eyelashes be

separated from each other—namely, the lower from the upper (*eyelashes*).

517. And when the lower eyelashes are separated from the upper, and disclose the abode of vision, then are the eyes opened in the same manner as when one awaketh from his sleep.

518. Then are the eyes rolled around, and (*Microprosopus*) looketh back upon the open eye (*of Macroprosopus*), and they are bathed in its white brilliance.

519. And when they are thus whitened, the Lords of the Judgments are turned aside from the Israelites. And therefore it is written, Ps. xliv. 24: "Awake: wherefore sleepest thou, O Tetragrammaton? Make haste," &c.

520. Four colours appear in those eyes; from which shine the four coverings of the phylacteries, which shine through the emanations of the Brain.

521. Seven, which are called the eyes of Tetragrammaton, and the inspection, proceed from the black colour of the eye; as we have said.

522. As it is written, Zach. iii. 9: "Upon one stone seven eyes." And these colours flame forth on this side.

523. From the red go forth others, the Lords of Examination for Judgment.

524. And these are called: "The eyes of Tetragrammaton going forth throughout the whole earth."

525. Where it is said (*in the feminine gender*) "MSHVTTVTH, *Meshotetoth*, going forth," and not "MSHVTTIM, *Meshotetim*," in the masculine, because all are judgment.

526. From the yellow proceed others who are destined to make manifest deeds as well good as evil.

527. As it is written, Job xxxiv. 21: "Since His eyes are upon the ways of man." And these Zach. iv. 10, are called "The eyes of Tetragrammaton, MSHVTTIM, *Meshotetim*, going forth around, but in the masculine gender, because these extend in two directions—towards the good and towards the evil.

528. From the white brilliance proceed all those mercies and all those benefits which are found in the world, so that through them it may be well for the Israelites.

529. And then all those three colours are made white, so that He may have pity upon them.

530. And those colours are mingled together mutually, and mutually do they adhere unto each other. Each one affecteth with its colour that which is next unto it.

531. Excepting the white brilliance wherein all are comprehended when there is need, for this enshroudeth them all.

532. So therefore no man can convert all the inferior colours—the black, red, and yellow—into the white brilliance.

533. For only with this glance (*of Macroprosopus*) are they all united and transformed into the white brilliance.

534. His eyelashes (*i.e., those of Microprosopus, for to the eye of Macroprosopus neither eyebrows nor eyelashes are attributed*) are not found, when (*his eyes*) desire to behold the colours; seeing that his eyelashes disclose the place (*of sight*) for beholding all the colours.

535. And if they disclose not the place (*of vision*) the (*eyes*) cannot see nor consider.*

536. But the eyelashes do not remain nor sleep, save in that only perfect hour, but they are opened and closed, and again closed and opened, according to that Open Eye (*of Macroprosopus*) which is above them.

537. And therefore is it written, Ezek. i. 14: "And the living creatures rush forth and return."

538. Now we have already spoken of the passage, Isa. xxxiii. 20: "Thine eye shall see Jerusalem quiet, even Thy habitation."

539. Also it is written, Deut. ii. 12: "The eyes of Tetra-

* The simple meaning of this and the preceding section is, that the eyes can only see when the upper eyelashes are separated from the lower ones by the lids being raised.

grammaton thy God are ever thereon in the beginning of the year," &c.

540. For so Jerusalem requireth it, since it is written, Isa. i. 21: "TzDQ, *Tzedeq*, Justice abideth in Her."

541. And therefore (*is it called*) Jerusalem, and not Zion. For it is written, Isa. i. 26: "Zion is redeemed in MShPT, *Meshephat*, Judgment, &c.," which are unmixed mercies.

542. Thine eye: (*therefore*) is it written "OINK, *Ayinakh* (*in the singular number*). Assuredly it is the eye of the Most Holy Ancient One, the Most Concealed of All (*which is here referred to*).

543. Now it is said: "The eyes of Tetragrammaton thy God are thereon;" in good, that is to say, and in evil; according as either the red colour or the yellow is required.

544. But only with the glance (*of Macroprosopus*) are all things converted and cleansed into the white brilliance.

545. The eyelids (*of Microprosopus*) are not found when (*His eyes*) desire to behold the colours. But here (*it is said*), "Thine eyes shall behold Jerusalem." Entirely for good, entirely in mercy.

546. As it is written, Isa. liv. 7: "And with great mercies will I gather thee."

547. The eyes of Tetragrammaton thy God are ever thereon from the beginning of the year." Here the word "MRShITh, *Marashith*, from the beginning," is written defectively without A, for it is not written RAShITh with the A.

548. Hence it remaineth not always in the same condition. What doth not? The inferior H, *He*, (*of IHVH*).

549.* And concerning that which is supernal it is written, Lam. ii. 1: "He hath cast down MShMIM,

* In this section evidently Shamaim is taken to symbolize the supernal H, *He*.

Me-Shamaim, from the heavens; ARTz, *Aretz*, the earth the Tiphereth, Israel."

550. Wherefore hath he cast down Aretz from Shamaim? Because it is written, Isa. l. 3: "I will cover the heavens, Shamaim, with darkness," and with the blackness of the eye (*of Microprosopus*), namely, with the black colour, are they covered.

551. "From the beginning of the year." What, then, s that place whence those eyes of Tetragrammaton behold Jerusalem?

552. Therefore he* hasteneth to expound this (*saying immediately*): "From the beginning, MRSʜITʜ, of the year," which (*word MRSʜITH* being written thus), without the Aleph, A,† symbolizeth judgment; for judgment is referred unto that side, although virtually (*the word Merashith*) is not judgment.

553. "Even unto the end of the year." Herein, properly speaking, is judgment found. For it is written, Isa. i. 21: "Justice dwelt in her." For this is "the end of the year."

554. Come and see! A, *Aleph*, only is called the first (*letter*). In A, *Aleph*, is the masculine power hidden and concealed; that namely, which is not known.

555. When this Aleph is conjoined in another place then is it called RASʜITʜ, *Rashith*, beginning.

556. But if thou sayest that (*A*) is conjoined herewith,‡ truly it is not so, but (*A*) is only manifested therein and illuminateth it; and in that case only is it called RASʜITʜ, *Rashith*, beginning.

557. Now therefore in this (*passage*) RASʜITʜ (*spelt with the A*) is not found as regards Jerusalem; for were (*the letter A*) herein, it would (*denote that it would*) remain for ever.

*Moses, in this passage of Deuteronomy.

†That is, MRSʜITʜ instead of MRASʜITʜ.

‡That is, irrevocably, so that the word would cease to bear the same meaning were A not there. In other words, were A a radical letter of it.

558. Hence it is written defectively MRSHITH, *Me-Rashith.* Also concerning the world to come it is written, Isa. xli. 27:* "The first shall say to Zion, Behold, behold them," &c.

CHAPTER XV.

CONCERNING THE NOSE OF MICROPROSOPUS.

559. THE nose of Microprosopus is the form of His countenance, for therethrough is His whole countenance known.

560. This nose is not as the nose of the most Holy Ancient One, the Concealed with all Concealments.

561. For the nose of Him, the Ancient One, is the life of lives for all things, and from His two nostrils rush forth the *Ruachin De-Chiin*, RVCHIN DCHIIN, spirits of lives for all.

562. But concerning this (*nose of*) Microprosopus it is written, Ps. xviii. 9: "A smoke ascendeth in His nose."

563. In this smoke all the colours are contained. In each colour are contained multitudes of lords of most rigorous judgment, who are all comprehended in that smoke.

564. Whence all those are not mitigated save by the smoke of the inferior altar.

565. Hence it is written, Gen. viii. 21: "And IHVH smelled a sweet savour." It is not written (*He smelled*) the odour of the sacrifice. What is "sweet" save "rest?" Assuredly the spirit at rest is the mitigation of the Lords of Judgment.

566. (*When therefore it is said*) "And IHVH smelled

* The first, RASHVN, *Rashon*, where this word, derived from the same root as RASHITH, is spelt with A.

the odour of rest," most certainly the odour of the sacrificed victim is not meant, but the odour of the mitigation of all those severities which are referred unto the nose.

567. And all things which adhere unto them, all things, I say, are mitigated. But most of these severities mutually cohere.

568. As it is written, Ps. cvi. 2: "Who shall recount GBVRVTH IHVH, the Geburoth of Tetragrammaton?"

569. And this nose (*of Microprosopus*) emitteth fire from the two nostrils, which swalloweth up all other fires.

570. From the one nostril (*goeth forth*) the smoke, and from the other nostril the fire, and they both are found on the altar, as well the fire as the smoke.

571. But when He the most Holy Ancient One is unveiled, all things are at peace. This is that which is said, Isa. xlviii. 9: "And for My praise will I refrain from thee" (*literally, "block up thy nostrils"* *).

572. The nose of the Most Holy Ancient One is long and extended, and He is called Arikh Aphim, Long of Nose.

573. But this nose (*of Microprosopus*) is short, and when the smoke commenceth, it issueth rapidly forth, and judgment is consummated.

574. But who can oppose the nose of Him the Ancient One? Concerning this, all things are as we have said in the Greater Assembly, where concerning this matter the Companions were exercised.

575. In the book of the treatise of Rav Hamenuna the Elder he thus describeth these two nostrils (*of Microprosopus*), saying that from the one proceed the smoke and the fire, and from the other, peace and the beneficent spirits.

576. That is, when (*Microprosopus*) is considered as having (*in Himself the symbolism of*) right side and left side.

* The Hebrew idiom for having mercy always refers to the nose, as "to defer anger" is in Hebrew "to lengthen the nose," &c.

As it is written, Hosea xiv. 7: "And his smell like Lebanon."

577. And concerning His Bride it is written, Cant. vii. 9: "And the smell of thy nostril like apples." Which if it be true concerning the Bride, how much more concerning Himself? And this is a notable saying.

578. When therefore it is said, "And Tetragrammaton smelled the odour of peace," the word HNIChCh, *Ha-Nichach*, of peace," can be understood in a double sense.

579. One sense is primary, when the Most Holy Ancient One, the Concealed with all Concealments, is manifested; for HVA, *Hoa*, He, is the peace and mitigation of all things.

580. And the other respecteth the inferior mitigation, which is done through the smoke and fire of the altar.

581. And because of this duplicate meaning is the word NIChCh, *Nichach*, written with a double Ch. And all these things are said concerning Microprosopus.

CHAPTER XVI.

CONCERNING THE EARS OF MICROPROSOPUS.

582. THERE are two ears for hearing the good and the evil, and these two can be reduced into one.

583. As it is written, 2 Kings xix. 18: "Incline, O Tetragrammaton, Thine ear, and hear."

584. The ear from within dependeth upon certain curves which are therein formed, so that the speech may be made clearer before its entrance into the brain.

585. And the brain examineth it, but not with haste. For every matter which is accomplished in haste cometh not from perfect wisdom.

586. From those ears depend all the Lords of Wings who receive the Voice of the Universe; and all those are called thus, the Ears of Tetragrammaton.

587. Concerning whom it is written, Eccles. x. 20: "For a bird of the air shall carry the voice," &c.

588. "For a bird of the air shall carry the voice." This text hath a difficult (*meaning*). And now (for so much is expressed) whence is the voice?

589. For in the beginning of the verse it is written: "Curse not the King even in thy thought." Where it is written concerning even the (*unexpressed*) thought, and concerning the secret thoughts of thy couch.

590. Wherefore? Because "a bird of the air shall carry the voice." Which (*voice*) as yet is unexpressed.

591. Assuredly this is the true meaning. Whatsoever a man thinketh and meditateth in his heart, he maketh not a word until he bringeth it forth with his lips. (*What the text intendeth is*) if any man attendeth not hereunto.

592. For that voice sent forward (*from inconsiderate thought*) cleaveth the air, and it goeth forth and ascendeth, and is carried around through the universe; and therefore is the voice.

593. And the Lords of Wings receive the voice and bear it on unto the King (*Microprosopus*), so that it may enter into His ears.

594. This is that which standeth written, Deut. v. 28: "And Tetragrammaton hath heard the voice of your words." Again, Num. xi. 1: "And Tetragammaton heard, and His wrath was kindled."

595. Hence every prayer and petition which a man poureth forth before God the Most Holy One—blessed be He!—requireth this, that he pronounce the words with his lips.

596. For if he pronounce them not, his prayer is no prayer, and his petition is no petition.

597. But as far as the words go forth, they cleave the

[redacted]

air asunder, and ascend, and fly on, and from them is the voice made; and that which receiveth the one receiveth also the other, and beareth it into the Holy Place in the head of the King (otherwise, beneath Kether, the Crown).

598. From the three cavities (*of the brain of Microprosopus*) distilleth a certain distillation, and it is called the Brook. As it is said in 1 Kings xvii. 3: "The brook Kherith," as it were an excavation or channel of the ears.

599. And the voice entereth into that curved passage, and remaineth in that brook of that distillation.

600. And then is it therein detained, and examined, whether it be good or whether it be evil. This is the same which is said, Job. xxxiv. 3: "Because the ear examineth the words."

601. For what cause doth the ear examine the words? Because the voice is detained in that brook distilling into the curved passage of the ears, and doth not swiftly enter into the body, and thereunto is an examination instituted between the good and the evil.

602. "As the palate tasteth meat." Wherefore can the palate taste meat? Because in the same manner it causeth it to delay, and (*the meat*) doth not enter so rapidly into the body. And hence (*the palate*) proveth and tasteth it (*to discern*) whether it be sweet and pleasant.

603. From this opening of the ears depend other openings (*namely*) the opening of the eye, the opening of the mouth, the opening of the nose.

604. From that voice which entereth into the opening of the ears, if it be necessary (*a certain part*) entereth into the openings of the eyes, and these pour forth tears.

605. From that voice, if it be necessary (*a certain part*) entereth into the opening of the nose, and from that voice it produceth smoke and fire.

606. This is that which is written, Num. xi. i.: "And Tetragrammaton heard, and His wrath was kindled, and the fire of Tetragrammaton turned against them."

607. And if it be necessary that voice goeth forth into the opening of the mouth, and it speaketh, and determineth certain things.

608. From that voice are all things: from that voice (*a certain part*) entereth into the whole body, and by it are all things affected. Whence doth this matter depend? From that ear.

609. Blessed is he who observeth his words. Therefore is it written, Ps. xxxiv. 13: "Keep thy tongue from evil, and thy lips from speaking guile."

610. Unto this ear is attributed hearing, and under (*the idea of*) hearing are those brains comprehended.*

611. Chokmah is contained therein, as it is written, 1 Kings iii. 9: "And wilt Thou give unto Thy servant a hearing heart."

612. Binah also, as it is written, 1 Sam. iii. 9: "Speak, for Thy servant heareth." Also 2 Kings xviii. 26: "Because we have heard." And hencefrom all things depend.

613. Däath also, as it is said, Prov. iv. 10, "Hear, O my son, and receive My sayings." And again, *ibid.* ii. 1, "Thou shalt hide My sayings with thee." And thereunto all things depend from the ears.

614. From these ears depend prayers and petitions, and the opening of the eyes.

615. This is the same which standeth written, 2 Kings xix. 16: "Incline, O Tetragrammaton, Thine ear, and hear; open Thine eyes, and see. Thus all things depend hencefrom.

616. From this ear depend the highest Arcana, which go not forth without, and therefore is (*this ear*) curved in the interior parts, and the Arcana of Arcana are con-

* The three divisions of the Brain of Microprosopus.

cealed therein. Woe unto him who revealeth the Arcana!

617. And because the Arcana come into contact with this ear, and follow the curvings of that region, hence the Arcana are not revealed unto those who walk in crooked paths, but unto those (*who walk in*) those which are not crooked.

618. Hence is it written, Ps. xxv. 14: "The SVD IHVH, *Sod Tetragrammaton*, Secret of Tetragrammaton, is with them that fear Him, and He will show them His covenant;" namely, unto such as keep their path and thus receive His words.

619. But they who are perverse in their ways receive certain words, and quickly introduce the same into themselves, but in them is no place where they can be detained (*for examination*).

620. And all the other openings are opened therein, until those words can issue forth from the opening of the mouth.

621. And such men are called the sinners of their generation, hating God the Most Holy One—blessed be He.

622. In Mischna, or our tradition, we have taught that such men are like unto murderers and idolaters.

623. And all these things are contained in one saying, where it is written, Lev. xix. 16: "Thou shalt not go up and down as a tale-bearer among thy people, neither shalt thou stand against the blood of thy neighbour: ANI IHVH, I am Tetragrammaton."

624. Therefore he who transgresseth the first part of that verse doth the same as if he were to transgress the whole.

625. Blessed is the portion of the just, concerning whom it is said, Prov. xi. 13: "A tale-bearer revealeth secrets, but he that is of a faithful spirit concealeth the matter."

626. "Spirit, RVCH, *Ruach*," properly (*is used here*)

for the Ruach of such is extracted from the Supernal Holy Place.

627. Now we have said that this is a symbol. Whosoever revealeth Arcana with fixed purpose of mind, he is not of the body of the Most Holy King.

628. And therefore to such a man nothing is an Arcanum, neither is from the place of the Arcanum.

629. And whensoever his soul departeth, the same adhereth not unto the body of the King, for it is not his place. Woe unto that man! woe unto himself! woe unto his Neschamah!" *

630. But blessed is the portion of the just who conceal secrets, and much more the Supernal Arcana of God the Most Holy One—blessed be He!—the highest Arcana of the Most Holy King.

631. Concerning them it is written, Isa. lx. 21: "Thy people also shall be all righteous; they shall inherit the land for ever.

CHAPTER XVII.

CONCERNING THE COUNTENANCE OF MICROPROSOPUS.

632. His countenance is as two abodes of fragrance, and all that I have before said is His testimony.

633. For the testimony, SHDVTHA, *Sahedutha*, dependeth from Him, and in all his testimony dependeth.

634. But these places of fragrance are white and red; the testimony of Ab the Father, and Aima the Mother; the testimony of the inheritance which He hath taken by right and obtained.

635. And in our tradition we have also established by

* See Introduction concerning the names of the parts of the Soul.

how many thousand degrees the whiteness differeth from the redness.

636. But yet at once they agree together in Him in one,* under the general form of the whiteness; for whensoever it is illuminated from the light of the white brilliance of the Ancient One, then that white brilliance overcloudeth the redness, and all things are found to be in light.

637. But whensoever judgments ascend (otherwise threaten) in the universe, and sinners are many, leprosy is found in all things (otherwise, throughout the universe), and the redness spreadeth over the countenance, and over-cloudeth all the whiteness.

638. And then all things are found in judgment, and then (*He putteth on*) the vestments of zeal, which are called "the garments of vengeance" (Isa. lix. 17), and all things depend herefrom.

639. And because the testimony existeth in all things, hence so many Lords of Shields are enshrouded by those colours, and attend upon those colours.

640. When those colours are resplendent, the worlds all and singular exist in joy.

641. In that time when the white brilliance shineth all things appear in this colour; and when He appeareth in redness, similarly all things appear in that colour.

CHAPTER XVIII.

CONCERNING THE BEARD OF MICROPROSOPUS.

642. IN those abodes (otherwise forms) of fragrance the beard beginneth to appear from the top of the ears, and it descendeth and ascendeth in the place of fragrance.

* *I.e.*, The various degrees of the whiteness.

643. The hairs of the beard are black, and beautiful in form as in (*that of*) a robust youth.

644. The oil of dignity of the supernal beard of the Ancient One (*floweth down*) in this beard of Microprosopus.

645. The beautiful arrangement of this beard is divided into nine parts. But when the most holy oil of dignity of the Most Holy Ancient One sendeth down rays into this beard, its parts are found to be twenty-two.*

646. And then all things exist in benediction, and thence Israel the patriarch (*i.e., Jacob*) took his blessing. And the symbol of this is to be found in these words, Gen. xlviii. 20: "BK, with the twenty-two shall Israel bless." (*The real translation of BK is "in thee," but the numerical value of BK is twenty-two; hence the symbolism here rendered.*)

647. We have described the conformations of the beard already, in the Conclave of the Assembly. Here also I desire to enter upon this matter in all humility.

648. Now we thus examined all the parts of the beard, that in the Conclave of the Assembly (*we found*) that they were all disposed from the parts of the beard of the Most Holy Ancient One.

649. Six there are; nine they are called. For the first conformation goeth forth through that Spark of the most refulgent Light-bearer,† and goeth down beneath the hair of the head, assuredly beneath those locks which overhang the ears.

650. And it descendeth before the opening of the ears unto the beginning of the mouth.

651. But this arrangement is not found in the Most Holy Ancient One. But when that fountain of Wisdom, CHKMTHA, *Chokmatha*, floweth down from MZLA, *Mezla*, the Influence of the Most Holy Ancient One, and dependeth

* Answering to the number of the letters of the Hebrew alphabet, which together with the ten Sephiroth form the thirty-two paths of wisdom of the "Sepher Yetzirah."

† See "Book of Concealed Mystery," ch. ii. § 31, 40, &c.

from Him, and when Aima, the Mother, ariseth, and is included in that subtle ether, then She, Aima, assumeth that white brilliance.*

652. And the Scintilla entereth and departeth, and together mutually are They bound, and thence cometh the One Form.

653. And when there is need, One ariseth above the Other, and the Other again is concealed in the presence of Its Companion.

654. And therefore there is need of all things; of one thing for performing vengeance, of another for showing forth mercy.

655. And therefore David the king hath sought out this beard, as we have shown already.

656. In this beard nine conformations are found, (*among which are*) six myriads which depend among them, and are extended throughout the whole body.

657. And those six which depend hang in the locks which are beneath the abodes of fragrance, three on this side and three on that.

658. And in the ornamentation of the beard hang the three remaining (*conformations*); one above the lips, and two in those locks which hang down upon the chest.

659. And all those six (*other conformations*), three on this side and three on that side, go forth, and all depend from those locks which hang down, and they are extended throughout the whole body.

660. But on account of those three (*conformations*), which are more connected with the ornament of the beard than all the others, the Holy Name is written in its purity.

661. When it is written thus. Ps. cxviii. 5: "I invoked IH, *Yah*, in my trouble: IH, *Yah*, heard me at large: Tetragrammaton is with me, therefore I will not fear."

* In the "Book of Concealed Mystery," ch. i. § 31, HVA and ALHIM are shown to be interchangeable, and they both are FEMININE. And now we come to the "Three Mothers," of the "Sepher Yetzirah," the Great Supernal Feminine Triad, which is even BEFORE THE TRIUNE FATHER. I may say no more here; in fact, I have almost revealed too much. Let the reader carefully meditate on § 651, for there the indicible Arcanum is shadowed.

662. But that which we have already laid down in the Conclave of the Assemby concerning these words, "In my trouble I invoked IH, *Yah,*" that this is to be referred to that place where the beard beginneth to be extended, which place is more remote, and before the ears, is also correct.

663. And in the book of the dissertation of the school of Rav Yeyeva the Elder it is thus said and established, that the beginning of the beard cometh from the supernal CHSD, *Chesed,* Mercy.

664. Concerning which it is written, "LK IHVH HGDVLH VHGBVRH VHTHPARTH, *Leka, Tetragrammaton, Ha-Gedulah, Ve-Ha-Geburah, Ve-Ha-Tiphereth,* Thine, O Tetragrammaton, Gedulah (*another name for Chesed*), Geburah, and Tiphereth (*the names of the fourth, fifth, and sixth Sephiroth, which Protestants usually add to the end of the Lord's Prayer, substituting, however, Malkuth for Gedulah*), Thine, O Tetragrammaton, are the Mercy, the Power, and the Glory (*or Beauty*)." And all these are so, and thus it (*the beard*) commenceth.

665. Therefore the nine (*conformations*) arise from and depend from the beard; and thus it commenceth from before the ears. But (*the conformations*) remain not in permanence save through another cause, as we have before laid down.

666. For whensoever the universe hath need of mercy, the Influence, Mezla, of the Ancient one is uncovered; and all those conformations which exist in the most adorned beard of Microprosopus are found to be entirely mercies, yet so that they can exercise vengeance against the haters of the Israelites, and against those who afflict them.

667. But the whole ornament of the beard consisteth in those locks which hang down, because all things depend thencefrom.

668. All those hairs which are in the beard of Microprosopus are hard and rigid, because they all subject

the judgments when the Most Holy Influence is manifested.

669. And when there is to be contention, then He appeareth like unto a brave hero, victorious in war. And then that becometh bare of hair which is bare of hair, and that becometh bald which is bald.

670. Moses commemorated these nine conformations a second time, Num. xiv. 17, when there was need to convert them all into mercy.

671. For although he recite not now the thirteen conformations (*of the beard of Macroprosopus*), yet from this idea the thing depended; for he did not allow himself to enter into those conformations simply that he might enumerate them.

672. But unto the Influence directed he his meditation, and made mention thereof. As it is written, Num. xiv. 17: "And now, I beseech thee, let KCH, *Kach*, the Power of Tetragrammaton, be great!"

673. What is to be understood by KCH IHVH, *Kach Tetragrammaton*, the Power of Tetragrammaton? Thus is MZLA QDISHA, *Mezla Qadisha*, the Holy Influence, called, even the Concealed with all Concealments. And from the Influence that Strength and that Light depend.

674. And since of this (*Influence*) Moses was speaking, and this (*Influence*) he was commemorating, and concerning this (*Influence*) he was meditating, he then immediately recited those nine conformations which belong unto Microprosopus.

675. So that they all might exist in light, and that judgment might not be found therein. And therefore this whole judgment (otherwise, this whole beard) dependeth from the Influence.

676. When the hairs begin to be restrained He Himself is as the hero of an army victorious in war.

677. In this beard (*of Microprosopus*) floweth down the oil of dignity from the Concealed Ancient One, as it is said, Ps. cxxxiii, 2: "Like excellent oil upon the head, descending upon the beard, the beard of Aaron."

CHAPTER XIX.

CONCERNING THE LIPS AND MOUTH OF MICROPROSOPUS.

678. THOSE hairs cover not the lips, and the entire lips are red and rosy. As it is written, Cant. v. 13: "His lips as roses." (*In the ordinary version* SHVSHNIM, *Shushanim, is translated "lilies," not "roses."*)

679. His lips murmur Geburah, Severity, but they also murmur Chokmah, Wisdom.

680. From those lips alike depend good and evil, life and death.

681. From these lips depend the Lords of Vigilance. For when those lips murmur, they all are excited to bring forth secret things, as well as the Lords of Judgment in all the tribunals wherein they have their abiding-place.

682. And therefore are these called the Watchers; as it is written, Dan. iv. 17: "This matter is by the decree of the Watchers, and the demand by the word of the Holy Ones."

683. What is a Watcher? In the book of the dissertation that is explained from this passage, 1 Sam. xxviii. 16: "And is become thine enemy."

684. Seeing that judgments are stirred up against those who obtain not mercy from the Supernals.

685. Hence are those stirred up who are the lords of the enmity of all things.

686. And, nevertheless, in each case is there mercy and judgment. And therefore is it said, Dan. iv. 13: "A watcher and a holy one;" judgment and mercy.

687. And between those lips when they are opened is the mouth disclosed.

688. By that RVCH, *Ruach*, breath, which goeth forth from His mouth, many thousands and myriads are enshrouded; and when it is extended by the same are the

true prophets enfolded, and all are called the mouth of Tetragrammaton.

689. When forth from His mouth the words proceed through His lips, the same are muttered through the whole circuit of eighteen thousand worlds,* until they are all bound together at once in the twelve paths and the known ways. And one thing ever expecteth another.

690. By the tongue is the vocal expression of the sublime spoken, in the middle nexus of the utterance.

691. And therefore is it written, Cant. v. 16: "His mouth is most sweet." And this same palate of His conveyeth a sweet taste; wherefore He smileth when He tasteth food (*which is pleasant*).†

692. "And He is altogether the desirablenesses (*or delights*)" (*of the powers of*) fire and (*the powers of*) water, because the fire and water are counterchanged with each other mutually (otherwise, are conformed together), and are beautiful in his conformation.‡

693. For the colours are mutually associated together.

* That is the number eighteen on the plane of Asiah. And 18 is the fourth part of 72. And 72 is the number of the Schemahamphrorasch (*see ante*), and the number of the Quinaries or sets of 5 degrees in the 360 degrees of the Zodiac. And there are 6 such sets in 30 degrees of each sign. And thus we return to the 12 signs of the Zodiac, and these are operated on from the 10 Sephiroth through the "7 paths of the Queen," and these again depend from the first 3 Sephiroth, and these again from Kether, and Kether is Macroprosopus, from whom backwards depend the Negative Existences in their Veils; and Macroprosopus is called HVA, *Hoa*, which = 12, and finds its expression in Aima Elohim. Thus rusheth through the Universe the Flux and Reflux of the Eternal Word.

† I am doubtful as to whether this is the best translation of the last clause of § 691. Rosenroth has not translated it at all. The Chaldee is MMTHQIM VDAI MAI CHKV KDA VCHIK ITOVM LAKVL, *Mamthaqim Vadeai Maai Chiko Kedea Vecheik Yitauom Leakol.*

‡ This whole section requires comment. I must first observe that Knorr de Rosenroth in his Latin version has supposed that in the word MCHMDIM, *Machemadim*, fire and water, ASH and MIM, are hidden as in a sort of anagram. Now while it is true that MIM can be thus extracted, ASH cannot, for the remaining letters, CHMD will by no exegetical rule I know of form a word signifying fire. The following I take to be the real meaning of the passage. Chokmah is the fire, I, and Binah is the water, H,

694. In His palate are the (*guttural*) letters (*of the Hebrew Alphabet—namely, A, H, Ch, O*) formed and constructed; in the circuit of His (*mouth*) are they condensed (*into the palatals G, I, K, Q*).*

695. The letter A, *Aleph*, which cast forth the kings and constituted the kings † (*i.e., that guttural letter which is referred to the First Sephira, Kether, the Crown, becometh the palatal letter G, Ghimel*).

696. The letter Ch, *Cheth*, which goeth forth and descendeth and ascendeth, and is crowned in the head (*referring to the Second Sephira, Chokmah, Wisdom*), and is fire condensed in ether (*i.e., developeth in the palatal letter I, Yod*).

697. The letter H, *He*, the golden-yellow colour (otherwise, germinating power) of the Mother, Aima, having been connected with the Female Power, is extended in the Greater Female Potency into the desire of the Holy City, which two (otherwise, for these places) are mutually bound together the one unto the other (*these two are Aima, the*

the Father and Mother Who, conjoined, produce the Son. Now the fire is symbolized by a triangle with the apex uppermost △, and water by ▽, these two together united form ✡ the sign of the Macrocosm, the external symbol of Vau, V, Microprosopus. And He inherits the double qualities of the Father and the Mother, shown by the word "delights" ("Machemadim") being written in the plural.

* The letters of the Hebrew alphabet are usually classed in the following manner:—

Gutturals = A, H, Ch, O (R by some).
Palatals = G, I, K, Q.
Einguals = D, Th, T, L, N.
Dentals = Z, S, Sh, Tz (R by others).
Labials = B, V, M, P.

The "Sepher Yetzirah" further classes them as—

3 Mothers (Primitives) = A, M, Sh.
7 Duplicated = B, G. D, K, P, R, Th.
12 Simples = H, V, Z, Ch, T, I, L, N, S, O, Tz, Q.

In the above classification it classes R as a dental.

† This section and § 698, contain references to the Edomite kings and their symbology—namely, as denoting the primal worlds which were destroyed (See "The Book of Concealed Mystery," ch. i. § 3; "The Greater Holy Assembly," ch. ii. and ch. xxvi.; and "The Lesser Holy Assembly," ch. x.).

supernal H of IHVH, and the Holy City, the Bride, as She is called in the Apocalypse, the final H of IHVH). (*And the guttural letter H, He, formeth the palatal letter K, Kaph, which is referred unto the Queen.*) As it is written, Cant. iv. 6: "Unto the mountain of myrrh, unto the hill of frankincense."

698. The letter O, *Ayin* (*which denoteth the seven Inferiors which were destroyed*) is the medium or splendour of mediation (*i.e., the internal Light of the broken vessels*), hath been formed forth in His lips by revolution therein (*and it hath been condensed in Q, Qoph, which goeth forth from the middle of the palate unto the lips*). For the branches (*of the Tree of Life, namely*) are connected in Him (*Microprosopus*) in the spirits (*such as they were in the prior world*) formed forth (*such as they are in the restored world*).

699. For in the mysteries of the letters of Solomon the King, those four letters, A, H, CH, O, are surrounded by GIKQ.

700. But it is written in Job vi. 6: "Can that which is unsavoury be eaten without salt?" &c.

701. Also it is written, Isa. xxxii. 17: "And the work of TzDQ, *Tzedeq*, Righteousness (*or Justice*), shall be peace." Also, Ps. xix. 10: "More to be desired are they than gold, yea, than much fine gold," &c.

702. But King David saith, *ibid.* 11: "Also by them is thy servant warned."

703. I affirm concerning myself, that I have been every day cautious concerning them, so that concerning them I might not err (*i.e., concerning the judgments, Meshephath, referred to in verse* 9).

704. Excepting a certain day when I was binding together the Crowns of the King * in the Cave of Maranæa, I beheld a Splendour of devouring Fire flashing from His

* *I.e.,* Tracing out the properties, &c., of the Sephiroth which form the King, Microprosopus, and, as appears from the latter part of this section, those only in their aspect of Judgment and Wrath.

wrathful Countenance of Flame, and with terror I trembled at the sight.

705. From that day forth I ever acted with caution in my meditations concerning them, neither have I omitted that all the days of my life.

706. Blessed is his portion who is prudent regarding Him who is more ancient than (otherwise, concerning the gentleness of) the King, so that he may taste thereof, as is fitting.

707. Therefore is it written, Ps. xxxiv. 9: "Taste and see that Tetragrammaton is good," &c.

708. Also it is written, Prov. ix. 5: "Come, eat of my bread," &c.

CHAPTER XX.

CONCERNING THE BODY OF MICROPROSOPUS.

709. The masculine power is extended through Däath; and the Assemblies and Conclaves are filled.

710. It commenceth from the beginning of the skull, and it is extended throughout the whole body, through the breast, and through the arms, and through all the other parts.

CHAPTER XXI.

CONCERNING THE BRIDE OF MICROPROSOPUS.

711. Unto His back adhereth closely a Ray of most vehement Splendour, and it flameth forth and formeth a certain skull, concealed on every side.

712. And thus descendeth the Light of the two brains, and is figured forth therein.

713. And She (*the Bride*) adhereth unto the side of the Male; wherefore also She is called, Cant. v. ii., "My dove, my perfect one." Read not, "THMTHI, *Thamathi*, My perfect one;" but "THAVMTHI, *Theomathi*, My twin sister," more applicably.

714. The hairs of the Woman contain colours upon colours, as it is written, Cant. vii. 5: "The hair of Thy head like purple."

715. But herewith is Geburah, Severity, connected in the five Severities (*i.e., which are symbolized in the numerical value*, 5, *of the letter H final of IHVH, which is the Bride*); and the Woman is extended on Her side, and is applied unto the side of the Male.

716. Until She is separated from His side, and cometh unto Him so that She may be conjoined with Him, face to face.

717. And when They are conjoined together, they appear to be only one body.

718. Hence we learn that the Masculine, taken alone, appeareth to be only half the body, so that all the mercies are half; and thus also is it with the Feminine.

719. But when They are joined together, the (*two together*) appear to form only one whole body. And it is so.

720. So also here. When the Male is joined with the Female, They both constitute one complete body, and all the Universe is in a state of happiness, because all things receive blessing from Their perfect body. And this is an Arcanum.

721. And therefore it is said, Gen. ii. 3: "Tetragrammaton blessed the seventh day and hallowed it." For then all things are found (*to exist*) in the one perfect Body, for MTRVNITHA, *Matronitha*, the Mother (*i.e., the Inferior Mother*) is joined unto the King, and is found to form the one Body with Him.

722. And therefore are there found to be blessings upon this day.

723. And hence that which is not both Male and Female together is called half a body. Now, no blessing can rest upon a mutilated and defective being, but only upon a perfect place and upon a perfect being, and not at all in an incomplete being.*

724. And a semi-complete being cannot live for ever, neither can it receive blessing for ever.

725. The Beauty of the Female is completed by the Beauty of the Male. And now have we established these facts (*concerning the perfect equality of Male and Female*), and they are made known unto the Companions.

726. With this Woman (*the inferior H*) are connected all those things which are below; from Her do they receive their nourishment, and from Her do they receive blessing; and She is called the Mother of them all.

727. Like as a mother containeth the body (*of her child before birth*), and that whole body deriveth its nourishment from her. (Otherwise, containeth a garden, and the whole garden is from her.) Thus is She unto all the other inferiors.

728. It is written, Prov. vii. 4: "Say unto Chokmah, Thou art my sister."† For there is given one Chokmah (*Male*), and there is also given another Chokmah (*Female*).

729. And this Woman is called the Lesser Chokmah in respect of the other.

730. And therefore is it written, Cant. viii. 8: "We have a little sister and she hath no breasts."

731. For in this exile (*i.e., separated from the King*) She appeareth unto us to be "our little sister." At first,

* This section is another all-sufficient proof of the teachings maintained throughout the Qabalah, namely, that Man and Woman are from the creation co-equal and co-existent, perfectly equal one with the other. This fact the translators of the Bible have been at great pains to conceal by carefully suppressing every reference to the *Feminine portion of the Deity*, and by constantly translating feminine nouns by masculine. And this is the work of so-called religious men!

† Chokmah, Wisdom, the second Sephirah, is Male in respect of Binah, but Female in respect of Kether. This is somewhat analogous to the Greek idea of the birth of Athené, Wisdom, from the brain of Zeus.

indeed, she is small, but she becometh great and greater, until she becometh the Spouse whom the King taketh unto Himself.

732. As it is written, Cant. viii. 10: "I am a wall, and my breasts are like towers.

733. "And my breasts," &c., since they are full with the nourishment of all things;* "like towers," because they are the great rivers which flow forth from Aima the Supernal.

CHAPTER XXII.†

CONCERNING THE REMAINING MEMBERS OF MICROPROSOPUS.

734. THE Male is extended in right and left, through the inheritance which He receiveth (*i.e., from Chokmah and Binah*).

735. But whensoever the colours are mingled together then is He called Tiphereth, and the whole body is formed into a tree (*the Autz Ha-Chaiim, or Tree of Life*),‡ great and strong, and fair and beautiful, Dan. iv. 11.

736. "The beasts of the field had shadow under it, and the fowls of the heaven dwelt in the boughs thereof, and all flesh was fed of it."

737. His arms are right and left. In the right arm is Chesed and Life; in the left is Geburah and Death.

738. Through Däath are His inner parts formed, and they fill the Assemblies and Conclaves, as we have said.

739. For thus is it written: "And through Däath shall the Conclaves be filled."

* Compare the symbolism of the many breasts of the Ephesian Diana.

† The "Idra Zuta" contains twenty-two chapters, the number of the letters of the Hebrew alphabet, of the chapters of St. John's Apocalypse, and of the verses of the 1st, 2nd, 4th, and 5th chapters of Lamentations of Jeremiah, &c. It is the number of the Qabalistical keys.

‡ Notice that the tree of life is the united body, and the tree of knowledge of good and evil the separated.

740. Afterwards is His body extended into two thighs, et intra hæc continentur duo renes, duo testiculi masculini.

741. Omne enim oleum, et dignitas, et vis masculi e toto corpore in istis congregatur; nam omnes exercitus, qui prodeunt ab iis, omnes prodeunt et morantur in orificio membri genitalus.

742. And therefore are they called Tzabaoth, the Armies; and they are Netzach (*Victory, the seventh Sephira*) and Hod (*Glory, the eighth*). For Tiphereth is Tetragrammaton, but Netzach and Hod are the armies; hence cometh that name, Tetragrammaton Tzabaoth.

743. Membrum masculi est extremitas totius corporis, et vocatur Yesod, fundamentum, et hic est gradus ille qui mitigat fœminam. For every desire of the Male is toward the female.

744. Per hoc fundamentum ille ingreditur in fœminam; in locum qui vocatur Tzion et Jerusalem. Nam hic est locus tegendus fœminæ, et in uxore vocatur uterus.

745. And hence is Tetragrammaton Tzabaoth called Yesod, the Foundation (*the ninth Sephira*). Also it is written, Ps. cxxxii. 13: "Since Tetragrammaton hath chosen Tzion to be a habitation for Himself, He hath desired Her."

746. When Matronitha, the mother, is separated, and conjoined with the King face to face in the excellence of the Sabbath, all things become one body.

747. And then the Holy One—blessed be He!—sitteth on His throne, and all things are called the Complete Name, the Holy Name. Blessed be His Name for ever, and unto the ages of the ages.

748. All these words have I kept back unto this day, which is crowned by them for the world to come. And now herein are they manifested, O blessed be my portion!

749. When this Mother is conjoined with the King, all the worlds receive blessing, and the universe is found to be in joy.

750. Like as the male (*Microprosopus*) existeth from the Triad (*Kether, Chokmah, and Binah*), and His beginning is with the Triad, in this same manner are all things disposed, and the end of the whole body is thus; also the Mother (*Inferior*) receiveth not the blessing except in the Syntagma of the Triad, and these paths are Netzach, Hod, and Yesod.

751. And she is mitigated, and receiveth blessing in that place which is called the Holy of Holies below.

752. As it is written, Ps. cxxxii. 3: "Since there Tetragrammaton giveth His blessing." For there are two paths; that which is above, and that which is below.

753. Hence there is permission granted unto none to enter therein, save unto the High Priest, who entereth from the side of Chesed, in order that none other might enter into that supernal place save that which is called Chesed.

754. And He entereth into the Holy of Holies, and the Bride is mitigated, and that Holy of Holies receiveth blessing, in the place which is called Tzion.

755. But Tzion and Jerusalem are two paths, one denoting Mercy, and the other Justice.

756. For concerning Tzion it is written, Isa. i. 27: "Through Meshephat, Judgment, it is redeemed." And concerning Jerusalem it is written, *ibid.* 21: "Justice, Tzedeq, abideth in Her," as we have before explained.

757. And every desire of the Male is toward the Female. But thus are these called, because hence proceed blessings for all the worlds, and all things receive blessing.

758. This place is called Holy, and all the holinesses of the Male enter therein, through that path of which we have spoken.

759. But they all come from the supernal head of the Male skull, from that portion of the supernal brain wherein they reside.

760. And this blessing floweth down through all the members of the body even unto those which are called Tzabaoth, the Armies.

761. And all that which floweth down throughout the whole body is congregated therein, and therefore are they called Tzabaoth, the Armies; because all the armies of the superiors and inferiors go forth therefrom.

762. And that which floweth down into that place where it is congregated, and which is emitted through that most holy Yesod, Foundation, is entirely white, and therefore is it called Chesed.

763. Thence Chesed entereth into the Holy of Holies; as it is written, Ps. cxxxiii. 3: "For there Tetragrammaton commanded the blessing, even life for evermore."

764. Rabbi Abba said: "Scarcely could the Holy Light-bearer (*i.e., Rabbi Schimeon*) finish the word, life' before his words ceased altogether. But I was still writing them down, and thought that there would still be more for me to write, but I heard nothing.

765. "But I raised not mine head, since the light around him was so great that hereunto I could not look that way.

766. "Therefore I trembled, and I heard a Voice, which cried aloud and said, Prov. iii. 2: 'Length of days and years of life,' &c.

767. "I heard another Voice, Ps. xxi. 5: 'Seeketh life from thee,' &c.

768. "Through that whole day the fire departed not from the house, and there was no one who could come near unto him, because they were unable, for the fire and the light encircled him through that whole day.

769. "But I tell upon my face on the ground, and cried aloud.

770. "When therefore the fire was withdrawn, I saw that that Holy Light-bearer, the Holy of the Holy Ones (*i.e., Rabbi Schimeon*) had been taken away from this world.

771. "But having been turned round, his body had fallen on his right side, and his face still bore a smile.

772. "And Rabbi Eleazar, his son, arose, and having

taken his hands in his, kissed him; but I kissed the dust which was beneath his feet.

773. The Companions wished to mourn for him, but they could not speak. Yet the Companions began to weep, and Rabbi Eleazar prostrated himself thrice, and could not open his mouth.

774. At last he began, and said: "O my father! O my father! there were Three,* and into One have they returned.

775. "Now shall the living creatures (*the Cherubim*) rush forth (*from the Name*); the birds shall fly upward and hide themselves in the opening of the Great Sea, and all the Companions shall drink their blood."

776. But Rabbi Chiya arose upon his feet and said: "Hitherto hath the Holy Light-bearer (*Rabbi Schimeon*) taken care of us (otherwise, hath occupied himself with us). Now is the time not fitting for any other thing save to pay him due honours."

777. Therefore Rabbi Eleazar and Rabbi Abba arose, and put upon him the sepulchral garment; and who ever saw such a disturbance and mingled crowd of learned men? Through the whole house ascended fragrant odours (*of spices brought for the dead*).

778. Then they placed him in the coffin; and no man except Rabbi Eleazar and Rabbi Abba did these services for him.

779. But the lictors and soldiers came from Kaphar (otherwise, from Tzipori and Tardaia, or doctors and learned men from the country), and drove them away.†

780. But the inhabitants of Maronæa rescued them with great tumult, because they thought that he was not to be buried there.

781. When therefore the sepulchral bier was borne

* Referring to Rabbi Schimeon, Rabbi Abba, and himself having symbolized Kether, Chokmah, and Binah.

† Knorr de Rosenroth adds a Latin note here to the effect that it is doubtful whether this was for insult, or because they were jealous of the honour of burying him.

forth, he (*i.e., the body of Rabbi Schimeon*) was raised above it in the air, and a fire flamed around him.

782. And a Voice was heard (*saying*): "Come ye and assemble together, and enter in unto the nuptials of Rabbi Schimeon. Isa. lvii.: 'Let him enter in with peace, and let them rest in their chambers.'"

783. When he was carried into the sepulchral cave, a Voice was heard in the cave saying: "This is He who disturbed the earth, and made the kingdoms tremble."

784. How many liberties are stored up in heaven for thee!

785. This is that Rabbi Schimeon Ben Yochai, concerning whom his Lord was glorified daily. Blessed is his portion above and below!

786. How many highest treasures are reserved for him!

787. Concerning him it is said, Dan. xii. 13: "But go thou thy way till the end be, for thou shalt rest, and stand in thy lot at the end of the days."

Hereunto is the Lesser Holy Assembly.

INDEX.

AARON, 146, 328
Ab, 8, 12, 13, 24, 25, 279, 288, 301, 302, 305, 306, 323
Abel, 146
Abraham, 5, 129, 140, 161, 164, 196, 232, 236
Absolute, 16, 17, 35, 38, 115, 156, 175, 205, 265, 266, 279
Abyss, 36, 48, 188, 198, 241, 245, 249, 266, 297
Achad, 7, 12, 22, 47, 67, 117, 137, 139, 166
Adam, 5, 13, 21, 24, 28, 34, 42, 84, 86, 92, 95, 101, 106, 103, 114, 152, 176, 177, 185, 208, 209, 210, 211, 212, 227, 228, 229, 239, 241, 242, 247, 248, 249, 250, 251
Adonai, 26, 30, 31, 32, 56, 60, 69, 71, 88, 89, 96, 103, 106, 149, 150, 168, 169, 170, 210, 214, 303
Agla, 31
Agrippa, Cornelius Henry, 5
Ahebah, 7, 166
Aima, 25, 285, 287, 288, 301, 302, 305, 306, 307, 308, 323, 326, 330, 331, 336
Ain, 16, 121, 266, 280
Ain Soph, 16, 38, 39, 40, 44, 48, 70, 280
Ain Soph Aur, 16, 70, 94
Air, 104, 177, 178, 179, 279
Aishim, 26
Alchemical, 27, 155, 189, 235, 289
Aleph, the letter, 11, 12, 31, 60, 74, 78, 79, 96, 98, 103, 111, 171, 178, 202, 210, 279, 314, 315, 316, 331, 332
Almighty, 105
Alphabet, 3, 11, 32, 34, 54, 63, 79, 80, 83, 87, 88, 93, 96, 103, 115, 119, 180, 185, 264, 325, 331, 336
Ama, 25, 272, 285, 288
Amath, 160, 217, 293, 308
Amen, 89, 90, 110, 168, 169, 289, 303
Amirah, 150, 151
Ancient of the Ancient Ones, 21, 23, 113, 115, 117, 125, 133, 136, 137, 139, 148, 153, 155, 156, 158, 160, 165, 167, 174, 175, 179, 184, 195, 202, 214, 225, 233, 252, 267

Ancient of Days, 231, 11, 112, 117, 119, 123, 124, 126, 129, 130, 131, 132, 133, 134, 141, 143, 144, 147, 153, 157, 158, 163, 167, 168, 173, 175, 178, 179, 180, 182, 183, 184, 186, 189, 191, 192, 202, 205, 213, 214, 216, 217, 218, 219, 239, 242, 251, 302, 307
Ancient One, 23, 31, 35, 44, 45, 47, 66, 70, 71, 73, 77, 85, 91, 97, 99, 115, 116, 117, 118, 119, 121, 127, 129, 130, 131, 132, 134, 144, 145, 146, 147, 153, 156, 157, 168, 179, 182, 195, 198, 206, 217, 219, 262, 265, 266, 267, 270, 272, 275, 279, 298, 303, 309, 316, 324, 325, 327, 328
Androgynous, 27, 34, 86, 95, 225
Angels, 26, 30, 37, 53, 103, 104, 106, 112, 149, 171, 172, 245, 253, 254
Ani, 59, 60, 78, 168, 322
Apocalypse, 24, 25, 96, 145, 332, 336
Aquarius, 24, 34
Aralim, 25
Arcanum, 101, 110, 113, 144, 175, 185, 196, 200, 209, 217, 224, 226, 227, 240, 249, 254, 284, 311, 321, 322, 323, 326, 334
Archetypal, 29, 35, 67, 69
Arikh Anpin, 24, 41, 44, 77, 117, 137
Asch Metzareph, 14, 15
Asiah, 29, 32, 33, 34, 35, 47, 62, 103, 164, 170, 194, 330
Atch, 31, 279, 280
Ath, 46, 86, 96, 194, 226, 227
Athené, 335
Atmosphere, 36
Atziloth, 29, 32, 33, 34, 35, 67, 69, 170
Aub, 32, 33, 73, 74, 78
Aunu, 256
Auphanim, 24
Aur, 45, 48, 168
Authiqa, 23, 44
Authiqa De-Authiqin, 23
Authiq Iomin, 23
Authiqa Qadisha, 23
Auza, 249
Auzael, 249
Axieros, 269
Axiochersa, 269
Axiochersos, 269
Ayin, the letter, 103, 171, 331, 332

B.

BARIETHA, 155, 195, 200, 219, 221
Bath, 286, 288

Beast, 30, 54, 91, 104, 248, 249
Beauty, 25, 26, 40, 46, 58, 65, 68, 88, 95, 97, 126, 148, 222, 225, 229, 230, 335
Behemoth, 248
Bela, 175
Ben, 8, 12, 32, 33, 72, 74, 282, 285, 286, 288
Beni Elohim, 26
Benignity, 46, 65, 88, 94, 96, 97, 103, 126, 219, 220, 223, 231, 232, 233, 234, 235, 239
Beor, 175
Berashith, 8, 12, 13, 46, 95, 96
Beth, the letter, 12, 103, 171, 286, 331
Beth Elohim, 14, 54
Bhagavadgita, 18
Binah, 24, 32, 40, 42, 53, 54, 55, 58, 59, 60, 67, 88, 94, 144, 147, 163, 189, 201, 225, 234, 267, 273, 278, 281, 282, 285, 286, 287, 288, 289, 298, 301, 302, 305, 307, 321, 330, 335, 336, 338, 340
Book of Concealed Mystery, 15, 16, 41, 43 to 108, 115, 128, 134, 137, 141, 144, 147, 151, 152, 157, 160, 161, 174, 180, 189, 191, 192, 201, 204, 208, 212, 219, 222, 224, 226, 231, 234, 239, 240, 243, 246, 248, 272, 278, 283, 284, 288, 291, 301, 303, 310, 325, 326, 331
Book of Formation, 119
Book of the Revolutions of Souls, 15, 86, 101
Briah, 29, 32, 33, 34, 35, 47, 52, 170, 285
Bride, 25, 31, 32, 35, 41, 42, 47, 49, 51, 52, 56, 57, 58, 60, 62, 63, 64, 65, 70, 71, 72, 74, 75, 78, 85, 86, 94, 95, 100, 105, 106, 164, 210, 233, 286, 287, 293, 300, 332, 334, 338
Buddhist, 37
Bull, 24

C

Cain, 86
Canaan, 100
Canticles, 74, 105, 116, 141, 147, 173, 181, 186, 190, 205, 215, 220, 224, 225, 229, 243, 247, 263, 271, 286, 287, 318, 329, 330, 332, 334, 335, 336
Ceridwen, 233
Chaioth-Ha-Qadesh, 24, 56, 104, 265
Chariot, 104, 172, 253, 257, 261
Chashmalim, 25
Chen, 9
Chesed, 25, 40, 51, 88, 103, 126, 174, 219, 223, 234, 243, 267, 270, 276, 289, 293, 297, 301, 308, 327, 336, 338, 339

Cheth, the letter, 103, 171, 309, 318, 331, 332
Chiah, 35, 40, 53, 83, 92, 228, 299
Chioa, 30
Chokmah, 9, 24, 25, 27, 32, 40, 53, 60, 67, 73, 88, 138, 167, 217, 250, 267, 273, 274, 278, 280, 281, 282, 284, 285, 287, 288, 289, 290, 291, 298, 301, 302, 305, 306, 307, 321, 325, 329, 330, 331, 335, 336, 338, 340
Cholom Yesodoth, 28
Christ, 146
Christian, 25, 31, 32, 284
Chronicles, 97, 194
Clef des Mysteres, 36
Commutations, Tables of the, 10
Companions, 109, 110, 113, 149, 251, 254, 256, 259, 260, 261, 262, 305, 335, 340
Concealed of the Concealed, 21, 23, 78, 113, 115, 167, 195, 252, 263, 269, 283, 298, 306, 316, 318
Creation, 29, 30, 50, 52, 94, 104, 160, 161, 172, 174, 284
Creative, 30, 35
Cremonensian Codex, 15, 210
Crown, 20, 23, 27, 28, 31, 34, 35, 41, 44, 45, 48, 60, 61, 66, 71, 72, 76, 85, 88, 94, 96, 97, 111, 126, 132, 145, 149, 156, 169, 175, 177, 226, 233, 242, 243, 244, 248, 256, 267, 268, 269, 287, 289, 293, 294, 304, 320, 331

D

DAATH, 26, 59, 60, 74, 106, 180, 278, 288, 289, 290, 291, 305, 321, 333, 336
Daleth, the letter, 11, 60, 75, 79, 80, 92, 93, 103, 171, 202, 210, 284, 285, 331
Daniel, 26, 58, 123, 130, 141, 143, 168, 178, 182, 223, 236, 245, 251, 289, 329, 336, 341
Daughter, 93, 101, 177, 232, 235, 249, 282, 286, 288, 290, 300, 301
David, 6, 54, 82, 102, 107, 131, 132, 207, 208, 209, 210, 211, 212, 236, 326, 332
Day, 52, 99, 109, 140, 167, 236, 257, 293
Death, 30, 52, 104, 109
Debur, 150, 151
Decad, 26, 65, 74, 99, 100, 105, 149, 160, 180, 214
Deity, 17, 21, 22, 30, 34, 43, 44, 46, 48, 78, 89, 139, 141, 168, 170, 208, 335
Demons, 30, 51, 54, 103, 240, 244, 249
Deuteronomy, 69, 78, 110, 111, 191, 193, 198, 204, 214, 242, 254, 313, 315, 319

Devils, 30, 51
Dew, 116, 117, 177, 178, 179, 265, 303
Diana, 336
Din, 25, 103, 301
Dinhabah, 175
Dragon, 50, 51, 52, 53, 152, 237
Duad, 24, 27, 92, 267, 268, 271
Duenech, 289

E

Eagle, 24, 75
Earth, 36, 37, 43, 46, 47, 69, 76, 82, 89, 90, 91, 94, 97, 100, 104, 105, 112, 125, 128, 150, 163, 178, 188, 227, 242, 248, 249, 250, 289, 297, 312, 315
Ecclesiastes, 101, 112, 139, 199, 251, 295, 319
Eden, 36, 96, 119, 123, 124, 131, 152, 156, 167, 180, 262, 270, 278, 279, 281, 284, 287, 293
Edom, 22, 29, 102, 113, 114, 174, 175, 233, 300
Edomite Kings, 22, 29, 43, 47, 48, 85, 102, 174, 176, 298, 331
Egypt, 5, 6, 176
Egyptians, 6, 163, 168, 289
Eheieh, 17, 23, 30, 31, 32, 41, 61, 66, 67, 79, 88, 91, 96, 141, 175
El, 25, 88, 143, 144, 171, 234, 291, 305, 310
El Chai, 26
Elements, 28, 104
Elihu, 255
Eliphaz Levi Zahad, 17, 35, 36
Eloh, 25, 209
Elohim, 7, 8, 21, 22, 25, 26, 46, 48, 54, 56, 61, 69, 70, 82, 84, 88, 90, 93, 96, 98, 101, 104, 105, 106, 107, 108, 124, 163, 167, 202, 209, 226, 227, 239, 242, 249, 265, 273, 280, 303, 326, 330
Enoch, 105
Equilibrium, 16, 29, 43, 44, 45, 55, 57, 66, 71, 73, 75, 92, 94, 96, 121, 135, 136, 138, 141, 183, 225, 242, 246, 266, 308
Esther, 155
Eucharist, 269
Eugenius Philalethes, 20
Eve, 42, 228, 241
Existence, 17, 23, 30, 31, 44, 63
Exodus, 23, 79, 88, 94, 107, 111, 117, 121, 122, 140, 145, 148, 150, 153, 170, 175, 188, 196, 197, 198, 216, 217, 218, 236, 237, 252, 289, 303
Ezekiel, 24, 34, 53, 56, 75, 86, 104, 132, 173, 226, 240, 245, 251, 265, 313

F

Father, 8, 12, 13, 22, 24, 25, 31, 32, 35, 41, 57, 58, 59, 60, 61, 62, 63, 64, 66, 67, 71, 73, 74, 75, 78, 80, 84, 85, 86, 89, 92, 93, 94, 95, 96, 107, 140, 156, 165, 180, 236, 279, 280, 281, 282, 283, 285, 286, 288, 289, 290, 291, 298, 299, 302, 304, 305, 306, 307, 323, 326, 331, 340
Fear, 25, 291
Female, 21, 22, 35, 55, 58, 62, 73, 84, 85, 86, 92, 93, 95, 100, 177, 227, 229, 244, 281, 282, 286, 295, 300, 301, 331, 334, 335, 338
Feminine, 21, 22, 24, 25, 26, 27, 46, 55, 61, 73, 82, 85, 92, 101, 209, 229, 231, 239, 312, 326, 334
Fire, 104, 177, 178, 196, 198, 200, 279, 318, 330, 331, 339
Fludd, Robert, 5
Formation, 29, 35, 50, 160
Foundation, 26, 40, 46, 56, 57, 59, 60, 62, 64, 72, 85, 88, 92, 97, 167, 243, 337, 339

G

GABRIEL, 7, 245
Garden, 67, 82, 98, 100, 131, 152, 167, 262, 278, 284, 285, 335
Gate, 32, 60, 64, 65, 69, 74, 106, 180, 184, 200, 201, 210, 234, 253
Geburah, 25, 51, 52, 88, 163, 174, 193, 194, 224, 243, 267, 289, 317, 327, 329, 334, 336
Gedulah, 25, 174, 194, 327
Gehenna, 261, 269
Gematria, 4, 7, 12, 31, 47, 51, 54, 67, 76, 111, 120, 137, 139, 143, 152, 155, 167, 170, 182, 194, 234, 277, 285, 303
Genesis, 22, 47, 48, 49, 69, 70, 76, 82, 83, 84, 86, 90, 91, 93, 96, 97, 98, 100, 105, 106, 107, 113, 114, 116, 119, 128, 129, 174, 175, 180, 193, 194, 195, 196, 197, 198, 202, 209, 226, 232, 233, 239, 241, 249, 250, 265, 284, 287, 300, 303, 305, 316, 325, 334
Ghimel, the letter, 31, 103, 331, 332
Giants, 100, 249
Glory, 46, 52, 61, 65, 68, 77, 88, 97, 125, 163, 168, 221, 222, 246, 262, 337
Gnomes, 104
God, 25, 26, 34, 37, 47, 57, 69, 88, 89, 95, 112, 124, 137, 140, 143, 144, 150, 151, 153, 154, 155, 169, 172, 173, 180, 182, 191, 199, 200, 204, 216, 218, 228, 232, 241, 242, 254, 256, 261, 262, 263, 282, 291, 292, 293, 296, 297, 303, 314, 319, 322, 323
Golgotha, 72, 303
Grace, 9, 268, 270, 279, 309
Greater Holy Assembly, 40, 41, 67, 77, 109 to 257, 260, 261, 278, 300, 317, 331
Greatness, 25

H

HABAKKUK, III, 202
Hadar, 175, 222, 234, 300
He, the letter, 11, 31, 32, 33, 34, 41, 54, 55, 56, 57, 58, 59, 60, 61, 62, 64, 65, 67, 69, 70, 71, 72, 73, 74, 75, 78, 79, 80, 84, 85, 86, 87, 88, 89, 92, 93, 95, 96, 98, 100, 101, 103, 107, 108, 147, 171, 179, 180, 194, 202, 210, 225, 231, 232, 246, 272, 273, 274, 282, 285, 286, 288, 304, 310, 314, 330, 331, 332, 334, 335
Heavens, 46, 96, 112, 242, 251, 265, 303, 315
Hell, 30
Hercules, 54
Hermes, 96, 155, 189, 242
Hertha, 233
Hexad, 74, 161, 243, 284
Histoire de la Magie, 17
Hoa, 54, 78, 79, 130, 156, 168, 185, 242, 263, 268, 279, 280, 283, 291, 292, 294, 298, 302, 318, 326, 330
Hod, 26, 40, 51, 61, 65, 88, 125, 163, 221, 222, 243, 267, 310, 337, 338
Horus, 269, 289
Hosea, 252, 283, 299, 318

I

IDDO, 262
Idra Rabba Qadisha, 14, 66, 67, 70, 71, 76, 77, 102, 109 to 257
Idra Zuta Qadisha, 14, 67, 77, 150, 259 to 341
IHVH, 9, 12, 26, 30, 31, 32, 35, 55, 56, 57, 59, 61, 63, 64, 66, 67, 69, 70, 71, 73, 82, 84, 88, 89, 96, 107, 141, 156, 168, 171, 179, 180, 196, 202, 208, 209, 210, 211, 214, 225, 227, 246, 276, 280, 282, 283, 285, 286, 303, 311, 314, 316, 317, 322, 327, 332, 334
Image, 36, 38, 248
Infinite, 18, 38, 44
Influence, 27, 64, 69, 102, 152, 274, 275, 276, 279, 283, 290, 292, 303, 325, 328
Influx, 61, 66, 71, 75, 76, 85, 88, 97, 98, 99, 101, 103, 104, 107, 160, 161, 162, 167
Inscrutable Height, 23, 40
Ior, 103, 194
Isaac, 236
Isaiah, 25, 50, 57, 69, 77, 78, 95, 97, 108, 112, 116, 127, 129, 130, 131, 144, 152, 157, 161, 163, 168, 179, 190, 193, 198, 237, 248, 257, 266, 273, 279, 284, 287, 291, 313, 314, 315, 316, 317, 323, 338, 341
Isheth Zenunim, 30
Isis, 233, 269, 289

[redacted]

Israel, 8, 12, 22, 23, 53, 94, 95, 106, 111, 113, 114, 121, 124, 125, 129, 141, 154, 183, 185, 187, 198, 204, 271, 289, 303, 312, 313, 315, 325, 327, 332

J

Jacob, 59, 60, 123, 137, 140, 163, 196, 197, 204, 236, 291, 305, 306, 325
Jehovah, 26, 30, 32, 55, 69, 71
Jellinek, Dr., 38
Jeremiah, 67, 71, 120, 123, 124, 131, 149, 161, 184, 230, 336
Jeroboam, 262
Jerusalem, 77, 190, 191, 247, 313, 314, 315, 337, 338
Jesus, 8, 72
Job, 51, 78, 124, 151, 153, 188, 201, 215, 218, 280, 301, 312, 320, 332
John, 24
Joseph, 128, 197
Joshua, 93, 94, 100, 107, 253
Jubilee, 107, 180, 288
Judgment, 28, 41, 49, 51, 51, 52, 53, 54, 55, 59, 72, 76, 85, 94, 95, 102, 103, 104, 105, 106, 122, 123, 141, 143, 153, 155, 164, 173, 175, 178, 182, 183, 184, 185, 187, 191, 194, 195, 196, 215, 216, 226, 230, 231, 232, 233, 234, 235, 240, 241, 244, 245, 247, 274, 277, 293, 294, 295, 296, 297, 300, 301, 309, 310, 312, 314, 315, 329, 332, 338
Jupiter, 27, 104
Justice, 25, 26, 40, 52, 141, 163, 191, 224, 238, 248, 289, 293, 294, 296, 297, 314, 315, 332, 338

K

Kaph, the letter, 103, 171, 325, 331, 332
Karma, 37, 38
Kerubim, 24, 26, 32, 34, 35, 172, 340
Kether, 20, 23, 24, 26, 27, 31, 32, 34, 41, 44, 45, 46, 48, 61, 66, 67, 70, 88, 91, 96, 111, 124, 145, 166, 169, 175, 177, 217, 248, 265, 266, 267, 280, 283, 289, 301, 302, 305, 320, 330, 331, 335, 338, 340
Khem, 289
Khorsia, 29
King, 26, 27, 28, 31, 32, 34, 35, 51, 53, 93, 98, 102, 108, 109, 113, 136, 145, 146, 149, 155, 158, 159, 210, 211, 218, 233, 236, 240, 248, 253, 256, 264, 269, 289, 292, 294, 295, 296, 300, 307, 319, 320, 323, 326, 332, 333, 334, 335, 336, 337
Kingdom, 20, 26, 46, 47, 48, 49, 50, 55, 62, 63, 73, 84, 88, 92, 94, 96, 97, 100, 101, 103, 104, 106, 107, 233, 234, 296

Kings, 26, 29, 43, 48, 84, 85, 88, 93, 101, 102, 103, 113, 114, 129, 132, 154, 174, 199, 200, 300, 307, 318, 320, 321
Kneph, 289
Knowledge, 58, 59, 60, 74, 76, 106, 115, 131, 132, 180, 278, 288, 289, 291, 305, 310
Kokab, 28

L

Lamed, the letter, 31, 103, 171, 331
Lamentations, 314, 336
Law, 8, 59, 83, 109, 110, 111, 115, 129, 140, 141, 146, 160, 161, 162, 182, 183, 205, 280
Leah, 59
Leo, 24, 34
Lernæan Hydra, 54
Lesser Countenance, 26, 32, 35, 41, 48, 118, 179
Lesser Holy Assembly, 40, 67, 77, 259 to 341
Levanah, 28
Leviathan, 42, 51, 53, 54, 85, 189, 237
Leviticus, 80, 91, 106, 157, 245, 285, 287, 300, 311, 322
Light, 20, 28, 36, 48, 50, 51, 54, 56, 62, 65, 66, 73, 74, 76, 82, 84, 85, 102, 103, 106, 107, 114, 115, 116, 122, 123, 125, 126, 127, 136, 145, 147, 148, 158, 159, 168, 177, 179, 195, 198, 218, 219, 222, 223, 234, 255, 256, 263, 266, 267, 268, 270, 279, 283, 289, 292, 294, 304, 306, 332
Limitless, 16, 19, 20, 44, 45, 48
Lion, 24
Lord, 26, 30, 31, 48, 59, 60, 69, 71, 83, 87, 88, 89, 90, 91, 94, 95, 96, 98, 109, 110, 125, 127, 128, 129, 132, 133, 150, 156, 159, 163, 167, 168, 183, 199, 201, 214, 216, 218, 230, 238, 242, 244, 251, 255, 308, 312, 319, 329, 341
Love, 7, 25, 40, 111, 166, 253, 286, 295
Lublinensian Codex, 15
Lully, Raymond, 5

M

Macrocosm, 36, 41, 155, 331
Macroprosopus, 24, 26, 31, 35, 41, 43, 44, 45, 46, 47, 48, 54, 57, 61, 65, 66, 69, 70, 71, 72, 73, 76, 77, 78, 81, 82, 83, 85, 91, 96, 97, 99, 102, 111, 112, 115, 116, 117, 118, 119, 121, 122, 123, 124, 125, 130, 133, 134, 136, 137, 138, 141, 142, 144, 145, 147, 148, 149, 153, 154, 156, 158, 160, 162, 163, 164, 166, 167, 168, 169, 170, 173, 182, 183, 184, 185, 187, 190, 192, 194, 204, 207, 216, 218, 222, 238, 266, 271, 280, 283, 303, 304, 307, 312, 313, 314, 328, 330

Madim, 27
Magnificence, 25
Mah, 32, 33, 73, 74, 78, 79, 251
Malachi, 112, 148, 195, 232
Male, 21, 35, 55, 58, 67, 84, 85, 86, 92, 93, 95, 177, 227, 229, 230, 231, 235, 239, 244, 247, 281, 282, 286, 287, 295, 300, 301, 334, 335, 338
Malkuth, 20, 25, 26, 27, 31, 32, 35, 46, 47, 49, 51, 52, 53, 55, 56, 57, 63, 78, 84, 88, 94, 96, 148, 160, 169, 233, 267, 296, 327
Man, 24, 25, 29, 34, 36, 37, 60, 67, 83, 84, 85, 86, 87, 88, 89, 90, 91, 92, 101, 102, 106, 126, 127, 134, 137, 139, 141, 152, 155, 168, 174, 175, 177, 186, 188, 207, 208, 209, 210, 211, 212, 216, 227, 228, 230, 233, 234, 235, 241, 242, 243, 245, 248, 251, 259, 281, 301, 305, 312, 335
Mantuan Codex, 15, 45, 46, 66, 67, 68, 70, 83, 100
Mars, 27, 104, 163, 194
Mary, 307
Masculine 21, 22, 24, 25, 27, 46, 55, 82, 85, 92, 101, 209 239, 312, 315, 334
Masloth, 27
Matred, 177, 235, 300
Matrona, 26, 337
Matter, 30, 35, 100, 112, 165
Mechetabel, 177, 234, 235, 300
Melakim, 26
Melchizedek, 295
Melekh, 26
Mem, the letter, 51, 103, 171, 178, 279, 310, 331
Mercury, 28, 104
Mercy, 25, 26, 28, 41, 49, 50, 52, 53, 55, 59, 69, 70, 89, 94, 102, 103, 104, 122, 125, 141, 143, 155, 157, 158, 160, 164, 174, 182, 183, 187, 191, 192, 195, 196, 203, 215, 216, 219, 220, 223, 224, 225, 230, 234, 235, 238, 239, 247, 266, 270, 274, 276, 293, 295, 297, 301, 308, 309, 314, 327, 329, 338
Meshephat, 293, 294, 295, 296, 297, 314, 338
Messiach, 7, 50, 131, 132, 133, 149, 273
Metatron, 7, 105, 106
Mezahab, 177, 235, 300, 301,
Mezla, 27, 279, 303, 325, 327, 328
Micah, 137, 140, 144, 151, 154, 158, 160, 165
Microcosm, 36, 155, 231
Microprosopus, 26, 31, 32, 35, 40, 41, 42, 43, 46, 47, 48, 49, 51, 56, 57, 58, 59, 61, 63, 64, 65, 66, 67, 70, 71, 72, 73, 74, 75, 76, 77, 78, 81, 82, 83, 84, 86, 91, 93, 94, 95, 97, 98, 99, 102, 103, 107, 114, 118, 119, 120, 121, 122, 124, 125, 129, 131, 132, 133, 134, 136, 137, 138, 141, 145, 146, 148, 152, 155, 159, 164, 166, 167, 168, 173, 177, 178, 179, 180,

181, 182, 183, 184, 185, 186, 187, 190, 191, 192, 195, 196, 198, 199, 200, 201, 202, 203, 204, 205, 207, 210, 212, 213, 214, 216, 217, 218, 219, 221, 222, 224, 225, 226, 227, 229, 232, 233, 235, 236, 238, 239, 243, 248, 265, 267, 268, 271, 272, 273, 274, 275, 278, 279, 283, 284, 289, 293, 298, 299, 302, 303, 304, 305, 306, 307, 309, 310, 311, 312, 313, 314, 315, 316, 317, 318, 319, 320, 321, 323 324, 325, 327, 328, 329, 331, 332, 333, 336, 338
Mikhael, 7, 37, 38
Mildness, 25, 28, 103, 169
Miölner, 302
Mirandola, J. P. de, 5
Mischna, 322
Moab, 310
Monad, 22, 99, 268, 271
Moon, 27, 28, 62, 104, 257
More, Dr. Henry, 5
Moses, 6, 54, 60, 94, 104, 105, 106, 107, 140, 141, 148, 151, 182, 196, 197, 198, 216, 217, 237, 252, 275, 315, 328
Most Holy Ancient One, 21, 23, 70, 73, 140, 198, 219, 223, 224, 226, 227, 240, 263, 264, 265, 266, 267, 268, 269, 270, 271, 272, 273, 274, 276, 277, 279, 280, 281, 283, 289, 294, 298, 299, 301, 302, 304, 305, 306, 310, 314, 316, 317, 318, 325
Most Holy One, 262, 263, 296, 303, 319, 322, 323
Mother, 22, 24, 25, 26, 32, 35, 41, 42, 53, 54, 57, 58, 59, 60, 61, 62, 63, 64, 65, 66, 67, 71, 72, 73, 74, 75, 78, 80, 82, 84, 86, 87, 92, 93, 94, 95, 96, 97, 98, 103, 106, 107, 180, 225, 233, 240, 269, 281, 282, 285, 286, 287, 288, 289, 290, 291, 298, 299, 301, 302, 304, 305, 306, 307, 308, 323, 326, 331, 334, 335, 337, 338

N

Name, 24, 25, 26, 30, 31, 61, 66, 69, 70, 72, 73, 76, 77, 78, 82, 84, 89, 90, 95, 96, 97, 98, 99, 100, 101, 102, 103, 105, 106, 108, 111, 129, 155, 167, 168, 169, 170, 172, 174, 197, 209, 210, 214, 220, 227, 232, 235, 241, 242, 249, 264, 272, 273, 283, 285, 292, 294, 299, 326, 337, 340
Negative, 16, 20, 43, 44, 45, 266
Negative Existence, 16, 18, 19, 20, 44, 117, 121, 266, 280, 330
Negative Subsistence, 18, 19
Nephesch, 34, 35, 36, 37, 40, 92, 228, 253, 299
Nephilim, 249
Nequdah Peshutah, 23
Nequdah Rashunah, 23
Neschamah, 34, 35, 36, 37, 40, 91, 228, 247, 253, 269, 299, 323

Netzach, 26, 40, 45, 46, 51, 88, 97, 126, 184, 185, 224, 243, 267, 310, 337, 338,
Noah, 5, 250.
Nogah, 27, 104, 105
Notariqon, 7, 9, 31, 55, 111
Numbers, 75, 89, 98, 100, 117, 127, 128, 152, 155, 159, 190, 199 200, 216, 217, 223, 265, 309, 319, 321, 328
Nun, the letter, 60, 64, 74, 78, 103, 171, 210, 286, 310, 331

O

Obadiah, 75.
Olahm, 28, 29, 31, 40, 158, 167, 203, 249
Osiris, 269, 289
Otz, 28, 267, 336

P

Paau, 234, 300
Pachad, 25, 40, 163, 174
Palace, 89, 94, 104, 252, 253, 256, 291, 292
Paradise, 42, 51, 67, 111, 152, 262, 270, 281
Path, 26, 54, 55, 57, 59, 60, 61, 62, 63, 64, 65, 66, 68, 70, 71, 75, 84, 87, 89, 92, 94, 95, 96, 97, 98, 99, 100, 101, 102, 103, 104, 105, 106, 107, 108, 119, 121, 122, 124, 126, 128, 151, 153, 154, 155, 156, 157, 180, 181, 182, 183, 189, 206, 210, 219, 220, 221, 226, 228, 231, 241, 256, 264, 266, 267, 269, 280, 282, 283, 293, 299, 307, 309, 310, 330, 338
Patriarch, 161, 236, 257, 325
Paul, 146
Pe, the letter, 103, 171, 331
Pentad, 74
Pentateuch, 6
Pistorius, 152, 169
Planets, 37, 104, 105
Positive Existence, 16, 19, 45, 266
Potential Existence, 19, 266
Primordial Point, 23
Primum Mobile, 27, 104
Proclus, 21
Prosper Rugere, 8
Proverbs, 57, 62, 68, 80, 112, 121, 127, 128, 129, 136, 138, 158, 175, 181, 213, 214, 222, 225, 243, 250, 266, 271, 278, 282, 288, 290, 291, 295 296, 297, 308, 309, 321, 322, 333, 335, 339

Psalms, 26, 53, 54, 78, 82, 91, 97, 98, 99, 104, 107, 109, 110, 120, 122, 123, 124, 125, 128, 129, 133, 146, 154, 156, 158, 159, 168, 183, 187, 188, 189, 192, 194, 199, 201, 203, 207, 218, 219, 221, 223, 226, 232, 236, 238, 239, 248, 261, 271, 273, 274, 277, 281, 285, 291, 293, 296, 297, 298, 299, 300, 305, 308, 310, 311, 312, 316, 317, 321, 322, 339
Pythagoras, 21, 214

Q

Qabalah, 1, 2, 4, 5, 6, 10, 11, 13, 14, 15, 17, 21, 22, 25, 28, 30, 38, 55, 72, 88, 100, 111, 173, 226, 272, 283, 284, 335
Quain, 241, 245
Qliphoth, 30, 51, 103
Qoph, the letter, 103, 171, 331, 332
Quaternary, 35, 266, 284, 304
Queen, 25, 26, 27, 28, 31, 32, 34, 35, 47, 39, 51, 55, 56, 57, 58, 59, 60, 71, 78, 92, 94, 95, 96, 97, 101, 105, 106, 107, 149, 233, 269, 330, 332

R

Rabbi Abba, 6, 110, 111, 125, 149, 150, 162, 218, 222, 254, 255, 259, 260 261, 262, 292, 339, 340
Rabbi Benchas Ben Yair, 256, 259, 262
Rabbi Chiya, 110, 149, 150, 152, 260, 340
Rabbi Chizqiah, 110, 147, 148, 149, 252
Rabbi Eleazar, 6, 110, 111, 122, 123, 149, 150, 160, 207, 212, 259, 260, 261, 262, 339, 340
Rabbi Moses Korduero, 36
Rabbi Schimeon Ben Yochai, 6, 109, 110, 112, 113, 122, 123, 125, 126, 130, 132, 134, 146, 148, 149, 150, 153, 156, 158, 162, 163, 166, 169, 172, 203, 204, 207, 218, 222, 224, 225, 242, 251, 252, 253, 254, 255, 256, 257, 259, 260, 261, 262, 263, 269, 281, 283, 290, 292, 299, 339, 340, 341
Rabbi Yehuda, 110, 130, 149, 150, 163, 212, 223, 255, 260
Rabbi Yisa, 110, 149, 157, 252
Rabbi Yitzchaq, 110, 137, 146, 149, 150, 260
Rabbi Yitzchaq Loria, 36
Rabbi Yosi, 110, 131, 149, 154, 252
Rabbi Yosi Ben Jacob, 110, 149, 150, 260
Rachel, 59, 305
Raphael, 7
Rashith Ha-Galgalim, 27
Ratzon, 122, 270

Rav Hammenuna, 133, 256, 262, 286, 300, 317
Rav Yeyeva, 273, 279, 282, 284, 309, 327
Rebekah, 305
Rechoboth, 234
Resh, the letter, 103, 171, 331
Reuchlin, John, 5
Revelation, 54, 189
Rhea, 233
Righteousness, 40, 77, 148, 332
Risha Havurah, 23
Rom Meolah, 23, 40
Royal Valley, 50, 53
Ruach, 7, 8, 9, 12, 22, 27, 34, 35, 36, 37, 40, 248, 249, 251, 273, 299, 302, 316, 322, 323, 329

S

SABBATH, 122, 123, 240, 255, 257, 269, 310, 337
Salamanders, 104
Samael, 30, 37, 38
Samekh, the letter, 103, 171, 331
Samuel, 88, 90, 98, 107, 185, 196, 197, 238, 251, 291, 305, 321, 329
Sandalphon, 103
Sarah, 232
Satan, 30, 51
Saturn, 27, 52, 104
Saul, 234
Scandinavians, 28
Schechinah, 26, 49, 55, 103, 111, 161, 197, 246, 250, 260
Schemahamphorasch, 111, 170, 171, 197, 330
Scintilla, 19
Scorpio, 24, 34
Scorpion, 24
Sea, 25, 42, 53, 90, 125, 144, 147, 188, 189, 225, 241, 307, 340
Seg, 32, 33, 74, 78
Sepher Yetzirah, 14, 22, 51, 61, 119, 161, 178, 180, 196, 243, 273, 279, 325, 326, 331
Sepher Sephiroth, 14, 15
Sephiroth, 16, 20, 21, 24, 25, 26, 27, 28, 29, 32, 38, 39, 40, 41, 42, 44, 45, 46, 47, 49, 50, 51, 52, 54, 58, 59, 60, 62, 63, 65, 66, 67, 69, 73, 84, 88, 89, 92, 94, 96, 97, 100, 104, 111, 126, 137, 145, 149, 150, 156, 160, 161, 163, 164, 166, 169, 172, 174, 179, 180, 197, 211, 214, 217, 228, 237, 243, 256, 261, 264, 267, 269, 280, 281, 282, 284, 289, 310, 325, 327, 330, 332

Seraphim, 25
Serpent, 42, 50, 51, 52, 85, 104, 152, 237, 241, 295
Seth, 246
Severity, 41, 46, 51, 88, 94, 96, 100, 106, 193, 194, 233, 235, 297, 309, 329, 334
Shabbathai, 27
Shaddaï, 7, 26, 88, 105
Shedim, 249
Shells, 30, 36, 50, 51, 53, 100, 102, 103, 104, 105
Shemesh, 27
Shiloh, 7
Shin, the letter, 7, 103, 171, 178, 196, 279, 331
Shinanim, 26
Sinai, 148, 252
Siphra Dtzenioutha, 14, 43 to 108, 115
Smooth Point, 23
Snake, 24
Solomon, 6, 66, 94, 101, 102, 132, 204, 233, 286, 287, 295, 332
Solomon Meir Ben Moses, 8
Son, 8, 12, 13, 22, 32, 35, 57, 61, 72, 93, 95, 96, 101, 131, 146, 156, 251, 253, 259, 261, 282, 284, 285, 286, 288, 289, 290, 307, 331
Song of Songs, 66, 68, 204
Soul, 34, 35, 36, 37, 40, 60, 65, 71, 72, 83, 87, 91, 92, 98, 103, 104, 106, 158, 228, 241, 242, 247, 253, 323
Sphinx, 24, 36
Spinoza, 38
Spirit, 8, 12, 13, 22, 27, 35, 36, 40, 46, 48, 51, 70, 71, 86, 91, 92, 98, 99, 100, 101, 102, 105, 107, 112, 114, 131, 132, 133, 150, 152, 153, 164, 165, 173, 180, 199, 200, 223, 224, 234, 240, 241, 242, 246, 248, 249, 251, 269, 273, 302, 316, 322
Splendour, 26, 40, 104, 148, 163
Strength, 25, 143, 163, 193, 194, 224, 225, 243, 251, 277, 291
Sun, 27, 37, 62, 104, 148
Sylphs, 104
Syntagma, 19, 245, 246, 247, 270, 282, 285, 338

T

TALMUD, 53
Tau, the letter, 51, 96, 103, 119, 171, 264, 331
Taurus, 24, 34
Temira De-Temirin, 23
Temple, 6, 89, 160, 161, 233
Temura, 7, 9, 11, 55

Teth, the letter, 103, 171, 331
Tetrad, 74, 161, 284
Tetragrammaton, 9, 12, 31, 32, 33, 34, 35, 41, 50, 51, 54, 55, 56, 57, 59, 60, 61, 62, 63, 64, 65, 67, 69, 70, 71, 72, 73, 74, 75, 76, 77, 78, 82, 85, 87, 89, 91, 95, 96, 98, 99, 100, 101, 102, 103, 104, 105, 106, 107, 108, 110, 111, 121, 122, 123, 127, 128, 129, 130, 131, 140, 147, 150, 151, 152, 153, 154, 155, 163, 165, 167, 168, 169, 170, 172, 179, 183, 188, 190, 191, 193, 194, 195, 196, 197, 198, 199, 200, 201, 202, 204, 207, 208, 209, 210, 211, 212, 214, 216, 223, 224, 226, 227, 228, 230, 231, 236, 237, 238, 239, 241, 242, 246, 249, 250, 251, 252, 254, 255, 257, 266, 267, 283, 291, 296, 297, 299, 304, 305, 307, 308, 311, 312, 314, 315, 317, 318, 319, 321, 322, 326, 327, 328, 330, 333, 334, 337 338, 339
Than, 152, 237
Thrashisim, 26, 245
Thashraq, 10
Thebunah, 286, 288, 290
Theli, 51
Thenanim, 53
Thor, 302
Thora, 210
Throne, 25, 29, 34, 52, 86, 116, 130, 132, 149, 173, 174, 226, 236, 251, 293, 294, 337
Tiphereth, 25, 34, 40, 51, 58, 60, 62, 88, 94, 97, 106, 126, 148, 152, 222, 225, 229, 230, 237, 243, 267, 284, 289, 315, 327, 336, 337
Tree of Knowledge of Good and Evil, 103, 104, 336
Tree of Life, 28, 98, 104, 197, 284, 332, 336
Triad, 24, 27, 267, 338
Trinity, 25, 26, 27, 28, 30, 31, 32, 34, 35, 45, 117, 149, 266, 304
Triune, 27, 267
Truth, 109, 122, 158, 160, 183, 188, 217, 218, 219, 247, 293, 294, 306, 308
Tzabaoth, 26, 88, 246, 310, 337, 339
Tzaddi, the letter, 103, 171, 331
Tzedeq, 27, 40, 289, 293, 294, 295, 296, 297, 314, 332, 338
Tzelem, 36, 38
Tziruph, 9, 10

U

Understanding, 24, 54, 55, 59, 60, 61, 62, 64, 67, 71, 73, 74, 76, 80, 82, 84, 87, 88, 94, 95, 98, 101, 106, 107, 109, 114, 131, 133, 163, 168, 180, 184, 201, 265, 273, 281, 282, 285, 288
Undines, 104

Unity, 7, 12, 22, 27, 39, 40, 47, 67, 78, 111, 117, 137, 139, 166, 226, 243, 246, 266, 268, 273, 283
Universe, 28, 29, 37, 43, 44, 46, 47, 66, 98, 100, 103, 108, 112, 135, 136, 148, 149, 155, 159, 161, 162, 183, 216, 228, 319, 330

V

VAN HELMONT, J. Baptist, 5
Vast Countenance, 24, 26, 31, 35, 41, 44, 45, 48, 91, 117, 266
Vau, the letter, 11, 32, 33, 34, 41, 54, 55, 56, 57, 58, 59, 60, 61, 62, 64, 65, 70, 71, 72, 73, 74, 75, 79, 80, 84, 85, 86, 87, 88, 89, 92, 93, 95, 96, 100, 103, 171, 179, 210, 246, 272, 282, 284, 285, 286, 288, 304, 331
Vaughan, Thomas, 20
Veil, 20, 36, 114, 115, 169, 170, 172, 330
Venus, 27, 104, 105
Victory, 26, 45, 46, 88, 97, 126, 184, 185, 224, 310, 337
Virgin, 32, 307

W

WATERS, 48, 49, 51, 53, 83, 84, 87, 97, 98, 104, 147, 178, 189, 196, 234, 279, 284, 287, 289, 293, 310, 330, 331
Wheels, 24, 52, 104
White Head, 23, 124, 125, 176, 177, 195, 264, 303
Wisdom, 24, 40, 53, 56, 58, 60, 61, 62, 64, 67, 76, 80, 87, 88, 93, 95, 96, 101, 107, 109, 118, 131, 132, 133, 138, 139, 161, 167, 173, 180, 189, 213, 214, 217, 240, 244, 250, 251, 256, 265, 266, 270, 273, 274, 276, 277, 280, 281, 282, 284, 285, 288, 291, 318, 325, 329, 331, 335
Woman, 25, 30, 63, 64, 85, 93, 94, 229, 230, 231, 233, 234, 235, 239, 247, 281, 286, 287, 334, 335
World, 28, 29, 30, 32, 33, 34, 35, 36, 37, 38, 40, 47, 48, 52, 59, 62, 67, 69, 72, 74, 80, 85, 90, 94, 97, 100, 101, 103, 104, 107, 108, 112, 113, 116, 120, 121, 132, 134, 142, 143, 144, 147, 150, 156, 159, 166, 170, 172, 174, 175, 178, 179, 185, 187, 188, 194, 203, 204, 222, 223, 228, 231, 233, 234, 238, 241, 243, 246, 248, 249, 252, 253, 257, 259, 260, 261, 263, 269, 283, 384, 295, 296, 297, 301, 302, 303, 310, 331, 337
Wrath, 51, 122, 155, 193, 198, 199, 200, 203, 223, 274, 321, 332

Y

YAH, 55, 64, 82, 83, 84, 85, 88, 96, 98, 171, 207, 208, 209, 210, 211, 212, 261, 282, 287, 311, 326, 327
Yekal, 89

Yesod, 26, 34, 40, 46, 51, 56, 57, 59, 60, 62, 63, 70, 78, 88, 167, 243, 267, 337, 338, 339
Yetzirah, 29, 32, 34, 35, 47, 161, 170, 251
Yggdrasil, 28
Yod, the letter, 11, 32, 33, 34, 35, 41, 54, 55, 56, 57, 58, 59, 60, 61, 62, 63, 64, 65, 67, 70, 71, 72, 73, 74, 75, 77, 78, 79, 80, 84, 85, 86, 87, 88, 89, 92, 93, 94, 95, 96, 98, 99, 100, 103, 107, 108, 171, 179, 180, 191, 202, 210, 227, 231, 232, 246, 272, 280, 282, 283, 284, 285, 286, 287, 304, 330, 331, 332

Z

Zauir Anpin, 26, 41, 77, 117, 137, 179, 195, 198, 203
Zayin, the letter, 103, 171, 331
Zechariah, 125, 128, 167, 187, 188, 244, 254, 312
Zephaniah, 154
Zeus, 335
Zion, 127, 191, 314, 316, 337, 338
Zodiac, 24, 27, 31, 34, 171, 214, 330
Zohar, 6, 14, 29, 41, 43, 55, 121, 174

FINIS.

Holland Rowbottom, Printer, "Graphic" Office, Bournemouth.

CPSIA information can be obtained at www.ICGtesting.com
Printed in the USA
LVOW112050110912

298391LV00018B/224/P

9 781141 940509